ALMANAC 2018

A young green turtle swims near the surface of a lagoon in French Polynesia in the South Pacific.

ALMANAC 2018

NATIONAL GEOGRAPHIC
WASHINGTON, D.C.

National Geographic Kids Books
gratefully acknowledges the following people for their help with the
National Geographic Kids Almanac 2018.

Anastasia Cronin of the
National Geographic Explorers program

Amazing Animals

Suzanne Braden, Director, Pandas International

Dr. Rodolfo Coria, Paleontologist, Plaza Huincul, Argentina

Dr. Sylvia Earle,
National Geographic Explorer-in-Residence

Dr. Thomas R. Holtz, Jr., Senior Lecturer, Vertebrate Paleontology,
Department of Geology, University of Maryland

Dr. Luke Hunter, Executive Director, Panthera

Dereck and Beverly Joubert,
National Geographic Explorers-in-Residence

Nizar Ibrahim, National Geographic Emerging Explorer

"Dino" Don Lessem, President, Exhibits Rex

Kathy B. Maher, Research Editor,
National Geographic magazine

Kathleen Martin, Canadian Sea Turtle Network

Barbara Nielsen, Polar Bears International

Andy Prince, Austin Zoo

Christopher Sloan

Julia Thorson, translator, Zurich, Switzerland

Dennis vanEngelsdorp, Senior Extension Associate,
Pennsylvania Department of Agriculture

Going Green

Eric J. Bohn, Math Teacher, Santa Rosa High School

Stephen David Harris,
Professional Engineer, Industry Consulting

Catherine C. Milbourn, Senior Press Officer, EPA

Brad Scriber, Senior Researcher, *National Geographic* magazine

Paola Segura and Cid Simões,
National Geographic Emerging Explorers

Dr. Wes Tunnell, Harte Research Institute for
Gulf of Mexico Studies, Texas A&M University–Corpus Christi

Natasha Vizcarra, Science Writer and Media Liaison,
National Snow and Ice Data Center

Culture Connection

Dr. Wade Davis, National Geographic Explorer-in-Residence

Deirdre Mullervy, Managing Editor,
Gallaudet University Press

Life Science / Space and Earth

Tim Appenzeller, Chief Magazine Editor, *Nature*

Dr. Rick Fienberg, American Astronomical Society,
Press Officer and Director of Communications

Dr. José de Ondarza, Associate Professor,
Department of Biological Sciences, State University
of New York, College at Plattsburgh

Lesley B. Rogers, Managing Editor (former),
National Geographic magazine

Dr. Enric Sala, National Geographic Visiting Fellow

Abigail A. Tipton, Director of Research (former),
National Geographic magazine

Erin Vintinner, Biodiversity Specialist,
Center for Biodiversity and Conservation at the
American Museum of Natural History

Barbara L. Wyckoff, Research Editor (former),
National Geographic magazine

Wonders of Nature

Anatta, NOAA Public Affairs Officer

Dr. Robert Ballard,
National Geographic Explorer-in-Residence

Douglas H. Chadwick, wildlife biologist and contributor to
National Geographic magazine

Susan K. Pell, Ph.D., Science and Public Programs Manager,
United States Botanic Garden

History Happens

Dr. Sylvie Beaudreau, Associate Professor,
Department of History, State University of New York

Elspeth Deir, Assistant Professor, Faculty of Education,
Queens University, Kingston, Ontario, Canada

Dr. Gregory Geddes, Professor, Global Studies,
State University of New York–Orange,
Middletown-Newburgh, New York

Dr. Fredrik Hiebert, National Geographic Visiting Fellow

Micheline Joanisse, Media Relations Officer,
Natural Resources Canada

Dr. Robert D. Johnston,
Associate Professor and Director of the
Teaching of History Program, University of Illinois at Chicago

Dickson Mansfield, Geography Instructor (retired),
Faculty of Education, Queens University,
Kingston, Ontario, Canada

Tina Norris, U.S. Census Bureau

Parliamentary Information and Research Service,
Library of Parliament, Ottawa, Canada

Karyn Pugliese, Acting Director, Communications,
Assembly of First Nations

Geography Rocks

Glynnis Breen, National Geographic Special Projects

Carl Haub, Senior Demographer,
Conrad Taeuber Chair of Public Information,
Population Reference Bureau

Dr. Toshiko Kaneda, Senior Research Associate,
Population Reference Bureau

Dr. Kristin Bietsch, Research Associate,
Population Reference Bureau

Dr. Walt Meier, National Snow and Ice Data Center

Dr. Richard W. Reynolds,
NOAA's National Climatic Data Center

United States Census Bureau, Public Help Desk

Contents

Your World 2018

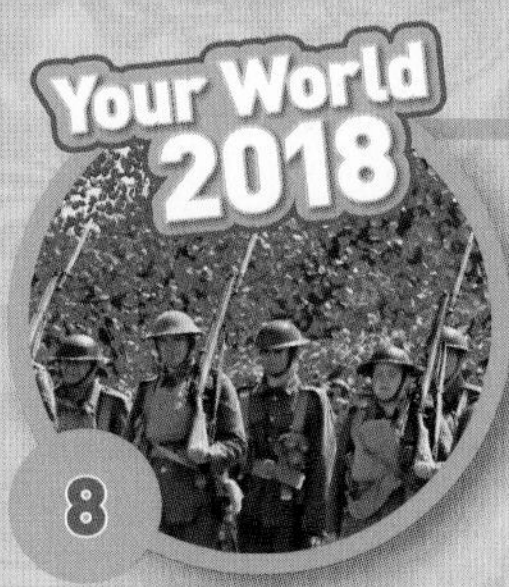

8

Awesome Exploration

18

Amazing Animals

36

Going Green

92

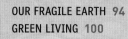

The results are in!

Who helped preserve our past with a virtual time capsule for the future in 2017? See page 28.

Want to become part of the 2018 Almanac Newsmaker Challenge? Go to page 29 to find out more.

Members of the Great War Society living history group in Bovington, England, stand under a shower of a million poppy flowers representing fallen soldiers. November 11, 2018, marks the 100th anniversary of the armistice that ended World War I.

Your World
2018

Octopus Intelligence

INKY AT THE NATIONAL AQUARIUM OF NEW ZEALAND

These eight-armed animals are as clever as they are curious.

It was a scene ripped straight from a movie: Under the cover of darkness on a quiet night, Inky the octopus made a great escape from New Zealand's National Aquarium. After crawling through a small gap in his enclosure, the soccer-ball-size cephalopod slithered some eight feet (2.4 m) across the floor before squeezing through a narrow drain pipe. From there, he wriggled along until the pipe ended, leading Inky into the ocean—and freedom.

A CALIFORNIA BIGEYE OCTOPUS

BRAIN POWER

Inky's after-hours escape wasn't just an example of an animal accidentally busting loose. It showcased an octopus's incredible intelligence, too. Researchers say that an octopus's complex brain and excellent eyesight give it the ability to form mental maps, navigate through mazes, recognize individual faces, and problem solve. And, like Inky, they are very curious and motivated by food, so it's not totally unusual for an octopus to figure a way out of its tank to seek out snacks—or simply a new scene. Other aquariums have reported octopuses breaking out of their enclosures to feast on fish in nearby tanks.

IN A SNAP

Inky isn't the only eight-armed animal to go viral recently: Rambo, a female octopus living in New Zealand's Kelly Tarlton's Sea Life Aquarium, charms visitors by snapping shots of them from her tank using a waterproof digital camera. Wanting to show off the mollusk's mega smarts, Rambo's trainer taught her to press a red button on a camera mounted to the side of her tank when she heard a buzzer. The photos are then sold as souvenirs, with the money going toward the aquarium's programs. Rambo's reward? Plenty of shrimp and crabs—and celebrity status in the animal world.

OLYMPIC FEVER

South Korea Set to Host the 2018 Winter Games

For 16 days in February, thousands of athletes from around the world will gather in PyeongChang, a county in South Korea. And some will be flying higher than ever, thanks to the addition of big air snowboarding. This event, which will be contested for the first time on an Olympic stage, has competitors flying off a ramp, then jumping, flipping, and spinning as many times as possible before hitting the ground. Meaning this year's Olympics may be the most extreme games yet.

Cold weather? Snow problem! From downhill skiing to sledding in your backyard, there are tons of ways to stay active over the winter. So break out your warmest coat and layer on the long underwear ... and check out some of the coolest sports around.

WELL, THIS IS ONE WAY TO PLAY LEAPFROG!

Athletes compete in men's Ski Cross at the Winter Olympic Games in Vancouver, British Columbia, Canada.

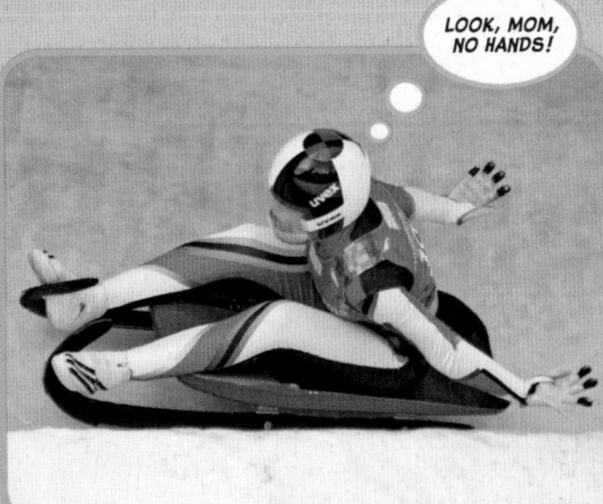

LOOK, MOM, NO HANDS!

Luge Mixed Relay Competition at the Youth Winter Olympics in Innsbruck, Austria.

Animal Roundup

Meet three critters making headlines around the world.

Piper the Airport Dog

Piper, a border collie, keeps watch on the runway at an airport in Michigan, U.S.A. His job? To chase away ducks, geese, snowy owls, and other creatures that could damage an airplane. Talk about paw patrol!

Larry the Cat

Larry may be the most famous feline in the U.K. Rescued by former Prime Minister David Cameron in 2011, Larry is now a permanent resident of 10 Downing Street. The cat's so cozy in "Number 10" that he even has his own title: Chief Mouser.

Mysterious Purple Orb

It's a blob. It's a ball. It's a pleurobranch! A mysterious purple orb discovered in the Pacific Ocean has stumped scientists. While no one has determined exactly what this orb is, most experts agree that it's likely a small mollusk, called a pleurobranch, in a rare purple hue.

HOT MOVIES in 2018*

- *Avatar 2*
- *How to Train Your Dragon 3*
- *Gnomeo and Juliet: Sherlock Gnomes*
- *Cruella*
- *The Secret Life of Pets 2*
- *Wreck-It Ralph 2*
- *Mulan* (live-action)

*Release dates and titles are subject to change.

PIGEONS TRACK AIR POLLUTION

Talk about a bird-brained idea: For a few days in London, a flock of 10 pigeons flew around town tracking air pollution. Known as the Pigeon Air Patrol, the birds were outfitted with tiny backpacks containing a sensor measuring harmful emissions in the air. As the pigeons took to the skies, people could monitor their progress—and pollution levels around the city—online. The Pigeon Air Patrol was just an experiment in London. But as air pollution continues to plague the planet, this approach could really take flight around the world.

ANCIENT DISCOVERY

An unsuspecting construction crew in Rome recently dug up the past, literally. While working to upgrade a subway station in a part of the city near the famed Colosseum, workers unearthed archaeological ruins dating back nearly 2,000 years lurking about 30 feet (9 m) belowground. The sizable site, which experts believe once housed elite military guards, includes a hallway as long as a football field with 39 rooms featuring frescoes on the wall and black-and-white mosaics on the floors. Other rare relics discovered in the dirt? A bronze bracelet and coin—plus the remains of 13 humans.

MISSION COMPLETE

Juno made a total of 37 orbits around Jupiter.

It took five years for Juno to reach Jupiter's orbit from Earth.

What's it like on Jupiter? We may soon find out, thanks to the Juno spacecraft, which is set to deorbit in February 2018 after circling the planet since July 2016. Seeking to unlock the secrets of the massive, mysterious planet, Juno's mission studied everything from Jupiter's magnetic field to its composition to the swirling clouds hovering above its surface. A high-tech camera aboard the spacecraft captured rare glimpses of Jupiter, including videos of some of the planet's many moons. Scientists hope that all of the data and images gathered by Juno will ultimately teach us more about how the planet formed—and, in turn, reveal more about how Earth came about, too.

JUNO APPROACHING JUPITER

AN IMAGE OF JUPITER CAPTURED BY JUNO

YEAR IN SPACE

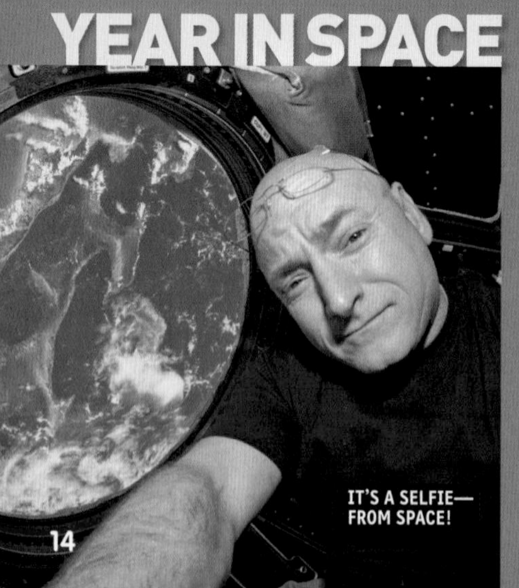

IT'S A SELFIE—FROM SPACE!

He's back! After 340 days living at the International Space Station, Captain Scott Kelly returned to Earth. His stay was twice as long as a typical stint on the Space Station—and a record for the longest time an American's spent orbiting Earth. Kelly's main mission? To get a grasp on how the body reacts to a long period of time in space. Scientists even studied Kelly's identical twin, Mark, to see if there were any obvious physical changes between Scott and his Earth-bound brother.

FUN WITH FRUIT IN MICRO-GRAVITY

Buildings in Disguise

These aren't your basic buildings! Around the world, some imaginative architects have gone way outside the box when it comes to their daring designs. From the "Big Pineapple"—originally built on a pineapple farm in Australia—to the Fish Building in India, these structures sure stand out!

Some of these buildings represent "novelty architecture," where a building is meant to resemble the items it sells (like the pineapple building), or they're intended to be a recognizable landmark, such as the "chicken church" (below right) in Indonesia, or the lotus flower-shaped ArtScience Museum in Singapore (below left). Whatever the inspiration behind these buildings, they are prime examples of designers daring to be different.

BIG PINEAPPLE IN WOOMBYE, AUSTRALIA

FISH BUILDING IN HYDERABAD, ANDHRA PRADESH, INDIA

LOTUS-SHAPED ARTSCIENCE MUSEUM IN SINGAPORE

CHICKEN CHURCH IN MAGELANG, INDONESIA

Cool Events in 2018

International Dance Day

GET YOUR BOOGIE ON during this celebration of types of dance around the world.

April 29

Olympic Winter Games

GO FOR THE GOLD! Athletes from all over the world will compete for coveted medals in PyeongChang, South Korea.

February 9–25

World Emoji Day

TEXT your favorite winky face or emoticon.

July 17

Dr. Seuss's Birthday

Break out your red-and-white-striped hat—the famous children's author would be 114 years old today.

March 2

World Cat Day

THIS HOLIDAY HONORING our favorite felines is **the cat's meow!**

August 8

Pingxi Sky Lantern Festival

The NIGHT SKY IS DOTTED with 100,000 to 200,000 lanterns, not stars, during this festival in Taiwan.

March 2

Festival of the Winds

GO FLY A KITE! Life's a breeze at this annual festival on AUSTRALIA'S BONDI BEACH.

September 9

Paralympic Winter Games

Athletes with physical disabilities chase their Olympic dreams in events like wheelchair curling and para-snowboarding.

March 9–18

International Mountain Day

There are hundreds of thousands of mountains on our planet. Find one and TAKE A HIKE TODAY!

December 11

OZONE HEALING

Just call it the incredible shrinking ozone hole. For decades, there's been a massive hole in the ozone layer that appears over the Antarctic. A result of chlorine-containing chemicals once used in products like hair spray and refrigerators, the depleted ozone region averaged an area of 8.7 million square miles (22 million sq km) in the 1996–2005 period. By 2016, the hole had shrunk more than 0.6 million square miles (1.6 million sq km), about three times the size of France. Scientists say this is due to the international ban on those chemicals in 1987. While researchers predict that the hole won't return to 1980 levels until 2070, this is definitely positive news for our planet.

VIEW OF OZONE OVER THE ANTARCTIC. PURPLE AND BLUE COVER AREAS WHERE THERE IS THE LEAST OZONE.

In-Ear Translator

IMAGINE THIS: You're visiting Paris, but you don't speak French. No problem, just pop the Pilot earpiece in and use the app to understand every word another user says to you. The device, which you wear in your ear like an earbud, translates foreign languages including Spanish, Italian, Portuguese, and English in real time. You simply select which language you want from an app on your phone and then let the Pilot do the translation. *C'est magnifique!*

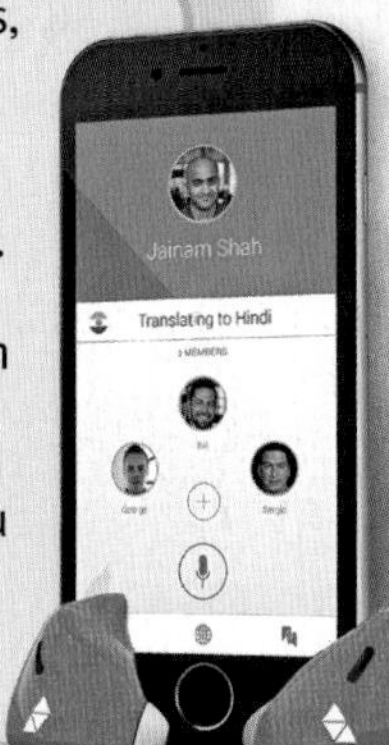

TEEN POLAR ADVENTURER

Jade Hameister recently glided into the record books by becoming the youngest person to ski to the North Pole. Just 14 at the time, Jade—with her father by her side—covered the trek in 11 days, facing bitter cold temperatures and biting winds while towing a 110-pound (50-kg) pack. And Jade, who documented her trip on Instagram, is just beginning: She plans to ski to the South Pole next.

An ice cave rises above trekkers exploring Lake Superior's frozen surface near Bayfield, Wisconsin, U.S.A.

Awesome Exploration

National Geographic Explorer **Kevin McLean** really goes out on a limb to collect data on small mammals such as porcupines, howler monkeys, and woolly opossums high in the treetops. Here, he shares his exploration essentials.

18 THINGS IN AN EXPLORER'S

1

CLIMBING HARNESS.

"I DESCRIBE THIS AS A CROSS BETWEEN A TOOL BELT AND A DIAPER. I SPEND HOURS IN MY HARNESS AND WILL EVEN FALL ASLEEP IN IT."

2

COMPASS.

"JUST A SIMPLE PLASTIC COMPASS TO HANG AROUND MY NECK AND QUICKLY GUIDE ME."

3

WATER BOTTLE.

"I sweat a lot when I'm climbing. To stay hydrated, I make sure to have at least two liters of water and sports drink with me at all times."

4

NOTEBOOK.

"I use **WATERPROOF** notebooks so I can jot down my observations in any weather."

5

GPS.

"So I know where I'm going! It has to have a strong signal, especially if I'm under a dense canopy cover."

6

CAMERA TRAPS.

"THIS IS ACTUALLY A MOTION-SENSITIVE CAMERA IN A CAMOUFLAGED BOX. ANYTHING THAT'S WARM OR MOVING WILL SET THEM OFF."

7

SLINGSHOT.

"I use this to help me get my rope into the tree. It's actually 8 feet (2.4 m) tall, but it breaks down into two pieces that I can fit in my backpack."

8

CARABINERS.

"I need these to chain myself to the rope. They're able to hold a lot of weight, and support me as I move around."

9

RECHARGEABLE BATTERIES.

"I always bring spare AA batteries for the camera."

BACKPACK

10

SMARTPHONE WITH A WRIST STRAP.

"TAKING PICTURES AND VIDEOS WITH MY PHONE IS EASY AND FAST WHEN I'M IN THE TREE. I ALWAYS HAVE A WRIST STRAP, BECAUSE EVEN THE STRONGEST CASE WON'T SAVE THE PHONE FROM A 150-FOOT (45-M) PLUMMET FROM THE CANOPY."

11

THROW BAG AND THROWLINE.

"A little beanbag attached to a string. I use my slingshot to shoot it around a branch, then I tie my rope to the string and pull it over the branch."

12

LONG-SLEEVE SHIRT.

"Insects are everywhere in the forest, and bug spray can damage the ropes I use. So I try to keep my skin as covered as possible."

13

PEANUT BUTTER AND JELLY SANDWICH.

"An easy and convenient snack, and it doesn't matter if it gets smashed or wet."

14

ROPE.

"I USE NYLON CLIMBING ROPES SPECIALLY MADE FOR TREE CLIMBING. I'M ALWAYS ATTACHED TO THEM."

15

HELMET.

"I ALWAYS WEAR A HELMET. BRANCHES, LEAVES, AND PIECES OF EQUIPMENT CAN FALL AT ANY GIVEN MOMENT."

16

ANTIBIOTIC OINTMENT AND BANDAGES.

"I get little nicks and scrapes from the branches and thorns on the trees, which can get easily infected in the field. It's good to treat them."

17

MOSQUITO NET.

"It attaches to my helmet when it gets really buggy out. But usually ticks are a bigger problem than mosquitos."

18

MAP.

"In case the GPS fails me. It's important to NEVER FULLY RELY on electronics, since they can fail you."

DARE to EXPLORE

Do you have what it takes to be a great explorer? Read these stories of four adventurers, and see how you can get started on the exploration path.

JENNY DALTRY
Herpetologist

WANT TO BE A HERPETOLOGIST?
STUDY: Biology, geography, and other sciences
WATCH: *AVATAR*
READ: *Not Your Typical Book About the Environment* by Elin Kelsey

Herpetologist Jenny Daltry has come face-to-fangs with venomous snakes and toothy crocodiles. Here, she talks about warming up to cold-blooded animals.

"One time while on the Caribbean Island of Montserrat, I was observing amphibians near the top of a volcano that hadn't erupted in over 350 years. Suddenly, I heard a tremendous roar and spun around to see a column of smoke shooting into the air. The volcano was erupting! I turned to run. Luckily, I found a path away from the rumbling mountain and made it to safety.

"Fleeing a lava-spewing volcano is one of many unforgettable moments I've had on the job. Another is helping to preserve the Antiguan racer—a small, harmless snake found on the island of Antigua. Twenty years ago only 50 were left on Earth, and today, over 1,200 Antiguan racers now exist. Helping to bring animals back from the brink of extinction makes you realize just how much is possible. Every single person has the power to make a difference."

"It doesn't matter who you are or where you're from. You have the potential to accomplish amazing things. Stay positive and focused, and you'll reach your goals."

ORIENTAL VINE SNAKE

SIAMESE CROCODILE

ANTIGUAN SPOTTED ANOLE

A CROCODILE CAN'T STICK ITS TONGUE OUT.

LALY LICHTENFELD
Conservationist

WANT TO BE A **CONSERVATIONIST?**

STUDY: Biology, ecology, and history

WATCH: *Game of Lions*, a National Geographic film

READ: *Facing the Lion* by Joseph Lemasolai Lekuton

"Stay curious and always try to **learn new things.** Being open to **new experiences** will lead to **amazing opportunities.**"

"Sitting in my tent during an expedition into the wilderness of Tanzania, I was startled by a big, beautiful lioness ambling through our campsite. Lions usually try to avoid close encounters with humans. But this one padded right up to me. I sat very still, but my heart was pounding. Would she pounce or swipe at me? The animal just stood motionless for some time, looking into my eyes. Then she turned around and trotted off. It was a very special moment.

"My job is to protect big cats such as lions in Tanzania. Humans pose a big threat to these animals. That's because the big cats sometimes hunt cows and other livestock owned by people. When the humans try to stop them, the felines can get hurt—or worse. My team and I work to resolve conflicts between people and cats peacefully. For instance, we teach farmers how to build special fences called living walls around their livestock that keep lions out.

"Big cats around the world face threats. But there's so much we can do to help."

BUILDING A BOMA

LIONS ARE THE ONLY CATS THAT LIVE IN GROUPS.

CORY RICHARDS
Adventure photographer

WANT TO BE A PHOTOGRAPHER?

STUDY: Photography, anthropology, and geology

WATCH: The documentary *Cave People of the Himalaya*

READ: *Banner in the Sky* by James Ramsey Ullman

RICHARDS SCALES A PEAK IN THE ROCKY MOUNTAINS IN CANADA ON A PHOTO EXPEDITION.

"Don't let **obstacles** discourage you from reaching your **goals.** Anything is **possible** if you put your **heart** into it."

RICHARDS' STUNNING PHOTOGRAPHY

CANADA

EUROPE'S CRIMEAN PENINSULA

"One time I was rappelling, or descending by rope, down a seaside cliff in Spain to photograph some climbers. Suddenly the rock that my rope was anchored to at the top of the cliff broke away. My stomach lurched as I went into a free fall, plummeting 50 feet (15 m) into the ocean. Once I hit the water, the heavy camera equipment strapped to my body dragged me under the waves. With my heart hammering, I freed myself from the gear and swam to the surface. My cameras were ruined, but I was alive.

"Working as a photographer can be a nonstop adventure. My career has taken me to every terrain imaginable, from icy peaks in Asia to the vast plains of Africa to coral reefs in the South Pacific Ocean. I've snapped pictures of people scaling mountains, diving, and skiing across Antarctica. I love using photography to show the incredible things humans are capable of doing.

"Getting the right shot involves creativity and sometimes danger. Stay open to new experiences, and you'll never be disappointed."

IN EXTREME COLD, CAMERAS CAN PACK UP WITH ICE.

DEE BOERSMA
Biologist

WANT TO BE A BIOLOGIST?
STUDY: Math, science, and technology
WATCH: The documentary *March of the Penguins*
READ: *Galápagos George* by Jean Craighead George

"No matter what you end up doing with your life, try to make the world a better place."

DEE BOERSMA OBSERVES MAGELLANIC PENGUINS IN ARGENTINA.

Conservation biologist Dee Boersma talks about working in remote locations to study penguins and sharing the planet with other animals.

"When I first went to the Galápagos Islands off the coast of Ecuador over 40 years ago to study the penguins that lived there, I camped by myself for two weeks to see what I could discover. Rats, venomous snakes, and three-foot-long iguanas were everywhere. No other humans were with me on the island, so it could get a little lonely. But I would talk to the sea lions that slept on the beach outside my tent—they snore so loud!"

"The lives of penguins aren't so different from our own: They raise families and take care of their loved ones. What we humans need to do is protect their habitats so they can thrive. Each one of us can do something to make life better for other creatures."

GALÁPAGOS PENGUIN

PENGUINS SWIM UP TO 3,100 MILES (5,000 KM) IN A YEAR.

What Kind of Explorer Are You?

Take this quiz and mark your answers on a piece of paper to find out the type of adventurous occupation that's the perfect fit for you!

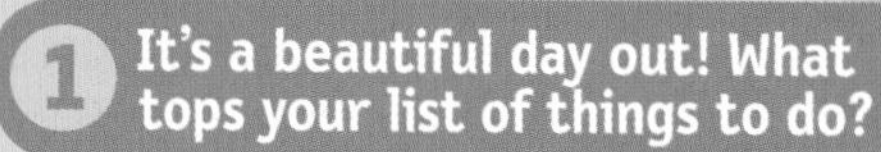

1 It's a beautiful day out! What tops your list of things to do?

A. taking a walk down to your neighborhood pond to look for turtles and ducks
B. grabbing your camera and snapping some pictures of the birds in your backyard
C. digging around your yard and looking for cool stones and creatures living underground
D. going for a hike

2 What's your dream vacation?

A. snorkeling with tropical fish in Tahiti
B. watching wildlife on a safari in Africa
C. digging for dinosaur bones in Argentina
D. climbing Mount Fuji in Japan

4 What's your favorite subject in school?

A. biology
B. visual arts
C. history
D. gym

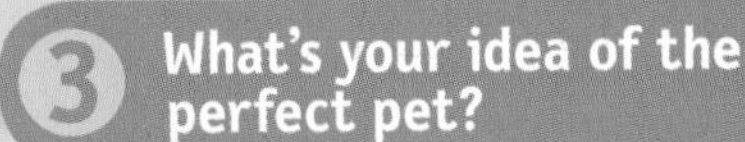

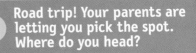

5 Road trip! Your parents are letting you pick the spot. Where do you head?

A. the beach
B. the zoo
C. a museum
D. a state park

3 What's your idea of the perfect pet?

A. a fish
B. a cat
C. a lizard
D. a dog

If You Chose Mostly ...

As

Oceanographer. You're meant for a life on the sea. Whether it's scuba diving with sharks or working on reducing ocean waste, your love for the water and life beneath the surface makes you a perfect match for a career in the marine world.

Bs

Wildlife Photographer. Wild about animals? Passionate about photography? As a wildlife photographer, you can combine your passion for both. Spending hours observing animals and documenting their every move from behind the lens could be the future you should focus on.

Cs

Archaeologist. History is never a mystery for you, and you love piecing together clues from the past. Collecting dinosaur bones or discovering ancient civilizations? Now that's something you'd definitely dig.

Ds

Mountaineer. Your sporty lifestyle and enthusiasm for all things active make you the perfect match for a career as a mountaineer. As a true trailblazer, you'd spend time scaling the planet's highest peaks, scampering over boulders, and exploring parts of Earth few people have ever been before.

Marine biologist Jessica Cramp needs your help.

We're sending out an SOS to help National Geographic Explorer Jessica Cramp and marine conservationists around the world save our sharks. This awesome (but often misunderstood) predator is a vital part of the ocean's ecosystem. When sharks thrive, the ocean thrives.

The more everyone knows about sharks, the more we can increase their chances for survival. So answer our SOS call! **Plunge into the world of sharks and join this year's Almanac Newsmaker Challenge at natgeokids.com/almanac.** When you emerge, you'll be a shark expert. Take a fun shark quiz, pledge to help save this important predator, and get tips on how you can help. You can also find out what kind of shark matches your personality, download shark masks and posters, and help us choose the coolest shark species to feature in next year's Almanac!

If you're looking for Jessica Cramp, you may find her working on a boat in the middle of the Pacific Ocean, or perhaps scuba diving off the coast of a remote atoll. Such is the life of a marine conservationist like Cramp. Here, the National Geographic Explorer shares more about her fin-tastic job—and why it's important to protect sharks.

We asked **Cramp** to answer some questions for our readers and young explorers:

How did you get your start in marine biology?

I used to work as a research biologist in a lab, which was challenging—but it wasn't my dream. I am a surfer and diver and wanted to spend more time outside and make a positive impact on the environment. Eventually, I got the opportunity to volunteer for a local marine conservation organization and help create a shark sanctuary in the Cook Islands. Becoming a marine biologist and conservationist allowed me to align my intentions with my actions—and work has never been so fun!

What is a typical day on the job like for you?

There's no typical day! Sometimes, I spend hours in front of my computer researching. When I'm in the field, I'm on a boat tagging sharks, fishing for bait, and dropping baited cameras into the ocean. We work from sunrise to sunset. At night, I'll look over the day's camera footage to look for shark presence—including new species or interesting behavior. I'm usually wet, salty, and smell like fish all day long, but it's worth it.

What do you like best about your job?
I like that it's always changing, but that the goal stays the same: solid research that informs policy, outreach that inspires outcomes, and advocating for what I believe in.

Any scary encounters with sharks?
I've had one or two uncomfortable moments, but most of my time spent in the water with sharks I feel relaxed and comfortable. The majority of sharks are quite afraid of us. They lose interest and swim away much sooner than I'd like, so I find myself wishing they'd hang around a little longer.

Tell us about a cool experience you've had in the field.
Freediving into a large school of sharks on a remote, submerged atoll called Beveridge Reef in Niue. I was leading the shark research on a recent expedition with National Geographic. The setting, the expedition, the abundance of sharks, it was unforgettable.

Why is it so important to shine the spotlight on sharks and make sure they're protected?
Unfortunately for sharks, the high value of the fins, meat, and liver oil drive overexploitation of many species. Because they are slow-growing, late to mature, and many species have very few offspring, they just aren't able to replenish the population as quickly as they are being fished. And without them in our ocean, the natural balance and order of life is upset, which can have unpleasant cascading effects on other animals and their habitat.

What can we do to help protect sharks?
Be curious! Understand how sharks are connected to the fish on your dinner plate. There are companies that fish responsibly, but we don't always know what effects our tuna sandwich may have had on sharks, seabirds, whales, manta rays, or other ocean creatures. The more we know about how fish are caught, the faster the changes will happen in the water.

Get smart about sharks at natgeokids.com/almanac.

View last year's challenge results

In last year's Almanac Newsmaker Challenge, we asked kids to create a time capsule, photograph it, and share it on My Shot. We received so many fantastic photos, from as far away as China, and together they present a fascinating window to the past for kids in 2050.

HIGHLIGHTS

Most popular items: headphones and earbuds, smartphones, computers and tablets, books, plushies, toys, games, sneakers

Top books: Harry Potter, *Diary of a Wimpy Kid*, and *Nat Geo Kids Almanac* and Weird But True books

Top toys/games: Legos, Rubik's Cube, Uno, Minions

Here are a few of our favorites. View the complete photo gallery at: natgeokids.com/almanac

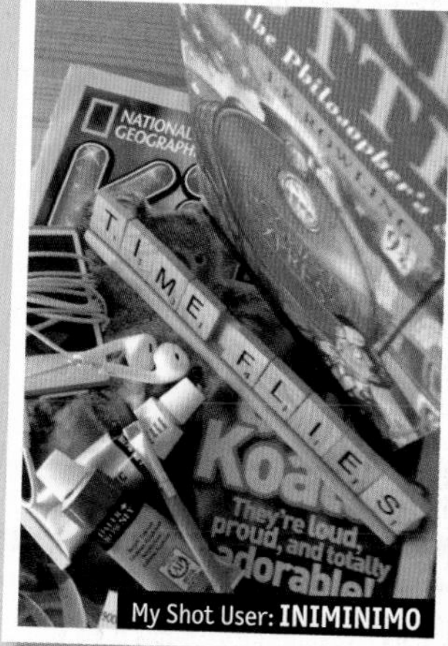

My Shot User: **INIMINIMO**

My Shot User: **Ferretopia**

My Shot User: **allid126**

Meerkat Close Encounter

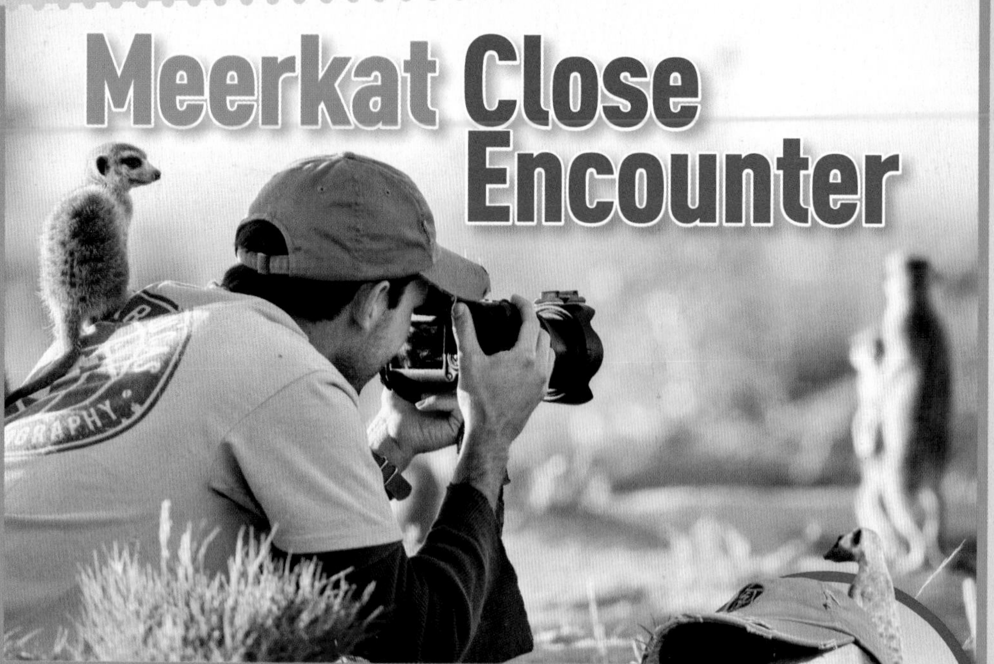

Wildlife photographer Will Burrard-Lucas gives new meaning to the term "up close and personal" while photographing meerkats in the wild.

Makgadikgadi Pans, Botswana
When a family of meerkats discovered a wildlife photographer on his stomach angling for a picture outside their burrow, they didn't hide. Instead they used him as a lookout rock!

Baby meerkat pups venturing aboveground for the first time took turns playing with photographer Will Burrard-Lucas's camera. One bold adult hoisted himself onto Burrard-Lucas's head and scaled to the top of the camera lens he was holding. "They were trying to get as high as they could to have a good look around," Burrard-Lucas says.

"For meerkats, the higher you get, the safer you are, because you can hopefully spot a predator before it spots you," says Kenton Kerns, a biologist at the Smithsonian's National Zoo in Washington, D.C. "If they can find a stable spot that's higher than their normal places, they'll do anything to get there—including climbing a human."

Before packing up for the day, Burrard-Lucas waited patiently while one curious meerkat peered through the lens of his camera on the ground. Another meerkat walked right in front of it. How's that for a close-up?

FROZEN IN TIME

ERNEST SHACKLETON'S PRESERVED HUT IN CAPE ROYDS, ANTARCTICA

ANTARCTIC EXPLORERS ERNEST SHACKLETON, ROBERT FALCON SCOTT, AND EDWARD WILSON, CIRCA 1903

When British adventurers Ernest Shackleton and Robert Falcon Scott explored Antarctica in the early 1900s, they set up camp in wooden huts, which they left behind in the icy environs once the expeditions were over.

One would think that over time, the huts would completely deteriorate in the harsh conditions of the coldest continent. But the structures remained upright, albeit damaged by water, wind, and snow over the years. Now, a team of conservationists have completely restored them, offering a time capsule into the explorers' lives a century ago.

So what's inside the huts? Thousands of artifacts, like clothes, scientific equipment, photographs, and even frozen butter. Here's a closer look at some of the items originally used then—and how they compare to the gear used by today's Antarctic explorers.

THE FOOD

THEN: Scott's crew mostly munched on pemmican, a mixture of dried beef and fat plus water, and plenty of biscuits.

NOW: Explorers eat a customized diet fine-tuned to give them enough calories to withstand the cold conditions and physical demands. On the menu? Porridge and cream for breakfast, energy bars, electrolyte drinks, and chicken curry for dinner.

THE SLEDS

THEN: Shackleton and Scott's teams hauled heavy loads in wooden sleds dragged by ponies and dogs.

NOW: Modern lightweight sleds are made of carbon fiber and are capable of carrying more equipment while still being sleek enough to smoothly travel over the ice.

THE CLOTHES

THEN: Early explorers wore wool, cotton, and animal fur. Gloves, boots, and sleeping bags were lined with reindeer fur.

NOW: High-tech mountaineering clothing is made from breathable fabrics that have been specially designed for the Antarctic's cold and dry environment.

Scientist at Base Orcadas in Antarctica

THE COMMUNICATION

THEN: Completely isolated in the Antarctic, explorers had no means of communicating with the outside world and could only write the details of their journey in notebooks.

NOW: Ultralight laptops connected to a mobile satellite hub help explorers stay connected, post pictures, and even watch movies.

PHOTO ARK

Joel Sartore and His Wild Project

Picture this: An elephant, set against a black backdrop, photographed at such a close angle that you can see every wrinkle and groove in its curled trunk. Then there's a stunning shot of a green tree python's eye, with scales layered around it like tiny flower petals. Or a portrait of a pair of baby fennec foxes, their beady-eyed gazes locked and giant ears perked as though they're listening to your every word.

As a longtime National Geographic photographer, Joel Sartore has captured it all. And in an effort to bring more focus on endangered species, he has photographed a growing collection of over 6,000 species of animals, from baboons to butterflies. Known as the Photo Ark, this project aims to capture every single animal living in captivity around the world (eventually, the project will include an estimated 12,000 species). Sartore, who has visited zoos, aquariums, and animal rehabilitation centers in more than 40 countries to find his subjects, hopes that the images will encourage people to be more aware of just how vulnerable these animals are.

"Every year I see more habitat loss, more species consumed for food, medicine or simply decoration," Sartore says. "The Photo Ark was born out of desperation to halt, or at least slow, the loss of global biodiversity."

Aside from awareness, Sartore also hopes to share a unique and intimate look at the animals—especially those that no longer live in the wild. And in the event that the species disappears altogether? "The goal is to see these animals as they actually looked in life," Sartore says.

Calling all shutterbugs!

Budding photographers can send their favorite pics to National Geographic Kids My Shot (ngkidsmyshot.com), where you can share, view, and rate cool images, like these animal photos taken by kids like you. So, what do you see through that lens? Break out your camera and start snapping away!

Owl's Eye
FishyMan

Beetles around their eggs
creatifxpressions

The Blue-eyed Fly
Lomax

Wolf
Funnysweetlicious

Bright Hummingbird
so7gra0983

Black Kitten
Bunny

QUIZ WHIZ

Explore just how much you know about adventure with this quiz!

Write your answers on a piece of paper. Then check them below.

1. **What does Joel Sartore's Photo Ark project feature pictures of?**
   a. animals living in captivity
   b. landscapes
   c. planets
   d. families

2. **True or false?** A crocodile can't stick its tongue out.

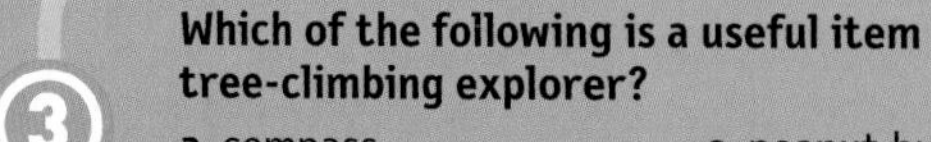

3. **Which of the following is a useful item for a tree-climbing explorer?**
   a. compass
   b. slingshot
   c. peanut butter and jelly sandwich
   d. all of the above

4. **A herpetologist studies** ____________________.

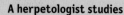

5. **Lions are the only cats that do what?**
   a. roar
   b. live in groups
   c. swim
   d. climb trees

Not **STUMPED** yet? Check out the *NATIONAL GEOGRAPHIC KIDS QUIZ WHIZ* collection for more crazy **ADVENTURE** questions!

ANSWERS: 1. a; 2. True; 3. d; 4. amphibians; 5. b

HOMEWORK HELP

How to Write a Perfect Essay

Need to write an essay? Does the assignment feel as big as climbing Mount Everest? Fear not. You're up to the challenge! The following step-by-step tips will help you with this monumental task.

1 **BRAINSTORM.** Sometimes the subject matter of your essay is assigned to you, sometimes it's not. Either way, you have to decide what you want to say. Start by brainstorming some ideas, writing down any thoughts you have about the subject. Then read over everything you've come up with and consider which idea you think is the strongest. Ask yourself what you want to write about the most. Keep in mind the goal of your essay. Can you achieve the goal of the assignment with this topic? If so, you're good to go.

2 **WRITE A TOPIC SENTENCE.** This is the main idea of your essay, a statement of your thoughts on the subject. Again, consider the goal of your essay. Think of the topic sentence as an introduction that tells your reader what the rest of your essay will be about.

3 **OUTLINE YOUR IDEAS.** Once you have a good topic sentence, you then need to support that main idea with more detailed information, facts, thoughts, and examples. These supporting points answer one question about your topic sentence—"Why?" This is where research and perhaps more brainstorming come in. Then organize these points in the way you think makes the most sense, probably in order of importance. Now you have an outline for your essay.

4 **ON YOUR MARK, GET SET, WRITE!** Follow your outline, using each of your supporting points as the topic sentence of its own paragraph. Use descriptive words to get your ideas across to the reader. Go into detail, using specific information to tell your story or make your point. Stay on track, making sure that everything you include is somehow related to the main idea of your essay. Use transitions to make your writing flow.

5 **WRAP IT UP.** Finish your essay with a conclusion that summarizes your entire essay and restates your main idea.

6 **PROOFREAD AND REVISE.** Check for errors in spelling, capitalization, punctuation, and grammar. Look for ways to make your writing clear, understandable, and interesting. Use descriptive verbs, adjectives, or adverbs when possible. It also helps to have someone else read your work to point out things you might have missed. Then make the necessary corrections and changes in a second draft. Repeat this revision process once more to make your final draft as good as you can.

Amazing Animals

A group of gray wolves gather in snowy woods in Norway.

EXTRAORDINARY Animals

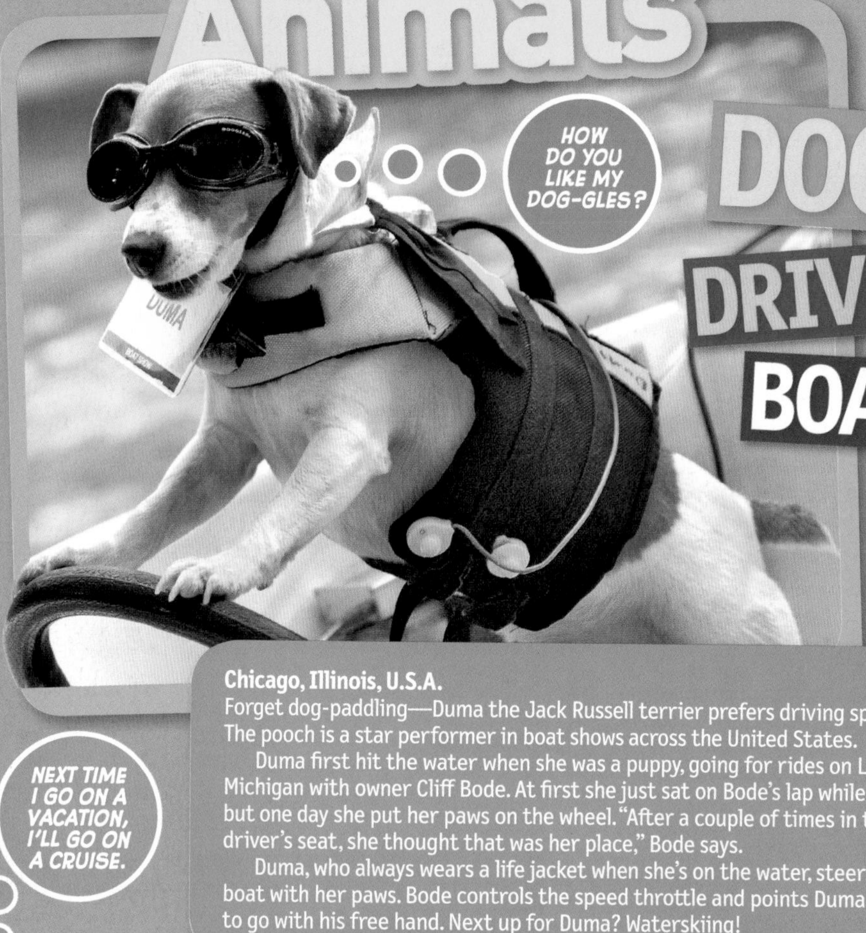

HOW DO YOU LIKE MY DOG-GLES?

DOG DRIVES BOAT

Chicago, Illinois, U.S.A.

Forget dog-paddling—Duma the Jack Russell terrier prefers driving speedboats. The pooch is a star performer in boat shows across the United States.

Duma first hit the water when she was a puppy, going for rides on Lake Michigan with owner Cliff Bode. At first she just sat on Bode's lap while he drove, but one day she put her paws on the wheel. "After a couple of times in the driver's seat, she thought that was her place," Bode says.

Duma, who always wears a life jacket when she's on the water, steers the boat with her paws. Bode controls the speed throttle and points Duma where to go with his free hand. Next up for Duma? Waterskiing!

NEXT TIME I GO ON A VACATION, I'LL GO ON A CRUISE.

LOST PARROT GIVES ADDRESS

Nagareyama, Japan

When Yosuke (YOH-su-kay) the parrot's owner took him outside for some fresh air, Yosuke flapped away. "We looked for Yosuke for three days, but we couldn't find him," Yoshio Nakamura says.

What Nakamura didn't know was that police had found the African gray parrot and took him to a veterinarian. At first Yosuke was shy. Then he started singing. Suddenly, after about 10 days, he squawked, "I'm Mr. Yosuke Nakamura" and recited his address. African grays are known for their intelligence and vocabulary. Yosuke knows about 50 phrases and took about a month to learn his address. Good thing he did—getting lost is strictly for the birds.

CHIMP OUTSMARTS HUMANS

YES, I AM SMARTER THAN A FIFTH GRADER.

Kyoto, Japan
Think you're brainier than a chimpanzee? Most people do—unless they've met Ayumu the chimp. According to researchers, he has a better memory than most humans.

Ayumu and three other chimps took the same memory test that college students did. Numbers in random order flashed on a screen, and then turned into white squares. Participants had to touch the squares in numerical order to demonstrate memory skills. Ayumu was so accurate he outscored chimps *and* students.

Scientist Tetsuro Matsuzawa, who led the study, says many people think humans are better than animals in every way. He says this test proves that isn't always true and hopes his research will motivate people to treat animals with more respect.

AYUMU PUTS HIS MEMORY SKILLS TO THE TEST.

YOU COULD SAY I RECEIVED KOALA-TY CARE.

KOALA SURVIVES WILD RIDE

STAFF AT THE AUSTRALIA ZOO WILDLIFE HOSPITAL TREAT TIMBERWOLF.

Gympie, Australia
Spotting a koala in Australia isn't unusual—but discovering one clinging to the front of your car is. That's just what a family of five found when they stopped for gas after a long night of driving.

The koala was likely crossing a freeway when the family's car struck him, and no one realized the vehicle had hit the animal. Instead of falling onto the road, the little marsupial survived the journey by gripping the front bumper of the car.

"Koalas live in trees and are able to hold on to branches in very strong winds," says Amber Gillett, a veterinarian at the Australia Zoo Wildlife Hospital where the koala, later named Timberwolf, was taken after the family called rescuers.

In fact, the only injury Timberwolf suffered was a broken nail. After just a few weeks of rest, he was ready to return to the wild.

Incredible Animal Friends

FOX PLAYS WITH TERRIER

Corwen, Wales, U.K.
Rosie the orphan fox pup loves playtime with her adopted sister, Maddy the Patterland terrier. They even frolic in the family's living room. "The fox likes to run along the top of the sofa and jump over the coffee table to meet Maddy. The room is usually a wreck," says owner Richard Bowler, who took in the fox after she was abandoned.

It's an odd friendship, since Maddy's parents were actually bred to hunt foxes. Nobody told *this* dog, though. She spends most of her time rolling around with Rosie in an outdoor vegetable garden.

The furry friends do settle down for nap time, though—but not before Maddy gives Rosie a sloppy good-night kiss.

PATTERLAND TERRIER

ORIGIN
Most likely England

WEIGHT
Between 10 and 17 pounds (4.5 and 7.7 kg)

DIG IT
Terriers love to dig. In fact the word "terrier" comes from *terra*, a Latin word for earth.

ONE OF MANY
There are more than 25 different terrier breeds.

RED FOX

RANGE
North America, Europe, Asia, and northern Africa

WEIGHT
Between 8 and 15 pounds (3.6 and 6.8 kg)

SOLO ACT
As solitary animals, red foxes don't typically form packs like wolves.

HERE I AM!
Red foxes often use their tails as signal flags for fox-to-fox communication.

NEXT TIME, I GET TO SPLASH THE TOURISTS.

DOLPHIN SWIMS WITH SEA LION

INDO-PACIFIC BOTTLENOSE DOLPHIN

RANGE
Waters off of Asia, Africa, and Australia

LENGTH
6 to 10 feet (1.8 to 3 m)

HIGH JUMP
They have been seen leaping as high as 16 feet (4.9 m) from the water's surface.

SCALING SEALS
This mammal sheds its outermost layer of skin every two hours.

Coffs Harbour, Australia
Miri the sea lion loves giving Jet the bottlenose dolphin smooches. "Miri has been known to stop whatever she's doing, glide over to Jet, and plant a big kiss on him," says Angela Van Den Bosch of Dolphin Marine Magic water park, where the friends live.

Jet and Miri became best buds during the marine center's playtime, when the park's sea lions hang out with the dolphins. Although some sea lions like to sun themselves outside the dolphin pool, Miri slides into the water to chill with her friend. The two enjoy chasing each other and munching on snacks. The pair even "talk" to one another. Jet makes clicking noises at his sea lion buddy, while Miri barks in response. Sounds like these two speak fluent BFF.

AUSTRALIAN SEA LION

RANGE
Waters off of western and southern Australia

LENGTH
4.5 to 8 feet (1.4 to 2.4 m)

SPECIES ALERT
Only 10,000 to 15,000 Australian sea lions remain in the wild.

SCALING SEALS
Great climbers, these creatures have been found on top of cliffs.

Frog VERSUS Fungus

Scientists race to save amphibians from a deadly threat.

FRINGED LEAF FROGS LIVE IN THE SOUTH AMERICAN COUNTRIES OF BRAZIL, COLOMBIA, ECUADOR, PERU, AND PROBABLY BOLIVIA.

You can call a group of frogs an army or colony.

More than 6,500 known species of frogs and toads exist.

A dark-green fringed leaf frog croaks softly as it sits on a tree branch in a wooded area of Brazil. Suddenly it jumps to another branch. As the frog soars, it flaunts its brilliant orange-yellow tummy. Other fringed leaf frogs hop around and show off their stomachs too, adding streaks of color to the green habitat.

The bright bellies of these small animals aren't their only attention-grabbing feature. The species, which lives in tropical forests of South America, has somehow been able to survive a threat endangering amphibians worldwide. The menace—a deadly fungus called chytrid (KIH-trid) that attacks amphibians' skin—has wiped out certain frog species in some forests. But the fringed leaf frog still remains healthy. Scientists are examining these frogs and others that seem less affected by chytrid to learn how other animals can beat the threat.

CROAKER SOAKER

Chytrid began spreading rapidly in the 1990s, according to some scientists. It thrives in rivers and streams, where amphibians typically hang out. By attacking the animals' delicate skin, the fatal fungus suffocates its victims.

CUBAN TREE FROG

Scientists estimate that when chytrid invades an area, 80 percent of the amphibian species can become infected. It's hit many countries, from Brazil to Japan to Australia. "Chytrid has had a devastating impact," conservation biologist and amphibian specialist Danté Fenolio says. The good news is that chytrid is easily cured. An infected frog can take a soak in an antifungal bath a few minutes a day for about 10 days to clear it up.

But first scientists have to find infected frogs, so they trek into forests. They scoop up as many animals with chytrid as possible and bring them to zoos and sanctuaries for treatment.

Once introduced to their new pads, relocated amphibians are treated like VIPs. Keepers give them healing baths and place them in superclean aquariums to prevent the fungus from spreading. They also provide their "guests" with tasty snacks of live crickets, grasshoppers, ants, and katydids—the same things that they'd eat in the wild.

Though a lot of the rescued animals have recovered completely, keepers haven't been able to return them to their natural habitat. Unfortunately, the antifungal baths don't provide immunity to chytrid. And scientists haven't figured out a way to remove the fungus from the animals' homes. So if they're brought back to the forests, they could be exposed to chytrid again and reinfected.

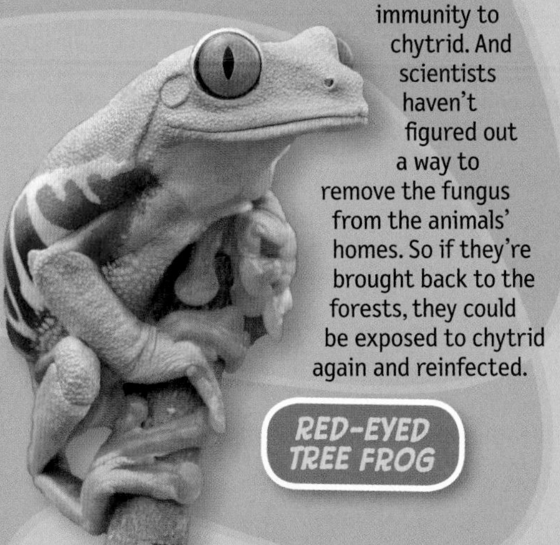
RED-EYED TREE FROG

Now scientists are turning to the frogs' cousins—amphibians that seem to be unaffected by chytrid—to lend a webbed hand.

REASONS FOR HOPE

The populations of certain amphibians such as the fringed leaf frog, marine toad, and red-eyed tree frog haven't declined because of chytrid. What's happening? For certain species such as the fringed leaf frog, the answer remains unclear. But scientists think that some of these animals may naturally host types of bacteria on their skin that prevent the fungus from growing. Other amphibians with poison glands might produce special chemicals along with their toxins that help the animals resist chytrid. And certain animals may simply have inherited a natural immunity to the fungus. To help animals that might get infected, researchers are trying to reproduce the fungus-fighting bacteria that naturally grow on some captive Panamanian golden frogs. They may then be able to transfer the bacteria to vulnerable amphibians. Researchers from the University of South Florida have also found that Cuban tree frogs can build more and more of a resistance to chytrid if they are repeatedly infected and treated. It's too early to know if these treatments will work on a large scale and allow relocated frogs to return to their homes. But they offer hope.

PANAMANIAN GOLDEN FROG

Frogs were the first land animals to have vocal cords.

"We look forward to the day when we can return rescued frogs and other amphibians to the wild where they belong," Fenolio says. Forests that host a chorus of croaks? That's definitely a reason to jump up and down!

SPYING ON SLOTHS

RESEARCHERS USE TECHNOLOGY TO LEARN ABOUT LIFE IN THE SLOW LANE.

A BROWN-THROATED THREE-TOED SLOTH IN COSTA RICA

Tucked in a tree canopy in Panama's rain forest, a three-toed sloth and the newborn baby clinging to her belly are all but invisible to the naked eye. This is the sloths' defense strategy: hiding from predators by camouflaging themselves. But their stealth behavior also makes it tricky for researchers to study sloths. Spying on the sloths has been hard to do, but now, cool technology allows sloth scientists to "see" what this animal does all day long.

COOL TOOLS

"Spying" tools include using a harmless, sticky substance to glue a tiny cap on a sloth's head. Inside is a monitor that records brain activity, so researchers can tell when the sloth is awake and asleep. Radio collars track a sloth's travel—they typically move just 80 feet (24 m) a day—to understand how much space a sloth needs to thrive. And outfitting the animals with custom backpacks help researchers record body temperature and geographic location. After four weeks, an automatic latch opens, and the backpack falls to the forest floor. The data inside gives clues about the best spots to set sloths free in the wild.

SAVING THE SLOTHS

Learning about the daily habits and routines of sloths is helpful in developing protected areas for these animals. And thanks to these high-tech tools, researchers have behind-the-scenes information that can help ensure that sloths hang around for a long time to come.

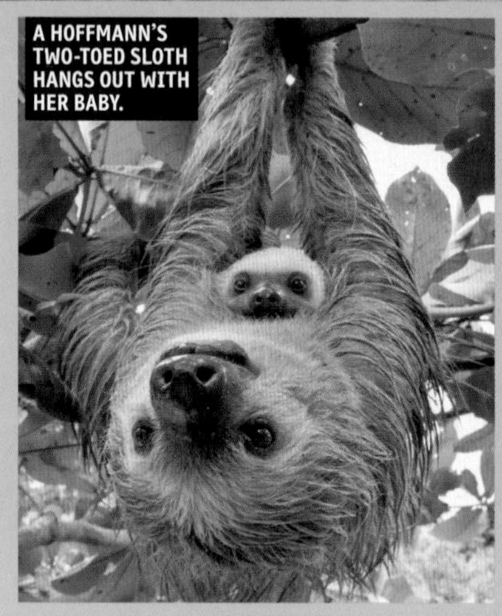

A HOFFMANN'S TWO-TOED SLOTH HANGS OUT WITH HER BABY.

How many toes? Sloths come in two models: two-toed and three-toed. They resemble each other, but they're two completely different families. Two-toed sloths are feistier and faster than three-toed sloths. Two-toed sloths can move quickly in the trees, while sloths with three toes usually move more slowly.

Scientists use **cool technology** to uncover clues about these **big cats.**

SNOW LEOPARD SELFIES

A SNOW LEOPARD'S COAT HELPS IT BLEND IN WITH ITS SURROUNDINGS.

In Mongolia, a snow leopard and her two cubs scamper along a rugged mountainside. One cub pushes his face up to a small metal object that's secured to a rock. The young snow leopard has no idea he's taking selfies—lots of them. The object that caught his attention is a camera that snaps his portrait every half second.

HIDDEN CAMERAS

Researchers have posted dozens of the cameras to trees and rocks throughout the areas of Central Asia where snow leopards are known to roam. With built-in sensors, the gadgets activate when they detect movement and heat. This surveillance gives researchers a window into the endangered cats' secret lives, exposing how they play, hunt, and relax.

The cameras also allow scientists to get to know individual snow leopards. Patterns in the fur of these big cats are very distinctive. Sharp observers can use them like fingerprints to identify the cats. If they catch glimpses of the same snow leopard with cameras in two different locations, they've tracked the snow leopard's movements.

STOPPING THE THREAT

To come up with conservation plans for these stealthy animals, scientists are turning to cutting-edge technology to learn all they can. Snow leopards—which live in Central Asian countries such as China, Bhutan, and Mongolia—are endangered. Humans are the biggest threat to these animals. Poachers kill snow leopards for their fur, and some herders attack any that try to eat their livestock. Some experts think as few as 4,000 snow leopards remain in the wild. Tools like these hidden cameras figure out what these cats need in their environments to thrive.

ADULT SNOW LEOPARDS ARE SOLITARY, BUT YOUNG SIBLINGS WILL CUDDLE AND PLAY.

WHAT IS Taxonomy?

Since there are billions and billions of living things, called organisms, on the planet, people need a way of classifying them. Scientists created a system called **taxonomy**, which helps to classify all living things into ordered groups. By putting organisms into categories we are better able to understand how they are the same and how they are different. There are seven levels of taxonomic classification, beginning with the broadest group, called a domain, followed by kingdom, down to the most specific group, called a species.

Biologists divide life based on evolutionary history, and they place organisms into three domains depending on their genetic structure: Archaea, Bacteria, and Eukarya. (See p. 207 for "The Three Domains of Life.")

Where do animals come in?

Animals are a part of the Eukarya domain, which means they are organisms made of cells with nuclei. More than one million species of animals have been named, including humans. Like all living things, animals can be divided into smaller groups, called phyla. Most scientists believe there are more than 30 phyla into which animals can be grouped based on certain scientific criteria, such as body type or whether or not the animal has a backbone. It can be pretty complicated, so there is another, less complicated system that groups animals into two categories: vertebrates and invertebrates.

Chinese stripe-necked turtle

SAMPLE CLASSIFICATION
JAPANESE MACAQUE

Kingdom:	Animalia
Phylum:	Chordata
Class:	Mammalia
Order:	Primates
Family:	Cercopithecidae
Genus:	*Macaca*
Species:	*fuscata*

TIP
Here's a sentence to help you remember the classification order:
King Phillip Came Over For Good Soup.

BY THE NUMBERS

There are 12,316 vulnerable or endangered animal species in the world. The list includes:

- **1,208 mammals**, such as the snow leopard, the polar bear, and the fishing cat.
- **1,375 birds**, including the Steller's sea eagle and the black-banded plover.
- **2,343 fish**, such as the Mekong giant catfish.
- **989 reptiles**, including the American crocodile.
- **1,156 insects**, including the Macedonian grayling.
- **2,063 amphibians**, such as the Round Island day gecko.
- **And more**, including 166 arachnids, 729 crustaceans, 239 sea anemones and corals, 175 bivalves, and 1,787 snails and slugs.

Vertebrates Animals WITH Backbones

Fish are cold-blooded and live in water. They breathe with gills, lay eggs, and usually have scales.

Amphibians are cold-blooded. Their young live in water and breathe with gills. Adults live on land and breathe with lungs.

Reptiles are cold-blooded and breathe with lungs. They live both on land and in water.

Bird: Bald eagle

Fish: Clown anemonefish

Birds are warm-blooded and have feathers and wings. They lay eggs, breathe with lungs, and usually are able to fly. Some birds live on land, some in water, and some on both.

Mammals are warm-blooded and feed on their mothers' milk. They also have skin that is usually covered with hair. Mammals live both on land and in water.

Invertebrates Animals WITHOUT Backbones

Sponges are a very basic form of animal life. They live in water and do not move on their own.

Echinoderms have external skeletons and live in seawater.

Mollusks have soft bodies and can live either in or out of shells, on land or in water.

Arthropods are the largest group of animals. They have external skeletons, called exoskeletons, and segmented bodies with appendages. Arthropods live in water and on land.

Worms are soft-bodied animals with no true legs. Worms live in soil.

Cnidaria live in water and have mouths surrounded by tentacles.

Worm: Earthworms

Cnidaria: West Coast sea nettle

Cold-blooded versus Warm-blooded

Cold-blooded animals, also called ectotherms, get their heat from outside their bodies.

Warm-blooded animals, also called endotherms, keep their body temperature level regardless of the temperature of their environments.

Tips for being a COATI

There comes a time, if you're a coati, that you'll join a band of other coatis. Here are five pointers for fitting in.

BE A TEAM PLAYER.

Your coati band has as many as 30 members, and you'll have to get along with everyone—that means females of all ages and immature males. (When males are two to three years old they leave the band.) So don't dawdle as you travel together searching for food. Have your pals' backs as you keep each other safe.

KEEP YOUR NAILS SHARP.

Shh. Hear the insect larvae squirming inside that log but have no idea how to get at them? Just use your long, sharp claws to gouge and rip into wood. Mounds of grubs are now yours any time you want.

BE COOL—DON'T BEG.

There's no sharing in coati bands; you'll have to find your own meals. Don't just stand there drooling if you see an adult eating something interesting. It's totally OK to put your nose right up to her mouth and take a big whiff. You can even follow her around to see how she finds more.

GO BACK FOR SECONDS— AND THIRDS, AND FOURTHS.

You can eat practically everything in the forest—as long as it's small enough. Meals include fruits, beetles, centipedes, scorpions, termites, insect larvae, and spiders. And it's not gross to crave something chewy on the outside and crunchy on the inside, such as a frog, lizard, rodent, or bird.

CROCODILE HATCHLING

CHILL OUT.

After a hard day of eating bugs and dodging predators, you deserve a little fun. So leap from branch to branch with your bandmates. Scale to the treetop, use your mighty tail to balance way up high, and scramble straight down. You might be having a blast, but playing also helps build muscle and speed. You'll need both to track down tasty frogs and escape hungry predators—and that's what being a full-fledged coati is all about.

TOUGH CATS

COUGAR KITTENS WATCH MOM TO SURVIVE.

Snowy footprints wind through the trees in Wyoming, U.S.A.'s Teton Mountains. They are the paw prints of a mother mountain lion following the scent of an elk. Her seven-month-old kittens romp alongside her. They're supposed to be learning to hunt by watching their mom. Shh! Mom chirps at her kittens to tell them to hide, then she freezes. She crouches down, ready to pounce. Then, the skillful hunter takes down the elk in a cloud of snow, and just a few seconds later dinner is served for this feline family.

TRACKING CATS

How young cougars learn to hunt is one of the things cougar researchers like Mark Elbroch of Panthera, a conservation organization, are working to figure out. They're keeping track of the mother cougar—who they call F51—using the satellite signal from her electronic collar. When she gave birth to her kittens, Elbroch put expandable tracking collars on them, too.

RAISING THE FAMILY

As the kittens grew older and stronger, they learn how to search for food by following their mother, watching her select an animal to stalk, and observing how she catches her prey. They also learn that meal plans can change quickly. Sometimes, wolves chase F51 and her kittens away from kills, and they also compete with coyotes, bears, wolves, and, in Wyoming, even other cougars for elk and mule deer.

Luckily, F51 is able to provide plenty of food for her kittens. Her territory overlaps with another female's, and they are friendly with each other, often sharing food.

FINAL CHALLENGE

In the spring, one of the researchers watches a couple of one-year-old cougars with a fawn they don't quite know what to do with. Their mother likely injured the fawn so that her kittens could use it to practice hunting skills. These two are just beginning to figure out how to make a kill.

Like these young cats, F51's kittens had watched their mom to learn survival skills. Elbroch's team spots one kitten, now on her own. The team is relieved to see her kill a ground squirrel by herself. Now they're hopeful that this tough young cat will survive.

GOOFBALLS

THE WAY ARMADILLOS BEHAVE WILL CRACK YOU UP.

If you held a contest for the funniest animal on the planet, the prize would have to go to an armadillo. Get ready to LOL as NG shows off the silly side of armadillos.

Armadillos live mostly in Central and South America. Only the nine-banded armadillo lives in the United States.

An armadillo looks hilarious.

Armadillos look like a mixture of a huge roly-poly bug, a pig, and a medieval knight—with a bit of giant insect mixed in. But they're actually mammals, closely related to anteaters and sloths. They have long snouts and piglike ears, and their bodies are covered with protective bony plates that look like a knight's armor.

Armadillos are mostly nocturnal. They stay inside their burrows when it's hot and come out at dawn or dusk or at night to look for food.

They leap straight up when startled.

If something startles a nine-banded armadillo by touching it on the back, it responds by jumping straight up into the air, sometimes as high as four feet (1.2 m). It's a reflex that probably helps them get away from predators. (Or maybe it just makes the predators laugh so hard they forget to chase the armadillo.)

They stick out their tongues to eat.

Armadillos use their long, sticky tongues to feel around in ant nests, slurping up lots of ants at a time. A nine-banded armadillo can eat thousands of ants at one meal. Ants may not be *your* favorite food, but don't make fun of an armadillo's snack—it might stick out that extra-long tongue at you!

They turn into balls.

Armadillos usually aren't fighters. When threatened, the three-banded armadillo protects itself by rolling into a ball. The result looks so much like a soccer ball that a three-banded armadillo named Fuleco was the mascot of the 2014 World Cup in Brazil.

They're likely to get into traffic jams.

If you frighten an armadillo, it might run away to hide in the nearest burrow. But sometimes when one armadillo is trying to get into the burrow, another armadillo (or two!) is trying to get out. They get stuck!

Armadillos have been around for at least 65 million years.

A nine-banded armadillo uses its huge front claws to dig its burrow. It might have several burrows but uses only one for its babies. That burrow is up to 25 feet (7.6 m) long and can have several rooms and connecting tunnels.

Mistaken Identity

Sugar gliders seem to think that they're birds and soccer players. Find out why.

The sugar glider appears to be one mixed-up mammal. Mostly found in the forests of Australia and on the nearby island of New Guinea, this tree-dweller exhibits a mishmash of traits seen in other animals and humans. Is it confused, or does it just have bizarre behaviors? Read on and decide for yourself.

A SUGAR GLIDER'S TAIL IS LONGER THAN ITS BODY.

THEY HAVE BIRDLIKE MOVES.

When the sugar glider wants to travel long distances, it leaps from its treetop home into the air and spreads its limbs as if they're wings. Luckily, skin flaps on either side of its body connect the front and back legs. With the flaps extended, the critter can sail on air. Sugar gliders aren't birds, but they definitely have soaring skills.

MALE SUGAR GLIDERS HAVE A BALD PATCH ON THEIR HEADS.

THEY ACT LIKE BALL PLAYERS.

Sugar glider families sleep inside tree hollows. At naptime they heap together like soccer stars who have just scored a big win. Huddling like this keeps the animals warm. But not just any glider is welcome on the "victory pile." If an unrelated sugar glider sneaks onto a family's turf, the clan will chase it away. Now that's good defense.

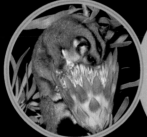

THEY BEHAVE LIKE KIDS.

You probably have a serious sweet tooth. And sugar gliders act like, well, a kid in a candy store when they're around sweet stuff. This animal devours foods that are high in sugar such as flower nectar and tree sap.

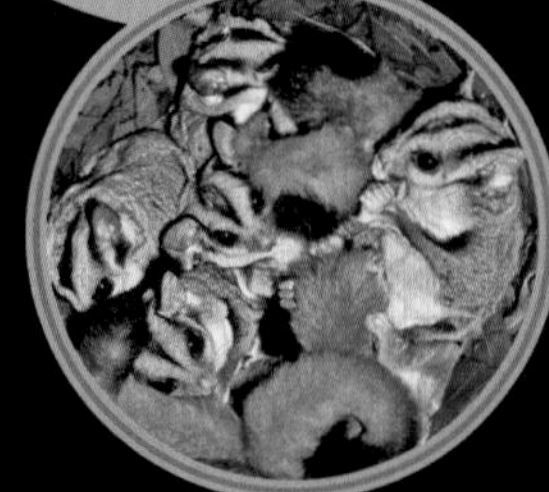

WOLVERINE!

How to track a wild, mysterious super-predator

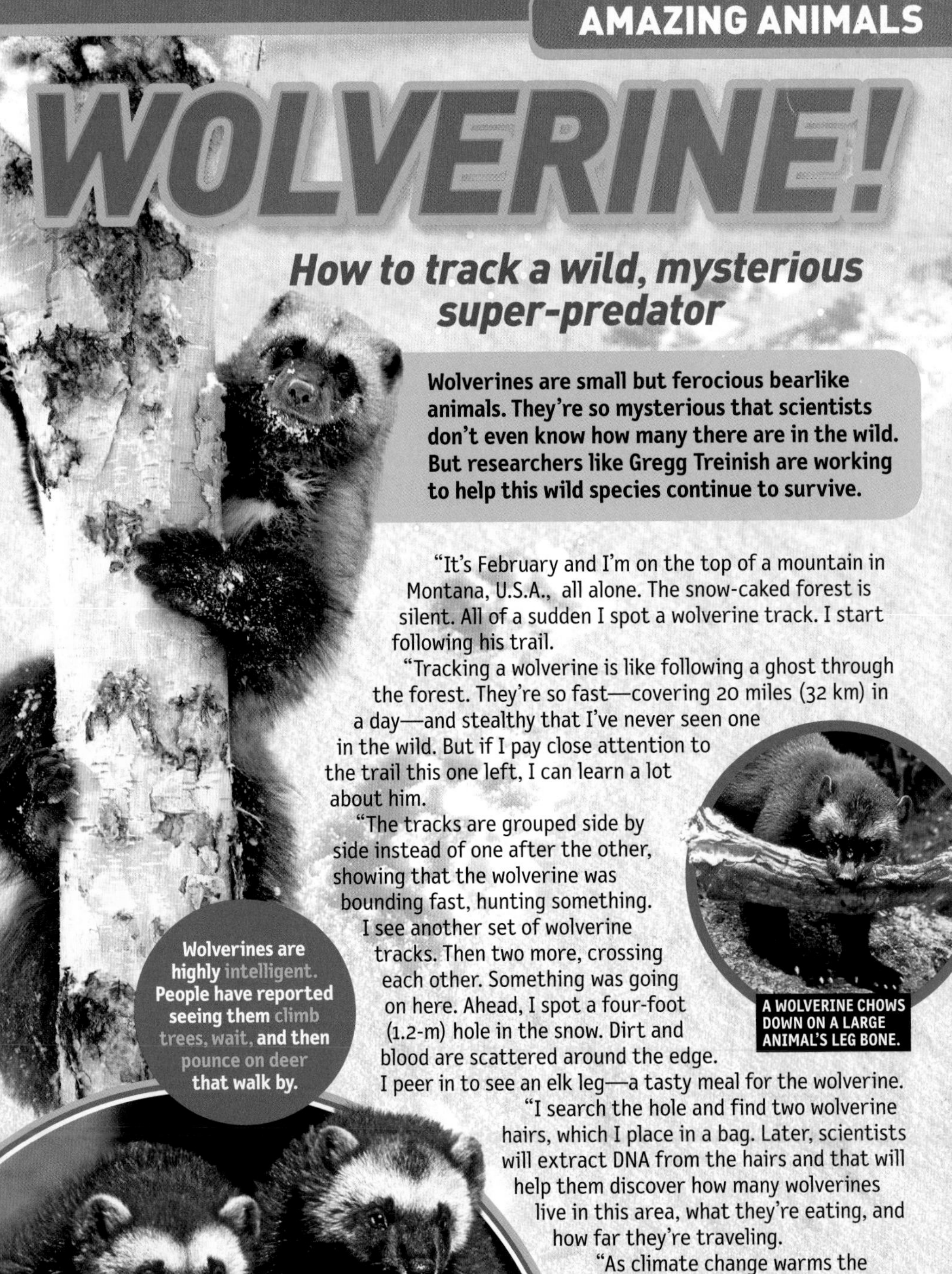

Wolverines are small but ferocious bearlike animals. They're so mysterious that scientists don't even know how many there are in the wild. But researchers like Gregg Treinish are working to help this wild species continue to survive.

"It's February and I'm on the top of a mountain in Montana, U.S.A., all alone. The snow-caked forest is silent. All of a sudden I spot a wolverine track. I start following his trail.

"Tracking a wolverine is like following a ghost through the forest. They're so fast—covering 20 miles (32 km) in a day—and stealthy that I've never seen one in the wild. But if I pay close attention to the trail this one left, I can learn a lot about him.

"The tracks are grouped side by side instead of one after the other, showing that the wolverine was bounding fast, hunting something. I see another set of wolverine tracks. Then two more, crossing each other. Something was going on here. Ahead, I spot a four-foot (1.2-m) hole in the snow. Dirt and blood are scattered around the edge. I peer in to see an elk leg—a tasty meal for the wolverine.

"I search the hole and find two wolverine hairs, which I place in a bag. Later, scientists will extract DNA from the hairs and that will help them discover how many wolverines live in this area, what they're eating, and how far they're traveling.

"As climate change warms the planet, wolverines' snowy habitat is disappearing. The clues I find will help scientists track the population to learn whether we need to take action to prevent these phantoms of the forest from disappearing forever."

A WOLVERINE CHOWS DOWN ON A LARGE ANIMAL'S LEG BONE.

Wolverines are highly intelligent. People have reported seeing them climb trees, wait, and then pounce on deer that walk by.

Wild Hamsters

FARMERS TRY TO MAKE PEACE WITH THESE PESKY CRITTERS.

In a sun-dappled wheat field in France, a prowling barn cat meets a black-bellied hamster. Too far from her burrow to run for shelter, the wild hamster rises on her hind legs to face her enemy. She puffs out her cheeks, flashes her black underbelly, growls, and bares her teeth. The cat backs away. That black-bellied hamster is one tough rodent.

"They're afraid of nothing," says Alexandre Lehmann, a biologist who has worked with these wild hamsters for the past 12 years. "They fight against cars and dogs and even farmers. They try to fight against tractors. The Germans call them small bears."

Good thing the black-bellied hamster won't go down without a fight. Because in France, where only 500 to 1,000 remain in the wild, these cranky critters are in a fight for their lives.

During hibernation a hamster's heart beats only about six times a minute.

There are around 25 different species of wild hamsters.

TWO-DAY-OLD HAMSTERS

The earliest hamsters lived more than 2.5 million years ago.

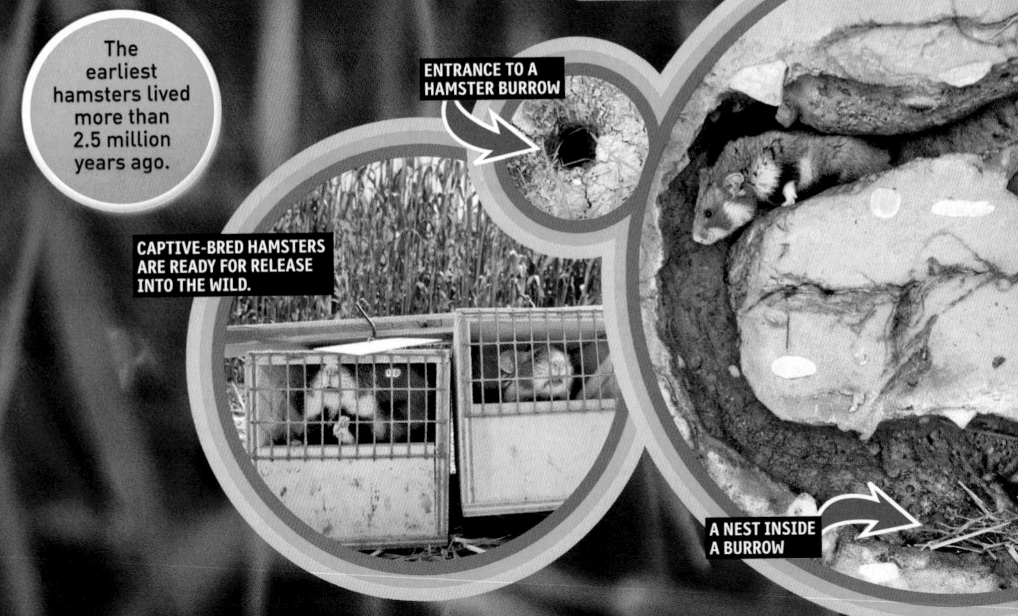
ENTRANCE TO A HAMSTER BURROW
CAPTIVE-BRED HAMSTERS ARE READY FOR RELEASE INTO THE WILD.
A NEST INSIDE A BURROW

FEISTY RODENTS

Don't confuse the black-bellied hamster with its puny tame relative, the golden hamster. At about 12 inches (30 cm) long, the black-bellied hamster is twice as big. And it's way more feisty.

In fact, black-bellied hamsters historically have been considered public enemy number one—rodents on the wrong side of the law. Ranging from the eastern steppes of Russia to the plains of Alsace in France, black-bellied hamsters have long been seen as pests because of their appetites for farmers' grains, beets, and cabbage. And since mother hamsters can give birth to as many as 14 babies a year, sometimes the population has exploded. The hamsters earned a bad rap, and humans tried everything to get rid of them. Some older farmers remember a time when, as kids, they were paid as bounty hunters to kill hamsters and bring their tails to city hall.

FRANCE
EUROPE
ATLANTIC OCEAN

The war on hamsters continued until just a few decades ago, when naturalists noticed the rodents were in trouble. Although plenty of hamsters were in Russia and the Ukraine, their numbers had been dwindling in western Europe. A movement began to save the hamsters. In 1993 France passed a law protecting them as an endangered species.

HELPING HANDS

At the Stork and Otter Reintroduction Centre in Alsace, Lehmann and his colleagues breed captive hamsters and release their pups into the wild. But breeding black-bellied hamsters isn't easy. Remember, these critters have attitude. Forget humans—they don't even like each other.

If all goes well, the mother hamster will give birth to a litter of about seven pups in three weeks' time. One year later the pups will be ready for release into the wild.

GROWING HABITAT

Black-bellied hamsters might think of themselves as tough guys. But to a fox or an eagle, they're just a four-legged snack. To survive, hamsters need to be released into a field with lots of leafy hiding places. That's a problem in Alsace, where most farmers plant corn. The corn hasn't sprouted in early spring, when hamsters come out from winter hibernation. In the bare fields the hamsters are easy targets for predators.

Some older farmers don't want hamsters on their property because of their reputation as pests. But most are willing to help, especially since the French government will pay farmers to grow early-sprouting crops such as alfalfa and winter wheat and allow hamsters to be released on their lands. It's a way to protect not just the hamsters, but also other small animals that thrive in a landscape of leafy fields.

Sounds like the bad beast on the block is up to some good after all.

18 Cool Things About

1

A SALTWATER CROCODILE'S BITING POWER IS NEARLY FOUR TIMES STRONGER THAN A LION'S.

2

THE CHINESE SOFT-SHELLED TURTLE PEES FROM ITS MOUTH.

3

THE RETICULATED PYTHON CAN GROW ABOUT THE SAME LENGTH AS CERTAIN FIRE ENGINES.

4

A shingleback skink's tail is shaped almost exactly like its head.

5

King cobras, which grow to 18 feet (5.5 m), can lift the upper third of their bodies off the ground.

6

A GILA MONSTER CAN EAT UP TO A THIRD OF ITS WEIGHT IN ONE MEAL.

7

A veiled chameleon's tongue can stretch one and a half times the length of its body.

8

Most male box turtles have **bright red eyes.**

9

The Namib web-footed gecko keeps hydrated by licking moisture from its eyeballs.

REPTILES

10

Crocodiles can climb trees.

11

AFRICAN EGG-EATING SNAKES SWALLOW BIRD EGGS WHOLE.

12

A FLYING DRAGON LIZARD can glide through the air for 30 FEET (9.1 m) on winglike skin flaps.

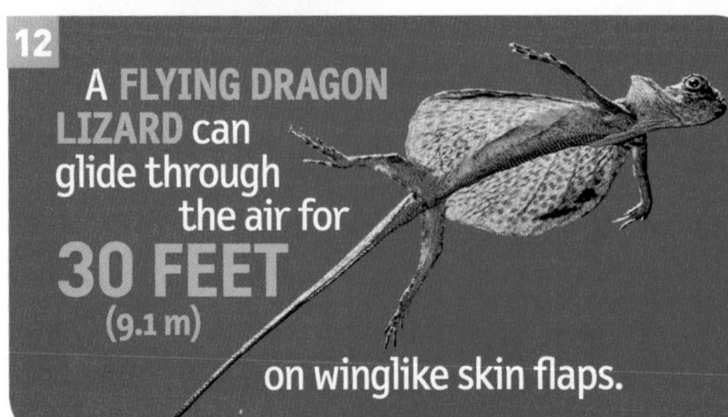

13

About HALF of all known CHAMELEON SPECIES can be found on the African island of MADAGASCAR.

14

Spectacled caimans blow bubbles at potential mates.

15

An ALLIGATOR SNAPPING TURTLE uses a WORMLIKE extension on its tongue to LURE FISH into its mouth.

16

Galápagos marine iguanas often swim in the ocean.

17

THE GABOON VIPER CARRIES ENOUGH VENOM TO KILL 30 PEOPLE.

18

Green basilisk lizards have specially designed feet that let them run on water without sinking.

BRAINWAVES

Inside the Amazing Minds of Dolphins

SCIENTISTS STUDY THE BEHAVIOR OF THESE AND OTHER BOTTLENOSE DOLPHINS AT THE ROATÁN INSTITUTE FOR MARINE SCIENCES IN HONDURAS, CENTRAL AMERICA.

ALFONZ AND KIMBIT EACH TAKE HOLD OF A ROPE TO PULL APART THE PIPE WITH A TREAT INSIDE.

In an experiment at a research center in Florida, U.S.A., two dolphins try to solve a puzzle. Named Alfonz and Kimbit, the dolphins examine a pipe that scientists have stuffed with tasty fish and dropped into the water. To get to the snack, each dolphin must tug on a rope connected to a cap on each end of the pipe. Neither dolphin can open the pipe alone, so to solve this puzzle, Alfonz and Kimbit must work together.

They don't waste any time. Gripping the ropes with their teeth, the dolphins yank off the caps. Success! They split the treat inside. Their feat reveals a lot about the amazing minds of these marine mammals. Alfonz and Kimbit demonstrate that they can communicate, cooperate, and plan—three behaviors scientists consider signs of intelligence in animals. But intelligence is tricky to measure in animals, and researchers are figuring out new ways to answer an old question. "We shouldn't be asking, 'How smart are dolphins?'" says Stan Kuczaj, an expert on dolphin intelligence. "We should be asking, 'How are dolphins smart?'"

STRANGE BRAINS

Scientists see signs of intelligent life throughout the animal kingdom. Octopuses can solve puzzles. Wolves communicate. Crows use tools. But dolphins possess *all* of these brainy abilities. Some people think that the only animals smarter than dolphins are humans.

But dolphin brains are very different from our own. Dolphins have adapted for life in the ocean. They sleep with half their brains awake to stay alert for sharks and other dangers. "These animals live in a very different world," underwater photographer Brian Skerry says. "They're best described as an alien intelligence."

They even have an otherworldly ability: echolocation, a way to "see" by bouncing sound waves of high-speed clicks off objects hundreds of yards away. Dolphins use this sixth sense in intelligent ways. They listen to each other's signals to cooperate while hunting. "I suspect they also use echolocation to read the emotions of other animals," Kuczaj says. Ever notice how your muscles grow tense when you're anxious or your heart races when you get scared? Using echolocation, dolphins can sense these characteristics in other animals. They can even tell if another dolphin is sick. "Knowing the mood of other animals in the group is an important ability when you're such a social animal," Kuczaj says.

PROBLEM SOLVERS

In the shallow waters off Florida, a group of dolphins goes fishing. One darts into action, swimming in speedy circles around a school of fish to kick up a netlike wall of mud. Trapped, the fish leap over the mud—and right into the open mouths of the other dolphins. In other places, dolphins have devised their own brainy means of landing lunch. Orcas in Argentina trap sea lions on the beach. Dolphins off another coast of South America cooperate to scare fish into easier-to-chomp schools. Like Alfonz and Kimbit, these wild dolphins are cooperating to solve problems.

SOCIAL SWIMMER

Dolphins form decades-long friendships and team up to hunt for food, find mates, and protect the group. Partnerships fall apart and re-form according to complex social rules that scientists are still figuring out. If a dolphin gets sick or hurt, the entire group will follow and look after it. "Social behavior is a key to their survival," Skerry says.

A PIECE OF SEAWEED BECOMES A TOY AS THESE BOTTLENOSE DOLPHINS PLAY TOGETHER.

AFTER FORCING FISH TO CLUMP TOGETHER, DUSKY DOLPHINS GRAB AN EASY MOUTHFUL. A PENGUIN (BOTTOM) EVEN SNEAKS IN FOR THE FEAST.

Signs of Dolphin Smarts

THEY COMMUNICATE. Scientists suspect dolphins "talk" about everything from basic facts like their age and gender to whether they're happy or sad. When faced with a shark or other threats, they'll even call group members for backup.

THEY COOPERATE. Intensely social animals, dolphins establish complex relationships that scientists still don't understand. They team up to hunt, protect each other, find mates, and just play.

THEY INVENT. Dolphins demonstrate a humanlike ability to adapt to different situations. Some even use tools. Dolphins in Australia wear sponges to protect their noses when they dig in the seafloor for food.

Name That TIDE POOL ANIMAL

When the tide goes out in rocky, coastal areas, some water gets left behind in pools and crevices. These spots are called tide pools, and many different creatures like to hang out in them. See if you can name these tide pool animals.

A

This creature is always on the lookout for a new home. Snail shells are usually its preference, but with five pairs of legs, you can't call it a slowpoke!

A tide pool is one tough neighborhood! When the tide is in, waves come crashing; when the tide is out, animals are exposed to sun, cold weather, and even freshwater from rain. When you look closely at tide pool creatures, you'll find they all have adaptations to survive these harsh conditions.

B

These drifters don't have much say about where they end up, but often they show up in tide pools. They may be soft and squishy, but their tentacles are stunning.

C

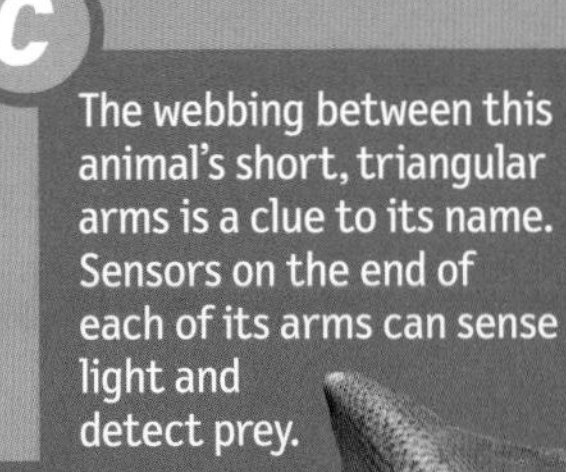

The webbing between this animal's short, triangular arms is a clue to its name. Sensors on the end of each of its arms can sense light and detect prey.

D

Nemo and his father lived inside one of these. When their tentacles are open they are ready for food; when they're folded in, they're likely munching.

E

After grazing on algae, this tide pool creature finds the perfect parking spot on a rock and hunkers down, sealing water underneath itself to keep its body moist during low tide.

F

Call it a tide pool salad. This leafy green creature can get dry and stiff at low tide, but it bounces right back once the water comes in.

A. Hermit crab; **B.** Jellyfish; **C.** Bat star; **D.** Sea anemone; **E.** Limpet; **F.** Sea lettuce

SEA TURTLE

A lost and freezing loggerhead gets help from warmhearted volunteers.

The freezing sea turtle can barely manage another stroke as she struggles to keep herself warm in the frigid waters of Cape Cod Bay off Massachusetts, U.S.A. The reptile is suffering from the turtle version of human hypothermia—when body temperature falls below normal levels. Her strength is fading fast.

She bobs lifelessly on the surface of the water before a gust of wind propels her toward land. Washed up on the shore of Crosby Landing Beach, she lies motionless in the sand, bitterly cold. If she doesn't get help soon, she won't have a chance.

LIFEGUARDS ARRIVE

Taking a morning stroll along the beach, Brian Long spots the large turtle. He can't tell if she's alive, so he immediately phones the Massachusetts Audobon Society, a conservation organization. The call reaches director Bob Prescott, who rushes to the beach in a pickup truck and identifies the two-and-a-half-foot (.76-m)-long creature as a loggerhead sea turtle. An endangered species, they spend their summers in the north and their winters in warmer southern waters, but this turtle likely got lost while navigating down the coast and missed the chance to migrate before cold weather set in.

The animal's eyes are closed, and she's not visibly breathing. But when

Some Pacific loggerheads migrate over 7,500 miles (12,000 km) between nesting beaches.

A cooler loggerhead nest will produce more male hatchlings, while a warmer one will produce more females.

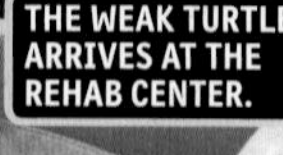
THE WEAK TURTLE ARRIVES AT THE REHAB CENTER.

Prescott gently touches her neck, the big-beaked reptile slowly raises her head. She's hanging on but urgently needs medical care. The two men hoist the huge animal onto the bed of the truck, and she's taken to New England Aquarium in Boston, Massachusetts. Here, she can begin her recovery.

SHELL-SHOCKED

At the aquarium's marine animal rehabilitation center, staff name the turtle Biscuits and give her an exam. She weighs in at 165 pounds (75 kg)—slightly underweight for a loggerhead of Biscuits's age. She has developed open wounds, she's dehydrated, and she has pneumonia. She is also cold-stunned, a condition that affects reptiles if their temperatures drop too low. As their bodies cool, the animals' blood circulation slows, causing the animals to enter a coma-like state, practically unable to move.

Now her caretakers' goal is to raise her body temperature from an extremely low 48°F (9°C) to between 70°F and 80°F (21°C and 25°C). But it won't be easy—warming her too quickly could be deadly. She's moved into a temperature-controlled pool set to 55°F (13°C).

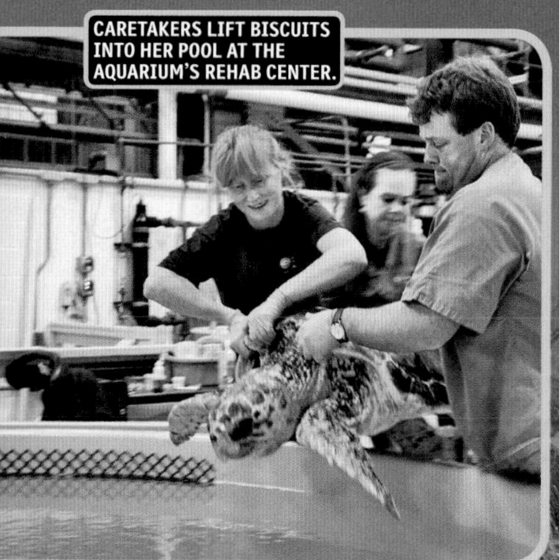

CARETAKERS LIFT BISCUITS INTO HER POOL AT THE AQUARIUM'S REHAB CENTER.

Each day the rehabbers raise the thermostat a little higher. As the temperature rises, Biscuits begins to move normally again.

To help her regain energy, the staff offer healthy meals of fish and squid, and they rehydrate her with daily injections of nutrient-filled fluids. Biscuits also receives antibiotics for her pneumonia and soothing ointment for her skin

These turtles may live for 50 years or more in the wild.

GEORGIA SEA TURTLE CENTER STAFF UNLOAD BISCUITS FROM THE PLANE.

TURTLE TAKEOFF

Soon, Biscuits is ready for to be moved to the Georgia Sea Turtle Center on Jekyll Island, which is located closer to her release site. Here the staff will continue to prepare her for reentry into the wild. Along with three other recovering turtles, she's flown to Georgia, U.S.A., on a private jet. Once there, Biscuits is placed in a tank where she can continue practicing her swimming strokes. Caretakers also put live blue crabs and horseshoe crabs in her tank so she can get used to catching prey again. These critters are some of a loggerhead's favorite foods in the wild, and Biscuits quickly remembers how to snatch up the tasty treats in her beak.

BISCUITS RETURNS TO THE SEA.

BACK TO THE SEA

A month later Biscuits is ready to return to the ocean. She's heavier, now weighing 180 pounds (82 kg), and has proven she can catch live prey. She's driven by her rehabilitation team to a release site in Florida, U.S.A. When the team lowers her onto the sand at the water's edge, she immediately crawls into the crashing waves and swims off, healthy and happy at last.

Awesome INSECT AWARDS

We're buggin' out! Our earth is crawling with over 800,000 species of insects. And whether they're teeny-tiny or superstrong, some of those six-legged species certainly stand out. Here are seven of the biggest, baddest, ickiest bugs out there!

Heavy Lifter

The ***rhinoceros beetle***, which gets its name from the hornlike structure on the male's head, is capable of carrying up to 850 times its own body weight.

Loud Mouth

The distinctive call of a male ***African cicada*** is about as loud as a rock concert or an ambulance siren. The call comes from special structures on the bug's belly, which vibrate to deter predators or attract another cicada's attention.

Is it a bird? A bat? No, it's the ***Atlas moth***, who has a wingspan wider than a dinner plate—the largest moth wings on the planet.

Biggest Wings

The ***monarch butterfly*** has a king-size appetite! A large monarch caterpillar can chomp an entire milkweed leaf in less than four minutes.

Big Eater

Sharpest Defense

When clustered with others on a branch, a tiny ***thorn bug*** becomes part of a prickly pack no bird wants a bite of!

Coolest Camo

It's common to mistake the ***walking leaf*** for an actual leaf, thanks to its large, feathery wings. This clever camouflage provides protection from potential predators.

Colossal Crawler

The ***Goliath beetle*** weighs about as much as a quarter-pound hamburger, making it one of the heaviest bugs on earth.

BIG CATS

A young male jaguar

Not all wild cats are big cats, so what are big cats? To wildlife experts, they are the four living members of the genus *Panthera:* tigers, lions, leopards, and jaguars. They can all unleash a mighty roar and, as carnivores, they survive solely on the flesh of other animals. Thanks to powerful jaws; long, sharp claws; and daggerlike teeth, big cats are excellent hunters.

Learn more about animals in peril and ways you can help with National Geographic Kids Mission: Animal Rescue series. Visit kids.nationalgeographic.com/mission-animal-rescue.

WHO'S WHO?

BIG CATS MAY HAVE a lot of features in common, but if you know what to look for, you'll be able to tell who's who in no time.

FUR

JAGUARS

A jaguar's coat pattern looks similar to that of a leopard, as both have dark spots called rosettes. The difference? The rosettes on a jaguar's torso have irregularly shaped borders and at least one black dot in the center.

TIGERS

Most tigers are orange-colored with vertical black stripes on their bodies. This coloring helps the cats blend in with tall grasses as they sneak up on prey. These markings are like fingerprints: No two stripe patterns are alike.

LEOPARDS

A leopard's yellowy coat has dark spots called rosettes on its back and sides. In leopards, the rosettes' edges are smooth and circular. This color combo helps leopards blend into their surroundings.

LIONS

Lions have a light brown, or tawny, coat and a tuft of black hair at the end of their tails. When they reach their prime, most male lions have shaggy manes that help them look larger and more intimidating.

JAGUAR
100 to 250 pounds
(45 TO 113 KG)
5 to 6 feet long
(1.5 TO 1.8 M)

LEOPARD
66 to 176 pounds
(30 TO 80 KG)
4.25 to 6.25 feet long
(1.3 TO 1.9 M)

BENGAL TIGER
240 to 500 pounds
(109 TO 227 KG)
5 to 6 feet long
(1.5 TO 1.8 M)

AFRICAN LION
265 to 420 pounds
(120 TO 191 KG)
4.5 to 6.5 feet long
(1.4 TO 2 M)

top spOt

How the jaguar's one-of-a-kind features make it stand out from other wild cats

The word jaguar comes from a Native American word meaning "he who kills with one leap."

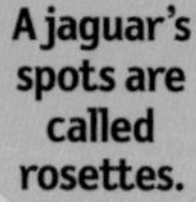

A jaguar's spots are called rosettes.

A STEALTHY PREDATOR glides along a river in South America. Noticing a group of alligator-like animals called caimans floating by the shore, the hunter silently cruises toward the reptiles. It swims between plants to mask its movements and pauses beside an unsuspecting caiman. Then the animal shoots through the water at its target, sinking its teeth into the reptile's scaly skin.

With its prey clamped between its jaws, the creature climbs from the water and onto the riverbank. In doing so, it reveals its true identity. The dripping-wet hunter is a jaguar.

"We knew jaguars were good swimmers," says wildlife ecologist Alan Rabinowitz, who runs a big cat conservation organization called Panthera and witnessed the splashy smackdown while on an expedition. "But we were astonished to learn that they can hunt as they swim."

Snagging prey while swimming is something no other feline does. Then again, the jaguar stands out from the rest of the cat crowd in many ways.

ON THE ON HUNT

One thing that makes a jaguar unique from other cats is its hunting techniques. This cat hunts for food on the ground, in trees, and while swimming in water. No other cat does this. "Even lions and tigers—the closest relatives of the jaguar—don't go after prey in all three spots," Rabinowitz says. "They usually just nab prey on the ground."

What's more, jaguars use a different hunting strategy from most other felines. A lot of cats chase targets over long distances. A jaguar silently sneaks up to prey such as tapirs before ambushing its meal. The animal creeps closer to its mark than even the tiger. When jaguars finally strike, they do so in their own special way. Most felines struggle with prey before overpowering it. But a jaguar has the largest jaws of any big cat, so its bite is so strong it's often able to take down its target with just one chomp.

But just because jaguars slay it with their hunting skills doesn't mean they like to fight. They only scuffle when necessary.

ADAPTATION NATION

So why is the jaguar so different from other felines? Over their four-million-year existence, jaguars have developed adaptations to help deal with unique challenges in their habitats. For instance, it's hard to chase prey through the forests where the cats live. That's why they creep right up to their target.

Deadly parasites thrive in the cat's habitat. If the jaguar is wounded, it could become exposed to infection. Um, no thank you! "Avoiding face-offs means that the jaguar is less likely to get a cut that could become infected," Rabinowitz says. That also may be why the cat developed its jumbo-size jaws, which allow it to quickly knock out prey. A swift takedown means less opportunity for infection-causing cuts. The jaguar's adaptations help it survive. "We're still figuring out everything. And we can't wait to uncover more jaguar secrets," Rabinowitz says.

The jaguar's roar sounds like a deep cough.

Jaguar Genetics

Scientists once thought that the jaguar species—like all other big cat species—was divided into smaller groups called subspecies. These form when groups of one type of animal become isolated from each other. The members within each group breed with one another. Over time, the groups develop slightly different genetics (codes passed from parents to offspring that determine traits).

In 2001 experts examined the DNA (or sets of genetics) in the fur and droppings of jaguars from Mexico to Argentina. Results revealed that no subspecies exist—all jaguars belong to one genetic group. "Every other big cat has subspecies," says wildlife ecologist Alan Rabinowitz. "This really makes the jaguar unique."

Scientists believe that jaguars move around so much that they don't have a chance to form isolated groups that can turn into subspecies. "That's good," Rabinowitz says. "Isolated animal groups are more vulnerable to extinction." Meaning that a jaguar's travel habits might actually take the species far in life.

Jaguars are near threatened. About 15,000 exist in the wild.

Lifestyles of the RICH and FURRY

OUTRAGEOUS WAYS TO PAMPER YOUR PET

From canine country clubs to tabby tiaras, pets today are living in the lap of luxury. In 2014, pet owners spent about $58 billion—almost twice what they spent in 2002—on supplies and services to pamper their pets. "Pets improve our lives," says Bob Vetere of the American Pet Products Association. "So we want to improve theirs." *NG Kids* tracks just how far some owners go to give their pets the royal treatment.

WHAT TO WEAR

When Selena Gomez and Amanda Seyfried need fashion for their dogs, they don't have to look far. That's because many stores now cater exclusively to the pampered pet. At Fifi & Romeo (left) in Los Angeles, California, dogs in handmade cashmere sweaters and colorful raincoats are considered fashionable, not funny-looking, and are sure to please the most finicky pooch.

Will your pet be less happy if you don't shower it with expensive stuff?

Absolutely not! "As long as your pet has food, comfort, and friendship, that's what's most important," says pet psychologist John C. Wright.

IN THE HOUSE

Skeeter the cairn terrier hangs out in a two-story doghouse with floor-to-ceiling windows, and heated floors. It's just one of many custom-made cribs owners are building for their pets. "One owner asked for a cat house with a separate dining room, litter box room, and bedroom," says Michelle Pollak of La Petite Maison, which builds luxury pet homes (above). "Some pet owners spare nothing to make sure their pets are comfortable and happy."

KENNEL—OR VACATION?

Sampson the Yorkshire terrier loves a good massage. His sister, Delilah, likes to get her toenails painted. They can do it all at the Olde Towne Pet Resort in Virginia, U.S.A. (below), one of many "pet spas" around the country that act more like luxury hotels than kennels.

CHOW TIME

Plain old dog chow just won't do for some canines. Gourmet pet food has become all the rage. Places like Three Dog Bakery offer biscuits made of carob chips, apples, oatmeal, and peanut butter, and cats munch on Alaskan salmon bites.

Pampering your pet could cost you an arm and a paw!

LUXURY SUITE AT PET SPA	$110 A NIGHT
PROFESSIONAL MASSAGE	$35
CUSTOM-BUILT DOGHOUSE	$10,000
HAND-KNITTED SWEATER	$280
GOURMET DOG TREATS	$6.99

PET TECH

Think you're tech-savvy? With all the gadgets owners are buying for their pets, some animals may have you beat. Some owners set up webcams so their pets can watch them at work. And Petzila, a company dedicated to connecting pets with their owners, offers a device that allows away-from-home owners to see, talk to, and surprise a pet with a treat—all through Wi-Fi and the click of an app.

NauGHty PETS

CAUGHT ON CAMERA

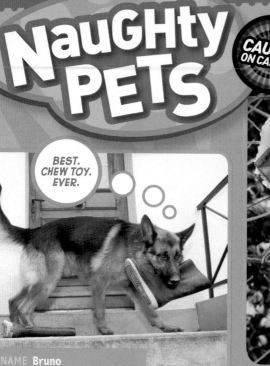

BEST. CHEW TOY. EVER.

NAME Bruno

FAVORITE ACTIVITY Testing out new chew toys

FAVORITE TOY Rubber ducky

PET PEEVE Stinky feet

I ENJOY BIRD-WATCHING... ESPECIALLY AT DINNERTIME.

NAME Mumford

FAVORITE ACTIVITY Making a list of birds to chase—um, watch

FAVORITE TOY Birdhouse scratching post

PET PEEVE Rainy days

THE PIANO ALWAYS SOUNDS BEST WHEN EVERYONE IS ASLEEP.

NAME Elton

FAVORITE ACTIVITY Composing piano *meow*-sic

FAVORITE TOY Piano pedals

PET PEEVE Keyboard cover

I FOUND MY COSTUME FOR NEXT HALLOWEEN: KING PUP THE MUMMY!

NAME Iggy

FAVORITE ACTIVITY Playing dress-up in household supplies

FAVORITE TOY Toilet plunger— a stick and a chew toy in one!

PET PEEVE Wipes

7 facts about pet rodents to nibble on

1 A golden hamster's cheek pouches extend all the way to its hips.

2 Gerbils can recognize each other by the taste of their saliva.

3 A gerbil ▶ may stomp its feet to communicate.

4 A rat's front teeth can grow up to five (12.7 cm) inches a year.

5 In Switzerland it's illegal to own just one guinea pig—you must have at least two.

6 A baby mouse is called a pinky.

7 Guinea pigs often sleep with their eyes open.

FAMOUS PETS OF HISTORY

History is full of legendary leaders, great thinkers—and famous fur balls. People have kept pets for thousands of years, and many have gained stardom for everything from saving lives to simply being supercute. Check out this timeline of famous pets.

1300s B.C.

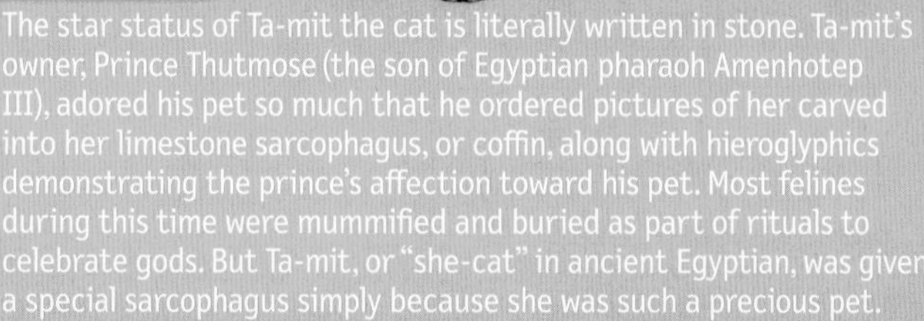

The star status of Ta-mit the cat is literally written in stone. Ta-mit's owner, Prince Thutmose (the son of Egyptian pharaoh Amenhotep III), adored his pet so much that he ordered pictures of her carved into her limestone sarcophagus, or coffin, along with hieroglyphics demonstrating the prince's affection toward his pet. Most felines during this time were mummified and buried as part of rituals to celebrate gods. But Ta-mit, or "she-cat" in ancient Egyptian, was given a special sarcophagus simply because she was such a precious pet.

100s

Chinese Emperor Ling of the Eastern Han loved his dog (which was possibly a Pekingese) so much that he gave it the rank of a senior court official. This meant that the dog was treated as royalty. The pooch supposedly was assigned a bodyguard to protect and wait on it, um, paw and foot. The dog ate the best quality rice and meat, and slept on cushy carpets. Ling even gave his dog a special hat to wear.

A PORTRAIT OF NEWTON PUTTING OUT FLAMES SET BY DIAMOND

1600s

Physicist Isaac Newton set the world on fire with his revolutionary experiments on the force of gravity. The scientist's dog, Diamond, became famous for setting real flames. Legend has it that when Newton left Diamond home alone one night, the mischievous pooch jumped on a desk and knocked over a candle, igniting and destroying stacks of Newton's research. The notes may have been destroyed, but the dog's reputation lived on: The story of Diamond has appeared in several books and magazine articles.

1700s

Russian ruler Peter the Great might not have been quite so great without his horse Lisette. In fact, the horse may have saved her owner's life during the Great Northern War, an 18th-century conflict between Russia and the empire of Sweden. The leader was seated on Lisette on the battlefield when a bullet was fired in his direction. Hearing the shot, Lisette quickly backed up so that the bullet hit her saddle rather than her owner. They were both unharmed, and the horse's act won her a place in history—plus plenty of treats from her grateful owner.

PORTRAIT OF LORY

1800s

Queen Victoria, whose reign in the United Kingdom lasted 63 years, owned two birds that were real rock stars. The queen loved her parrot Lory so much that she had an artist create a portrait of the bird, which today is part of the Royal Collection. And the queen's African gray parrot Coco was taught how to sing the British national anthem. Coco became famous for supposedly belting out the patriotic tune most mornings.

1900s

Lump the dachshund cuddled his way into his caretaker's heart—and art. The affectionate pooch lived in France with Pablo Picasso, a renowned 20th-century artist who helped develop a new painting style called cubism. Picasso adored Lump so much he featured the dog in many of his paintings. The artist also drew a picture of Lump on a dinner plate, which is now thought to be worth up to $90,000. While Picasso's paintings of Lump are expensive, the real dog was clearly priceless.

PICASSO AND LUMP

BO (LEFT) AND SUNNY CHILL OUT ON THE WHITE HOUSE LAWN.

2000s

Photographers were always snapping pics of U.S. president Barack Obama's pooches, Bo and Sunny. While the Portuguese water dogs didn't mind posing for the camera, they preferred roaming the White House lawn or taking naps in their historic home. They even had some duties, such as going to hospitals to cheer up patients and greeting world leaders who had come to visit. Being first dog also meant getting cuddles from the commander in chief, even after Bo chewed up the president's gym shoes.

Prehistoric TIMELINE

HUMANS HAVE WALKED on Earth for some 200,000 years, a mere blip in Earth's 4.5-billion-year history. A lot has happened during that time. Earth formed, and oxygen levels rose in the millions of years of the Precambrian time. The productive Paleozoic era gave rise to hard-shelled organisms, vertebrates, amphibians, and reptiles. Dinosaurs ruled the Earth in the mighty Mesozoic. And 64 million years after dinosaurs became extinct, modern humans emerged in the Cenozoic era. From the first tiny mollusks to the dinosaur giants of the Jurassic and beyond, Earth has seen a lot of transformation.

THE PRECAMBRIAN TIME

4.5 billion to 542 million years ago

- The Earth (and other planets) formed from gas and dust left over from a giant cloud that collapsed to form the sun. The giant cloud's collapse was triggered when nearby stars exploded.
- Low levels of oxygen made Earth a suffocating place.
- Early life-forms appeared.

THE PALEOZOIC ERA

542 million to 251 million years ago

- The first insects and other animals appeared on land.
- 450 million years ago (m.y.a.), the ancestors of sharks began to swim in the oceans.
- 430 m.y.a., plants began to take root on land.
- More than 360 m.y.a., amphibians emerged from the water.
- Slowly the major landmasses began to come together, creating Pangaea, a single supercontinent.
- By 300 m.y.a., reptiles had begun to dominate the land.

What Killed the Dinosaurs?

It's a mystery that's boggled the minds of scientists for centuries: What happened to the dinosaurs? While various theories have bounced around, a new study confirms that the most likely culprit is an asteroid or comet that created a giant crater. Researchers say that the impact set off a series of natural disasters like tsunamis, earthquakes, and temperature swings that plagued the dinosaurs' ecosystem and disrupted their food chain. This, paired with intense volcano eruptions that caused drastic climate changes, is thought to be why half of the world's species—including the dinosaurs—died in a mass extinction.

DINO TIMES

THE MESOZOIC ERA

251 million to 65 million years ago

The Mesozoic era, or the age of the reptiles, consisted of three consecutive time periods (shown below). This is when the first dinosaurs began to appear. They would reign supreme for more than 150 million years.

TRIASSIC PERIOD

251 million to 199 million years ago

- Appearance of the first mammals. They were rodent-size.
- The first dinosaur appeared.
- Ferns were the dominant plants on land.
- The giant supercontinent of Pangaea began breaking up toward the end of the Triassic.

JURASSIC PERIOD

199 million to 145 million years ago

- Giant dinosaurs dominated the land.
- Pangaea continued its breakup, and oceans formed in the spaces between the drifting landmasses, allowing sea life, including sharks and marine crocodiles, to thrive.
- Conifer trees spread across the land.

CRETACEOUS PERIOD

145 million to 65 million years ago

- The modern continents developed.
- The largest dinosaurs developed.
- Flowering plants spread across the landscape.
- Mammals flourished, and giant pterosaurs ruled the skies over the small birds.
- Temperatures grew more extreme. Dinosaurs lived in deserts, swamps, and forests from the Antarctic to the Arctic.

THE CENOZOIC ERA—TERTIARY PERIOD

65 million to 2.6 million years ago

- Following the dinosaur extinction, mammals rose as the dominant species.
- Birds continued to flourish.
- Volcanic activity was widespread.
- Temperatures began to cool, eventually ending in an ice age.
- The period ended with land bridges forming, which allowed plants and animals to spread to new areas.

Who Ate What?

Herbivores

- Primarily plant-eaters
- Weighed up to 100 tons (91 t)—the largest animals ever to walk on Earth
- Up to 1,000 blunt or flat teeth to grind vegetation
- Many had cheek pouches to store food.
- Examples: *Styracosaurus, Mamenchisaurus*

Carnivores

- Meat-eaters
- Long, strong legs to run faster than plant-eaters; ran up to 30 miles an hour (48 km/h)
- Most had good eyesight, strong jaws, and sharp teeth.
- Scavengers and hunters; often hunted in packs
- Grew to 45 feet (14 m) long
- Examples: *Velociraptor, Gigantoraptor, Tyrannosaurus rex*

What if dinos hadn't gone extinct?

If dinos still roamed Earth, they'd likely be the world's most dominant animals. And it's possible that they'd have picked up a few more skills. For instance, some species might have learned to use simple tools. (After all, types of birds—the dinosaur's closest living relatives—developed the ability to use tools such as sticks and leaves to dig or "fish" for food.) If humans were around in a dino-filled world, we'd need to avoid getting eaten by carnivorous dinosaurs. And plant-eating dinos would gobble up lots of leafy greens, leaving us with way less to eat. If these guys still existed, it would be anything but *dino*-mite.

DID YOU KNOW?

Tyrannosaurus means "tyrant lizard." At about 40 feet (12 m) long and about 15 to 20 feet (4.6 to 6 m) tall, the *T. rex* was one of the largest meat-eating dinosaurs that ever lived. If it roamed the Earth today, its bite would be strong enough to dent a car.

Machairoceratops cronusi

A Great Discovery!

Researchers in Utah, U.S.A. recently discovered a horned, plant-eating creature as long as a pickup truck and weighing about as much as a rhino. Named *Machairoceratops cronusi*, the dino is thought to have lived about 77 million years ago. The creature's crowning glory? Two massive curved spikes sticking out on top of its head may have been used to attract potential mates.

Bet you didn't know

Giant prehistoric snakes sometimes preyed upon dinosaur eggs and hatchlings.

DINO Classification

Classifying dinosaurs and all other living things can be a complicated matter, so scientists have devised a system to help with the process. Dinosaurs are put into groups based on a very large range of characteristics.

Scientists put dinosaurs into two major groups: the bird-hipped ornithischians and the reptile-hipped saurischians.

SOME DINOSAURS HAD 1,000 TEETH.

Ornithischian

"Bird-hipped"
(pubis bone in hips points backward)

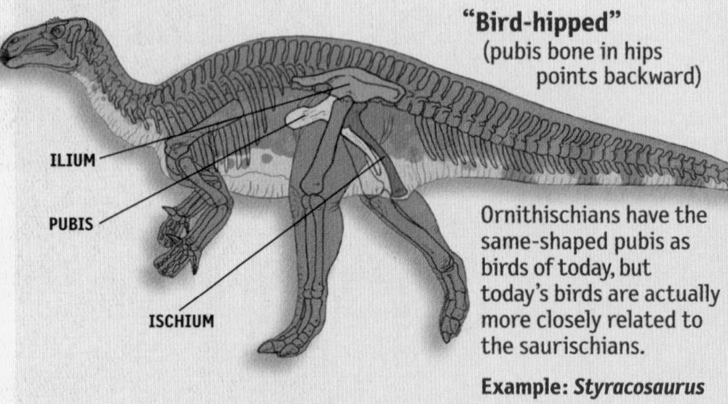

Ornithischians have the same-shaped pubis as birds of today, but today's birds are actually more closely related to the saurischians.

Example: ***Styracosaurus***

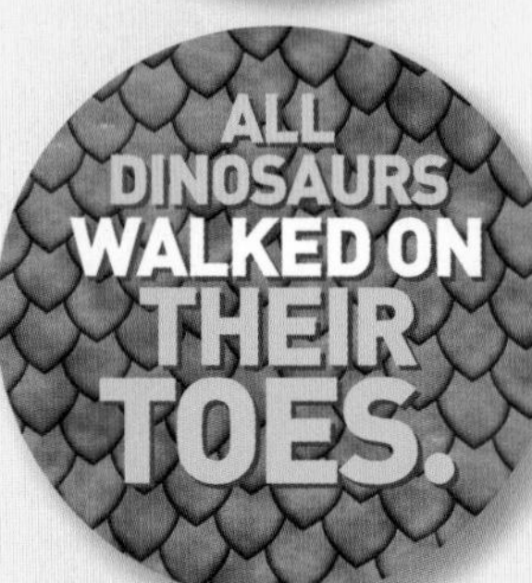

ALL DINOSAURS WALKED ON THEIR TOES.

Saurischian

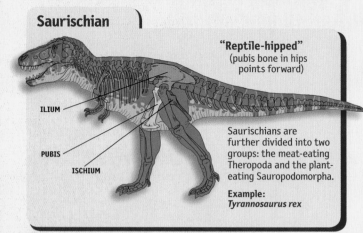

"Reptile-hipped"
(pubis bone in hips points forward)

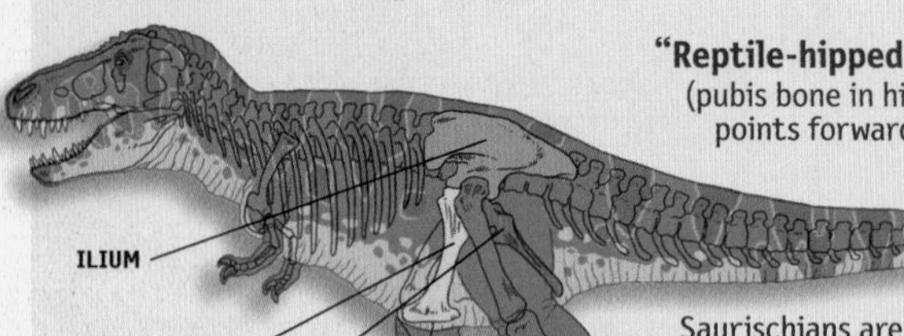

Saurischians are further divided into two groups: the meat-eating Theropoda and the plant-eating Sauropodomorpha.

Example:
Tyrannosaurus rex

LIKE BABY HUMANS, PSITTACOSAURUS CRAWLED BEFORE IT WALKED.

Within these two main divisions, dinosaurs are then separated into orders and then families, such as Stegosauria. Like other members of the Stegosauria, *Stegosaurus* had spines and plates along the back, neck, and tail.

3 NEWLY DISCOVERED DINOS

Humans have been searching for—and discovering—dinosaur remains for hundreds of years. In that time, at least 1,000 species of dinos have been found all over the world, and thousands more may still be out there waiting to be unearthed. Recent discoveries include the *Sarmientosaurus musacchioi*. Found in Argentina, it is one of the world's largest dinosaurs. For more exciting dino discoveries, read on.

1 ***Sarmientosaurus musacchioi***
(Saurischian)

Sarmiento, Argentina, and the late Dr. Eduardo Musacchio

Length: 40 feet (12.2 m)

Time Range: Late Cretaceous

Where: Argentina

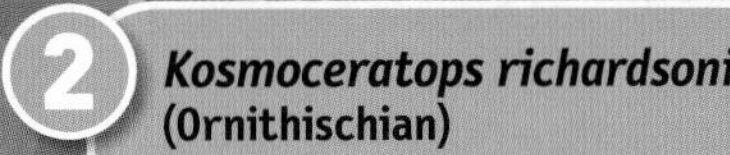

2 ***Kosmoceratops richardsoni***
(Ornithischian)

Ornamented horned face, and Scott Richardson, the dino's discoverer

Length: 15 feet (4.5 m)

Time Range: Late Cretaceous

Where: Utah, U.S.A.

3 ***Gualicho shinyae*** **(Saurischian)**

Named for Gualichu, a local goddess of animals and the dino's discoverer, Akiko Shinya

Length: 25 feet (7.6 m)

Time Range: Late Cretaceous

Where: Argentina

DINOSAUR FAMILY TREE

Dinosaurs evolved 230 million years ago from small, two-legged, meat-eating reptiles. The earliest dinosaurs soon branched off into two groups, Ornithischia and Saurischia. The groups are based on dinosaurs' hip bones (see p. 80). These groups kept branching as dinosaurs developed and changed to live in almost every environment on Earth.

HETERODONTOSAURS

THYREOPHORANS

ORNITHISCHIANS
Bird-hipped dinosaurs

DINOSAURIA

SAUROPODS

SAUROPODOMORPHS

SAURISCHIANS
Lizard-hipped dinosaurs

THEROPODS

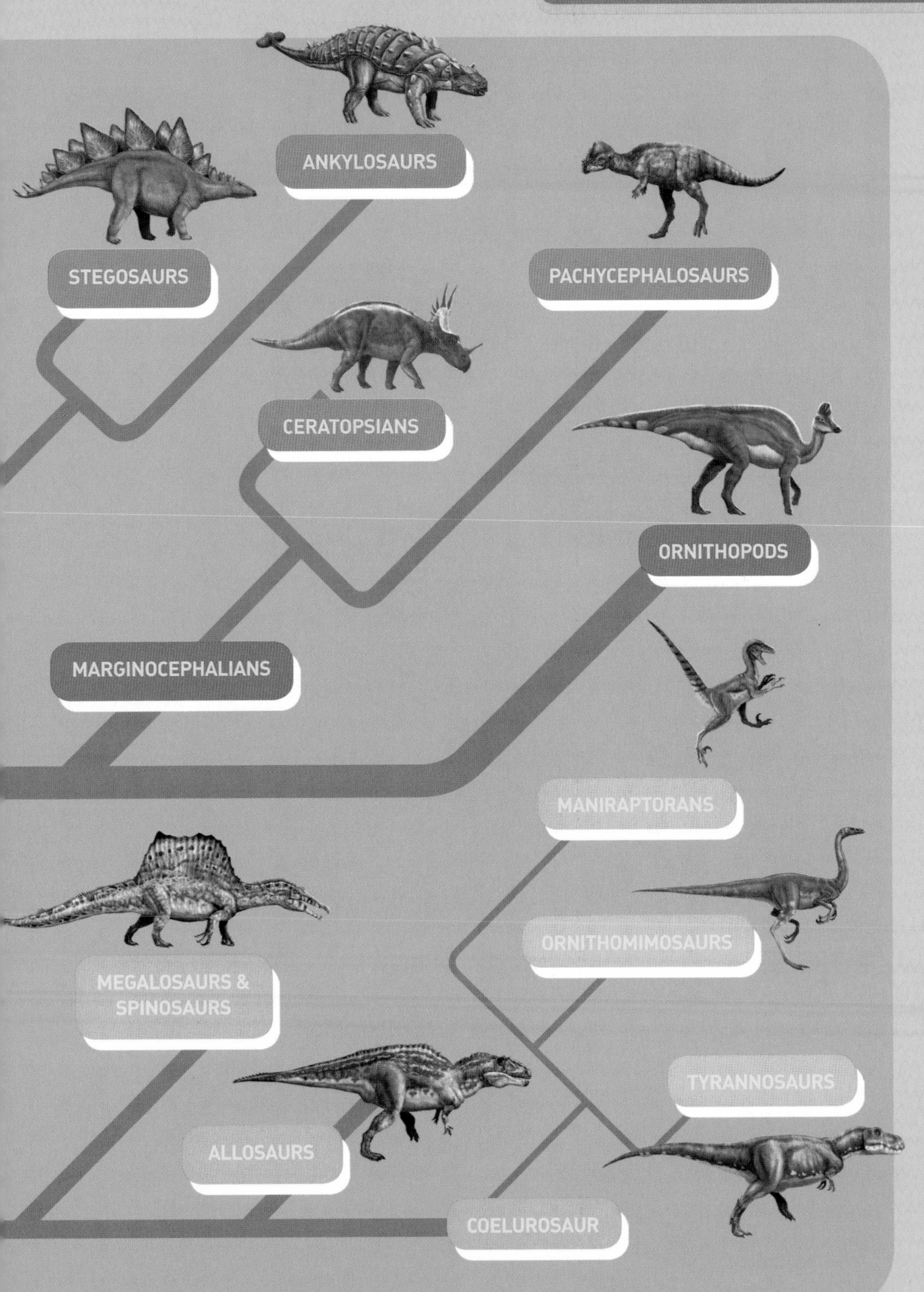
ANKYLOSAURS
STEGOSAURS
PACHYCEPHALOSAURS
CERATOPSIANS
ORNITHOPODS
MARGINOCEPHALIANS
MANIRAPTORANS
ORNITHOMIMOSAURS
MEGALOSAURS & SPINOSAURS
TYRANNOSAURS
ALLOSAURS
COELUROSAUR

18 Cutest Animals of 2018

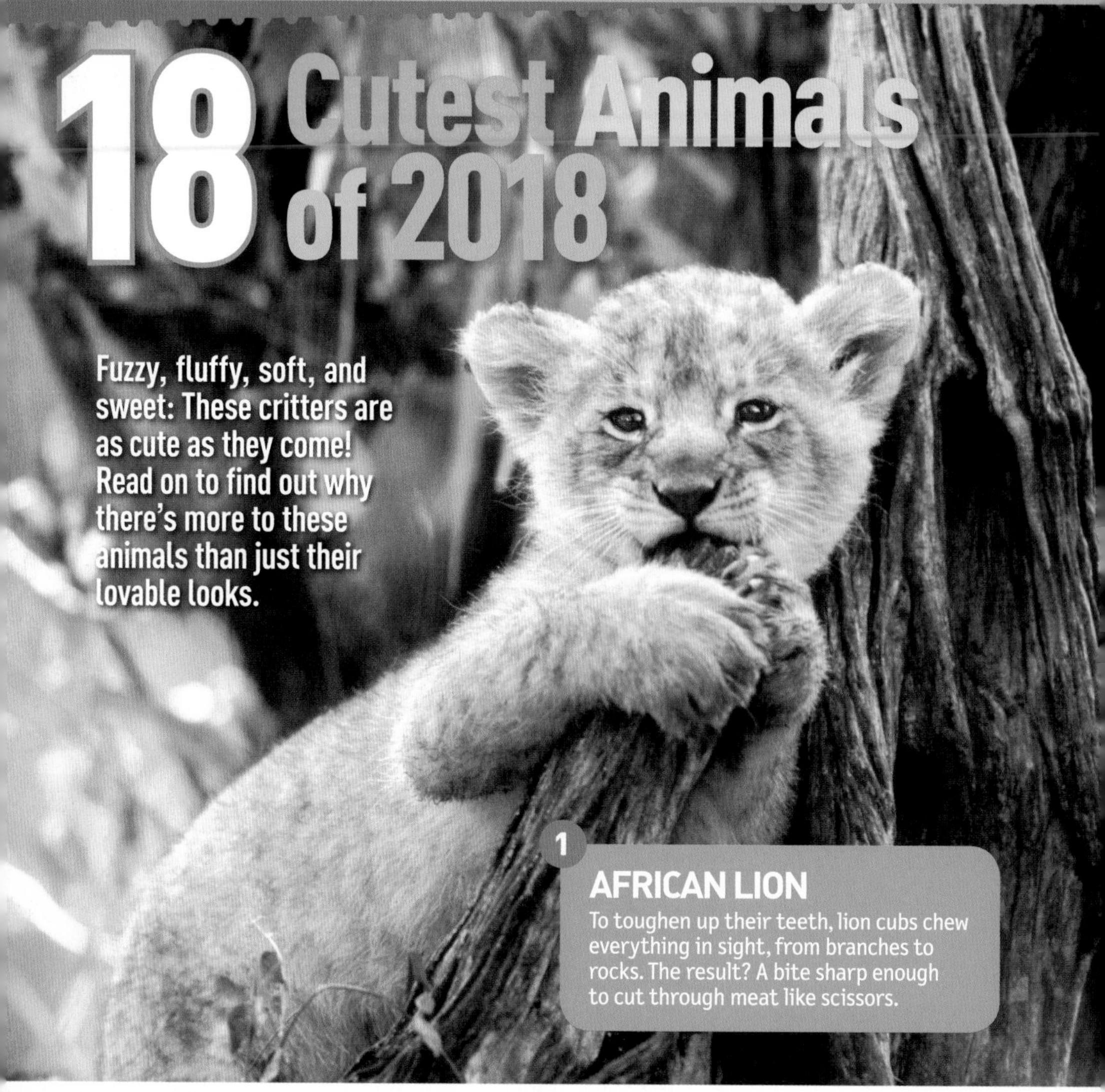

Fuzzy, fluffy, soft, and sweet: These critters are as cute as they come! Read on to find out why there's more to these animals than just their lovable looks.

1

AFRICAN LION

To toughen up their teeth, lion cubs chew everything in sight, from branches to rocks. The result? A bite sharp enough to cut through meat like scissors.

2

GROUND SQUIRRELS

It may look like these ground squirrels are exchanging a quick smooch, but this is likely more than just a friendly hello. Scientists say a quick sniff lets the squirrels recognize their relatives through glands near their mouths.

3

GRIZZLY BEAR

Sometimes you just have to stop and smell the daisies, like this grizzly cub. As omnivores, grizzlies feast on everything from fish and deer to seeds, berries—and even flowers.

4

EMPEROR PENGUIN

This chick's fluffy feathers keep it warm against the Arctic chill. Born unable to fly or swim, the chicks stay close to mom and other adults until they moult—or grow real, waterproof feathers.

5

HULK

Topping the scales at close to 200 pounds (91 kg), Hulk's considered the world's largest pit bull. But this gentle giant—who recently fathered a litter of eight puppies—is a sweet family pet who even takes bubble baths with his human.

6 WHITE-LEGGED DAMSELFLY

What big eyes you have! This bug's massive peepers provide a 360-degree field of vision, allowing it to track prey with an impressive 97 percent success rate.

7 VERVET MONKEY

Born with a pink face and dark hair, this little climber will soon develop the light hair and dark face distinctive to this species of monkey, found in East Africa.

8 ASIAN SMALL CLAWED OTTER

Smooch! A mama otter appears to plant a peck on her tiny pup. The smallest of all otter species, these playful swimmers—native to Asia—are often spotted sliding down muddy banks by the rivers, lakes, streams, and swamps they call home.

9

ANCHIETA'S DESERT LIZARD

What a grin on this guy! While it looks like this lizard is smiling wide, it's actually displaying a defensive stance. When threatened, the reptiles try to make themselves look as large as possible to scare off predators like birds and large snakes.

10

ILI PIKA

With perky ears and chubby cheeks, this pika could be mistaken for a teddy bear! Researchers recently discovered the rare rodent-like animal—who's about the size of a guinea pig—high in the mountains of China.

11

SQUIRREL GLIDER

Time for a quick rest! The acrobatic young squirrel glider can glide some 130 feet (40 m) from limb to limb—even longer if they launch from an extra-tall tree.

12

HARVEST MICE

This pair of mice are so mini, they can both rest on a thin wheat stem. The smallest rodents in Europe, these golden brown mice are no bigger than an adult's thumb.

13

INDIAN RHINOCEROS

This rhino may look little now, but it won't be for long! The animal—which lives in Nepal and India—will grow to be as tall as a grown man and weigh as much as a car.

14

GOSLING

Waddle, waddle everywhere! While a baby goose can swim and dive deep underwater just days after birth, it can take another three months before it learns to fly.

15

HEDGEHOG

This hoglet looks rather regal with its floral crown! While hedgehogs mostly hang out on the ground in bushes foraging for food, the spiky species can also climb trees and even swim.

16

EUROPEAN TREE FROG

Here's a whole *bunch* of cute! This frog is so tiny—only about the size of a coin—that it can perfectly perch on a berry. Typically found in meadows and shrubs throughout Europe, these frogs feed on insects, spiders, and worms.

17

BURROWING OWL

Hoo are you looking at? This burrowing owl strikes a curious pose. These birds typically nest underground, taking over burrows dug out by squirrels and prairie dogs.

18

LEOPARD

This young leopard may already have its telltale spots, but it wasn't born that way! At birth, cubs have soft, grayish fur. The spots—known as rosettes—eventually pop up as the leopard grows.

QUIZ WHIZ

How much do you know about all things animals? Quiz yourself!

Write your answers on a piece of paper. Then check them below.

1. **True or false?** Sloths typically move just 80 feet (24 m) a day.

2. **Which one of these cats is considered a big cat?**
   a. leopard
   b. lion
   c. jaguar
   d. all of the above

3. **Giant prehistoric ____________ sometimes preyed upon dinosaur eggs and hatchlings**
   a. sloths
   b. snakes
   c. hamsters
   d. horses

4. **True or false?** The Chinese soft-shelled turtle pees from its mouth.

5. **More than __________ known species of frogs and toads exist.**
   a. 650,000
   b. 650
   c. 6,500
   d. 65

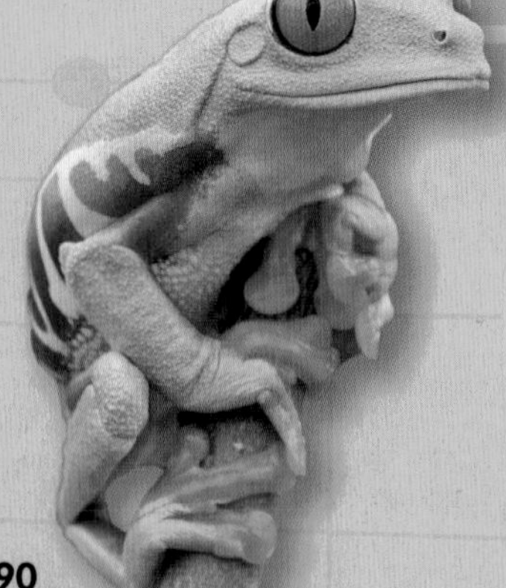

Not **STUMPED** yet? Check out the *NATIONAL GEOGRAPHIC KIDS QUIZ WHIZ* collection for more crazy **ANIMAL** questions!

ANSWERS: 1. True ; 2. d; 3. b; 4. True; 5. c

HOMEWORK HELP

Wildly Good Animal Reports

beluga whale

Your teacher wants a written report on the beluga whale. Not to worry. Use these organizational tools so you can stay afloat while writing a report.

STEPS TO SUCCESS: Your report will follow the format of a descriptive or expository essay (see p. 35 for "How to Write a Perfect Essay") and should consist of a main idea, followed by supporting details and a conclusion. Use this basic structure for each paragraph as well as the whole report, and you'll be on the right track.

1. Introduction

State your **main idea.**

The beluga whale is a common and important species of whale.

2. Body

Provide **supporting points** for your main idea.

The beluga whale is one of the smallest whale species.

It is also known as the "white whale" because of its distinctive coloring.

These whales are common in the Arctic Ocean's coastal waters.

Then **expand** on those points with further description, explanation, or discussion.

The beluga whale is one of the smallest whale species.

Belugas range in size from 13 to 20 feet (4 to 6.1 m) in length.

It is also known as the "white whale" because of its distinctive coloring.

Belugas are born gray or brown. They fade to white at around five years old.

These whales are common in the Arctic Ocean's coastal waters.

Some Arctic belugas migrate south in large herds when sea ice freezes over.

3. Conclusion

Wrap it up with a **summary** of your whole paper.

Because of its unique coloring and unusual features, belugas are among the most familiar and easily distinguishable of all the whales.

KEY INFORMATION

Here are some things you should consider including in your report:

What does your animal look like?
To what other species is it related?
How does it move?
Where does it live?
What does it eat?
What are its predators?
How long does it live?
Is it endangered?
Why do you find it interesting?

SEPARATE FACT FROM FICTION: Your animal may have been featured in a movie or in myths and legends. Compare and contrast how the animal has been portrayed with how it behaves in reality. For example, penguins can't dance the way they do in *Happy Feet.*

PROOFREAD AND REVISE: As with any great essay, when you're finished, check for misspellings, grammatical mistakes, and punctuation errors. It often helps to have someone else proofread your work, too, as he or she may catch things you have missed. Also, look for ways to make your sentences and paragraphs even better. Add more descriptive language, choosing just the right verbs, adverbs, and adjectives to make your writing come alive.

BE CREATIVE: Use visual aids to make your report come to life. Include an animal photo file with interesting images found in magazines or printed from websites. Or draw your own! You can also build a miniature animal habitat diorama. Use creativity to help communicate your passion for the subject.

THE FINAL RESULT: Put it all together in one final, polished draft. Make it neat and clean, and remember to cite your references.

Going Green

A rain barrel collects water in a garden.

THE ARCTIC'S DISAPPEARING ICE

In the past few decades, sea ice cover in the Arctic has shrunk because of global climate change. Arctic sea ice freezes up and expands in the winter and melts and shrinks in the summer. It typically reaches its smallest size every September. Scientists call this the "Arctic sea ice minimum." This minimum has shrunk from 3.02 million square miles (7.83 million sq km) in 1980 to about 1.4 million square miles (3.62 million sq km) in 2012. The change is so significant that cartographers at the *National Geographic Atlas of the World* redrew the map of the Arctic to reflect the smaller sea ice coverage. So what's behind this ice loss in the Arctic? Scientists point to a phenomenon known as the "positive feedback loop."

Sea ice's bright surface reflects sunlight back into space. This means icy areas absorb less solar energy and remain cool. But when air and ocean temperatures rise over time and more sea ice melts, fewer bright surfaces reflect sunlight back into space. The ice and exposed seawater absorb more solar energy, and this causes a feedback loop of more melting and more warming.

If the ice loss continues at the current rate, scientists are concerned the Arctic will become ice free during the summer at some point within this century. As the ice melts, it's essential that we find ways to protect the indigenous people and animals—such as polar bears and seals—that rely on the Arctic's ice for food and survival.

ARCTIC SEA ICE MINIMUM IN 1980

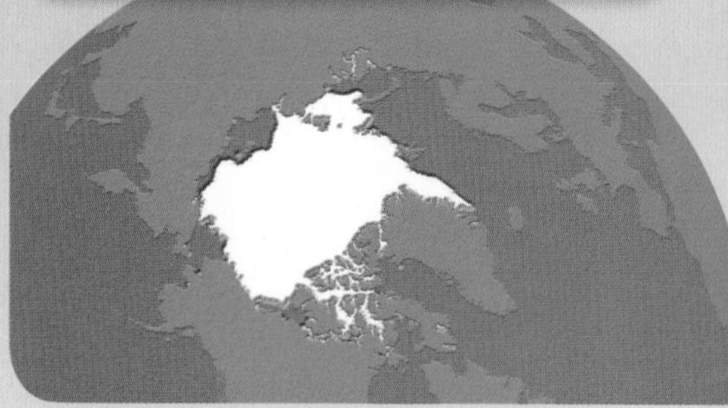

ARCTIC SEA ICE MINIMUM IN 2012

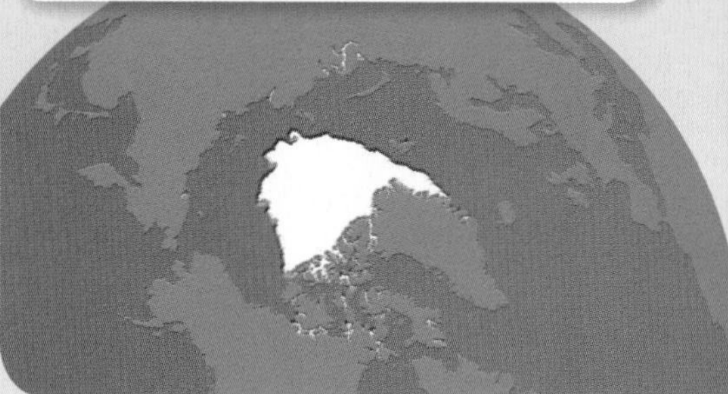

COMPARISON OF ARCTIC SEA ICE MINIMUMS

Arctic sea ice minimum in 1980

Arctic sea ice minimum in 2012

A MELTING WORLD

If all the ice on Earth melted, the world's oceans would rise 216 feet (66 m). But how high is that exactly? Check this chart to see out what might end up underwater.

THE STATUE OF LIBERTY 305 feet (93 m)

12 GIRAFFES 216 feet (66 m)

5 SCHOOL BUSES 200 feet (61 m)

6 ORCAS 192 feet (59 m)

5 Animals Battling Climate Change

1 Polar Bear

WHERE IT LIVES: Canada, Greenland, Russia, Norway, and Alaska, U.S.A.

WHY IT'S THREATENED: Due to shrinking amounts of sea ice in the Arctic, polar bears are losing their habitat—and changing sea temperatures are reducing the prey that polar bears rely on for food.

HOPE FOR THE FUTURE: Areas of the Arctic have been declared nature preserves, and work is being done to conserve dens and other important habitat areas used by polar bears.

2 Adélie Penguin

WHERE IT LIVES: Antarctica

WHY IT'S THREATENED: By 2099, 58 percent of the habitat where Adélie penguins lay their eggs could be too warm and too wet to host colonies.

HOPE FOR THE FUTURE: Research shows that Adélie penguins have endured the warmer temperatures in East Antarctica's Cape Adare peninsula, which may be a sign that they can survive the threat of global warming.

3

American Pika

WHERE IT LIVES: Mountaintops of the western U.S. and southwestern Canada.

WHY IT'S THREATENED: Rising temperatures are causing changes in vegetation in the pika's range, making it difficult for the animal to find food.

HOPE FOR THE FUTURE: Scientists have observed that some pikas have adapted by changing their diets. Pikas that eat unusual foods such as moss might be able to remain in cool, rocky areas at lower elevations year-round.

4

Orange-Spotted Filefish

WHERE IT LIVES: Indo-Pacific coral reefs

WHY IT'S THREATENED: Not only are coral reefs—the fish's habitat—in decline, but filefish are especially sensitive to warmer waters.

HOPE FOR THE FUTURE: Conservationists are working together to save the coral reefs (and all of the animals that thrive off of them), by expanding marine protected areas and taking steps to reverse global warming.

5

Gila Monster

WHERE IT LIVES: Southwestern U.S., northwest Mexico

WHY IT'S THREATENED: Hotter, drier conditions in the deserts means this colorful lizard is not getting enough water to survive, causing a decline in its numbers.

HOPE FOR THE FUTURE: Conservationists urge people to set aside a special gila monster habitat in higher regions of the southwest where there is more rainfall.

6 TIPS to Save the Earth

The Earth needs your help! Here are six ways to protect our planet.

1 Take a Walk – Usually get a ride to your friend's house down the street? Ask your parents if you can walk or ride your bike there instead. Skipping the car ride not only saves gas, but it also cuts back on air pollution. Just make sure to always have an adult with you on longer walks or rides, and stick to the sidewalks—especially on busy roads.

2 Fill It Up – Of the billions of bottles of water consumed in the United States every year, only about 30 percent are actually recycled. The rest clog up landfills or wind up in the ocean, where they may harm sea animals. An easy fix? Drink from a reusable water bottle. Experts say tap water is totally safe to drink, and you'll do your part to reduce the waste.

3 Bag It – Like water bottles, plastic grocery bags are likely to become hazards to the environment, as they take many years to degrade. Next time you go the grocery store with Mom or Dad, remind them to bring along reusable shopping totes.

4 Eat Up – Mom's right: You really should eat everything on your plate! Around the world, 1.4 billion tons (1.3 billion t) of food is lost or wasted every year. And all of that rotting food is filling up landfills and releasing harmful greenhouse gases into the environment. Coming up with creative ways to use up food that would otherwise be tossed—like making muffins out of ripe bananas—can make a big impact on the future of our planet.

5 Go Portable – Laptop computers use 50 to 90 percent less energy than desktop computers.

6 Pick It Up – Every year, people around the world generate 2.6 trillion pounds (1.2 trillion kg) of garbage—equal to the weight of more than 6 million blue whales. And some of that will wind up in your local creeks and playgrounds. So grab some gloves and a trash bag and pick up trash. You'll get some fresh air and exercise—and help the environment, too.

DID YOU KNOW?

If food waste were a country, it would be the third largest emitter of greenhouse gases behind China and the United States.

TRY MAKING YOUR OWN SOAP

Don't trash your leftover bits of soap! Combine soap slivers to keep pieces of soap from going into the garbage—and adding to landfill. Squish the slivers into cool shapes when they're wet.

Pollution

Cleaning Up Our Act

So what's the big deal about a little dirt on the planet? Pollution can affect animals, plants, and people. In fact, some studies show that more people die every year from diseases linked to air pollution than from car accidents. And right now nearly one billion of the world's people don't have access to clean drinking water.

A LITTLE POLLUTION = BIG PROBLEMS

You can probably clean your room in a couple of hours. (At least we hope you can!) But you can't shove air and water pollution under your bed or cram them into the closet. Once released into the environment, pollution—whether it's oil leaking from a boat or chemicals spewing from a factory's smokestack—can have a lasting environmental impact.

KEEP IT CLEAN

It's easy to blame things like big factories for pollution problems. But some of the mess comes from everyday activities. Exhaust fumes from cars and garbage in landfills can seriously trash the Earth's health. We all need to pitch in and do some house-cleaning. It may mean bicycling more and riding in cars less. Or not dumping water-polluting oil or household cleaners down the drain. Look at it this way: Just as with your room, it's always better not to let Earth get messed up in the first place.

What a Prince!

The heir to the British throne is doing his part to save Earth's oceans. Working to combat both overfishing and the amount of plastic that lands in the ocean every year—8.8 million tons (8 million t) by some estimates—Prince Charles is leading a charitable drive to protect the seas with a focus on sustainable fishing. We'd say that's a quite a royal effort.

Here's some food for thought: Around the world, approximately 3.97 million tons (3.6 million t) of fruits, veggies, and other food waste is tossed away every day.

And plenty of those scraps—especially produce—is perfectly good to eat. In fact, the amount of food that winds up wasted could feed two billion hungry people around the world. On top of food scraps, imperfect produce also often ends up in landfills, contributing to food waste, which, in turn, is a major source of greenhouse gas emissions. That's why advocates like Tristram Stuart are trying to change the way we look at imperfect food. From misshapen melons to bruised bananas, Stuart says it's just fine to fill up on ugly food.

Ugly FOOD

And he's demonstrating just that through his Feeding the 5,000 campaign—free public feasts made entirely of orphaned food. He's also encouraging major food corporations and grocery stores to stop throwing away so-called "ugly" fruits and veggies. "Today, there are major food corporations agreeing that it's unacceptable to throw so much away, and the United States recently announced a food waste reduction goal, calling for a 50-percent reduction by 2030," says Stuart. "In the United Kingdom, food waste has been reduced by 21 percent."

Even better news? You can help, too. "Anyone can take that slightly brown banana and turn it into a smoothie instead of tossing it," says Stuart. "But you also have the power to call the industry into account as well. It can be as easy as going into your local grocery store and asking about how much they are throwing away." Another simple step: Sign Stuart's pledge to reduce food waste (check it out at feedbackglobal.org) and share it with your friends and family to let them know that eating ugly food can be a beautiful thing.

By the Numbers
TRASH BREAKDOWN

After you toss out a banana peel, a soda can, or a smelly sock, it's out of sight, but it's still around—sometimes for weeks, and other times for hundreds of years! Here's a timeline of how long it takes everyday trash to decompose—or completely break down—in a landfill.

BANANA PEEL
2–5 WEEKS

APPLE CORE
2 MONTHS

WOOL SOCKS
1–5 YEARS

PLASTIC BAG
10–20 YEARS

LEATHER
50 YEARS

RUBBER BOOT SOLE
50–80 YEARS

ALUMINUM CAN
80–200 YEARS

GLASS BOTTLE
1 MILLION YEARS OR MORE

PLASTIC FISHING LINE
600 YEARS

18 THINGS ABOUT GREEN

1 Vatican City—the world's smallest country—uses solar energy to power several of its buildings.

2 THE BULLITT CENTER IN SEATTLE, WASHINGTON, U.S.A., INSTALLED AN "IRRESISTIBLE STAIRWAY" THAT LURES PEOPLE AWAY FROM ELEVATORS WITH PANORAMIC VIEWS.

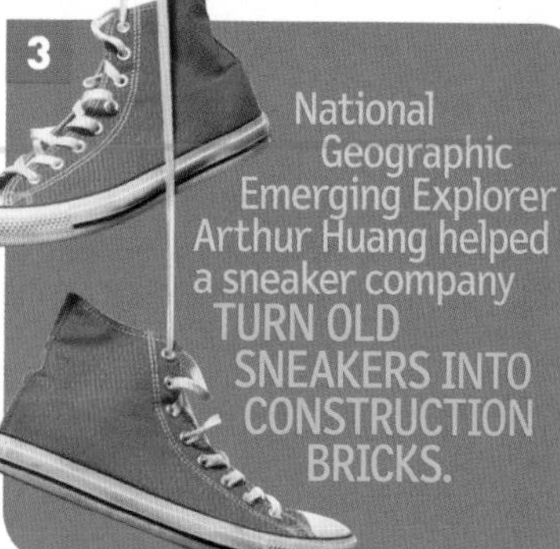

3 National Geographic Emerging Explorer Arthur Huang helped a sneaker company TURN OLD SNEAKERS INTO CONSTRUCTION BRICKS.

4 **1.5 million** plastic bottles were used to construct an exhibition hall in Taiwan.

5 Researchers are experimenting with ways **to use corn cobs** as building material.

6 BUILDERS IN SACRAMENTO, CALIFORNIA, U.S.A., TRANSFORMED SODA BOTTLES, SUNFLOWER SEEDS, AND DIAPER TABS INTO CONSTRUCTION MATERIALS.

7 **The White House**—home to the President of the United States—uses solar energy to heat its hot tub, outdoor shower, and pool.

8 Seawater is used to cool the Vancouver Aquarium in Vancouver, B.C., Canada.

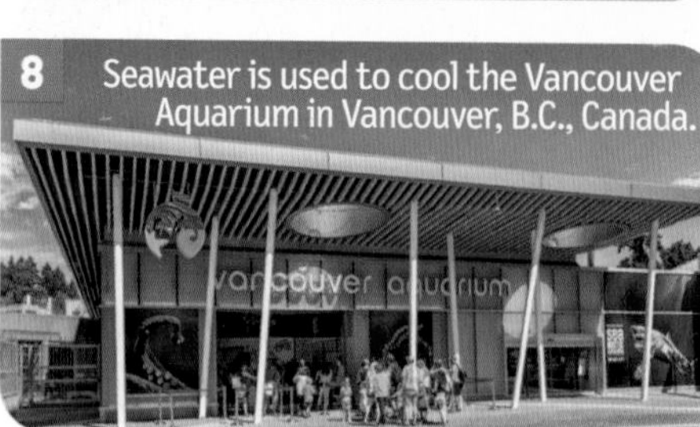

9 An Earthship house is the ultimate in living "green." One family built theirs out of **aluminum cans and tires packed with dirt.**

10

The Eiffel Tower has two wind turbines inside. They power the gift shop, museum, and restaurants on the first floor.

11

At 1,667 feet (508 m), TAIPEI 101 IS ONE OF THE TALLEST green buildings in the world.

12

LEVI'S STADIUM in San Francisco, California, U.S.A., features a 27,000-SQUARE-FOOT (2,508-SQ-M) "GREEN ROOF" WITH SOME 40 SPECIES OF VEGETATION.

13

GOATS GRAZE ON THE GREEN ROOF OF A RESTAURANT IN SISTER BAY, WISCONSIN, U.S.A.

BUILDINGS

14

A man in Washington, U.S.A., built a "Junk Castle" out of materials such as washing machine parts and old car doors.

15

Iceland has so many volcanoes and hot springs, it uses geothermal energy to power **nine out of ten homes.**

16

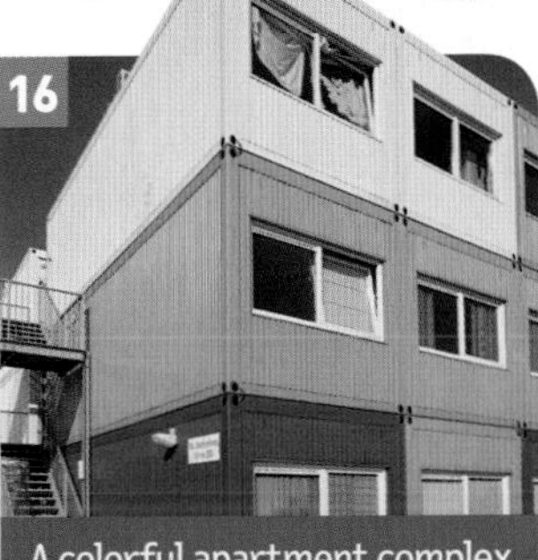

A colorful apartment complex in Amsterdam, Netherlands, is constructed of **recycled shipping containers.**

17

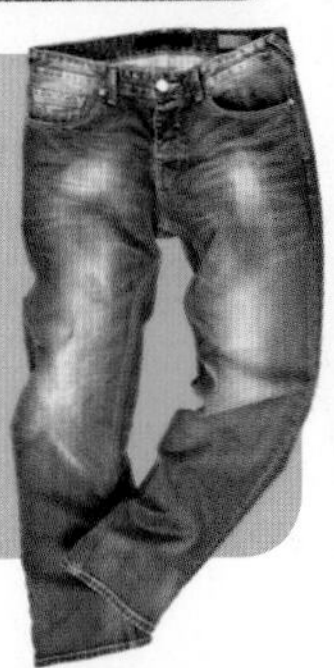

RECYCLED DENIM JEANS CAN BE USED AS INSULATION IN THE WALLS OF GREEN HOMES.

18

TWO TURBINES ON THE THAMES RIVER USE WATER TO CREATE ELECTRICITY FOR ENGLAND'S WINDSOR CASTLE.

What's your eco-friendly IQ? Find out with this quiz!

Write your answers on a piece of paper. Then check them below.

1. **If all the ice on Earth melted, which landmark would wind up partly underwater?**
   a. Freedom Tower
   b. Eiffel Tower
   c. Statue of Liberty
   d. Space Needle

2. **True or false?** Plastic bags take longer to decompose than wool socks.

3. **Which animals' habitats are facing serious threat due to climate change?**
   a. American pika
   b. Gila monster
   c. polar bear
   d. all of the above

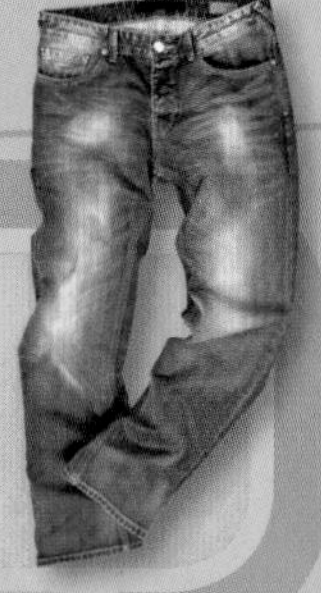

4. **True or false?** Old denim jeans can be used as insulation in the walls of homes.

5. **National Geographic cartographers recently redrew the map of the Arctic to reflect ______.**
   a. ice loss
   b. new glaciers
   c. expanded territory
   d. land that fell into the ocean

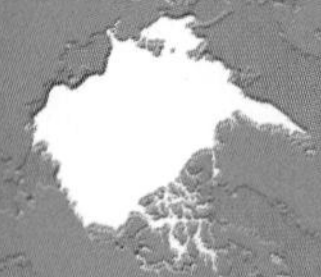

Not **STUMPED** yet? Check out the *NATIONAL GEOGRAPHIC KIDS QUIZ WHIZ* collection for more crazy **ENVIRONMENT** questions!

ANSWERS:
1. c; 2. True; 3. d; 4. True; 5. a

HOMEWORK HELP

Write a Letter That Gets Results

Knowing how to write a good letter is a useful skill. It will come in handy anytime you want to persuade someone to understand your point of view. Whether you're emailing your congressperson or writing a letter for a school project or to your grandma, a great letter will help you get your message across. Most important, a well-written letter leaves a good impression.

Check out the example below for the elements of a good letter.

Your address

Date

Salutation Always use "Dear" followed by the person's name; use Mr., Mrs., Ms., or Dr. as appropriate.

Introductory paragraph Give the reason you're writing the letter.

Body The longest part of the letter, which provides evidence that supports your position. Be persuasive!

Closing paragraph Sum up your argument.

Complimentary closing Sign off with "Sincerely" or "Thank you."

Your signature

Abby Jones
1204 Green Street
Los Angeles, CA 90045

March 31, 2018

Dear Mr. School Superintendent,

I am writing to you about how much excess energy our school uses and to offer a solution.

Every day, we leave the computers on in the classroom, the TVs are plugged in all the time, and the lights are on all day. All of this adds up to a lot of wasted energy, which is not only harmful for the Earth, as it increases the amount of harmful greenhouse gas emissions into the environment, but is also costly to the school. In fact, I read that schools spend more on energy bills than on computers and textbooks combined!

I am suggesting that we start an Energy Patrol to monitor the use of lighting, air-conditioning, heating, and other energy systems within our school. My idea is to have a group of students dedicated to figuring out ways we can cut back on our energy use in the school. We can do room checks, provide reminders to students and teachers to turn off lights and computers, replace old lightbulbs with energy-efficient products, and even reward the classrooms that do the most to save energy.

Above all, I think our school could help the environment tremendously by cutting back on how much energy we use. Let's see an Energy Patrol at our school soon. Thank you.

Sincerely,

Abby Jones

Abby Jones

COMPLIMENTARY CLOSINGS

Sincerely, Sincerely yours, Thank you, Regards, Best wishes, Respectfully,

Engineering and Technology

Delegates at the Mobile World Conference in Barcelona, Spain, experience a roller coaster ride using virtual reality headsets.

PILOT SITS HERE

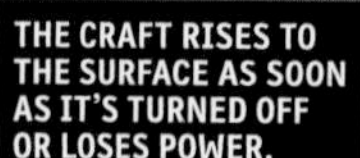
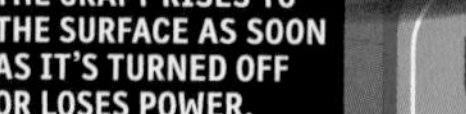

THE CRAFT RISES TO THE SURFACE AS SOON AS IT'S TURNED OFF OR LOSES POWER.

PARKING

UNDERWATER PLANE

The DeepFlight Super Falcon Mark II may look like an airplane, but it was built to brave the oceans. The diving machine's wings are similar to a jet's, only turned upside down. As the two-person craft dives underwater, the inverted wings generate negative lift—a force that helps push the craft downward, creating an extra smooth ride. And the craft's superquiet motor won't scare away marine animals. The sleek submersible can glide up to 400 feet (122 m) below the water's surface and even do tricks such as barrel rolls. With this plane-like diver, fun under the sea will really take off.

LAMP PUZZLE

What a bright idea! Inspired by the classic *Tetris* video game, the Tetris Stackable LED Desk Lamp is divided into seven differently shaped pieces that can fit together in several ways. Plug in the lamp's base and flip on its switch. Then pile the other pieces on top of it. The base feeds electricity to an LED bulb in any block directly touching it, causing it to illuminate. When more blocks are added, pieces below pass electricity up, and the new blocks light up too. You can create various formations with the blocks, and each piece glows a different color. It's no puzzle why this light is so cool.

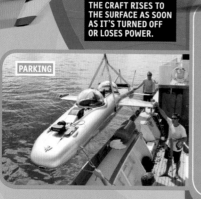

TENT ISN'T A PUSHOVER

A huge storm won't put a damper on your camping trip if you bring along the Heimplanet Mavericks inflatable tent. After unrolling the tent from the bag it comes in, use a hand pump to inflate it. It takes about 10 minutes for one person to blow up the 142-square-foot (13-sq-m) structure, which can comfortably fit 10 campers. And it's superhard to knock over, thanks to the way the weight of this dome-shaped tent is distributed. What's more, inflatable poles bend and crisscross over the exterior, giving the shelter extra reinforcement. In fact the Mavericks is so sturdy, it can withstand 112-mile-an-hour (180-km/h) winds. Who wouldn't be blown away by this awesome tent?

GENIUS WATCH

This gadget provides round-the-clock fun. The souped-up Kidizoom Smartwatch not only tells time—it also lets you snap photos, play games, and record voices, all with the touch of a finger. Stuck on a boring car ride with nothing to do? Pull up a puzzle game, or tap the microphone icon to record your friends and family. You can even add sound effects to the recorded conversation using the watch's special voice-altering function. It's about time a watch this awesome came along.

CAR SAILING

Driving along the beach in the SkyCar, you spot a pod of whales breaching in the distance. You want a closer look, so like a scene out of a futuristic sci-fi movie, you and your car take flight. On the ground the SkyCar drives like a regular car. To turn it into a plane, just switch it into fly mode, which activates the propeller. Next pull the parachute-like wing out of the back and find about a hundred yards (91 m) of space to use as a runway. Then accelerate to 40 miles an hour (64 km/h) and take off. Flying the SkyCar is just like driving it—the steering wheel is connected to the wing and controls your direction. The pedal controls altitude. (The more you push down, the higher you go.) The sky really *is* the limit.

You're playing at the park when you hear a buzz in the air. You look up and see a miniature flying saucer hovering above you. It's a drone, one of millions sold around the world in recent years. And whether they're used for toys or top-secret missions, it seems like drones are everywhere.

The Buzz on DRONES

DRONE DETAILS

Equipped with high-tech cameras, microphones, and sensors, drones can capture scenes from unique angles. They've proven to be useful in emergencies, like natural disasters, where they can be flown into unstable areas to provide instant feedback on damage and search for survivors. Drones are also used as an "eye in the sky" for sporting events like the Olympics and professional golf and soccer games, giving fans at home a closer-than-ever view of key plays and their favorite players. They're key in science, too: Researchers use drones for everything from studying critically endangered Sumatran orangutans high in the treetops of Indonesia to discovering ancient ruins in hard-to-reach locations.

NO-DRONE ZONE

But not everyone is flying high over drones. Crashing drones have injured people on the ground, and there have been reports of people using them to peep on private residences. They can also pose a huge threat to airplanes and helicopters. There have been many near misses in the sky due to drones flying dangerously close to aircraft.

Because of the risk they cause, many cities around the world have banned the buzzing drones. Police in the Netherlands have trained a bald eagle to fly to the gadget, clasp it in its claws, and bring it down to the ground. In Tokyo, Japan, where drones are forbidden in certain parts of the city, cops are attaching a 10-foot (3-m) net to their own drones to nab illegal flyers. Want to fly a drone in India? You must first get a license, like you'd need to drive a car or pilot a plane.

So will drones be as popular as smartphones and iPods one day? Possibly. But the hope is that a focus on laws and flying smart will keep the sky—and those below it—safe.

ROBOTICS

Robots may soon reboot the entire way you live. Over the past 50 years, these machines have mainly been used by NASA, or in places such as factories. But scientists are developing humanlike bots that can do so much more. Check out the science behind three awesome robots.

BENEBOT

WHAT IT'S WIRED FOR:
Storing information

Benebot operates by connecting through Wi-Fi to the cloud. The cloud uses the Internet to access networks of computer servers to perform tasks like storing data and supporting video chats. Benebot is able to share things with you that are kept on the cloud—for instance, information about products.

HOW IT WILL CHANGE YOUR LIFE:
Not sure which video game to buy while shopping at the electronics store? Using data from the cloud, Benebot will give you the scoop about each of your options so you can make a decision. It'll also stream videos of cool new items.

CHIMP

WHAT IT'S WIRED FOR:
Moving around obstacles

CHIMP uses a system called LIDAR to find objects and move around. As the machine moves, it shoots pulses of light from its head. These beams bounce off objects back to CHIMP's built-in sensors, and it then measures how long the light takes to return to figure out the distance of objects and how to navigate around them.

HOW IT WILL CHANGE YOUR LIFE: The five-foot (1.5-m)-tall, 400-pound (181-kg) droid was designed to aid people affected by disasters such as tornadoes. CHIMP could use its navigation skills to deliver supplies to disaster victims. Or, if something was broken in your house, someday CHIMP might swing into handyman-mode and fix it.

PR2

WHAT IT'S WIRED FOR:
Storing information

When PR2 comes across a rumpled piece of clothing, it uses pattern recognition to search for similar shapes programmed into its database. If it finds a match, it receives steps on how to fold it.

HOW IT WILL CHANGE YOUR LIFE: In addition to folding your laundry, PR2 can use its pattern recognition technology for other tasks such as tying shoelaces. With its agile hands, PR2 can even pour pancake batter into a frying pan and flip flapjacks.

PR2 SHOWS OFF ITS SKILLS: GRABBING A BEVERAGE, AND FLIPPING PANCAKES.

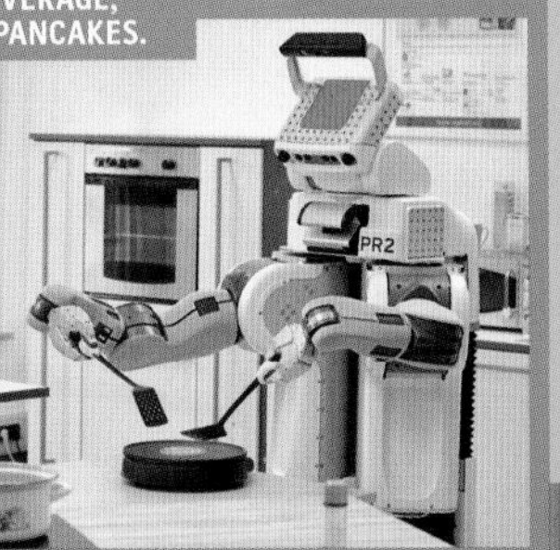

18 FACTS ABOUT 3-D

1

USING LAYERS OF A SUPERFINE NYLON POWDER, AN ENGINEER WAS ABLE TO CREATE AN ACOUSTIC GUITAR WITH HIS 3-D PRINTER.

2

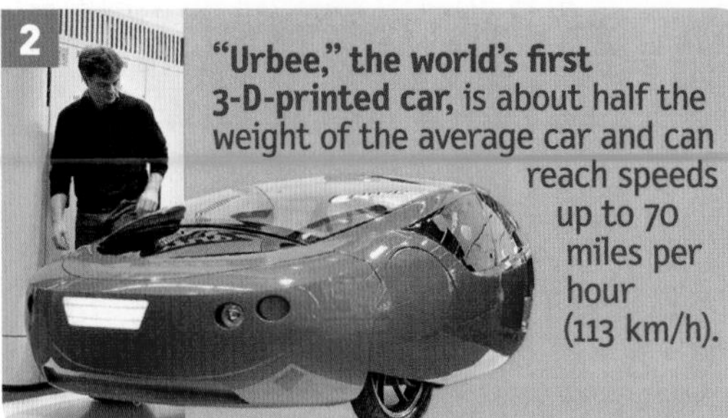

"Urbee," the world's first 3-D-printed car, is about half the weight of the average car and can reach speeds up to 70 miles per hour (113 km/h).

3

Engineers at Cornell University in New York, U.S.A., have figured out how to print **REPLACEMENTS FOR HUMAN EARS** that look and act like real ones.

4

ENGINEERS IN EUROPE RECENTLY REVEALED "THOR," THE WORLD'S FIRST 3-D-PRINTED AIRCRAFT.

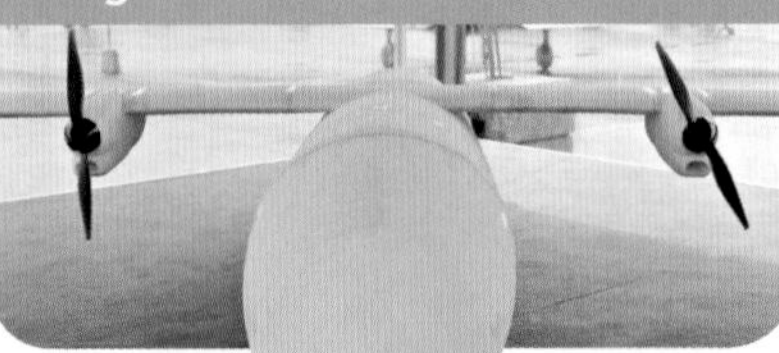

5

College students at the University of Maryland, U.S.A., **used a 3-D printer to make a flying robotic bird** called Robo Raven.

6

SOON, ASTRONAUTS IN SPACE WILL BE ABLE TO PRINT OUT OBJECTS LIKE CLIPS, BUCKLES—EVEN REPLACEMENT PARTS—**THANKS TO A 3-D PRINTER ON THE INTERNATIONAL SPACE STATION.**

7

THERE ARE 3-D PRINTERS THAT USE CHOCOLATE FOR "INK" TO CREATE MORSELS IN THE SHAPE OF YOUR FACE, FLOWERS, HEARTS, SNOWMEN, AND MORE.

8

A watchmaker has created a program that prints 18-carat gold by fusing bits of gold powder together.

9

TINY ENOUGH TO FIT ON YOUR FINGERTIP, THE **WORLD'S SMALLEST WORKING CIRCULAR SAW** WAS BUILT USING A 3-D PRINTER.

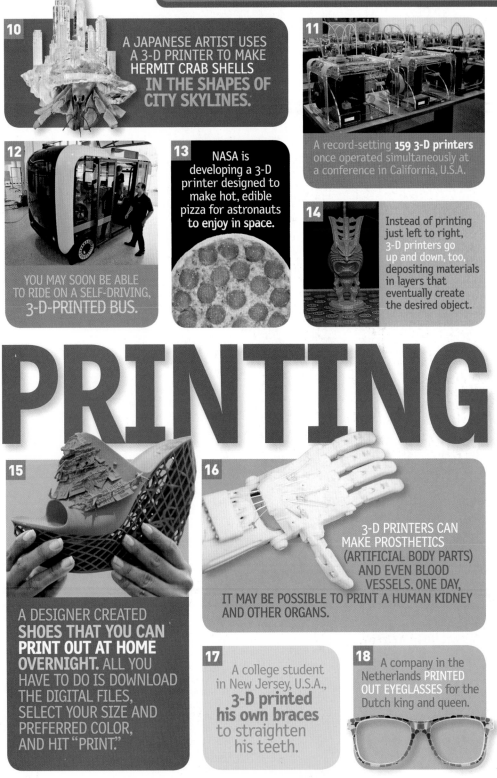

PRINTING

10

A JAPANESE ARTIST USES A 3-D PRINTER TO MAKE HERMIT CRAB SHELLS **IN THE SHAPES OF CITY SKYLINES.**

11

A record-setting **159 3-D printers** once operated simultaneously at a conference in California, U.S.A.

12

YOU MAY SOON BE ABLE TO RIDE ON A SELF-DRIVING, 3-D-PRINTED BUS.

13

NASA is developing a 3-D printer designed to make hot, edible pizza for astronauts to enjoy in space.

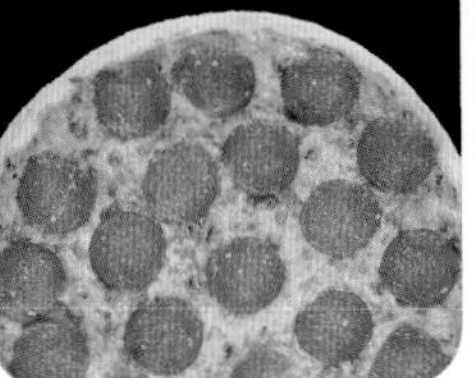

14

Instead of printing just left to right, 3-D printers go up and down, too, depositing materials in layers that eventually create the desired object.

15

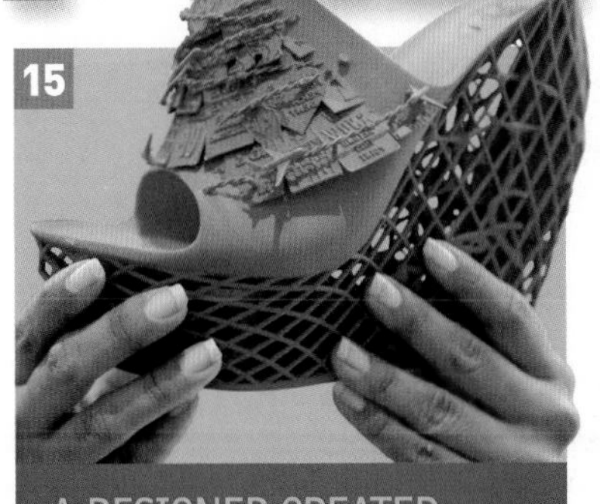

A DESIGNER CREATED **SHOES THAT YOU CAN PRINT OUT AT HOME OVERNIGHT.** ALL YOU HAVE TO DO IS DOWNLOAD THE DIGITAL FILES, SELECT YOUR SIZE AND PREFERRED COLOR, AND HIT "PRINT."

16

3-D PRINTERS CAN MAKE PROSTHETICS (ARTIFICIAL BODY PARTS) AND EVEN BLOOD VESSELS. ONE DAY, IT MAY BE POSSIBLE TO PRINT A HUMAN KIDNEY AND OTHER ORGANS.

17

A college student in New Jersey, U.S.A., **3-D printed his own braces** to straighten his teeth.

18

A company in the Netherlands PRINTED OUT EYEGLASSES for the Dutch king and queen.

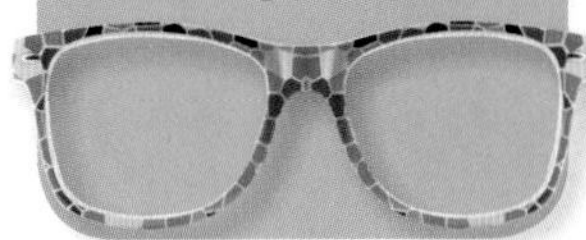

History's Greatest Hits

George Washington Carver

George Washington Carver's quest for knowledge made him a world-famous scientist and inventor. Find out about the groundbreaking life of this American hero.

START

Around 1864

George Washington Carver is born into slavery on a farm in Missouri, U.S.A. When slavery is abolished in 1865, his former owners, Moses and Susan Carver, decide to raise the orphaned George as their son.

1891 to 1896

Carver becomes the first black student accepted at Iowa State University, where he studies agriculture, the science of farming.

1896

Carver becomes a teacher at Tuskegee University in Alabama, U.S.A. He invents hundreds of products, including new kinds of paints and insecticides (chemicals used to kill insects).

1906

Discovering more than 300 ways to use peanut plants, Carver turns the nuts into glue, medicine, and paper. He shares his knowledge with farmers. (Fun fact: Carver did not invent peanut butter.)

PEANUT POWER

NO, TEDDY, I SAID MORE WATER, NOT LESS.

WHOOPS.

1915

Carver becomes famous for his farming smarts, and even advises the former U.S. president Theodore Roosevelt on agricultural matters.

1943

By the end of his career, Carver is a symbol of the important contributions of African Americans and inspires people all over, no matter what their skin color is.

ACCIDENTS Happen

Hey, they happen. Sometimes accidents are totally embarrassing. But other times they lead to something awesome. Check out these fortunate mistakes.

BUT SOMETIMES THEY RESULT IN **AMAZING DISCOVERIES.**

THE INVENTION: ARTIFICIAL SWEETENER

THE MOMENT OF "OOPS": Dirty hands

THE DETAILS: In the late 1870s, Constantin Fahlberg was working in his lab when he tipped over a beaker of chemicals, spilling them all over his hands. Without pausing to wash, Fahlberg went on with his work. When he went home to eat, the chemical residue was still on his fingers. After biting into a piece of bread, he noticed that it tasted strangely sweet. It wasn't the bread—it was something on his hands.

Fahlberg rushed back to work and found that the substance in the beaker that had spilled was sweet—much sweeter than sugar. He named his discovery saccharin—the first artificial sweetener.

THE INVENTION: MICROWAVE OVEN

THE MOMENT OF "OOPS": Accidentally melting a chocolate bar in a pocket

THE DETAILS: In the 1940s, Percy Spencer was experimenting with radar—radio waves used to detect objects. When he stepped in front of a magnetron—a device that makes waves called microwaves—the chocolate bar in his pocket melted! Spencer then aimed a beam of microwaves at some kernels of popping corn. They burst. Then he zapped a raw egg, which exploded. This proved that microwaves could heat food superfast, leading to the first microwave oven.

QUIZ WHIZ

Discover your tech-savvy smarts by taking this quiz!

Write your answers on a piece of paper. Then check them below.

1. **True or false?** The microwave oven was invented by accident.

2. **Which of the following has been created using 3-D printing?**
   a. artificial body parts
   b. an airplane
   c. pizza
   d. all of the above

3. **George Washington Carver turned _____ into glue, medicine, and paper.**
   a. apples
   b. potatoes
   c. peanuts
   d. carrots

4. **Researchers use __________ to study endangered Sumatran orangutans high in the treetops of Indonesia.**
   a. blimps
   b. kites
   c. pigeons
   d. drones

5. **What makes the PR2 robot helpful around the house?**
   a. It folds your laundry.
   b. It scrubs toilets.
   c. It takes your dog for a walk.
   d. It does the dishes.

Not **STUMPED** yet? Check out the *NATIONAL GEOGRAPHIC KIDS QUIZ WHIZ* collection for more crazy **TECHNOLOGY** questions!

ANSWERS:
1. True; 2. d; 3. c; 4. d; 5. a

HOMEWORK HELP

This Is How It's Done!

Sometimes, the most complicated problems are solved with step-by-step directions. These "how to" instructions are also known as a process analysis essay. While scientists and engineers use this tool to program robots and write computer code, you also use process analysis every day, from following a recipe to putting together a new toy or gadget. Here's how to write a basic process analysis essay.

Step 1: Choose Your Topic Sentence

Pick a clear and concise topic sentence that describes what you're writing about. Be sure to explain to the reader why the task is important—and how many steps there are to complete it.

Step 2: List Materials

Do you need specific ingredients or equipment to complete your process? Mention these right away so the readers will have all they need to do this activity.

Step 3: Write Your Directions

Your directions should be clear and easy to follow. Assume that you are explaining the process for the first time, and define any unfamiliar terms. List your steps in the exact order the reader will need to follow to complete the activity. Try to keep your essay limited to no more than six steps.

Step 4: Restate Your Main Idea

Your closing idea should revisit your topic sentence, drawing a conclusion relating to the importance of the subject.

EXAMPLE OF A PROCESS ANALYSIS ESSAY

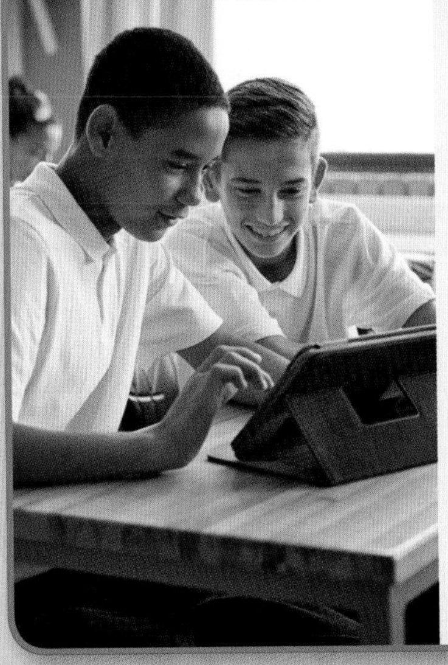

Downloading an app is a simple way to enhance your tablet. Today, I'd like to show you how to search for and add an app to your tablet. First, you will need a tablet with the ability to access the Internet. You'll also want to ask your parents' permission before you download anything onto your tablet. Next, select the specific app you're seeking by going to the app store on your tablet and entering the app's name into the search bar. Once you find the app you're seeking, select "download" and wait for the app to load. When you see that the app has fully loaded, tap on the icon and you will be able to access it. Now you can enjoy your app and have more fun with your tablet.

Wonders of Nature

Two bannerfish glide past an enormous sponge in the colorful coral reefs of the Solomon Islands in the South Pacific Ocean.

Weather and Climate

Weather is the condition of the atmosphere—temperature, wind, humidity, and precipitation—at a given place at a given time. Climate, however, is the average weather for a particular place over a long period of time. Different places on Earth have different climates, but climate is not a random occurrence. It is a pattern that is controlled by factors such as latitude, elevation, prevailing winds, the temperature of ocean currents, and location on land relative to water. Climate is generally constant, but evidence indicates that human activity is causing a change in the patterns of climate.

WEATHER EXTREMES

RAINBOW SHOW: The longest-lasting rainbow reportedly shone for six hours over England.

LIGHTNING HOT: Temperatures in the air around a lightning bolt can hit 50,000°F (27,760°C)

RAINIEST DAY: 72 inches (183 cm) of rain was recorded in a 24-hour period in 1966 on Reunion Island, a French island in the Indian Ocean, during Tropical Cyclone Denise.

GLOBAL CLIMATE ZONES

Climatologists, people who study climate, have created different systems for classifying climates. One often-used system is called the Köppen system, which classifies climate zones according to precipitation, temperature, and vegetation. It has five major categories—Tropical, Dry, Temperate, Cold, and Polar—with a sixth category for locations where high elevations override other factors.

ARCTIC OCEAN
ARCTIC CIRCLE
TROPIC OF CANCER
ATLANTIC OCEAN
PACIFIC OCEAN
EQUATOR
PACIFIC OCEAN
INDIAN OCEAN
TROPIC OF CAPRICORN
ANTARCTIC CIRCLE

Climate

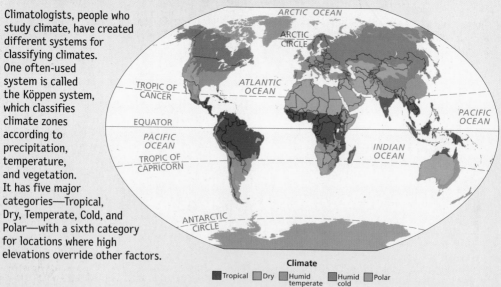

Tropical | Dry | Humid temperate | Humid cold | Polar

WATER CYCLE

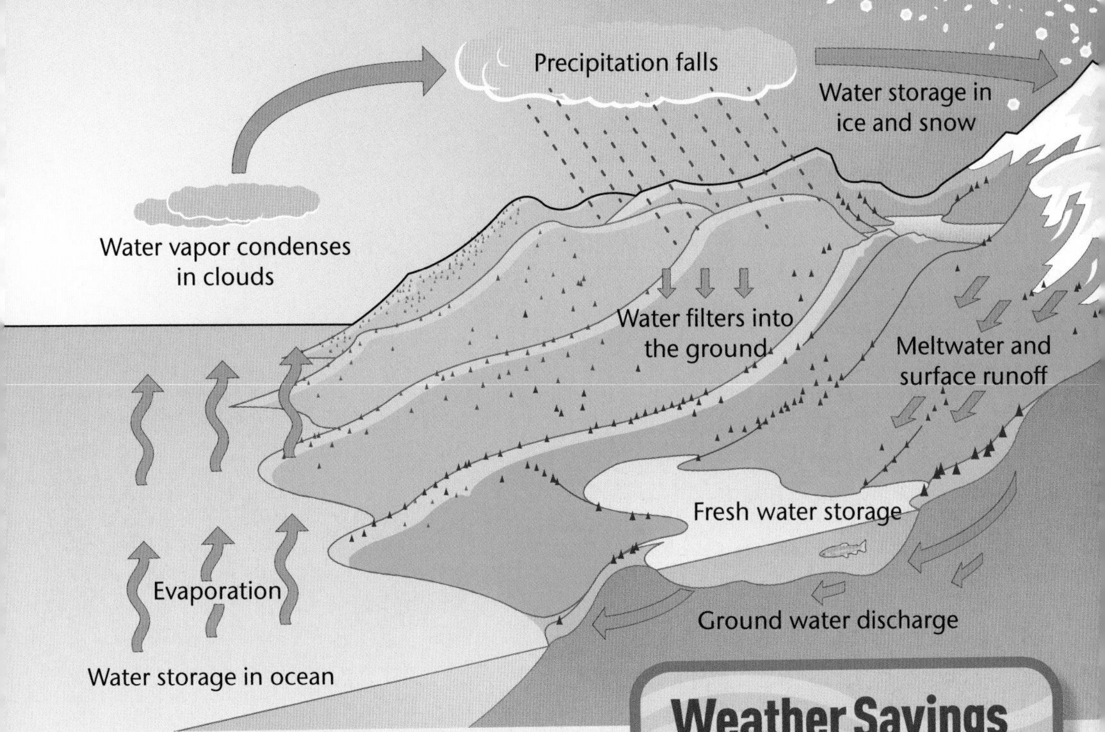

Precipitation falls

Water storage in ice and snow

Water vapor condenses in clouds

Water filters into the ground

Meltwater and surface runoff

Fresh water storage

Evaporation

Ground water discharge

Water storage in ocean

The amount of water on Earth is more or less constant—

only the form changes. As the sun warms Earth's surface, liquid water is changed to water vapor in a process called **evaporation.** Water on the surface of plants' leaves turn into water vapor in a process called **transpiration.** As water vapor rises into the air, it cools and changes form again. This time it becomes clouds in a process called **condensation.** Water droplets fall from the clouds as **precipitation,** which then travels as groundwater or runoff back to the lakes, rivers, and oceans, where the cycle (shown above) starts all over again.

To a meteorologist—a person who studies the weather—a "light rain" is less than 1/48 of an inch (0.5 mm). A "heavy rain" is more than 1/6 of an inch (4 mm).

Weather Sayings

These words of weather wisdom have been passed down for generations. But they're not always accurate—be sure to check the forecast!

- Red sky in the morning, sailors take warning. Red sky at night, sailors' delight.
- Clear nights mean cold days.
- If a circle forms 'round the moon, then it will rain very soon.
- Rain before seven stops by eleven.
- In a green sky, the cows will fly.

Types of Clouds

If you want a clue about the weather, look up at the clouds. They'll tell a lot about the condition of the air and what weather might be on the way. Clouds are made of both air and water. On fair days, warm air currents rise up and push against the water in clouds, keeping it from falling. But as the raindrops in a cloud get bigger, it's time to set them free. The bigger raindrops become too heavy for the air currents to hold up, and they fall to the ground.

4

3

1

2

How Much Does a Cloud Weigh?

A light, fluffy, cumulus cloud typically weighs about 216,000 pounds (97,975 kg). That's about the weight of 18 elephants. A rain-soaked cumulonimbus cloud typically weighs 105.8 million pounds (48 million kg), or about 9,000 elephants.

1 STRATUS These clouds make the sky look like a bowl of thick gray porridge. They hang low in the sky, blanketing the day in dreary darkness. Stratus clouds form when cold, moist air close to the ground moves over a region.

2 CIRRUS These wispy tufts of clouds are thin and hang high up in the atmosphere where the air is extremely cold. Cirrus clouds are made of tiny ice crystals.

3 CUMULONIMBUS These are the monster clouds. Rising air currents force fluffy cumulus clouds to swell and shoot upward, as much as 70,000 feet (21,000 m). When these clouds bump against the top of the troposphere, or the tropopause, they flatten out on top like tabletops.

4 CUMULUS These white, fluffy clouds make people sing, "Oh, what a beautiful morning!" They form low in the atmosphere and look like marshmallows. They often mix with large patches of blue sky. Formed when hot air rises, cumulus clouds usually disappear when the air cools at night.

Make a Barometer

ARE YOU FASCINATED BY WEATHER? Then you should make your own barometer to track the weather where you live!

SUPPLY LIST

- Ruler
- Tall glass
- Drinking straw
- Bubble gum
- Tape
- Water and blue food coloring

STEPS

1. Tape a clear drinking straw to a ruler. The bottom of the straw should line up with the 1/2-inch (12–13 mm) mark on the ruler.

2. Stand the ruler up in a tall glass and tape it to the inside of the glass so it stays straight. Fill the glass 3/4 full with water.

3. Here's the fun part: Chew on a piece of gum for a while, then stick it to the top of the straw.

4. Pour out 1/4 of the water so that the water in the straw is higher than the water in the cup.

5. Keep an eye on your barometer. When atmospheric pressure increases, the water level in your straw will rise (which usually means fair weather). When atmospheric pressure decreases, the water level will fall (and can mean clouds or rain are on the way). Record your findings in your meteorologist notebook!

Barometers were invented in Italy in the early 1600s by Evangelista Torricelli.

Time: about 10 minutes

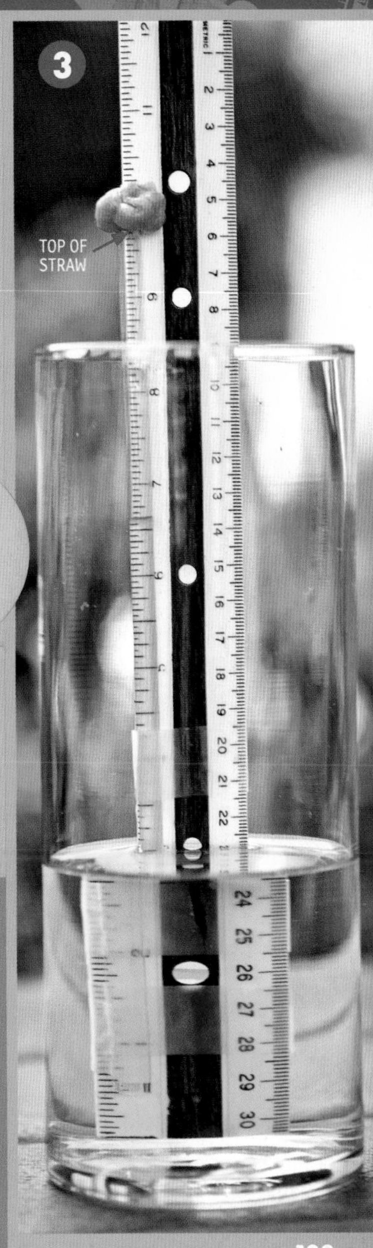

KEEP A WEATHER JOURNAL

Recording the daily temperature, rainfall, and barometric changes will help you track patterns in the weather. Try to take a measurement every day and record it in a journal. Set up a chart for each component of your weather station. After a few weeks, you might start to see some patterns, and soon you'll be making predictions—like a regular meteorologist!

18 FACTS ABOUT NATURAL

1

SOME 20,000 PEOPLE LIVED OUT HURRICANE KATRINA IN THE SUPERDOME IN NEW ORLEANS, LOUISIANA, U.S.A.

2

In just one forceful minute, the 1906 earthquake in California, U.S.A., became the deadliest in the state's history.

3
The Great Famine in Ireland in the mid-1800s was **caused by a fungus** that destroyed the potato crop.

4
THE MOST FAMOUS ERUPTION OF ITALY'S MOUNT VESUVIUS, THE ONLY ACTIVE VOLCANO ON THE MAINLAND OF EUROPE, OCCURRED IN A.D. 79.

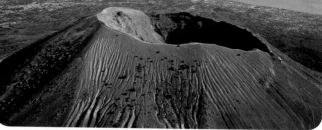

5
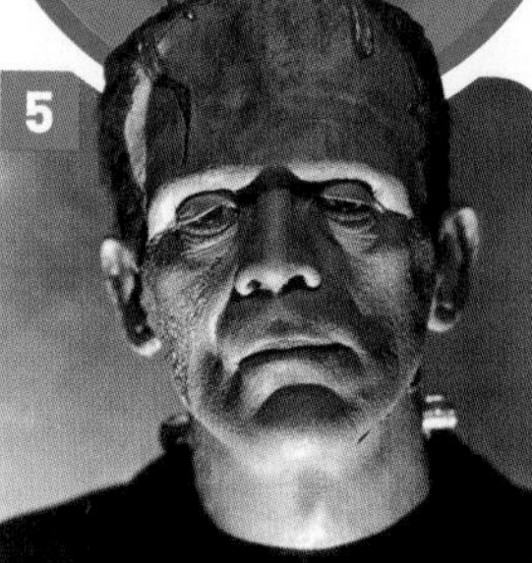
THE DARK AND GLOOMY WEATHER OF 1816 INSPIRED MARY SHELLEY TO WRITE ***FRANKENSTEIN.***

6

At 9.5 on the Richter scale, Chile's 1960 earthquake is the **STRONGEST QUAKE ON RECORD.**

7

THE SWISS ARMY BEGAN TRAINING DOGS TO SEARCH FOR VICTIMS BURIED BY AVALANCHES IN THE 1930s.

8
A monster, multi-vortex, F5 tornado—a large tornado with smaller ones inside it—**ripped through Joplin, Missouri, U.S.A.,** in May 2011.

9
FOR THE FIRST TIME SINCE 1888, WEATHER, IN THE FORM OF SUPERSTORM SANDY, SHUT DOWN THE NEW YORK STOCK EXCHANGE FOR TWO DAYS.

10 **DUST** FROM THE APRIL 1815 ERUPTION OF INDONESIA'S MOUNT TAMBORA **BLOCKED LIGHT FROM THE SUN,** AFFECTING CLIMATE WELL INTO 1816.

11

KANSAS AND OKLAHOMA, U.S.A., WERE HIT BY A TOTAL OF **74 TORNADOES** **IN A SINGLE DAY**—MAY 3, 1999.

12

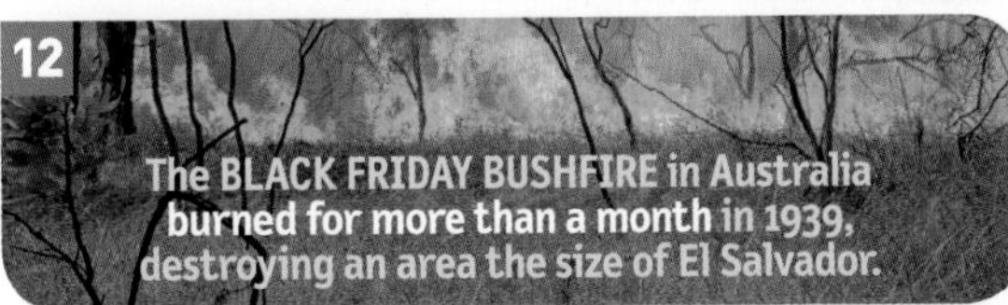

The **BLACK FRIDAY BUSHFIRE** in Australia **burned for more than a month** in 1939, destroying an area the size of El Salvador.

13

TORNADOES USUALLY SPIN IN THE OPPOSITE DIRECTION ABOVE AND BELOW THE EQUATOR.

14

The largest hurricanes can measure 10 miles (16 km) from top to bottom.

DISASTERS

15

CHINA'S 1931 FLOODS WERE THE **WORST DISASTER** IN THE COUNTRY'S HISTORY.

16

France has had the greatest number of **AVALANCHE FATALITIES.**

17

In 2012, **Superstorm Sandy** wiped out the famous boardwalk in Atlantic City, New Jersey, U.S.A.

18 **Hurricane Iniki, in 1992, was the most powerful to hit the Hawaiian Islands in their recorded history.**

Natural Disasters

Every world region has its share of natural disasters—the mix just varies from place to place. And the names of similar storms may vary as well. Take, for example, cyclones, typhoons, and hurricanes. The only difference among these disasters is where in the world they strike. In the Atlantic and the Northeast Pacific, they're hurricanes; in the Northwest Pacific near Asia they're typhoons; and in the South Pacific and Indian Oceans, they're cyclones.

Despite their distinct titles, these natural disasters are each classified by violent winds, massive waves, torrential rain, and floods. The only obvious variation among these storms? They spin in the opposite direction if they're south of the Equator.

HURRICANES IN 2018

HELLO, MY NAME IS . . .

Hurricane names come from six official international lists. The names alternate between male and female. When a storm becomes a hurricane, a name from the list is used, in alphabetical order. Each list is reused every six years. A name "retires" if that hurricane caused a lot of damage or many deaths.

- Alberto
- Beryl
- Chris
- Debby
- Ernesto
- Florence
- Gordon
- Helene
- Isaac
- Joyce
- Kirk
- Leslie
- Michael
- Nadine
- Oscar
- Patty
- Rafael
- Sara
- Tony
- Valerie
- William

TYPHOON!

A monster storm with gusts of 235 miles an hour (380 km/h) barrels down onto a cluster of islands in the heart of the Philippines in November 2013. Howling winds whip debris into the street as palm trees bend nearly in half, and seawater rises as high as a two-story building. This is Super Typhoon Haiyan, and it's about as dangerous as they come.

When does a typhoon become a super-typhoon? According to the U.S. National Oceanic and Atmospheric Administration (NOAA), winds must sustain speeds of over 150 miles an hour (240 km/h) for at least a minute. And not only is Haiyan powerful, it's also gigantic: The storm's clouds cover at least two-thirds of the Philippines, which is roughly the size of Arizona, U.S.A.

The word "typhoon" comes from the Greek *typhon,* meaning "whirlwind." These superstrong storms form when tropical winds suck up moisture as they pass over warm water. Increasing in speed and strength as they near the coast, typhoons can topple homes and cause massive flooding once they hit land.

The Philippines endures an average of eight or nine tropical storms every year. But none have been as disastrous as Haiyan. Resulting in over 6,300 casualties, affecting 16 million people, and racking up millions of dollars in damage, the storm was one of the strongest typhoons to ever hit land anywhere in the world.

Scale of Hurricane Intensity

CATEGORY	ONE	TWO	THREE	FOUR	FIVE
DAMAGE	Minimal	Moderate	Extensive	Extreme	Catastrophic
WINDS	74–95 mph (119–153 kph)	96–110 mph (154–177 kph)	111–129 mph (178–208 kph)	130–156 mph (209–251 kph)	157 mph or higher (252+ kph)
(DAMAGE refers to wind and water damage combined.)					

EARTHQUAKE!

From one moment to the next, life dramatically changed in the town of Pedernales, Ecuador. In an instant, the streets shook and buildings began to rattle. Restaurants and hotels, filled with tourists and villagers, crumbled to the ground. It was the worst disaster to hit Ecuador in decades: A magnitude 7.8 earthquake rocked the South American nation in April 2016, amassing a death toll of some 650 and injuring thousands more.

So why is Ecuador vulnerable to such epic earthquakes? Blame the country's location. It lies on the eastern rim of the Pacific Ring of Fire, a chain of active volcanoes in the Pacific Ocean where some 90 percent of all earthquakes on the planet occur. Ring of Fire activity is the result of tectonic plates, large slabs on Earth's crust that are constantly in motion. Sometimes, the plates slide next to each other, collide, or move apart, causing a release of energy in the earth's crust that forms a quake.

As the country seeks to rebuild its crumbled cities and villages, the hope is that such a powerful quake remains a rare occurrence.

FLOOD

In December 2015, up to a foot of rain (0.3 m) soaked the central United States. Missouri and surrounding states were the most affected. Soon, floodwaters from the nearby Mississippi River and its tributaries had risen to historical levels, spilling over the river-banks and severely damaging homes, businesses, and farms. Hundreds of buildings were washed away, leaving thousands of people without homes.

Although the floodwater began to recede, and life slowly returned to normal in the Midwest, the disaster left devastation in its wake. The damage was so severe, the cleanup bill hovered somewhere around $1 billion.

Recovering from a flood is a lengthy—and tough—ordeal. But thanks to help from the community—and an emergency declaration for federal disaster funds signed by President Barack Obama—the affected areas were able to rebound from what is now considered one of the most severe wintertime floods in U.S. history.

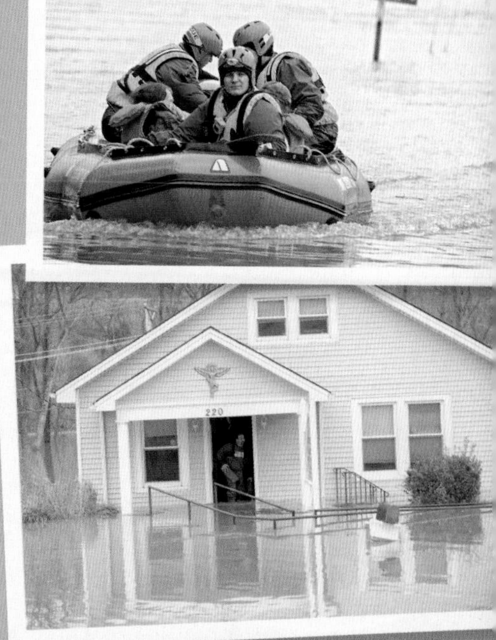

WILDFIRES!

The five coolest tools for battling blazes

For 20 years, John Kovalicky has worked as a smokejumper, an elite firefighter who parachutes out of airplanes to get as close as possible to remote and dangerous wildland blazes. Using hand tools like axes and shovels, smokejumpers work to stop the fire.

Most years more than 100,000 wildfires burn in the United States. Moving more than 14 miles per hour (22 km/h), these fires can scorch 9 million acres (3.6 million ha) of land each year. Wilderness firefighters like Kovalicky are constantly looking for smarter ways to battle the blazes. Here are some new ways they're getting the job done.

BIGGER, FASTER TANKERS

Until recently, planes from as far back as World War II would release a steady red stream of flame retardant to slow wildfires. Now, the U.S. Forest Service has new jet-powered tankers that can carry more than 3,000 gallons (11,350 L) of retardant and fly 345 miles an hour (555 km/h). That's about 40 percent faster than the old planes!

A FIREFIGHTER FLIES OVER A WILDFIRE.

BETTER GEAR

Smokejumpers need advanced gear, including parachutes. In the future, parachutes may be square instead of round, which will make it easier to maneuver in windy conditions so firefighters don't have to wait for calmer skies.

Smokejumpers will also wear data recorders to give them instant feedback on altitude, airspeed, and temperature with every jump. This way, aerial firefighters can perfect their technique and improve the next generation of parachutes.

PSYCHIC SOFTWARE

Wildfires are unpredictable. Wind can quickly turn a small fire into an out-of-control inferno. Large wildfires can create their own weather, some generating hurricane-force winds that spread the flames faster than a firefighter can run.

New mapping technology keeps firefighters a step ahead of the flames. Using weather data, this psychic software predicts where wildfires will spread. That lets firefighters stay ahead of the fire. They can clear fuel and other extremely flammable materials from the fire's path and drop retardant in the places most likely to stop the blaze before it can spread.

A CLOSED SHELTER

SUPERSHELTERS

What happens when firefighters get trapped in the path of a deadly blaze? They climb into fire shelters, small tents made of aluminum foil glued to special materials. They're designed to reflect the heat of a nearby fire and trap breathable air inside to help save the firefighter's life.

The U.S. Forest Service is developing new super shelters that will have upgrades like stronger glue and materials that can better protect the firefighter from higher temperatures.

FUTURE DRONES WILL BE WAY SMALLER THAN THIS VERSION.

EYES IN THE SKY

Firefighters face disaster when flames block their escape routes. Someday soon, drones may help them out. The small vehicles, which fly without a pilot on board, would use sophisticated imaging to find exit routes or pinpoint ponds and wells where crews could get water. The drone could also send info about the blaze back to its operator, and eventually to the firefighters on the ground.

WILDFIRE REGIONS IN THE U.S.

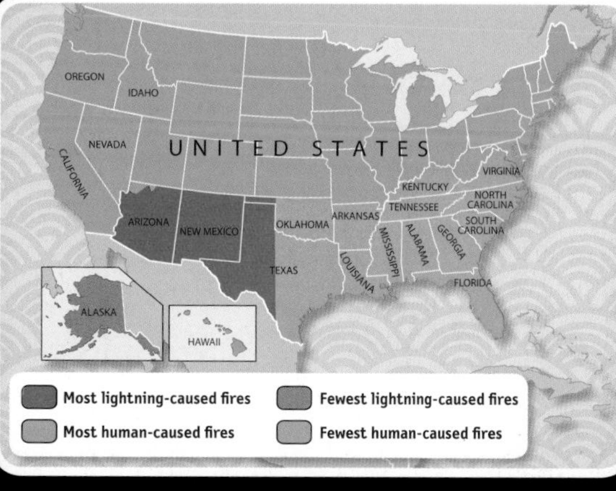

Map based on 13-year average of fires and acres reported to the National Interagency Coordination Center at the National Interagency Fire Center

HOW DOES YOUR GARDEN GROW?

The plant kingdom is more than 300,000 species strong, growing all over the world: on top of mountains, in the sea, in frigid temperatures—everywhere. Without plants, life on Earth would not be able to survive. Plants provide food and oxygen for animals and humans.

Three characteristics make plants distinct:

1. Most have chlorophyll (a green pigment that makes photosynthesis work and turns sunlight into energy), while some are parasitic.
2. They cannot change their location on their own.
3. Their cell walls are made from a stiff material called cellulose.

Photosynthesis

Plants are lucky—they don't have to hunt or shop for food. Most use the sun to produce their own food. In a process called photosynthesis, the plant's chloroplast (the part of the plant where the chemical chlorophyll is located) captures the sun's energy and combines it with carbon dioxide from the air and nutrient-rich water from the ground to produce a sugar called glucose. Plants burn the glucose for energy to help them grow. As a waste product, plants emit oxygen, which humans and other animals need to breathe. When we breathe, we exhale carbon dioxide, which the plants then use for more photosynthesis—it's all a big, finely tuned system. So the next time you pass a lonely houseplant, give it thanks for helping you live.

Check out these outrageous facts.

YOU CAN SEE COLORFUL LEAVES FROM SPACE.

Palm trees grew at the North Pole about 55 million years ago.

A BRITISH MAN GREW A GIANT ZUCCHINI THAT WEIGHED AS MUCH AS A LARGE SHEEPDOG.

APPLES ARE ONE-QUARTER AIR.

A peanut is not a nut.

PUMPKINS ALSO COME IN RED, GREEN, YELLOW, BLUE, TAN, AND WHITE.

Bees visit about five million flowers to make one average-size jar of honey.

PEACHES AND ALMONDS ARE RELATED.

CHECK OUT THIS BOOK!

weird
but
true!
GROSS
300 slimy, sticky, and smelly facts

Biomes

A BIOME, OFTEN CALLED A MAJOR LIFE ZONE, is one of the natural world's major communities where plants and animals adapt to their specific surroundings. Biomes are classified depending on the predominant vegetation, climate, and geography of a region. They can be divided into six major types: forest, freshwater, marine, desert, grassland, and tundra. Each biome consists of many ecosystems.

Biomes are extremely important. Balanced ecological relationships among biomes help to maintain the environment and life on Earth as we know it. For example, an increase in one species of plant, such as an invasive one, can cause a ripple effect throughout the whole biome.

FOREST

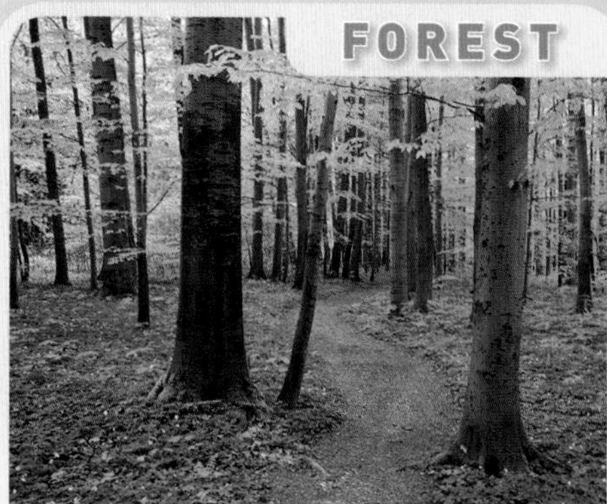

Forests occupy about one-third of Earth's land area. There are three major types of forests: tropical, temperate, and boreal (taiga). Forests are home to a diversity of plants, some of which may hold medicinal qualities for humans, as well as thousands of animal species, some still undiscovered. Forests can also absorb carbon dioxide, a greenhouse gas, and give off oxygen.

The rabbit-size royal antelope lives in West Africa's dense forests.

FRESHWATER

Most water on Earth is salty, but freshwater ecosystems—including lakes, ponds, wetlands, rivers, and streams—usually contain water with less than one percent salt concentration. The countless animal and plant species that live in a freshwater biome vary from continent to continent, but they include algae, frogs, turtles, fish, and the larvae of many insects.

The place where fresh and salt water meet is called an estuary.

MARINE

The marine biome covers almost three-fourths of Earth's surface, making it the largest habitat on our planet. Oceans make up the majority of the saltwater marine biome. Coral reefs are considered to be the most biodiverse of any of the biome habitats. The marine biome is home to more than one million plant and animal species.

Estimated to be up to 100,000 years old, sea grass growing in the Mediterranean Sea may be the oldest living thing on Earth.

DESERT

Covering about one-fifth of Earth's surface, deserts are places where precipitation is less than 10 inches (25 cm) per year. Although most deserts are hot, there are other kinds as well. The four major kinds of deserts are hot, semiarid, coastal, and cold. Far from being barren wastelands, deserts are biologically rich habitats.

Some sand dunes in the Sahara are tall enough to bury a 50-story building.

GRASSLAND

Biomes called grasslands are characterized by having grasses instead of large shrubs or trees. Grasslands generally have precipitation for only about half to three-fourths of the year. If it were more, they would become forests. Grasslands can be divided into two types: tropical (savannas) and temperate. Some of the world's largest land animals, such as elephants, live there.

Grasslands in North America are called prairies; in South America, they're called pampas.

TUNDRA

The coldest of all biomes, a tundra is characterized by an extremely cold climate, simple vegetation, little precipitation, poor nutrients, and a short growing season. There are two types of tundra: arctic and alpine. A tundra is home to few kinds of vegetation. Surprisingly, though, there are quite a few animal species that can survive the tundra's extremes, such as wolves, caribou, and even mosquitoes.

Formed 10,000 years ago, the arctic tundra is the world's youngest biome.

THE OC

PACIFIC OCEAN

STATS

Surface area
65,436,200 sq mi (169,479,000 sq km)

Portion of Earth's water area
47 percent

Greatest depth
Challenger Deep (in the Mariana Trench) -36,070 ft (-10,994 m)

Surface temperatures
Summer high: 90°F (32°C)
Winter low: 28°F (-2°C)

Tides
Highest: 30 ft (9 m) near Korean peninsula
Lowest: 1 ft (0.3 m) near Midway Islands

Cool creatures: **giant Pacific octopus, bottlenose whale, clownfish, great white shark**

GREAT WHITE SHARK

ATLANTIC OCEAN

STATS

Surface area
35,338,500 sq mi (91,526,300 sq km)

Portion of Earth's water area
25 percent

Greatest depth
Puerto Rico Trench -28,232 ft (-8,605 m)

Surface temperatures
Summer high: 90°F (32°C)
Winter low: 28°F (-2°C)

Tides
Highest: 52 ft (16 m) Bay of Fundy, Canada
Lowest: 1.5 ft (0.5 m) Gulf of Mexico and Mediterranean Sea

Cool creatures: **blue whale, Atlantic spotted dolphin, sea turtle**

GREEN SEA TURTLE

EANS

INDIAN OCEAN

STATS

Surface area
28,839,800 sq mi (74,694,800 sq km)

Portion of Earth's water area
21 percent

Greatest depth
Java Trench
-23,376 ft (-7,125 m)

Surface temperatures
Summer high: 93°F (34°C)
Winter low: 28°F (-2°C)

Tides
Highest: 36 ft (11 m)
Lowest: 2 ft (0.6 m)
Both along Australia's west coast

Cool creatures: **humpback whale, Portuguese man-of-war, dugong (sea cow)**

DUGONG

ARCTIC OCEAN

STATS

Surface area
5,390,000 sq mi (13,960,100 sq km)

Portion of Earth's water area
4 percent

Greatest depth
Molloy Deep
-18,599 ft (-5,669 m)

Surface temperatures
Summer high: 41°F (5°C)
Winter low: 28°F (-2°C)

Tides
Less than 1 ft (0.3 m) variation throughout the ocean

Cool creatures: **beluga whale, orca, harp seal, narwhal**

ORCA

To see the major oceans and bays in relation to landmasses, look at the map on pages 258 and 259.

PRISTINE SEAS

Explorers work to protect the last truly wild places in the ocean.

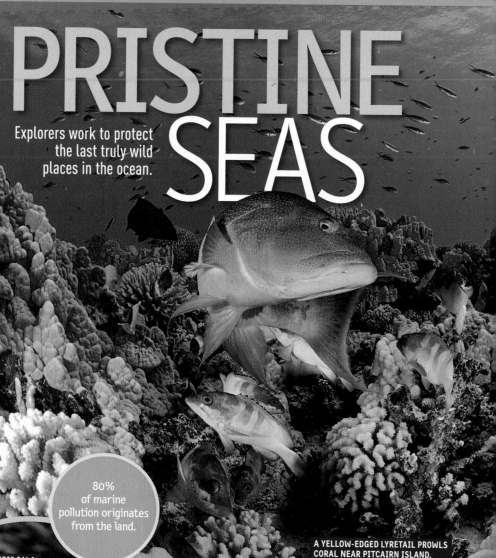

80% of marine pollution originates from the land.

A YELLOW-EDGED LYRETAIL PROWLS CORAL NEAR PITCAIRN ISLAND.

DR. ENRIC SALA

KEEPING OUR OCEANS PRISTINE

Oceans cover more than 70 percent of Earth's surface. Even with all of that water, only a tiny percentage is not impacted by human activity—but conservationists are working to change that. The National Geographic Pristine Seas team, led by National Geographic Explorer-in-Residence Enric Sala, travels to some of the most remote parts of the oceans to explore life underwater and create protected areas. One such location? The Pitcairn Islands in the South Pacific, where the Pristine Seas squad created the world's largest marine reserve, setting aside a swath of sea bigger than the entire state of California, U.S.A., for special protection. That means there is no fishing or seafloor mining allowed in the reserve, a move meant to keep the thousands of fish, plants, and coral living there healthy and thriving.

PITCAIRN ISLAND

So far, Pristine Seas has protected more than 1.16 million square miles (3 million sq km) of ocean territory.

A DIVER EXPLORES BOUNTY BAY NEAR PITCAIRN ISLAND.

GREY REEF SHARK

The goal of Pristine Seas is to help fully protect 10% of the world's oceans by 2020.

SAVING THE SHARKS

The Pristine Seas expedition has also made its mark on the uninhabited Southern Line Islands, an archipelago deep in the South Pacific. Dozens of grey reef sharks swirl around these islands, feeding on the fish around the coral reefs. But they face constant danger. Sought out by humans for their fins—considered a delicacy in some parts of Asia—these sharks are vulnerable to overfishing, which is when people catch them at too fast a rate for the species to replace themselves. But by working with the local government, Sala and his crew have established a 12-nautical-mile fishing exclusion zone around each island. It's a step in the right direction for protecting the ecology of the island and, ultimately, boosting the shark's dwindling population.

Quiz yourself to find out if you're a natural when it comes to nature knowledge!

Write your answers on a piece of paper. Then check them below.

1. **True or false?** Tornadoes usually spin in the same direction above and below the equator.

2. **_____ percent of all earthquakes on the planet occur in the Pacific Ring of Fire, a chain of active volcanoes in the Pacific Ocean.**

   a. 10 **b.** 50 **c.** 90 **d.** 1

3. **Deserts cover about ________ of Earth's surface.**

   a. one-fifth
   b. half
   c. one-quarter
   d. two-thirds

4. **Aside from orange, pumpkins also come in which colors?**

   a. green
   b. yellow
   c. blue
   d. all of the above

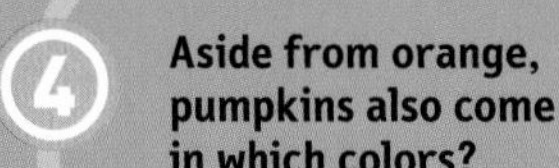

5. **True or false?** The Philippines endures an average of eight or nine tropical storms every year.

Not **STUMPED** yet? Check out the *NATIONAL GEOGRAPHIC KIDS QUIZ WHIZ* collection for more crazy **NATURE** questions!

ANSWERS:
1. False. They spin in the opposite direction; 2. c; 3. a; 4. d ; 5. True

HOMEWORK HELP

SPEAK NATURALLY

Oral Reports Made Easy

Does the thought of public speaking start your stomach churning like a tornado? Would you rather get caught in an avalanche than give a speech?

Giving an oral report does not have to be a natural disaster. The basic format is very similar to that of a written essay. There are two main elements that make up a good oral report—the writing and the presentation. As you write your oral report, remember that your audience will be hearing the information as opposed to reading it. Follow the guidelines below, and there will be clear skies ahead.

TIP: Make sure you practice your presentation a few times. Stand in front of a mirror or have a parent record you so you can see if you need to work on anything, such as eye contact.

Writing Your Material

Follow the steps in the "How to Write a Perfect Essay" section on p. 35, but prepare your report to be spoken rather than written. Try to keep your sentences short and simple. Long, complex sentences are harder to follow. Limit yourself to just a few key points. You don't want to overwhelm your audience with too much information. To be most effective, hit your key points in the introduction, elaborate on them in the body, and then repeat them once again in your conclusion.

An oral report has three basic parts:

- **Introduction**—This is your chance to engage your audience and really capture their interest in the subject you are presenting. Use a funny personal experience or a dramatic story, or start with an intriguing question.
- **Body**—This is the longest part of your report. Here you elaborate on the facts and ideas you want to convey. Give information that supports your main idea, and expand on it with specific examples or details. In other words, structure your oral report in the same way you would a written essay so that your thoughts are presented in a clear and organized manner.
- **Conclusion**—This is the time to summarize the information and emphasize your most important points to the audience one last time.

Preparing Your Delivery

1 Practice makes perfect.

Practice! Practice! Practice! Confidence, enthusiasm, and energy are key to delivering an effective oral report, and they can best be achieved through rehearsal. Ask family and friends to be your practice audience and give you feedback when you're done. Were they able to follow your ideas? Did you seem knowledgeable and confident? Did you speak too slowly or too fast, too softly or too loudly? The more times you practice giving your report, the more you'll master the material. Then you won't have to rely so heavily on your notes or papers, and you will be able to give your report in a relaxed and confident manner.

2 Present with everything you've got.

Be as creative as you can. Incorporate videos, sound clips, slide presentations, charts, diagrams, and photos. Visual aids help stimulate your audience's senses and keep them intrigued and engaged. They can also help to reinforce your key points. And remember that when you're giving an oral report, you're a performer. Take charge of the spotlight and be as animated and entertaining as you can. Have fun with it.

3 Keep your nerves under control.

Everyone gets a little nervous when speaking in front of a group. That's normal. But the more preparation you've done—meaning plenty of researching, organizing, and rehearsing—the more confident you'll be. Preparation is the key. And if you make a mistake or stumble over your words, just regroup and keep going. Nobody's perfect, and nobody expects you to be.

KNOCK,
KNOCK.
Who's there?
Yam.
Yam who?
I yam so happy to see you!
Animal Jam
EXPLORE!
NATIONAL GEOGRAPHIC KIDS' virtual world online:
AnimalJam.com
Enter the special code NGKAJ18 for a bonus!

FUN and
GAMES

Find the HIDDEN ANIMALS

ANIMALS OFTEN BLEND into their environments for protection. Find the animals listed below in the photographs. Write the letter of the correct photo on a separate sheet of paper.

ANSWERS ON PAGE 338

1. seal
2. owl
3. frog
4. lizard
5. orchid mantis

CHECK OUT THIS BOOK!

TICKLED PINK

These photos show close-up views of pink things. On a separate sheet of paper, unscramble the letters to identify what's in each picture. Bonus: Use the highlighted letters to solve the puzzle below. ANSWERS ON PAGE 338

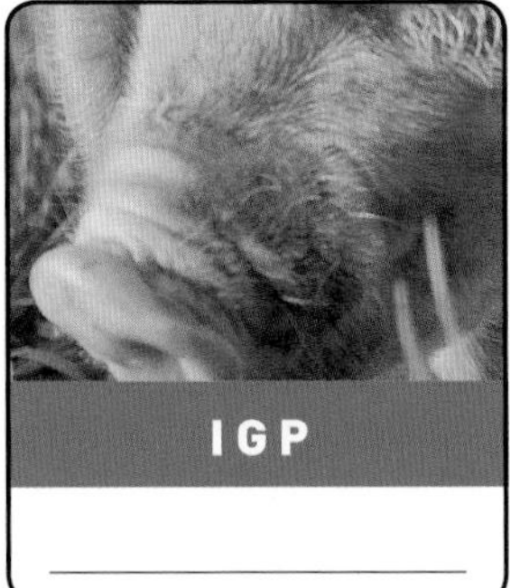

IGP

NAKLGIW MWRO

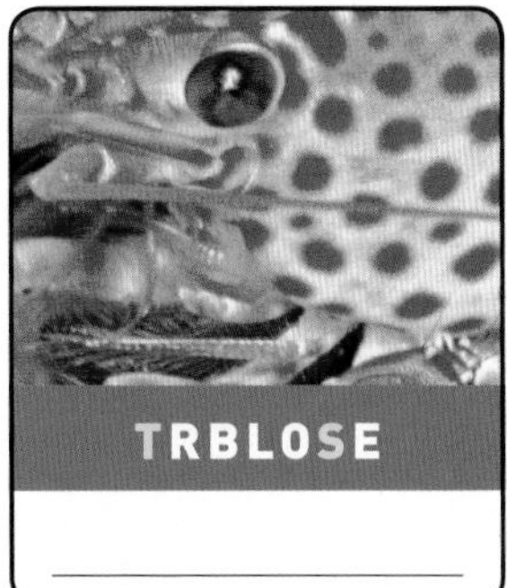

TRBLOSE

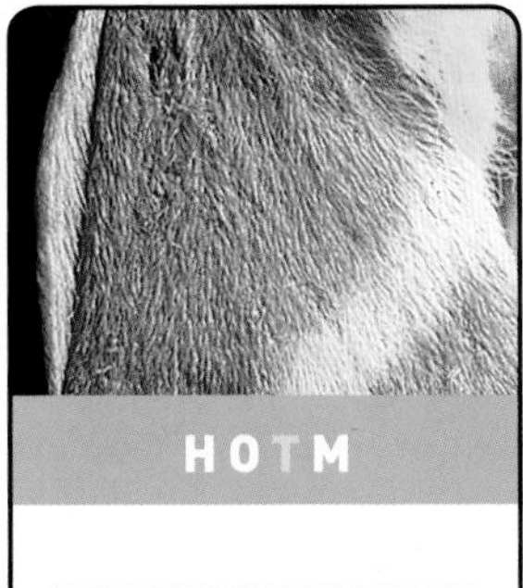

HOTM

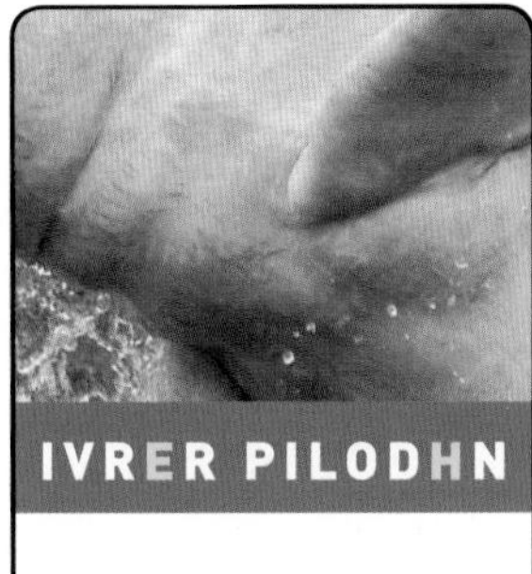

IVRER PILODHN

YAKIDDT

ONMLGIAF

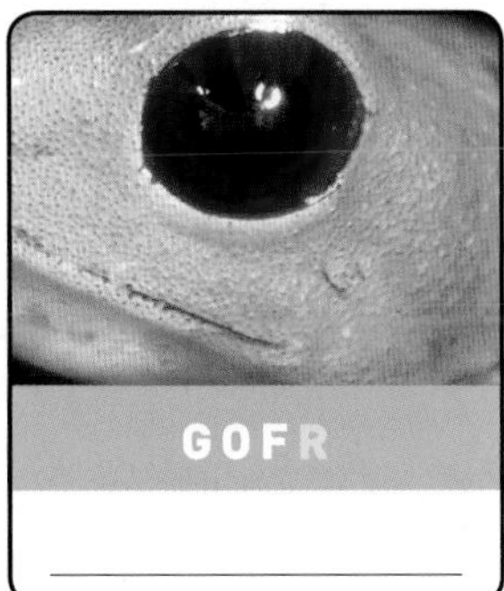

GOFR

LORAC

HINT: What do you call two birds in love?

ANSWER: _ _ E _ _ _ E _ _ _ _

Grand Teton Adventure

The visitors (below) to Grand Teton National Park in Wyoming, U.S.A., need to get to the park ranger. Use your finger to trace the way through the maze while avoiding the people, animals, and other obstacles blocking their path.

ANSWER ON PAGE 338

Funny Fill-In

Hawaiian Hullabaloo

Ask a friend to give you words to fill in the blanks in this story and write them on a separate sheet of paper. Then read the story out loud and fill in the words for a laugh.

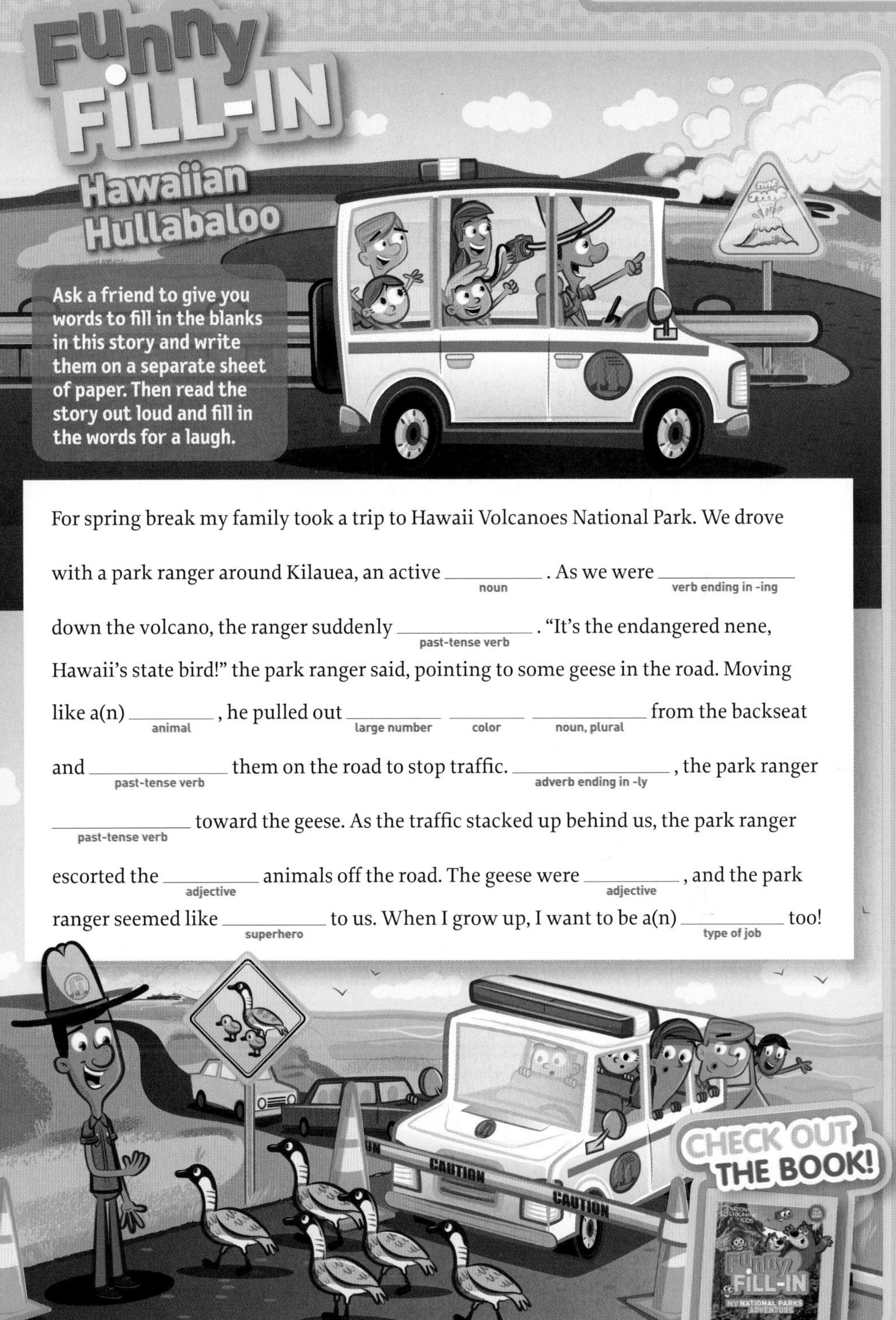

For spring break my family took a trip to Hawaii Volcanoes National Park. We drove with a park ranger around Kilauea, an active ________ (noun). As we were ________ (verb ending in -ing) down the volcano, the ranger suddenly ________ (past-tense verb). "It's the endangered nene, Hawaii's state bird!" the park ranger said, pointing to some geese in the road. Moving like a(n) ________ (animal), he pulled out ________ (large number) ________ (color) ________ (noun, plural) from the backseat and ________ (past-tense verb) them on the road to stop traffic. ________ (adverb ending in -ly), the park ranger ________ (past-tense verb) toward the geese. As the traffic stacked up behind us, the park ranger escorted the ________ (adjective) animals off the road. The geese were ________ (adjective), and the park ranger seemed like ________ (superhero) to us. When I grow up, I want to be a(n) ________ (type of job) too!

Spring Fever

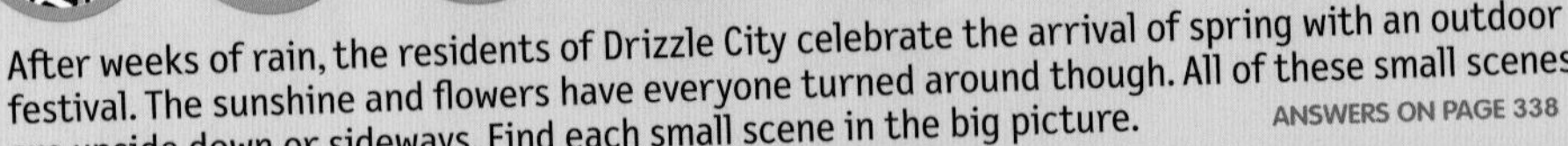

After weeks of rain, the residents of Drizzle City celebrate the arrival of spring with an outdoor festival. The sunshine and flowers have everyone turned around though. All of these small scenes are upside down or sideways. Find each small scene in the big picture.

ANSWERS ON PAGE 338

Penguin Party

The loudmouthed penguins at this party have a lot to say. Use the clues in the word balloons to match each penguin to its species name. Find and write down the correct letters on a separate sheet of paper. ANSWERS ON PAGE 338

1. Rockhopper
2. African
3. Chinstrap
4. Emperor
5. Erect-crested
6. Little
7. King
8. Macaroni
9. Magellanic
10. Yellow-eyed

ROUND UP **These photos show close-up views of round things. On a separate sheet of paper, unscramble the letters to identify what's in each picture.**
Bonus: Use the highlighted letters to solve the puzzle below. ANSWERS ON PAGE 338

WOBNALSL

______

BEGOL

______

KEBASTALLB

______

ERABML

______

RASUNT

______

NOGLBIW LABL

______

BEBRUR DBNA ALBL

______

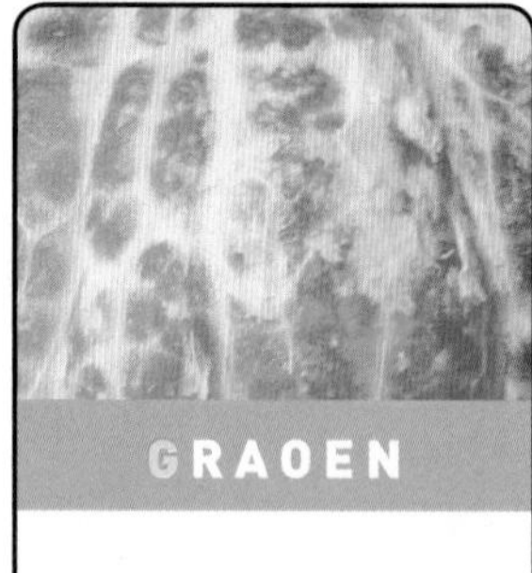

GRAOEN

______

CIDOS LBAL

______

HINT: What do you call a pig that plays basketball?

ANSWER: __ __ __ __ __ H __ __ __.

Just Joking

Pufferfish

Q What would you get if you crossed a dinosaur with a pig?

A Jurassic pork

TONGUE TWISTER!

Say this fast three times:

Felix finds fresh french fries finer.

CHECK OUT THIS BOOK!

KNOCK, KNOCK.

Who's there?

Gorilla.

Gorilla who?

Gorilla me a steak.

ANOTHER LAME JOKE

Two farms are next to each other. One is in Canada and one is in the United States. A rooster runs from the farm in Canada to the farm in the United States and lays an egg. So which country does the egg actually belong to? The answer is below.

ANSWER: Neither. Roosters don't lay eggs.

Fishy Business

Gil and his family are going on vacation. But first he has to run some errands. Use your finger to find the route that gets him from his home to the entrances of the places on his list in order. He can't swim along the same path twice and can't pass the park or the bank's door.

ANSWER ON PAGE 338

TO DO:
1. RETURN BOOK TO LIBRARY
2. BUY SWIMSUIT AT MALL
3. PICK UP SUNSCREEN AT CONVENIENCE STORE
4. GET HAIRCUT
5. CATCH SUB

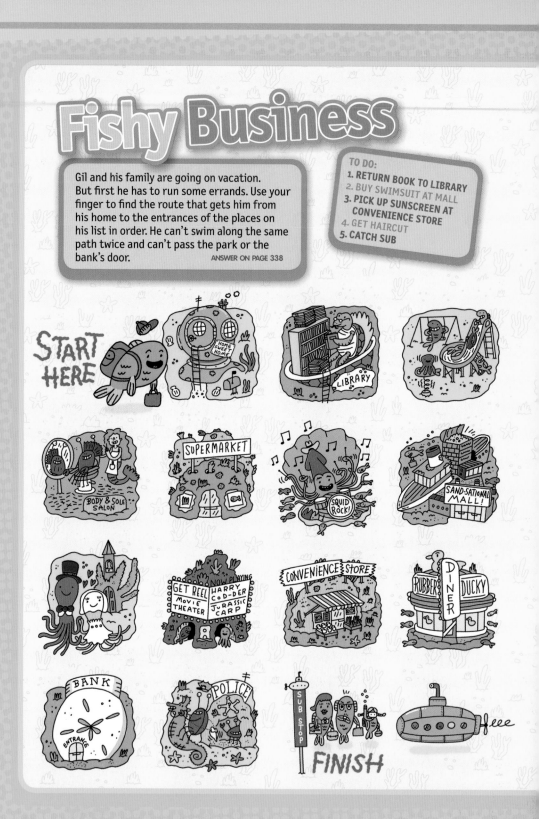

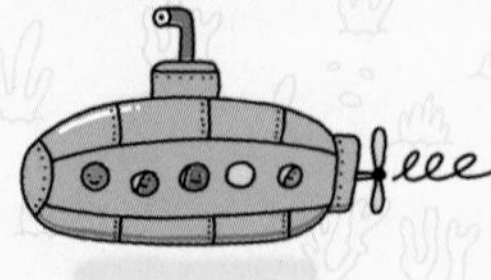

Laugh Out Loud

"HOW DO YOU KEEP YOUR SOCKS UP?"

"IT'S NOT *THAT* COLD OUTSIDE."

"NOT EVERYONE'S A DOG PERSON."

COME ON IN GUYS, IT'S NOT DEEP AT ALL!

Funny Fill-In

On Thin Ice

Ask a friend to give you words to fill in the blanks in this story and write them on a separate sheet of paper. Then read the story out loud and fill in the words for a laugh.

I tried ice-skating for the first time today, and I guess you could say I had beginner's luck. I picked out the ________ (adjective ending in -est) ________ (color) skates and laced them up in ________ (adjective) knots. ________ (adverb ending in -ly) I stepped onto the ice. I ________ (past-tense verb) off the wall and into the middle of the rink. So far, so good. Then, out of nowhere, a group of ________ (adjective) athletes ________ (past-tense verb) by me at about ________ (big number) miles an hour. Somehow I had skated into the middle of an ice ________ (sport) game! The next thing I knew, I was ________ (verb ending in -ing) all over the ice. As I attempted to ________ (verb) around the players, I saw a(n) ________ (type of sports equipment) coming straight toward me. Before I could move out of the way, it hit my ________ (body part) and ________ (past-tense verb) off my ________ (different body part). I tried to stay on my feet, but began ________ (verb ending in -ing) around and around. Instead of creating a figure eight, I was making a figure ________ (number). When I finally came to a stop, a loud buzzer sounded and the players yelled, "________ (exclamation)!" That's when I discovered I had accidentally scored a goal and won the game!

PLAY Funny Fill-In AND MORE! natgeokids.com/ffi

Redwood Roundup

These hikers are trekking around towering trees in Redwood National and State Parks in California, U.S.A. Join the fun by finding the 15 items listed to the right. ANSWERS ON PAGE 338

1. banana slug
2. skunk
3. binoculars
4. yellow raincoat
5. Roosevelt elk
6. porcupine
7. sunglasses
8. blue tent
9. park ranger
10. red backpack
11. trekking poles
12. toy airplane
13. lantern
14. frogs
15. map

CHECK OUT THE BOOK!

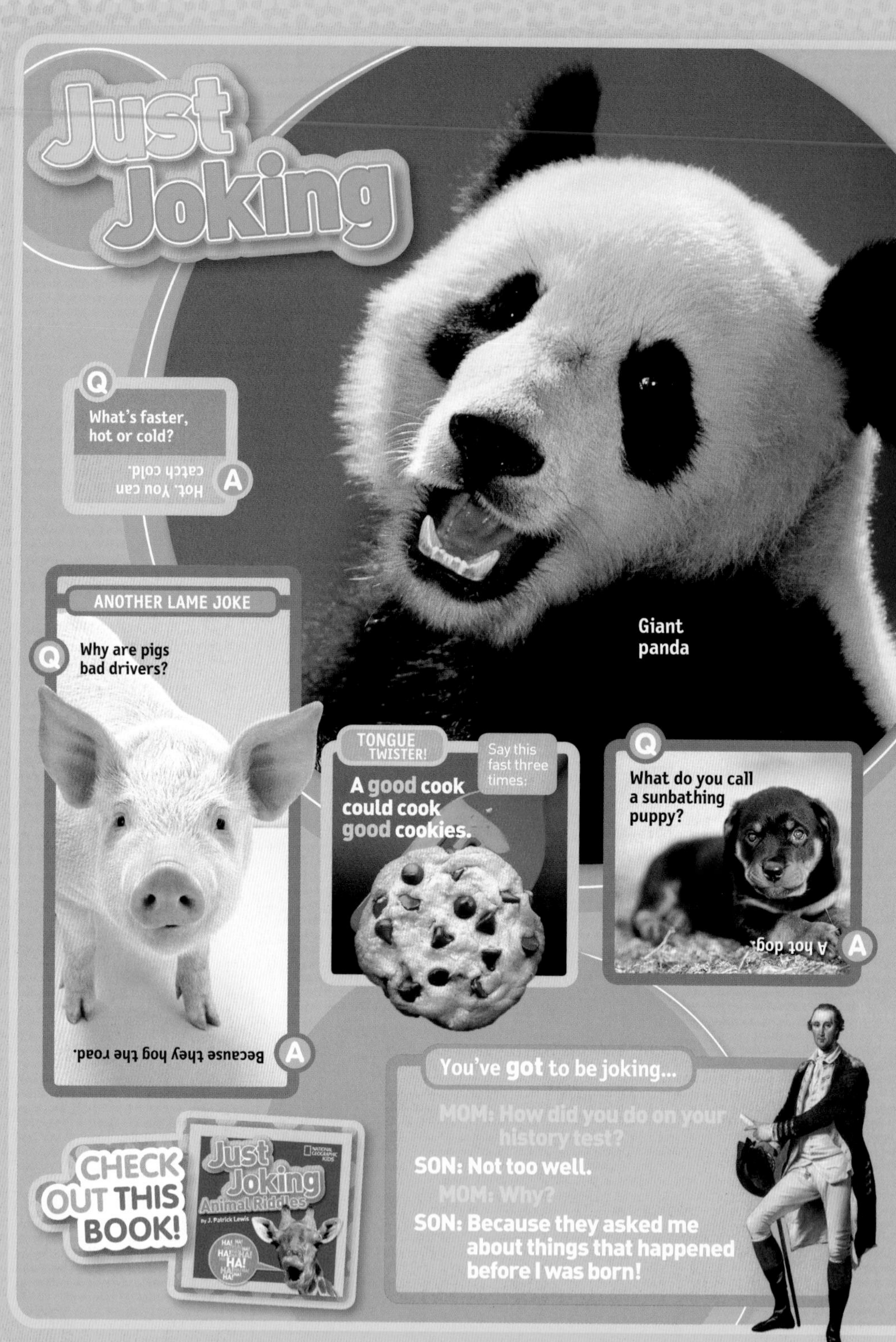

Just Joking
Q What's faster, hot or cold?
A Hot. You can catch cold.
Giant panda
ANOTHER LAME JOKE
Q Why are pigs bad drivers?
A Because they hog the road.
TONGUE TWISTER!
Say this fast three times:
A good cook could cook good cookies.
Q What do you call a sunbathing puppy?
A A hot dog.
You've got to be joking...
MOM: How did you do on your history test?
SON: Not too well.
MOM: Why?
SON: Because they asked me about things that happened before I was born!
CHECK OUT THIS BOOK!
Just Joking
Animal Riddles
By J. Patrick Lewis
NATIONAL GEOGRAPHIC KIDS

Go Fish!
Something's fishy at this aquarium. Find and write down on a separate sheet of paper the following items that are hidden in this scene.
surfboard
cowboy hat
sunflower
wrapped gift
bike wheel
teacup and saucer
plate of spaghetti
soft pretzel
guitar
ANSWERS ON PAGE 338

UnLeaShed
1
BEFORE HUMANS TRAVELED BEYOND EARTH, ANIMALS WERE SENT TO EXPLORE OUTER SPACE.
ANIMALS IN SPACE
IT'S TRUE. A DOG WAS THE FIRST ANIMAL TO ORBIT THE EARTH. WE MAKE THE BEST SPACE PETS!
IMPOSSIBLE, ATLAS! GUINEA PIGS HAVE ALWAYS BEEN THE BEST IN SPACE TRAVEL. THAT'S WHY WE WENT UP AFTER DOGS... TO GET IT RIGHT!
2
ACCORDING TO THIS SHOW THEY SENT SPIDERS AFTER GUINEA PIGS. SO I GUESS SPIDERS PERFECTED IT, NEVILLE.
I'LL PROVE THAT WE ARE THE BEST SPACE PETS.
I'LL LAUNCH MYSELF INTO SPACE!
3
LIFTOFF IN THREE...
WHOMP!
4
...TWO...
CREAK!
5
...ONE...
THIS IS NOT GOING TO BE PRETTY...
6
...ZERO...
7
LATER...
HMM... IF YOU CAN'T BRING THE PET TO THE MOON, BRING THE MOON TO THE PET!
8
THE NEXT MORNING...
HAVEN'T YOU GIVEN UP YET, NEVILLE?
NOT QUITE, PRINCESS TALLULAH.
IT'S JUST LULU.
I'VE FINALLY DEVISED THE PERFECT PLAN.

9
NEVILLE GOES TO THE NEIGHBOR'S YARD...
JUST DON'T COME BEHIND THIS WALL. THE TAKEOFF COULD BE TOO MUCH FOR YOU UNSCIENTIFIC PETS.
10
LIFTOFF!
11
WHOOOOOSH!
12
A BRAVER GUINEA PIG THERE NEVER WAS. DO YOU THINK WE'LL SEE HIM AGAIN?
SURE. HE'S LIVE STREAMING FROM SPACE.
13
REC
CAPTAIN'S LOG. STAR DATE... UM...TODAY.
WHILE I TAKE MY FIRST HISTORIC TRIP FOR GUINEA PIGS, I CAN'T HELP BUT FEEL THE VAST EMPTINESS OF THE UNIVERSE.
14
THIS TRULY IS THE LONELIEST TRIP.
15
IS THAT MAJOR? WHAT'S HE DOING IN SPACE?
IS IT JUST ME OR AM I SPINNING OUT OF CONTROL?
REC
HOUSTON, WE'VE GOT A PROBLEM.
16
SOMEONE, STOP THIS THING!
WE'VE GIVEN HER TOO MUCH POWER, CAPTAIN. SHE'S GONNA BLOW!
OH, I'LL PUT A STOP TO THIS.
17
WHOA!
LOOKS LIKE NEVILLE GOT THE LIFTOFF HE WANTED.
WHOOSH!
NEVILLE'S FINALLY AIRBORNE. FIND OUT WHAT HE, LULU, ATLAS, AND THE MAJOR ARE UP TO IN THE NEXT UNLEASHED!

Funny Fill-In

Beach Patrol

Ask a friend to give you words to fill in the blanks in this story and write them on a separate sheet of paper. Then read the story out loud and fill in the words for a laugh.

My friend ______ (friend's name) and I wanted to help save the environment, so we volunteered for a beach cleanup day. We stocked up on ______ (adjective) trash bags and ______ (adjective) gloves, and headed for the shores of the ______ (body of water). You wouldn't believe some of the junk we found. We picked up ______ (large number) aluminum ______ (noun, plural), ______ (adjective) plastic ______ (noun, plural), a soggy ______ (food) sandwich, a rusty ______ (type of transportation), and even a(n) ______ (slimy substance) -covered *National Geographic* magazine. Suddenly a(n) ______ (adjective) wave ______ (past-tense verb) onto the beach and washed up a treasure chest covered with ______ (beach item from nature, plural). My heart started ______ (verb ending in -ing) as we pried open the chest with a(n) ______ (noun). There were at least ______ (number) coins inside! My friend and I yelled, "We're rich!" and started ______ (verb ending in -ing) up and down like ______ (animal, plural). But when I scooped up some of the coins, they ______ (past-tense verb) all over my hands. The coins turned out to be ______ (type of candy, plural) wrapped in colored foil. But we had a great day anyway, because we helped protect the environment.

Just Joking
Q
Why did the boy's mother knit him three socks?
A
Because he grew another foot.
Mouse opossum
Q
What do you call terrified tyrannosaurs?
A
Nervous rex.
TONGUE TWISTER!
Say this fast three times:
Roscoe rescued Rosie from roaring rapids.
Q
Why do pilgrims' pants keep falling down?
A
Because their belt buckles are on their hats.
You've got to be joking...
Q
Where does a polar bear keep money?
A
In a snowbank.
CHECK OUT THIS BOOK!
Just Joking CATS
HA! HA! HA!

Space and Earth

Space agencies and private companies are working to establish colonies on Mars by the 2030s. This artist's rendition illustrates what a colony on the red planet might look like.

THE UNIVERSE BEGAN WITH A BIG BANG

Clear your mind for a minute and try to imagine this: All the things you see in the universe today—all the stars, galaxies, and planets—are not yet out there. Everything that now exists is concentrated in a single, incredibly hot, dense state that scientists call a singularity. Then, suddenly, the basic elements that make up the universe flash into existence. Scientists say that actually happened about 13.8 billion years ago, in the moment we call the big bang.

For centuries scientists, religious scholars, poets, and philosophers have wondered how the universe came to be. Was it always there? Will it always be the same, or will it change? If it had a beginning, will it someday end, or will it go on forever?

These are huge questions. But today, because of recent observations of space and what it's made of, we think we may have some of the answers. Everything we can see or detect around us in the universe began with the big bang. We know the big bang created not only matter but also space itself. And scientists think that in the very distant future, stars will run out of fuel and burn out. Once again the universe will become dark.

POWERFUL PARTICLE

It's just one tiny particle, but without it the world as we know it would not exist. That's what scientists are saying after the recent discovery of the Higgs boson particle, a subatomic speck related to the Higgs field, which is thought to give mass to everything around us. Without the Higgs boson, all the atoms created in the big bang would have zipped around the cosmos too quickly to collect into stars and planets. So you can think of it as a building block of the universe—and of us!

EARLY LIFE ON EARTH

About 3.5 billion years ago Earth was covered by one gigantic reddish ocean. The color came from hydrocarbons.

The first life-forms on Earth were Archaea that could live without oxygen. They released large amounts of methane gas into an atmosphere that would have been poisonous to us.

About 3 billion years ago erupting volcanoes linked together to form larger landmasses. And a new form of life appeared—cyanobacteria, the first living things that used energy from the sun.

Some 2 billion years ago the cyanobacteria algae filled the air with oxygen, killing off the methane-producing Archaea. Colored pools of greenish brown plant life floated on the oceans. The oxygen revolution that would someday make human life possible was now under way.

About 530 million years ago the Cambrian explosion occurred. It's called an explosion because it's the time when most major animal groups first appeared in our fossil records. Back then, Earth was made up of swamps, seas, a few active volcanoes, and oceans teeming with strange life.

More than 450 million years ago life began moving from the oceans onto dry land. About 200 million years later dinosaurs began to appear. They would dominate life on Earth for more than 150 million years.

PLANETS

MERCURY

Average distance from the sun: 35,980,000 miles (57,900,000 km)
Position from the sun in orbit: first
Equatorial diameter: 3,030 miles (4,878 km)
Length of day: 59 Earth days
Length of year: 88 Earth days
Surface temperatures: -300°F (-184°C) to 800°F (427°C)
Known moons: 0
Fun fact: The planet Mercury is made mostly of metals.

VENUS

Average distance from the sun: 67,230,000 miles (108,200,000 km)
Position from the sun in orbit: second
Equatorial diameter: 7,520 miles (12,100 km)
Length of day: 243 Earth days
Length of year: 224.7 Earth days
Average surface temperature: 864°F (462°C)
Known moons: 0
Fun fact: Venus is sometimes known as Earth's "twin sister" because the planets are similar in size and mass.

EARTH

Average distance from the sun: 93,000,000 miles (149,600,000 km)
Position from the sun in orbit: third
Equatorial diameter: 7,900 miles (12,750 km)
Length of day: 24 hours
Length of year: 365 days
Surface temperatures: -126°F (-88°C) to 136°F (58°C)
Known moons: 1
Fun fact: Our planet, Earth, is about 4.55 billion years old.

MARS

Average distance from the sun: 141,633,000 miles (227,936,000 km)
Position from the sun in orbit: fourth
Equatorial diameter: 4,221 miles (6,794 km)
Length of day: 25 Earth hours
Length of year: 1.9 Earth years
Surface temperatures: -270°F (-168°C) to 80°F (27°C)
Known moons: 2
Fun fact: There were once superhot and explosive volcanoes on Mars.

This artwork shows the eight planets and five dwarf planets in our solar system. The relative sizes and positions of the planets are shown but not the relative distances between them.

JUPITER

Average distance from the sun: 483,682,000 miles (778,412,000 km)
Position from the sun in orbit: sixth
Equatorial diameter: 88,840 miles (142,980 km)
Length of day: 9.9 Earth hours
Length of year: 11.9 Earth years
Average surface temperature: -235°F (-148°C)
Known moons: 67*
Fun fact: Jupiter's moon Europa has a deep, ice-covered ocean.

SATURN

Average distance from the sun: 890,800,000 miles (1,433,500,000 km)
Position from the sun in orbit: seventh
Equatorial diameter: 74,900 miles (120,540 km)
Length of day: 10.7 Earth hours
Length of year: 29.5 Earth years
Average surface temperature: -218°F (-139°C)
Known moons: 62*
Fun fact: Saturn's outermost ring is made up of fine dust particles and rocks the size of soccer balls.

*Includes provisional moons, which await confirmation and naming from the International Astronomical Union.

URANUS

Average distance from the sun: 1,784,000,000 miles (2,870,970,000 km)
Position from the sun in orbit: eighth
Equatorial diameter: 31,760 miles (51,120 km)
Length of day: 17.2 Earth hours
Length of year: 84 Earth years
Average surface temperature: -323°F (-197°C)
Known moons: 27
Fun fact: Uranus receives less than 0.3 percent of the sun's energy that Earth gets.

NEPTUNE

Average distance from the sun: 2,795,000,000 miles (4,498,250,000 km)
Position from the sun in orbit: ninth
Equatorial diameter: 30,775 miles (49,528 km)
Length of day: 16 Earth hours
Length of year: 164.8 Earth years
Average surface temperature: -353°F (-214°C)
Known moons: 14*
Fun fact: Neptune has storms with winds whipping around at 1,600 miles an hour (402 km/h).

For information about dwarf planets—Ceres, Pluto, Haumea, Makemake, and Eris—see p. 166.

DWARF PLANETS

Haumea

Eris

Pluto

Thanks to advanced technology, astronomers have been spotting many never-before-seen celestial bodies with their telescopes. One new discovery? A population of icy objects orbiting the sun beyond Pluto. The largest, like Pluto itself, are classified as dwarf planets. Smaller than the moon but still massive enough to pull themselves into a ball, dwarf planets nevertheless lack the gravitational "oomph" to clear their neighborhood of other sizable objects. So, while larger, more massive planets pretty much have their orbits to themselves, dwarf planets orbit the sun in swarms that include other dwarf planets as well as smaller chunks of rock or ice.

So far, astronomers have identified five dwarf planets: Ceres, Pluto, Haumea, Makemake, and Eris. There is also a newly discovered dwarf planet beyond Neptune that will need additional study before it is named. Astronomers are observing hundreds of newly found objects in the frigid outer solar system. As time and technology advance, the family of known dwarf planets will surely continue to grow.

CERES
Position from the sun in orbit: fifth
Length of day: 9.1 Earth hours
Length of year: 4.6 Earth years
Known moons: 0

PLUTO
Position from the sun in orbit: tenth
Length of day: 6.4 Earth days
Length of year: 248 Earth years
Known moons: 5

HAUMEA
Position from the sun in orbit: eleventh
Length of day: 3.9 Earth hours
Length of year: 282 Earth years
Known moons: 2

MAKEMAKE
Position from the sun in orbit: twelfth
Length of day: 22.5 Earth hours
Length of year: 305 Earth years
Known moons: 1*

ERIS
Position from the sun in orbit: thirteenth
Length of day: 25.9 Earth hours
Length of year: 561 Earth years
Known moons: 1

*Includes provisional moons, which await confirmation and naming from the International Astronomical Union.

DESTINATION SPACE

BLACK HOLE

This is your most dangerous mission yet. You've traveled to the galaxy M82 to get a close-up view of one of the strangest and deadliest things in the universe: a black hole. This one is called M82 X-1.

Most black holes are born when a giant star runs out of nuclear fuel and implodes, causing an explosion. After that, the black hole's gravity is so strong that it pulls in anything that gets too close. Nothing can escape a black hole's intense gravity—even light, the fastest thing in the universe.

You want to get a better look, so you put on a special space suit and exit your spacecraft. When you're 943 miles (1,518 km) away from the black hole, you notice something strange. Your legs are becoming longer and skinnier. Oh no! You're being "spaghettified." The black hole's gravity is stretching your body like a long noodle. You fire up your suit's rockets and zoom away from the black hole before it can tear you apart and swallow you up. You don't want to spend your life looking like spaghetti.

Scientists now think that almost every galaxy has a big black hole in its center. Our galaxy, the Milky Way, has a black hole called Sagittarius A*. (A* is scientist-code for "A-star.") At 26,000 light-years from Earth, it's much too far away to be dangerous to humans.

Destination
The black hole M82 X-1

Location
The galaxy M82

Distance
12 million light-years from Earth (a light-year is the distance light travels in one year)

Time to reach
325 billion years

Weather
Superheated gas clouds and bright x-rays

BLACK HOLE TIME TRAVEL

The intense gravity near a black hole makes time behave in strange ways. If an astronaut left his spacecraft to explore a black hole up close, he'd see the hands on his watch ticking at normal speed. But if anyone back on the spacecraft could observe the spacewalker's watch from far away, they'd see its hands slow down as the spacewalker got closer to the black hole. When the spacewalker returned to the spaceship after an hour, years would have passed for those aboard the spacecraft.

Someday humans may be able to use black holes to travel forward in time. An astronaut could take a short trip near a black hole and return to Earth after years, decades, or even centuries had passed there. A black hole time machine could allow a time traveler to find out what the world will be like in the future.

Sky Calendar 2018

Jupiter

Leonid meteor shower

Partial solar eclipse

January 2 Supermoon, Full Moon. The moon will be full and at its closest approach to Earth, likely appearing bigger and brighter than usual.

January 3–4 Quadrantids Meteor Shower Peak. Featuring up to 40 meteors an hour, it is the first meteor shower of every new year.

January 31 Total Lunar Eclipse. Visible throughout most of western North America, eastern Asia, Australia, and the Pacific.

March 15 Mercury at Greatest Eastern Elongation. Visible low in the western sky just after sunset, Mercury will be at its highest point on the horizon.

May 6–7 Eta Aquarids Meteor Shower Peak. View about 30 to 60 meteors an hour.

June 27 Saturn at Opposition. Your best chance to view Saturn in 2018. The planet will appear bright in the sky and be visible throughout the night.

July 13 Total Lunar Eclipse. Visible throughout most of Europe, western Australia, western and central Asia, and Africa.

July 27 Mars at Opposition. The best time to view the red planet. It makes its closest approach to Earth.

August 12–13 Perseid Meteor Shower Peak. One of the best! Up to 60 meteors an hour. Best viewing is in the direction of the constellation Perseus.

October 21–22 Orionid Meteor Shower Peak. View up to 20 meteors an hour. Look toward the constellation Orion for the best show.

November 17–18 Leonid Meteor Shower Peak. View up to 15 meteors an hour.

December 13–14 Geminid Meteor Shower Peak. A spectacular show! Up to 120 multicolored meteors an hour.

Various dates throughout 2018 View the International Space Station. Visit spotthestation.nasa.gov to find out when the ISS will be flying over your neighborhood.

Dates may vary slightly depending on your location. Check with a local planetarium for the best viewing time in your area.

6 stellar facts about stars

1 Our galaxy, known as the Milky Way, contains an estimated 200 to 400 billion stars.

2 The fastest spinning star ever discovered, VFTS 102, rotates at a million miles an hour (1.6 million km/h).

3 A "zombie star" is a surviving fragment of a star that exploded.

4 Scientists have created pieces of white dwarf stars in a lab.

5 Harry Potter characters Sirius Black and Bellatrix Lestrange were named after stars.

6 The star VY Canis Majoris is so large a plane would take more than a thousand years to orbit it.

18 ROCK-SOLID

1

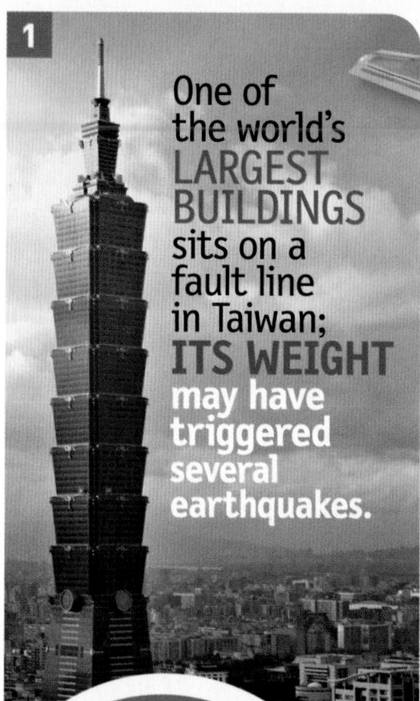

One of the world's LARGEST BUILDINGS sits on a fault line in Taiwan; **ITS WEIGHT may have triggered several earthquakes.**

2

EARTH MOVES AROUND THE SUN AT A SPEED THAT'S 100 TIMES FASTER THAN A JET.

3

THE IDEA that the Earth's crust was made up of moving continents was first published by German scientist Alfred Wegener in 1912.

4

IF EARTH WERE THE SIZE OF A GRAIN OF SAND, THE SUN WOULD BE **THE SIZE OF AN ORANGE.**

5

SOME ROCKS IN THE JACK HILLS OF WESTERN AUSTRALIA ARE 4.4 BILLION YEARS OLD.

6

At any single moment, there are about 20 volcanoes erupting worldwide—not counting the seafloor.

7

Boiling Lake on Dominica, a volcanic island in the Caribbean, is actually a flooded fumarole—an opening in Earth's crust where molten rock is close to the surface.

8

A GALLON OF VOLCANIC ASH IS TEN TIMES HEAVIER THAN A GALLON OF SNOW.

9

THERE IS A 100% CHANCE that there **will be an earthquake** somewhere on Earth **today!**

10

EARTH—WHICH GETS ITS NAME FROM THE MIDDLE ENGLISH WORLD *ERTHA* MEANING "GROUND"—IS THE ONLY PLANET IN OUR SOLAR SYSTEM NOT NAMED FOR A ROMAN GOD.

11

About one-fifth of Earth's land surface is desert, but only about 10 percent of deserts have sand dunes.

12

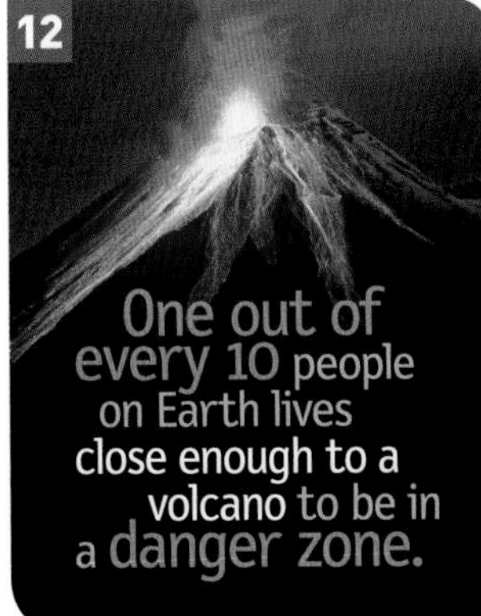

One out of every 10 people on Earth lives close enough to a volcano to be in a danger zone.

13

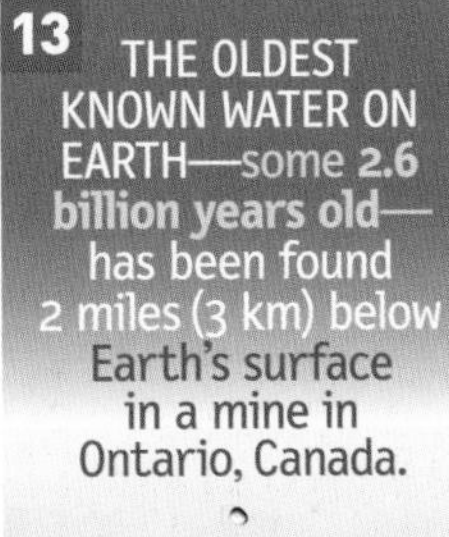

THE OLDEST KNOWN WATER ON EARTH—some **2.6 billion years old**—has been found 2 miles (3 km) below Earth's surface in a mine in Ontario, Canada.

14

THE LARGEST MUDFLOW EVER—98 FEET (30 M) THICK—BEGAN ATOP MOUNT RAINIER IN WASHINGTON STATE, U.S.A.

EARTH FACTS

15

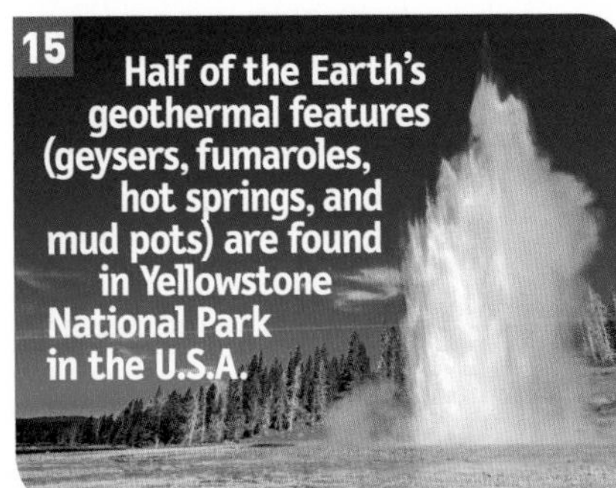

Half of the Earth's geothermal features (geysers, fumaroles, hot springs, and mud pots) are found in Yellowstone National Park in the U.S.A.

16

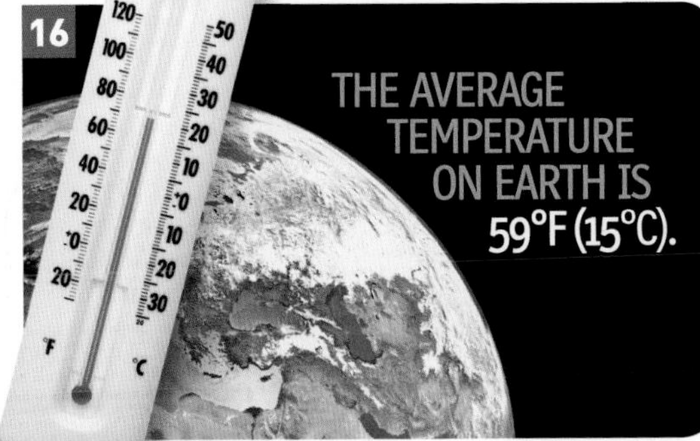

THE AVERAGE TEMPERATURE ON EARTH IS 59°F (15°C).

17

Almost 97% of Earth's water is salt water.

18

The area between the surface of the oceans and the seafloor makes up **99 percent of the living space on Earth.**

ROCK STARS

The world is full of rocks—some big, some small, some formed deep beneath the Earth, and some formed at the surface. While they may look similar, not all rocks are created equal. Look closely, and you'll see differences between every boulder, stone, and pebble. Here's more about the three top varieties of rocks.

Igneous

Named for the Greek word meaning "from fire," igneous rocks form when hot, molten liquid called magma cools. Pools of magma form deep underground and slowly work their way to the Earth's surface. If they make it all the way, the liquid rock erupts and is called lava. As the layers of lava build up they form a mountain called a volcano. Typical igneous rocks include obsidian, basalt, and pumice, which is so chock-full of gas bubbles that it actually floats in water.

OBSIDIAN

PUMICE

Metamorphic

Metamorphic rocks are the masters of change! These rocks were once igneous or sedimentary, but thanks to intense heat and pressure deep within the Earth, they have undergone a total transformation from their original form. These rocks never truly melt; instead, the heat twists and bends them until their shapes substantially change. Metamorphic rocks include slate as well as marble, which is used for buildings, monuments, and sculptures.

MARBLE

SLATE

Sedimentary

When wind, water, and ice constantly wear away and weather rocks, smaller pieces called sediment are left behind. These are sedimentary rocks, also known as gravel, sand, silt, and clay. As water flows downhill it carries the sedimentary grains into lakes and oceans, where they get deposited. As the loose sediment piles up, the grains eventually get compacted or cemented back together again. The result is new sedimentary rock. Sandstone, gypsum, limestone, and shale are sedimentary rocks that have formed this way.

SANDSTONE

GYPSUM

A LOOK INSIDE

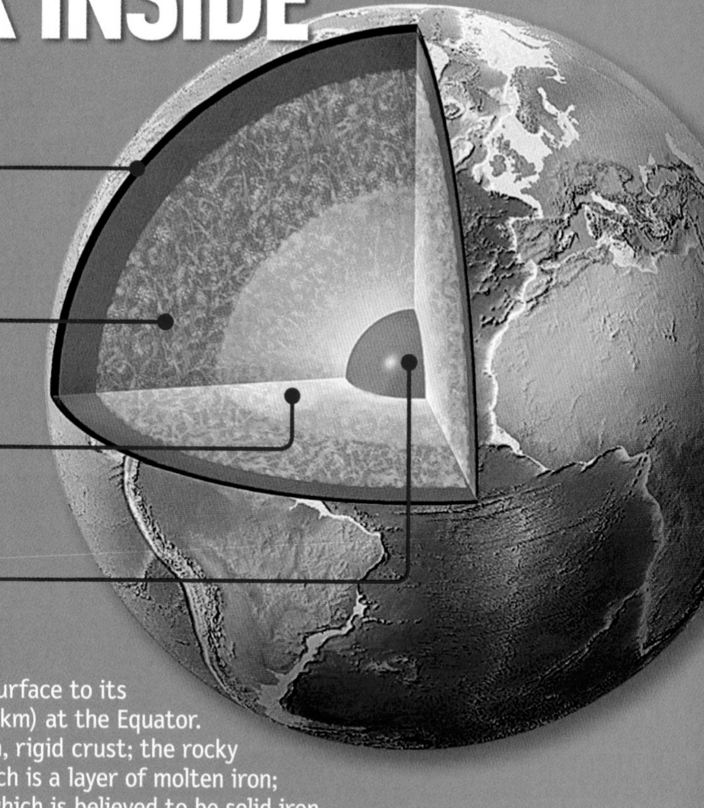

The **CRUST** includes tectonic plates, landmasses, and the ocean. Its thickness varies from 3 to 62 miles (5 to 100 km).

The **MANTLE** is about 1,800 miles (2,897 km) of hot, thick, solid rock.

The **OUTER CORE** is liquid molten lava made mostly of iron and nickel.

The **INNER CORE** is a solid center made mostly of iron and nickel.

The distance from Earth's surface to its center is 3,963 miles (6,378 km) at the Equator. There are four layers: a thin, rigid crust; the rocky mantle; the outer core, which is a layer of molten iron; and finally the inner core, which is believed to be solid iron.

What if you could dig to the other side of Earth?

Got a magma-proof suit and a magical drill that can cut through any surface? Then you're ready to dig some 8,000 miles (12,875 km) to Earth's other side. First you'd need to drill about 25 miles (40 km) through the planet's ultra-tough crust to its mantle. The heat and pressure at the mantle are intense enough to turn carbon into diamonds—and to, um, crush you. If you were able to survive, you'd still have to bore 1,800 more miles (2,897 km) to hit Earth's Mars-size core that can reach 11,000°F (6,093°C). Now just repeat the journey in the opposite order to resurface on the planet's other side. But exit your tunnel quickly. A hole dug through Earth would quickly close as surrounding rock filled in the empty space. The closing of the tunnel might cause small earthquakes, and your path home would definitely be blocked. Happy digging!

What is a Volcano?

IT'S SERIOUSLY HOT 4,000 MILES (6,437 KM) DOWN AT THE CENTER OF THE EARTH.

The temperature there ranges from 9,032°F to 12,632°F (5,000 to 7,000°C). That kind of heat melts rock into liquid, or molten, form. Sometimes molten rock gushes up and bursts through an opening in Earth's surface—a volcano—in a fiery flow of lava. Sometimes a volcano takes the shape of a mountain. Sometimes it even forms underwater.

MAGMA AND LAVA

Magma is molten rock before it reaches Earth's surface. Lava is molten rock after it reaches the surface. When lava erupts from a volcano, it can be liquid, semiliquid, or solid rock, depending on its temperature. The outer layer of rock can cool within minutes, but thick lava can take years to cool completely.

BUBBLING AND BOILING

Mud pots like these bubble and steam at the base of some volcanic mountains.

The Karymsky volcano in Russia is the most active volcano in its region. It's been actively erupting for more than 500 years. The volcano produces a fine, powdered rock called ash, which looks like black smoke.

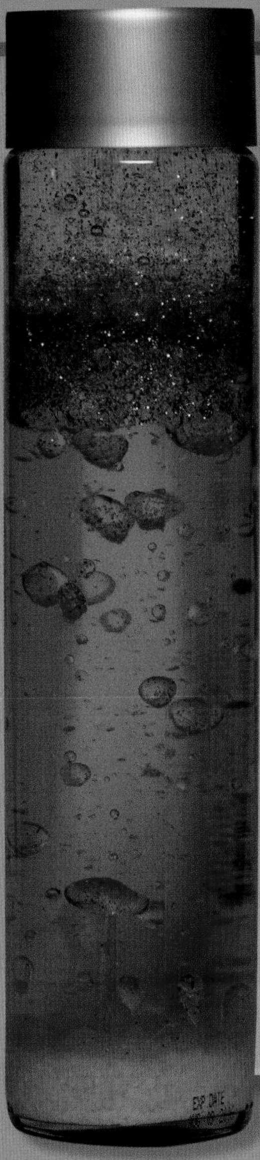

TRY THIS!

LAVA LAMP

To make a groovy lava lamp, first you'll need a tall jar.

1. Pour about 6 inches (15 cm) of water into the jar.
2. Add 2/3 cup of vegetable oil.
3. Wait until the oil rises to the top. Then add two drops of red food coloring to the oil.
4. To make your oily "lava" flow, shake some salt into the jar. Continue adding salt for as long as you want to make the bubbles sink and float in the water. Place the jar in front of a lamp for best results.

WHAT JUST HAPPENED?

Your lava lamp doesn't contain real lava—it just looks like it. Here's how it works. The oil floats on the water because it is less dense. The salt is denser, so it sinks to the bottom, pulling some oil along with it. As the salt dissolves, the oil floats back to the top. Now you have a cool lava flow that won't burn your hands!

Great Heights

Mauna Loa Volcano in Hawaii, U.S.A.

30,080 feet (9,170 m) is the height of Mauna Loa volcano, which makes up part of Hawaii. It begins below the ocean.

19,340 feet (5,895 m) is the height of Kilimanjaro, the tallest mountain in Africa—and also a volcano.

19 miles (30 km) is the height reached by the ash cloud over the volcano Hekla, in Iceland, in a 1947 eruption.

1,640 feet (500 m) is the height to which some lava fountains rose in the eruption of Askja, a volcano in Iceland.

HOT SPOT

FOUNTAINS OF SUPERHEATED WATER CREATE A WEIRD LANDMARK.

A bizarre blob of steaming fountains bursts with water and color from the barren landscape. It may look like a scene from another planet, but the surreal Fly Geyser unexpectedly gushes up from the Nevada, U.S.A., desert. The mounds stand 12 feet (3.7 m) tall, spouting scalding water 5 feet (1.5 m) higher. At first glance, Fly Geyser seems to be a natural wonder, but it's not quite natural. It's technically not a geyser either. It's an accident.

BIRTH OF FLY GEYSER Although Fly Geyser is powered by nature, it got a kick start from humans. The fountains spew water that continuously flows from a single underground hole, which was drilled by workers about 50 years ago. They had hoped to strike water that was so hot it could power an electrical plant with geothermal energy. The boiling water spurting from the Fly Geyser originates deep below the surface, where it is heated by shallow magma—hot, liquid rock. This wet zone is covered by a hard layer of rock, which traps the hot water. Because it can't escape as steam, the pressurized water's temperature rises far above the normal boiling point. The artificial, drilled hole gives the water a way out, like the opening of a soda bottle.

IT'S ALIVE! Even though the water spewing from Fly Geyser tops 200°F (93°C), the temperature turned out to be too low for a geothermal plant. The hole was plugged, but the hot water eventually forced its way up. Minerals that dissolved in the exiting water gradually built the mounds and surrounding terraces.

Fly Geyser's mounds and terraces aren't only alive with color—they're literally alive. The brilliant reds, yellows, and greens are caused by organisms called thermophiles, or "heat lovers." They are the only life-forms that can survive in such high, deadly temperatures. Different colors of thermophiles live in water at different temperatures, creating Fly Geyser's changing colors.

THEY'RE GONNA BLOW!

Natural geysers are more complicated than Fly Geyser. The world's most famous geyser, Wyoming's Old Faithful in Yellowstone National Park, doesn't spray continuously like Fly Geyser. Instead, it erupts about 16 times a day, shooting a steamy torrent of water more than 130 feet (40 m) into the air. What makes Old Faithful and other natural geysers different from Fly Geyser is their complex plumbing systems. The hot water's path to the surface becomes constricted, and the pressure builds. The heated water begins to bubble, and then explodes up and out. "It's like a volcano," explains U.S. Geological Survey researcher Shaul Hurwitz. "Once it starts erupting, all the stored water is released rapidly."

HOT PURSUIT Fly Geyser wasn't hot enough to support a geothermal plant, but it was a necessary step in a hit-or-miss process. Other heat-seeking holes in the area tapped into hotter water and were put to use. That water makes steam that cranks big machines to create electricity. Most power plants use steam, but geothermal ones don't burn coal or gas to make it, so they're much cleaner.

QUIZ WHIZ

Are your space and Earth smarts out of this world? Take this quiz!

Write your answers on a piece of paper. Then check them below.

1 **True or false?** Marble is a sedimentary rock.

2 **Earth moves around the sun at a speed that's 100 times faster than a ________.**

a. cheetah
b. speeding car
c. jet
d. merry-go-round

3 **True or false?** About 3.5 billion years ago Earth was covered by one gigantic reddish ocean.

4 **What do you call an opening in Earth's crust where molten rock is close to the surface?**

a. fumarole
b. hot spring
c. mud pot
d. sauna

5 **A _______ is a surviving fragment of a star that exploded.**

a. survivor star
b. dusty star
c. lonesome star
d. zombie star

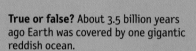

Not **STUMPED** yet? Check out the *NATIONAL GEOGRAPHIC KIDS QUIZ WHIZ* collection for more crazy **SPACE AND EARTH** questions!

ANSWERS:
1. False. It's a metamorphic rock.
2. c; 3. True; 4. a; 5. d

HOMEWORK HELP

ACE YOUR SCIENCE FAIR

You can learn a lot about science from books, but to really experience it firsthand, you need to get into the lab and "do" some science. Whether you're entering a science fair or just want to learn more on your own, there are many scientific projects you can do. So put on your goggles and lab coat, and start experimenting.

Most likely, the topic of the project will be up to you. So remember to choose something that is interesting to you.

THE BASIS OF ALL SCIENTIFIC INVESTIGATION AND DISCOVERY IS THE SCIENTIFIC METHOD. CONDUCT THE EXPERIMENT USING THESE STEPS:

Observation/Research—Ask a question or identify a problem.

Hypothesis—Once you've asked a question, do some thinking and come up with some possible answers.

Experimentation—How can you determine if your hypothesis is correct? You test it. You perform an experiment. Make sure the experiment you design will produce an answer to your question.

Analysis—Gather your results, and use a consistent process to carefully measure the results.

Conclusion—Do the results support your hypothesis?

Report Your Findings—Communicate your results in the form of a paper that summarizes your entire experiment.

Bonus!

Take your project one step further. Your school may have an annual science fair, but there are also local, state, regional, and national science fair competitions. Compete with other students for awards, prizes, and scholarships!

EXPERIMENT DESIGN

There are three types of experiments you can do.

MODEL KIT—a display, such as an "erupting volcano" model. Simple and to the point.

DEMONSTRATION—shows the scientific principles in action, such as a tornado in a wind tunnel.

INVESTIGATION—the home run of science projects, and just the type of project for science fairs. This kind demonstrates proper scientific experimentation and uses the scientific method to reveal answers to questions.

Culture Connection

A carved bird balances atop a First Nations totem pole at Brockton Point in Vancouver, British Columbia, Canada.

Food That FOOLS YOU

COOL TOPPING

Whipped cream has too much air to hold up for long. So this banana split is topped with whipped topping. Some stylists use sour cream or—*yum!*—shaving cream.

Does this banana split look good enough to eat? Hold on to your spoon, because things aren't exactly as they appear.

In the two hours it takes to do a photo shoot, ice cream melts, bananas turn brown, whipped cream sags, and the cherry slides right off. What to do? Call in the experts.

"Real food starts to look yucky after sitting out for a while," food stylist Linda Garrido says. Garrido's job is to make food look great for the camera. It could mean substituting something that *looks* like food for the real thing. Or it could mean "doctoring" the real food to make it look better longer.

Keep in mind, though: If it's a specific food being advertised, then that food has to be real. "A soup company once put marbles in the soup to prop up the vegetables," food photographer Taran Z says. "You can't do that." But if the food is not being advertised, then anything goes.

National Geographic Kids got the inside scoop on the tricks of the trade. So go ahead and dig into this banana split—just beware of the vegetable shortening and lemon juice!

JAM SESSION

Food stylists create strawberry ice cream by stirring strawberry jam into the vanilla ice-cream mixture.

SOUR SOLUTION

No one wants a bruised-looking banana. So this banana is painted with lemon juice to keep the fruit from turning brown.

STICK 'EM UP

It's tough being at the top. That's why this cherry is held in place by a toothpick to keep it from sliding off. If the cherry's not perfect, red lipstick can be used for touch-ups.

NUTCASE

Each hand-selected nut is carefully placed with tweezers. Sometimes nuts are touched up with a brown eyebrow pencil.

"ICING" CREAM

What appears to be chocolaty frozen goodness is really store-bought chocolate cake icing that was thickened with powdered sugar.

PLAIN VANILLA

Nothing's worse than mushy ice cream. This vanilla is a mixture of vegetable shortening, corn syrup, and powdered sugar. It'll look real for days.

FLYING SAUCES

Real chocolate, caramel, and strawberry sauces slide to the bottom of the bowl. But *these* sauces are thickened with corn syrup. That makes them less drippy so they stay put.

CHEW ON THIS

MANGO LASSI

India's version of the smoothie can be mixed with fruit or spices, but it's almost always blended with yogurt. It's a favorite refreshment in the summertime, when India's temperatures can hit triple digits. Sip up these facts about the mango lassi.

Some people chew **CARDAMOM** pods to fight bad breath.

A **MANGO** tree can grow up to a hundred feet (30 m) tall.

In the 11th century, German peasants paid for goods with **HONEY.**

LIME juice has been used to clean the walls of the Taj Mahal, India's most famous landmark.

YOGURT was once thought to bring a long life and good looks to those who ate it.

CHECK OUT THE BOOK!

NATIONAL GEOGRAPHIC KIDS COOKBOOK

COOL THINGS ABOUT INDIA

- Many buildings in the village of Shani Shingnapur have no doors.
- India has more post offices than any other country.
- The game of chess was likely invented in India.
- Cows—considered sacred by many in India—are often seen roaming city streets.
- The country's national bird is the peacock.

7 bite-size facts to chew on

1 A pizza topped with 24-karat gold sold for more than $4,000.

2 A head of broccoli is made up of hundreds of small flower buds.

3 Applesauce was the first food eaten in space by an American astronaut.

4 Strawberries contain more VITAMIN C than oranges.

5 The holes in Swiss cheese are called eyes.

6 Chewing gum burns about 11 calories an hour.

7 The largest corned beef sandwich on record weighed 5,440 pounds. (2,468 kg)

CELEBRATIONS

1 CHINESE NEW YEAR

February 16

Also called Lunar New Year, this holiday marks the new year according to the lunar calendar. Families celebrate with parades, feasts, and fireworks. Young people may receive gifts of money in red envelopes.

2 HOLI

March 2

This festival in India celebrates spring and marks the triumph of good over evil. People cover one another with powdered paint, called *gulal*, and douse one another with buckets of colored water.

3 DAY OF THE SEA

March 23

Bolivia may be a landlocked country, but it boasts a Navy, which it honors every March. On this day, also known as *Día del Mar*, people march through the streets carrying model ships and pictures of the ocean.

4 EASTER

April 1

A Christian holiday that honors the resurrection of Jesus Christ, Easter is celebrated by giving baskets filled with gifts, decorated eggs, or candy to children.

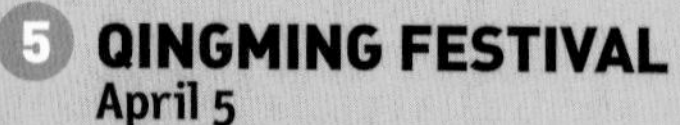

5 QINGMING FESTIVAL

April 5

Also known as "Grave Sweeping Day," this Chinese celebration calls on people to return to the graves of their deceased loved ones. There, they tidy up the grave, as well as light firecrackers, burn fake money, and leave food as an offer to the spirits.

6 KONINGSDAG

April 27

Orange you glad it's King's Day? People across the Netherlands celebrate the monarchy with street parties and by wearing all things orange.

7 RAMADAN AND EID AL-FITR

May 15*–June 15**

A Muslim holiday, Ramadan is a month long, ending in the Eid Al-Fitr celebration. Observers fast during this month—eating only after sunset. People pray for forgiveness and hope to purify themselves through observance.

8 CHEUNG CHAU BUN FESTIVAL

May 22

Revelers march in parades, eat vegetarian food, and climb towers covered in sweet steamed buns throughout this three-day festival marking the end of a plague that devastated Hong Kong 100 years ago.

9 TANABATA

July 7

To commemorate this Star Festival, people in Japan first write wishes on colorful strips of paper. Then, they hang the paper on bamboo branches in their yards and around their homes in the hopes that their wishes will come true.

10 BASTILLE DAY

July 14

The French call this day *La Fête Nationale*, as it is the celebration of the start of the French Revolution in 1789. In Paris, fireworks light up the night skies while dance parties spill into the streets.

*Begins at sundown.

**Dates may vary slightly by location.

Around the World

11 VERSLUNARMANNAHELGI

August 4–6

During Verslunarmannahelgi—also known as Iceland's Labor Day—people head to the great outdoors for camping trips, cookouts, and massive music festivals.

12 NAG PANCHAMI

August 15

In Nepal and India, Hindus worship snakes—and keep evil spirits out of their homes—by sticking images of serpents on their doors and making offerings to the revered reptiles.

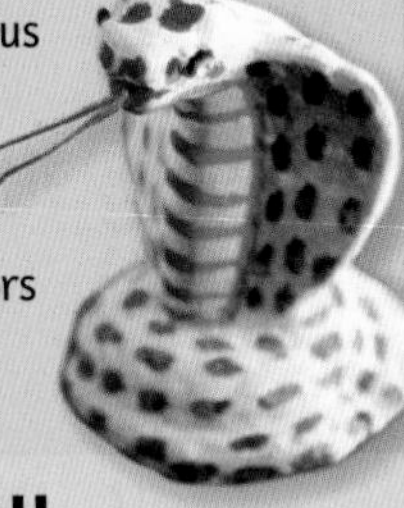

13 ROSH HASHANAH

September 9*–11

A Jewish holiday marking the beginning of a new year on the Hebrew calendar. Celebrations include prayer, ritual foods, and a day of rest.

14 HANUKKAH

December 2*–10

This Jewish holiday is eight days long. It commemorates the rededication of the Temple in Jerusalem. Hanukkah celebrations include the lighting of menorah candles for eight days and the exchange of gifts.

15 CHRISTMAS DAY

December 25

A Christian holiday marking the birth of Jesus Christ, Christmas is usually celebrated by decorating trees, exchanging presents, and having festive gatherings.

2018 CALENDAR

JANUARY

S	M	T	W	T	F	S
	1	2	3	4	5	6
7	8	9	10	11	12	13
14	15	16	17	18	19	20
21	22	23	24	25	26	27
28	29	30	31			

FEBRUARY

S	M	T	W	T	F	S
				1	2	3
4	5	6	7	8	9	10
11	12	13	14	15	16	17
18	19	20	21	22	23	24
25	26	27	28			

MARCH

S	M	T	W	T	F	S
				1	2	3
4	5	6	7	8	9	10
11	12	13	14	15	16	17
18	19	20	21	22	23	24
25	26	27	28	29	30	31

APRIL

S	M	T	W	T	F	S
1	2	3	4	5	6	7
8	9	10	11	12	13	14
15	16	17	18	19	20	21
22	23	24	25	26	27	28
29	30					

MAY

S	M	T	W	T	F	S
		1	2	3	4	5
6	7	8	9	10	11	12
13	14	15	16	17	18	19
20	21	22	23	24	25	26
27	28	29	30	31		

JUNE

S	M	T	W	T	F	S
					1	2
3	4	5	6	7	8	9
10	11	12	13	14	15	16
17	18	19	20	21	22	23
24	25	26	27	28	29	30

JULY

S	M	T	W	T	F	S
1	2	3	4	5	6	7
8	9	10	11	12	13	14
15	16	17	18	19	20	21
22	23	24	25	26	27	28
29	30	31				

AUGUST

S	M	T	W	T	F	S
			1	2	3	4
5	6	7	8	9	10	11
12	13	14	15	16	17	18
19	20	21	22	23	24	25
26	27	28	29	30	31	

SEPTEMBER

S	M	T	W	T	F	S
						1
2	3	4	5	6	7	8
9	10	11	12	13	14	15
16	17	18	19	20	21	22
23	24	25	26	27	28	29
30						

OCTOBER

S	M	T	W	T	F	S
	1	2	3	4	5	6
7	8	9	10	11	12	13
14	15	16	17	18	19	20
21	22	23	24	25	26	27
28	29	30	31			

NOVEMBER

S	M	T	W	T	F	S
				1	2	3
4	5	6	7	8	9	10
11	12	13	14	15	16	17
18	19	20	21	22	23	24
25	26	27	28	29	30	

DECEMBER

S	M	T	W	T	F	S
						1
2	3	4	5	6	7	8
9	10	11	12	13	14	15
16	17	18	19	20	21	22
23	24	25	26	27	28	29
30	31					

What's Your Chinese Horoscope?

Locate your birth year to find out.

In Chinese astrology the zodiac runs on a 12-year cycle, based on the lunar calendar. Each year corresponds to one of 12 animals, each representing one of 12 personality types. Read on to find out which animal year you were born in and what that might say about you.

RAT

1972, '84, '96, 2008

Say cheese! You're attractive, charming, and creative. When you get mad, you can have really sharp teeth!

HORSE

1966, '78, '90, 2002, '14

Being happy is your "mane" goal. And while you're smart and hardworking, your teacher may ride you for talking too much.

OX

1973, '85, '97, 2009

You're smart, patient, and as strong as an . . . well, you know what. Though you're a leader, you never brag.

SHEEP

1967, '79, '91, 2003, '15

Gentle as a lamb, you're also artistic, compassionate, and wise. You're often shy.

TIGER

1974, '86, '98, 2010

You may be a nice person, but no one should ever enter your room without asking—you might attack!

MONKEY

1968, '80, '92, 2004, '16

No "monkey see, monkey do" for you. You're a clever problem-solver with an excellent memory.

RABBIT

1975, '87, '99, 2011

Your ambition and talent make you jump at opportunity. You also keep your ears open for gossip.

ROOSTER

1969, '81, '93, 2005, '17

You crow about your adventures, but inside you're really shy. You're thoughtful, capable, brave, and talented.

DRAGON

1976, '88, 2000, '12

You're on fire! Health, energy, honesty, and bravery make you a living legend.

DOG

1970, '82, '94, 2006, '18

Often the leader of the pack, you're loyal and honest. You can also keep a secret.

SNAKE

1977, '89, 2001, '13

You may not speak often, but you're very smart. You always seem to have a stash of cash.

PIG

1971, '83, '95, 2007, '19

Even though you're courageous, honest, and kind, you never hog all the attention.

3 Fun Kits for Mom & Dad

On Mother's Day or Father's Day, give the gift of family time together. Make these cool kits as presents and have tons of family fun!

1 Herb Garden

YOU WILL NEED: SMALL HERB PLANTS SUCH AS THYME, BASIL, AND ROSEMARY • SANDWICH BAG FULL OF SMALL STONES • POTTING SOIL • TROWEL OR LARGE SPOON • HOMEMADE LABELS FOR HERBS (WE MADE THEM BY GLUING CRAFT FOAM ONTO WOODEN SKEWERS) • GARDENING GLOVES • LARGE FLOWERPOT TO DISPLAY ALL THE ITEMS

HOW TO GROW YOUR HERB GARDEN: Cover the bottom of the flowerpot with stones for drainage. Fill the pot partway with soil. Carefully remove the plants from their containers and position them in the larger pot, leaving some space between each plant. Fill in soil around the plants. Water until the soil is damp, then place the flowerpot in a sunny spot. Water the herbs when the soil dries out—about once a week. Then watch your garden grow.

2 Car Wash

YOU WILL NEED: PAPER TOWELS • SPONGE • OLD TOWELS TO USE AS RAGS • INGREDIENTS FOR HOMEMADE CAR SHAMPOO (DISHWASHING LIQUID, POWDERED LAUNDRY DETERGENT—BELOW) • SPRAY BOTTLE OF WINDOW CLEANER • HOMEMADE CAR AIR FRESHENER—BELOW • NICE BUCKET TO DISPLAY ALL THE ITEMS

HOW TO MAKE CAR SHAMPOO: In a bucket, mix one-third cup (80 mL) of dishwashing liquid, one-quarter cup (50 g) of powdered laundry detergent, and one gallon (3.8 L) of water.

HOW TO MAKE AN AIR FRESHENER Trace the shape of a cookie cutter onto craft foam, then cut out the shape. With an adult's permission, spray the foam with perfume or cologne several times. Let dry. Punch a hole at the top and tie a string through the hole. Then hang the air freshener from the car's rearview mirror.

3 Movie Night

Fill a basket with DVDs, bags of microwave popcorn, candy, and a blanket for curling up on the couch. Include homemade movie tickets for each member of your family.

HOWL-OWEEN PET PARTY

SOME BUNNY HAS A GREAT COSTUME.

You expect to see ghosts, vampires, and pirates on Halloween. What you *don't* expect is for those creatures to have four legs. Millions of pets will be dressed up for the holiday—here are some of the funniest getups.

BAT-WHO? JOEY THE DWARF SIAMESE RABBIT STEALS ATTENTION AS SUPERHERO SIDEKICK ROBIN.

WHAT DOES A PIRATE DOG DO? IT B-AAARGH-KS.

These pets like wearing costumes but yours may not. Never force your pet to do something it doesn't want to do.

PINK IS SO MY COLOR.

YEEHAW! BETTY THE ENGLISH BULLDOG IS A COLORFUL COWGIRL.

DUQUE THE COCKER SPANIEL IS SWASHBUCKLING IN HIS PIRATE GETUP.

I WOULDN'T SAY NO TO A COMB.

FEROCIOUS LION? MAYBE NOT. BUT CHILI THE BOSTON TERRIER IS STILL HAVING A GOOD HAIR DAY.

WHAT? NO KETCHUP?

BOSTON THE LONG-HAIRED DACHSHUND HAS WISELY HELD THE ONIONS FROM HIS COSTUME.

TREAT YOUR PET

Instead of candy, which will hurt your pet's tummy, give your furry friend its own Halloween snack. Check out pet stores for ideas, or grab a parent and try one of the recipes below from the American Society for the Prevention of Cruelty to Animals.

CREEPY CAT COOKIES

- ¼ cup (60 ml) of warm water
- 5 tablespoons (75 ml) of grated Parmesan cheese
- 3 tablespoons (45 ml) of margarine
- 1 tablespoon (15 ml) of cod liver oil
- 1 cup (240 ml) of white flour
- ¼ cup (80 ml) of soy flour

Preheat the oven to 300°F (150°C). Combine the water, cheese, margarine, and oil, then add the flour. Roll the dough ¼ inch (6 mm) thick and cut it with spooky-shaped cookie cutters. Bake the cookies on an ungreased cookie sheet for 20 to 25 minutes.

PUMPKIN POOCH BITES

- 2½ cups (600 ml) of whole wheat flour
- ½ cup (120 ml) of fresh or canned pumpkin
- ½ cup (120 ml) of peanut butter
- 2 teaspoons (10 ml) of cinnamon
- 1 teaspoon (5 ml) of baking powder
- ½ cup (120 ml) of water

Preheat the oven to 350°F (180°C). In a bowl, whisk together the flour, pumpkin, peanut butter, cinnamon, and baking powder. Add water as needed, but the dough should be stiff and dry. Roll the dough until it's ½ inch (1 ¼ cm) thick and cut it with cookie cutters. Bake the treats for about 40 minutes.

If you dress up your pet, check that the outfit is comfortable and allows the animal to breathe and walk safely.

These recipes should not replace your pet's regular meals. Check with your veterinarian if your pet has special dietary needs or food allergies.

Jordan's HALF-DINAR COIN has seven sides.

A $3 BILL is used in the Bahamas.

A British businessman created his own currency—named the PUFFIN—for an island he owned off of England.

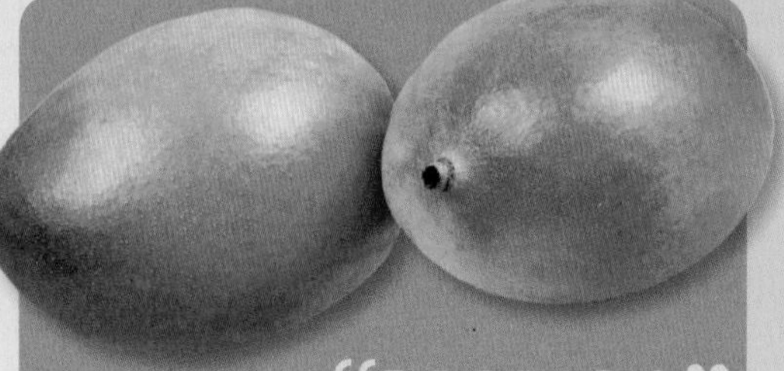

IN ARGENTINA, "MANGO" IS SLANG FOR "PESO."

THE NEW U.S. $20 FEATURES former slave and abolitionist HARRIET TUBMAN. She will be the first woman to APPEAR on a MODERN U.S. BANKNOTE.

The INCA called gold "THE SWEAT OF THE SUN" and silver "THE TEARS OF THE MOON."

A PORCUPINE APPEARED ON A COLLECTIBLE **50-TENGE COIN** FROM KAZAKHSTAN.

I KNEW I SHOULD'VE TRIED A FAKE ATM INSTEAD.

IN 2002, A MAN OPENED A FAKE BANK AND TOOK IN **$650,000** BEFORE HE WAS CAUGHT.

In Spain, "PASTA" is a slang term for "money."

A 1913 U.S. LIBERTY HEAD NICKEL—ONE OF ONLY FIVE IN EXISTENCE—**SOLD AT** AUCTION FOR MORE THAN $3.1 MILLION.

THE PHRASE **"BRING HOME THE BACON"** STARTED AFTER A 12TH-CENTURY PRIEST REWARDED A MARRIED COUPLE **WITH A SIDE OF BACON.**

BRICKS OF COMPRESSED TEA LEAVES WERE ONCE USED AS CURRENCY IN SIBERIA, MONGOLIA, AND CHINA.

MONEY TIP!

ANY TIME YOU BUY SOMETHING **ON SALE,** PUT WHAT YOU SAVED IN YOUR PIGGY BANK.

12 Ways to Say Friend

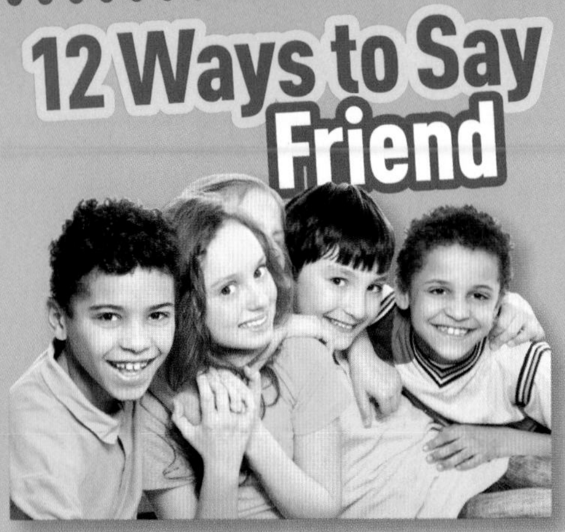

1. AFRIKAANS: **vriend** (male) / **vriendin** (female)
2. CANTONESE: **pung yau**
3. GERMAN: **Freund** (male) / **Freundin** (female)
4. HAWAIIAN: **hoaloha**
5. HINDI: **dost**
6. ICELANDIC: **vinur** (male) / **vinkona** (female)
7. MALAY: **kawan**
8. SPANISH: **amigo** (male) / **amiga** (female)
9. SWAHILI: **rafiki**
10. TAGALOG (Filipino): **kaibigan**
11. AKUAPIM TWI (Ghana): **adamfo**
12. WELSH: **ffrind**

LANGUAGES IN PERIL

TODAY, there are more than 7,000 languages spoken on Earth. But by 2100, more than half of those may disappear. In fact, experts say one language dies every two weeks, due to the increasing dominance of larger languages, such as English, Spanish, and Mandarin. So what can be done to keep dialects from disappearing? Efforts like National Geographic's Enduring Voices Project are now tracking down and documenting the world's most threatened indigenous languages, such as Tofa, spoken only by people in Siberia, and Magati Ke, from Aboriginal Australia. The hope is to preserve these languages—and the cultures they belong to.

10 LEADING LANGUAGES

Approximate population of first-language speakers (in millions)

1. Chinese*	1,197
2. Spanish	414
3. English	335
4. Hindi	260
5. Arabic	237
6. Portuguese	203
7. Bengali	193
8. Russian	167
9. Japanese	122
10. Javanese	83

Some languages have only a few hundred speakers, while Chinese has nearly one billion two hundred million native speakers worldwide. That's about triple the next largest group of language speakers. Colonial expansion, trade, and migration account for the spread of the other most widely spoken languages. With growing use of the Internet, English is becoming the language of the technology age.

*Includes all forms of the language.

By the Numbers
HIT THE BOOKS

Got a minute?

If you spend a little time reading each day, by the time you reach high school you'll be a reading wizard. Check out how many times you can read *Harry Potter and the Sorcerer's Stone* if you read a little—or a lot—every day.

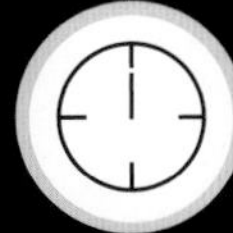

IF YOU READ **1 HOUR** EVERY DAY

EVERY YEAR, A SIXTH GRADER WILL HAVE READ: 3,285,000 words

THAT'S THE SAME AS READING *HARRY POTTER AND THE SORCERER'S STONE:* 42 times

FROM KINDERGARTEN THROUGH HIGH SCHOOL GRADUATION, YOU'LL HAVE READ FOR NEARLY: 198 days

IF YOU READ **20 MINUTES** EVERY DAY

EVERY YEAR, A SIXTH GRADER WILL HAVE READ: 1,095,000 words

THAT'S THE SAME AS READING *HARRY POTTER AND THE SORCERER'S STONE:* 14 times

FROM KINDERGARTEN THROUGH HIGH SCHOOL GRADUATION, YOU'LL HAVE READ FOR NEARLY: 66 days

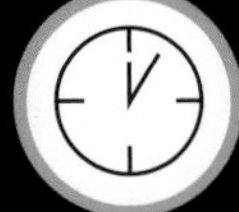

IF YOU READ **5 MINUTES** EVERY DAY

EVERY YEAR, A SIXTH GRADER WILL HAVE READ: 273,750 words

THAT'S THE SAME AS READING *HARRY POTTER AND THE SORCERER'S STONE:* 3.5 times

FROM KINDERGARTEN THROUGH HIGH SCHOOL GRADUATION, YOU'LL HAVE READ FOR NEARLY: 14 days

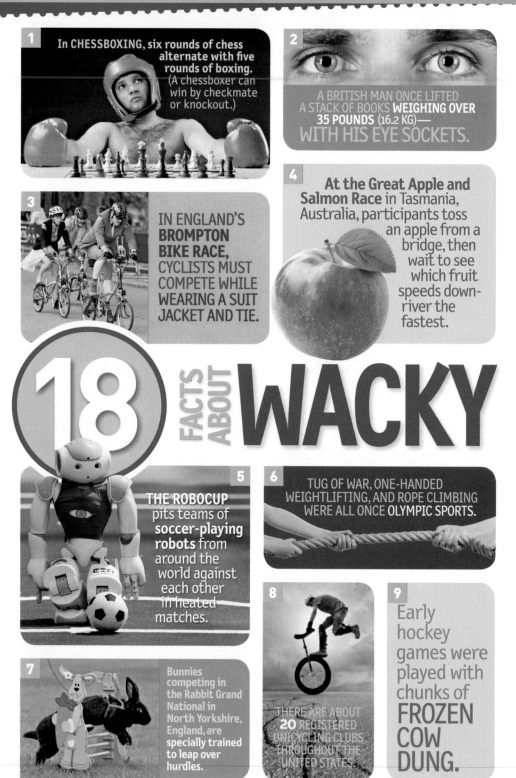

18 FACTS ABOUT WACKY

1

In CHESSBOXING, six rounds of chess alternate with five rounds of boxing. (A chessboxer can win by checkmate or knockout.)

2

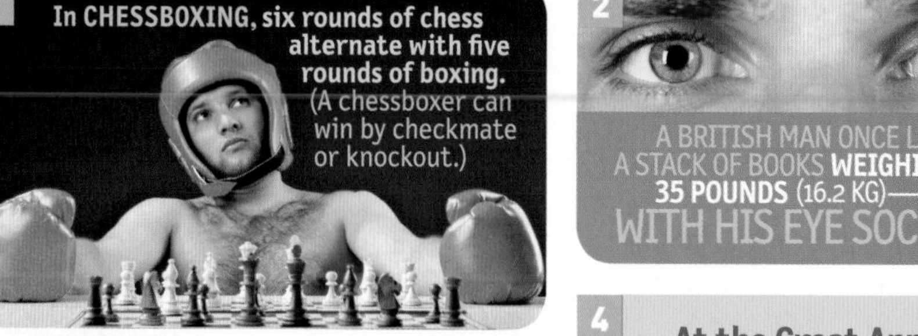

A BRITISH MAN ONCE LIFTED A STACK OF BOOKS **WEIGHING OVER 35 POUNDS** (16.2 KG)— WITH HIS EYE SOCKETS.

3

IN ENGLAND'S **BROMPTON BIKE RACE,** CYCLISTS MUST COMPETE WHILE WEARING A SUIT JACKET AND TIE.

4

At the Great Apple and Salmon Race in Tasmania, Australia, participants toss an apple from a bridge, then wait to see which fruit speeds down-river the fastest.

5

THE ROBOCUP pits teams of **soccer-playing robots** from around the world against each other in heated matches.

6

TUG OF WAR, ONE-HANDED WEIGHTLIFTING, AND ROPE CLIMBING WERE ALL ONCE **OLYMPIC SPORTS.**

7

Bunnies competing in the Rabbit Grand National in North Yorkshire, England, are specially trained to leap over hurdles.

8

THERE ARE ABOUT **20** REGISTERED UNICYCLING CLUBS THROUGHOUT THE UNITED STATES.

9

Early hockey games were played with chunks of **FROZEN COW DUNG.**

10

TWO BRITISH MEN ONCE PASSED A GIANT INFLATABLE VOLLEYBALL BACK AND FORTH 583 TIMES WITHOUT LETTING IT TOUCH THE GROUND.

11

Cattle go head to head while speeding down muddy rice fields during Indonesia's cow races, also known as Pacu Jawi.

12

Watching **RHINOCEROS BEETLES** wrestle is a popular sport in Laos.

13

THE FIRST ICE SKATES WERE MADE BY ATTACHING ANIMAL BONES TO THE FEET WITH LEATHER STRAPS.

14

A 61-year-old potato farmer from Australia once won a 543.7-mile (875-km) ultra-marathon after doing most of his **training in rain boots.**

SPORTS FROM AROUND THE WORLD

15

In **snow polo,** teams on horseback aim to whack the ball into the goal while PLAYING ON A FROZEN FIELD.

16

KITE FLYING IS A COMPETITIVE SPORT IN THAILAND.

17

In giant pumpkin kayaking competitions, paddlers race around the water in huge, hollowed-out gourds.

18

Three American brothers set the world record for the HIGHEST TRAMPOLINE BOUNCE by a team—sending one of them **soaring 22 feet** (6.7 m) in the air.

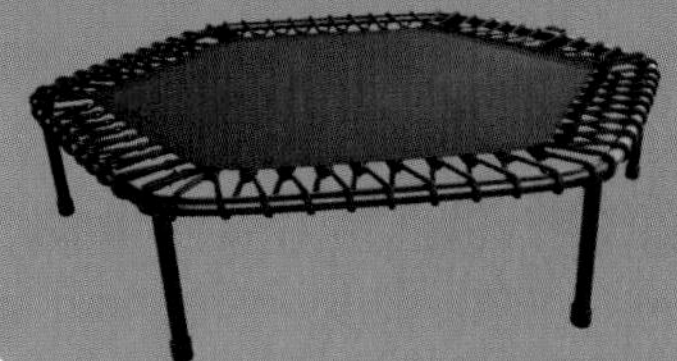

MONSTER MYTHS BUSTED!

5 TERRIFYING TALES DEBUNKED

Are monsters more than just the stuff of freaky films? Some people think so. They believe that big, bad beasts—hairy giants, pterodactyl-like brutes, and more—lurk just out of sight in areas around the world. Luckily, scientists have explanations that bust these tales. Check out five monster myths that have been defanged.

MYTH 1

THE LOVELAND FROG, A BIG AMPHIBIOUS CREATURE, PROWLS AN OHIO, U.S.A., TOWN.

HOW IT MAY HAVE STARTED

This slimy, froglike beast is said to stand four feet (1.2 m) tall and walk on two legs. In 1972 a police officer claimed he caught sight of it on a roadside while driving through Loveland, Ohio, U.S.A., at night. When another officer also reported seeing the freaky frog, the rumor took off.

WHY IT'S NOT TRUE

An investigation by local police found no evidence of the creature. Later, one of the police officers stated that he didn't actually believe that he had seen a monster, and that people had exaggerated his story. It's probable that the Loveland Frog was actually an escaped pet monitor lizard—some types can stretch 10 feet (3 m).

The Nepali name for Mount Everest in the Himalaya means "Forehead of the Sky."

MYTH 2

SHAGGY-HAIRED BEASTS CALLED YETIS ROAM ASIA'S PEAKS.

HOW IT MAY HAVE STARTED

Yetis are allegedly hairy ogres that look like a human-bear hybrid with jagged fangs. The legend of the yeti probably originated in Tibet, a territory nestled near Asia's Himalaya mountain range. Sherpas, a once nomadic people from the area, may have spread the myth during their travels in the 16th century. People still claim to see yetis today.

WHY IT'S NOT TRUE

In 2014 scientists did DNA tests on strands of hair found where yetis were supposedly spotted. Results showed that the hairs came not from an unknown beast, but from a rare subspecies of brown bear that lives in the area. It's likely that those who claimed to have seen a yeti really just saw this bear.

MYTH 3

THE DOBHAR-CHÚ—PART DOG, PART OTTER, ALL MONSTER—LURKS IN IRELAND.

Lough Corrib, a huge lake in western Ireland, contains more than 360 islands.

HOW IT MAY HAVE STARTED

An otter-dog mix, the Dobhar-chú (Gaelic for "water hound") supposedly inhabits Ireland's lakes. It's known for unleashing eerie whistles and having an appetite for humans. No one knows where the legend of this beast came from, but it dates back to at least the 1700s, when a carved image of the creature appeared on the tombstone of one of its alleged victims.

WHY IT'S NOT TRUE

It's more likely that Dobhar-chú is a Eurasian otter. The animal is found in Ireland's rivers and lakes and often whistles to communicate.

The wetlands of Lake Bangweulu in Zambia are home to roughly 390 species of birds.

MYTH 4

THE KONGAMATO, A FLYING REPTILIAN MONSTER, ATTACKS BOATERS IN AFRICA.

HOW IT MAY HAVE STARTED

Reportedly seen soaring over southern and central African swamps, the Kongamato is said to have leathery wings, sharp teeth, and a bad habit of swooping down to smash boats that paddle into its territory. Some say the creature is a pterodactyl—a prehistoric flying reptile. Although the myth has circulated for about a century, its origins are unknown.

WHY IT'S NOT TRUE

Scientists know the Kongamato couldn't be a long-extinct pterodactyl. It's more likely a swamp-dwelling hammerhead bat, the largest bat in Africa. It could also be a big type of stingray that tips boats as it leaps from the water.

MYTH 5

IN THE AMERICAS, THE BEASTLY CHUPACABRA DRINKS THE BLOOD OF FARM ANIMALS.

HOW IT MAY HAVE STARTED

When several goats and chickens in areas of Puerto Rico turned up dead with their blood seemingly drained in the 1990s, rumors spread that the culprit was a vampire-like monster with fangs, a forked tongue, and quills running down its back. A rash of similar deaths that occurred a few years later in Texas were also blamed on the Chupacabra (which roughly translates to "goat sucker" in Spanish).

WHY IT'S NOT TRUE

Investigators looking into the deaths of chickens in Texas found no real evidence that the animals' blood had been drained, making the possibility of a vampire-like slayer way less likely. And sightings of the Chupacabra have usually turned out to be sickly coyotes or dogs suffering from mange, a skin condition that gives them a sinister appearance.

World Religions

Around the world, religion takes many forms. Some belief systems, such as Christianity, Islam, and Judaism, are monotheistic, meaning that followers believe in just one supreme being. Others, like Hinduism, Shintoism, and most native belief systems, are polytheistic, meaning that many of their followers believe in multiple gods.

All of the major religions have their origins in Asia, but they have spread around the world. Christianity, with the largest number of followers, has three divisions—Roman Catholic, Eastern Orthodox, and Protestant. Islam, with about one-fifth of all believers, has two main divisions—Sunni and Shiite. Hinduism and Buddhism account for almost another one-fifth of believers. Judaism, dating back some 4,000 years, has more than 13 million followers, less than one percent of all believers.

CHRISTIANITY

Based on the teachings of Jesus Christ, a Jew born some 2,000 years ago in the area of modern-day Israel, Christianity has spread worldwide and actively seeks converts. Followers in Switzerland (above) participate in an Easter season procession with lanterns and crosses.

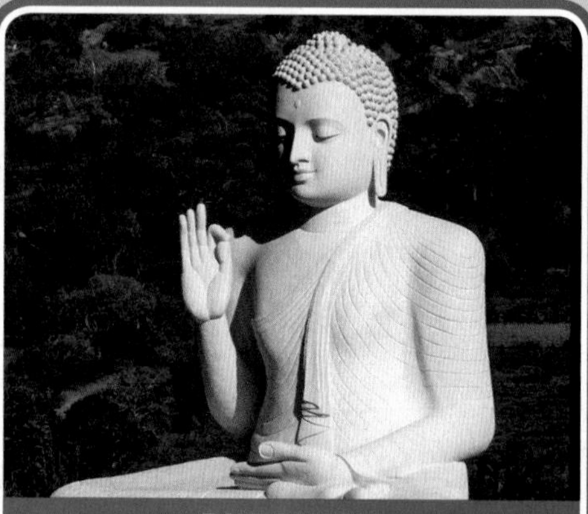

BUDDHISM

Founded about 2,400 years ago in northern India by the Hindu prince Gautama Buddha, Buddhism spread throughout East and Southeast Asia. Buddhist temples have statues, such as the Mihintale Buddha (above) in Sri Lanka.

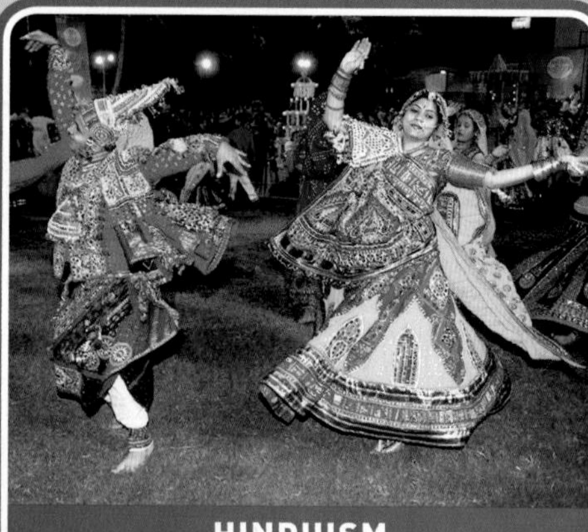

HINDUISM

Dating back more than 4,000 years, Hinduism is practiced mainly in India. Hindus follow sacred texts known as the Vedas and believe in reincarnation. During the festival of Navratri, which honors the goddess Durga, the Garba dance is performed (above).

CLOSE-UP

Technology Meets Tradition

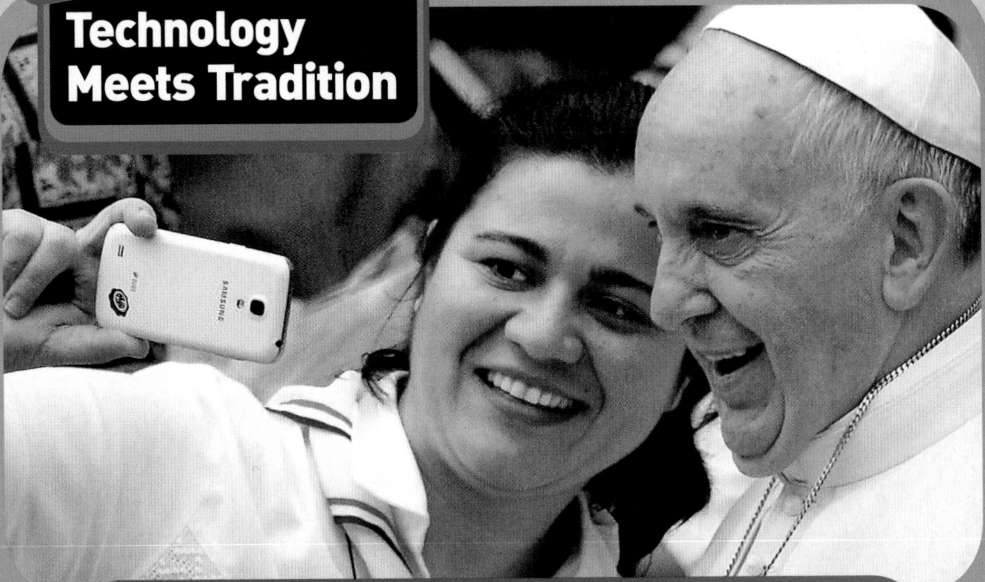

It has been 1,200 years since the bishop of Rome became known as the pope. Pope Francis became the head of the Roman Catholic Church in 2013 and has embraced technology as a way to reach Catholics around the globe. He's the first pope to pose for a selfie and has more than 22 million Twitter followers.

ISLAM

Muslims believe that the Koran, Islam's sacred book, records the words of Allah (God) as revealed to the Prophet Muhammad beginning around A.D. 610. Believers (above) circle the Kaaba in the Haram Mosque in Mecca, Saudi Arabia, the spiritual center of the faith.

JUDAISM

The traditions, laws, and beliefs of Judaism date back to Abraham (the Patriarch) and the Torah (the first five books of the Old Testament). Followers pray before the Western Wall (above), which stands below Islam's Dome of the Rock in Jerusalem.

QUIZ WHIZ

Take this quiz to find out how much you know about the world around you!

Write your answers on a piece of paper. Then check them below.

1. **True or false?**
Kite flying is a competitive sport in Thailand.

2. **The holes in Swiss cheese are called _________?**
   a. mouse bites
   b. windows
   c. eyes
   d. globes

3. **Who will be the first woman to appear on a modern U.S. banknote?**
   a. Betsy Ross
   b. Pocahontas
   c. Hillary Clinton
   d. Harriet Tubman

4. **True or false?**
According to Chinese astrology, 2018 is the Year of the Dog.

5. **In Spain "pasta" is a slang term for_________.**
   a. curls
   b. smartphones
   c. homework
   d. money

Not **STUMPED** yet? Check out the *NATIONAL GEOGRAPHIC KIDS QUIZ WHIZ* collection for more crazy **CULTURE** questions!

ANSWERS:
1. True; 2. c; 3. d; 4. True; 5. d

HOMEWORK HELP

Explore a New Culture

STAMPS OF SOUTH AFRICA

CURRENCY AND COINS OF SOUTH AFRICA

THE FLAG OF SOUTH AFRICA

You're a student, but you're also a citizen of the world. Writing a report on a foreign nation or your own country is a great way to better understand and appreciate how different people live. Pick the country of your ancestors, one that's been in the news, or one that you'd like to visit someday.

Passport to Success

A country report follows the format of an expository essay because you're "exposing" information about the country you choose.

Simple Steps

1. **RESEARCH** Gathering information is the most important step in writing a good country report. Look to Internet sources, encyclopedias, books, magazine and newspaper articles, and other sources to find important and interesting details about your subject.

2. **ORGANIZE YOUR NOTES** Put the information you gathered into a rough outline. For example, sort everything you found about the country's system of government, climate, etc.

3. **WRITE IT UP** Follow the basic structure of good writing: introduction, body, and conclusion. Remember that each paragraph should have a topic sentence that is then supported by facts and details. Incorporate the information from your notes, but make sure it's in your own words. And make your writing flow with good transitions and descriptive language.

4. **ADD VISUALS** Include maps, diagrams, photos, and other visual aids.

5. **PROOFREAD AND REVISE** Correct any mistakes, and polish your language. Do your best!

6. **CITE YOUR SOURCES** Be sure to keep a record of your sources.

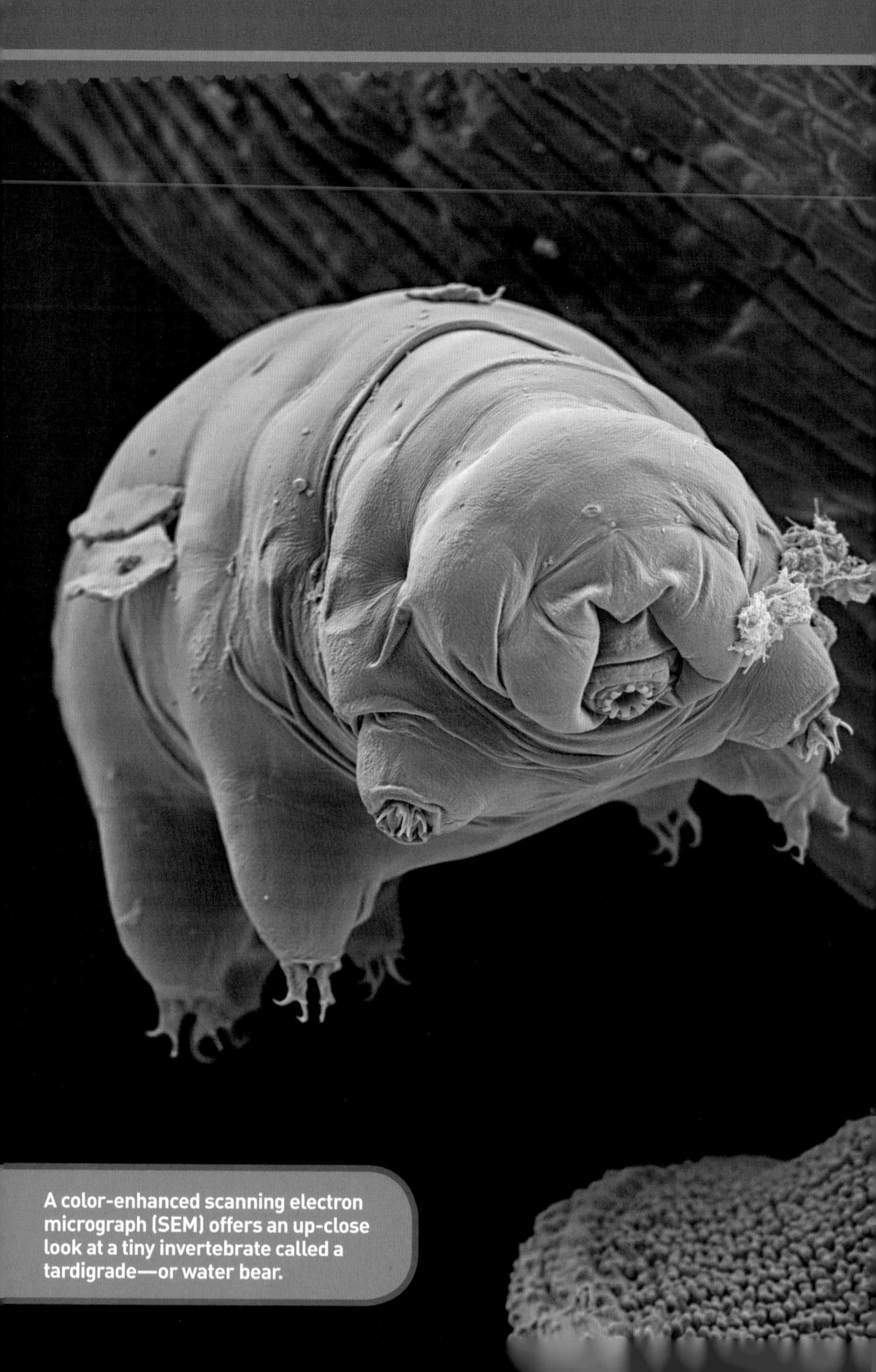

A color-enhanced scanning electron micrograph (SEM) offers an up-close look at a tiny invertebrate called a tardigrade—or water bear.

Life Science

WHAT IS LIFE?

This seems like such an easy question to answer. Everybody knows that singing birds are alive and rocks are not. But when we start studying bacteria and other microscopic creatures, things get more complicated.

SO WHAT EXACTLY IS LIFE?

Most scientists agree that something is alive if it can do the following: reproduce; grow in size to become more complex in structure; take in nutrients to survive; give off waste products; and respond to external stimuli, such as increased sunlight or changes in temperature.

KINDS OF LIFE

Biologists classify living organisms by how they get their energy. Organisms such as algae, green plants, and some bacteria use sunlight as an energy source. Animals (like humans), fungi, and some Archaea use chemicals to provide energy. When we eat food, chemical reactions within our digestive system turn our food into fuel.

Living things inhabit land, sea, and air. In fact, life also thrives deep beneath the oceans, embedded in rocks miles below the Earth's crust, in ice, and in other extreme environments. The life-forms that thrive in these challenging environments are called extremophiles. Some of these draw directly upon the chemicals surrounding them for energy. Since these are very different forms of life than what we're used to, we may not think of them as alive, but they are.

HOW IT ALL WORKS

To try and understand how a living organism works, it helps to look at one example of its simplest form—the single-celled bacterium called *Streptococcus*. There are many kinds of these tiny organisms, and some are responsible for human illnesses. What makes us sick or uncomfortable are the toxins the bacteria give off in our bodies.

A single *Streptococcus* bacterium is so small that at least 500 of them could fit on the dot above this letter *i*. These bacteria are some of the simplest forms of life we know. They have no moving parts, no lungs, no brain, no heart, no liver, and no leaves or fruit. Yet this life-form reproduces. It grows in size by producing long chain structures, takes in nutrients, and gives off waste products. This tiny life-form is alive, just as you are alive.

What makes something alive is a question scientists grapple with when they study viruses, such as the ones that cause the common cold and smallpox. They can grow and reproduce within host cells, such as those that make up your body. Because viruses lack cells and cannot metabolize nutrients for energy or reproduce without a host, scientists ask if they are indeed alive. And don't go looking for them without a strong microscope—viruses are a hundred times smaller than bacteria.

Scientists think life began on Earth some 3.9 to 4.1 billion years ago, but no fossils exist from that time. The earliest fossils ever found are from the primitive life that existed 3.6 billion years ago. Other life-forms, some of which are shown below, soon followed. Scientists continue to study how life evolved on Earth and whether it is possible that life exists on other planets.

MICROSCOPIC ORGANISMS*

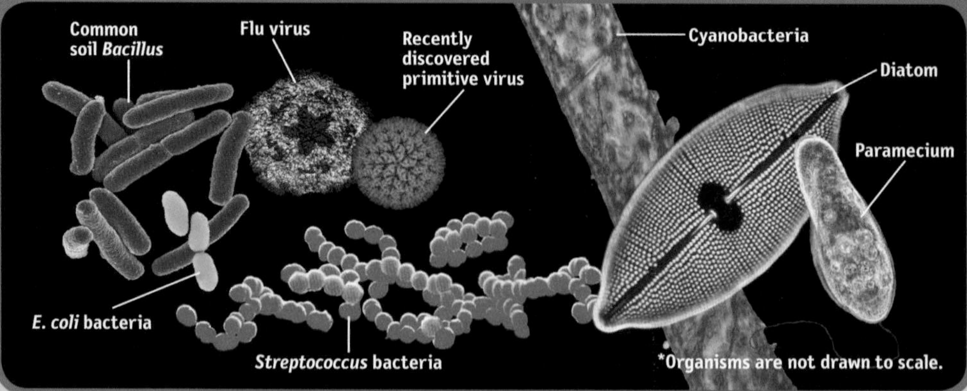

Common soil *Bacillus*

Flu virus

Recently discovered primitive virus

Cyanobacteria

Diatom

Paramecium

E. coli bacteria

Streptococcus bacteria

*Organisms are not drawn to scale.

The Three Domains of Life

Biologists divide all living organisms into three domains: Bacteria, Archaea, and Eukarya. Archaean and Bacterial cells do not have nuclei; they are so different from each other that they belong to different domains. Since human cells have a nucleus, humans belong to the Eukarya domain.

1 BACTERIA

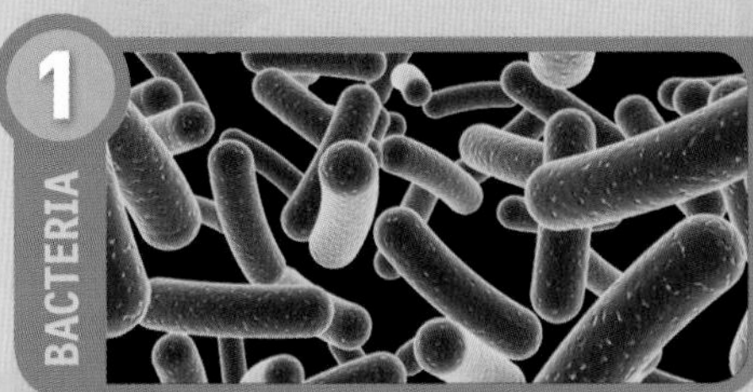

Domain Bacteria: These single-celled microorganisms are found almost everywhere in the world. Bacteria are small and do not have nuclei. They can be shaped like rods, spirals, or spheres. Some of them are helpful to humans, and some are harmful.

2 ARCHAEA

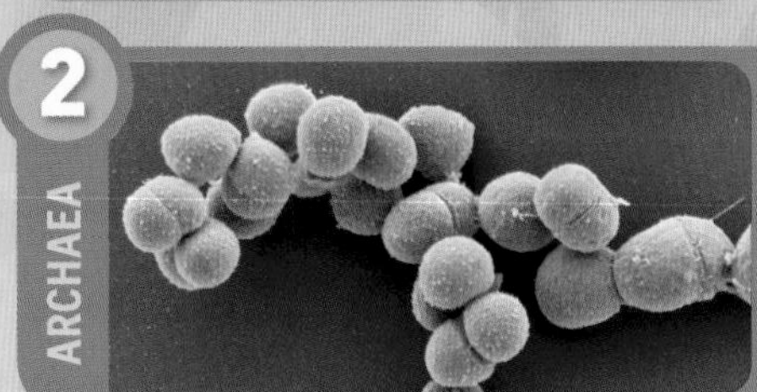

Domain Archaea: These single-celled microorganisms are often found in extremely hostile environments. Like Bacteria, Archaea do not have nuclei, but they have some genes in common with Eukarya. For this reason, scientists think the Archaea living today most closely resemble the earliest forms of life on Earth.

3 EUKARYA

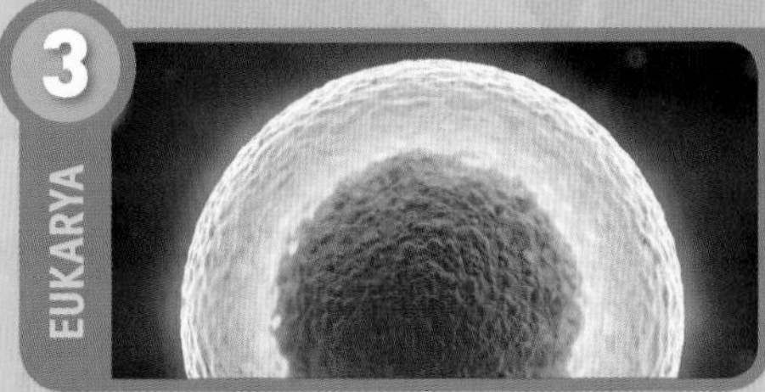

Domain Eukarya: This diverse group of life-forms is more complicated than Bacteria and Archaea, as Eukarya have one or more cells with nuclei. These are the tiny cells that make up your whole body. Eukarya are divided into four groups: fungi, protists, plants, and animals.

FYI

What is a domain? Scientifically speaking, a domain is a major taxonomic division into which natural objects are classified (see p. 46 for "What Is Taxonomy?").

FUNGI

Kingdom Fungi (about 100,000 species): Mainly multicellular organisms, fungi cannot make their own food. Mushrooms and yeast are fungi.

PROTISTS

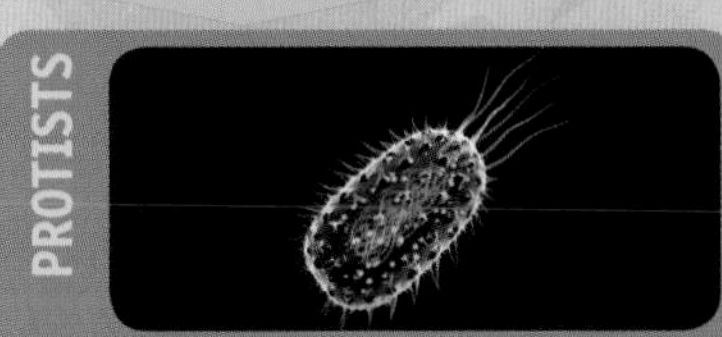

Protists (about 250,000 species): Once considered a kingdom, this group is a "grab bag" that includes unicellular and multicellular organisms of great variety.

PLANTS

Kingdom Plantae (about 300,000 species): Plants are multicellular, and many can make their own food using photosynthesis (see p. 130 for "Photosynthesis").

ANIMALS

Kingdom Animalia (about 1,000,000 species): Most animals, which are multicellular, have their own organ systems. Animals do not make their own food.

18 FANTASTIC FACTS ABOUT

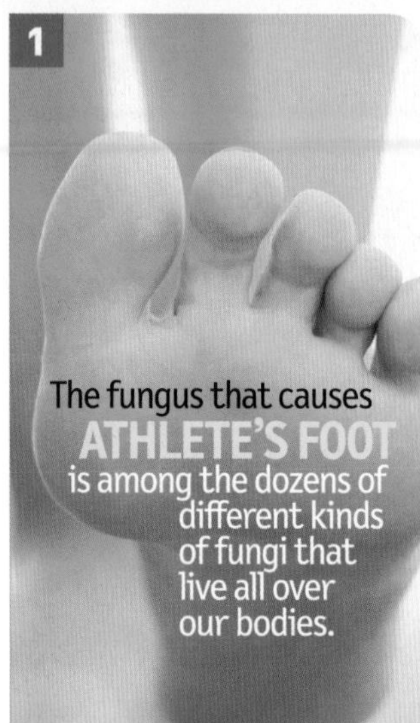

1 The fungus that causes **ATHLETE'S FOOT** is among the dozens of different kinds of fungi that live all over our bodies.

2 **FUNGI ARE NOT PLANTS OR ANIMALS.** They're so different from other organisms that they belong **TO THEIR OWN KINGDOM.**

3 **THE SECOND MOST FAVORITE PIZZA TOPPING IN THE UNITED STATES is a fungus:** mushrooms!

4 **Many mushrooms are safe to eat, but a few wild varieties can cause death. Some of them are known as "destroying angels" or "death caps."**

5 **Some fungi** not only grow but also thrive in **POLLUTED WATER.**

6 **Fungi** include organisms like YEASTS, MOLDS, MILDEW, AND **MUSHROOMS.**

7 THE GIANT "HONEY MUSHROOM" IS A FUNGUS THAT HAS KILLED THOUSANDS OF EVERGREEN TREES IN OREGON, U.S.A.

8 **Fungi**—and the bacteria buddies that grow with them—**CAN DECOMPOSE EVERYTHING** from food scraps to blue jeans and jet fuel.

9 **Lichens are organisms made up of both FUNGI AND ALGAE. One kind is named after U.S. president Barack Obama.**

10

MUSHROOMS ARE 80–90 PERCENT WATER.

11

Some types of mushrooms grow on HORSE POOP.

12

There is a mushroom that glows 24 hours a day and is bright enough to read by at night.

FUNGI

13

WILD MUSHROOMS can be **boiled** to produce BEAUTIFUL, NATURAL CLOTH DYES.

14

The ancient Romans **held an** annual festival for Robigus, **the** god of rust fungi.

15

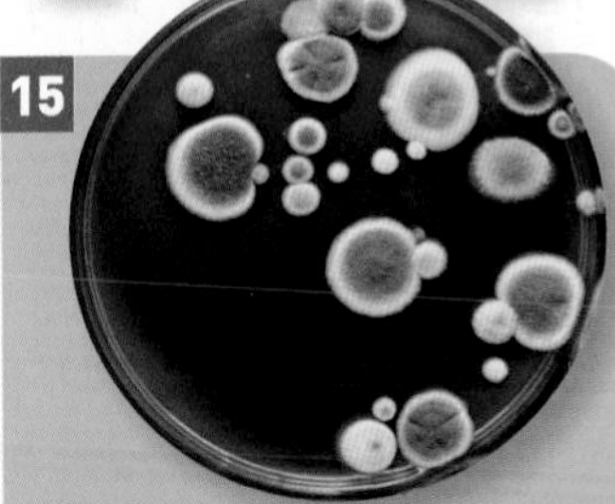

You can't see most fungi. **THEY ARE MICROSCOPIC.**

16

There are some **100,000 KNOWN SPECIES OF FUNGI,** living everywhere from the steamy tropics to the wood huts built by explorers in frigid Antarctica.

17

In China's Yunnan Province, more than **100 MUSHROOM CAPS** grew on a single stem to create a gigantic mushroom top that **WEIGHED 33 POUNDS** (15 kg).

18

MOLDS ARE USED TO RIPEN CHEESES, such as blue cheese, Brie, and Roquefort.

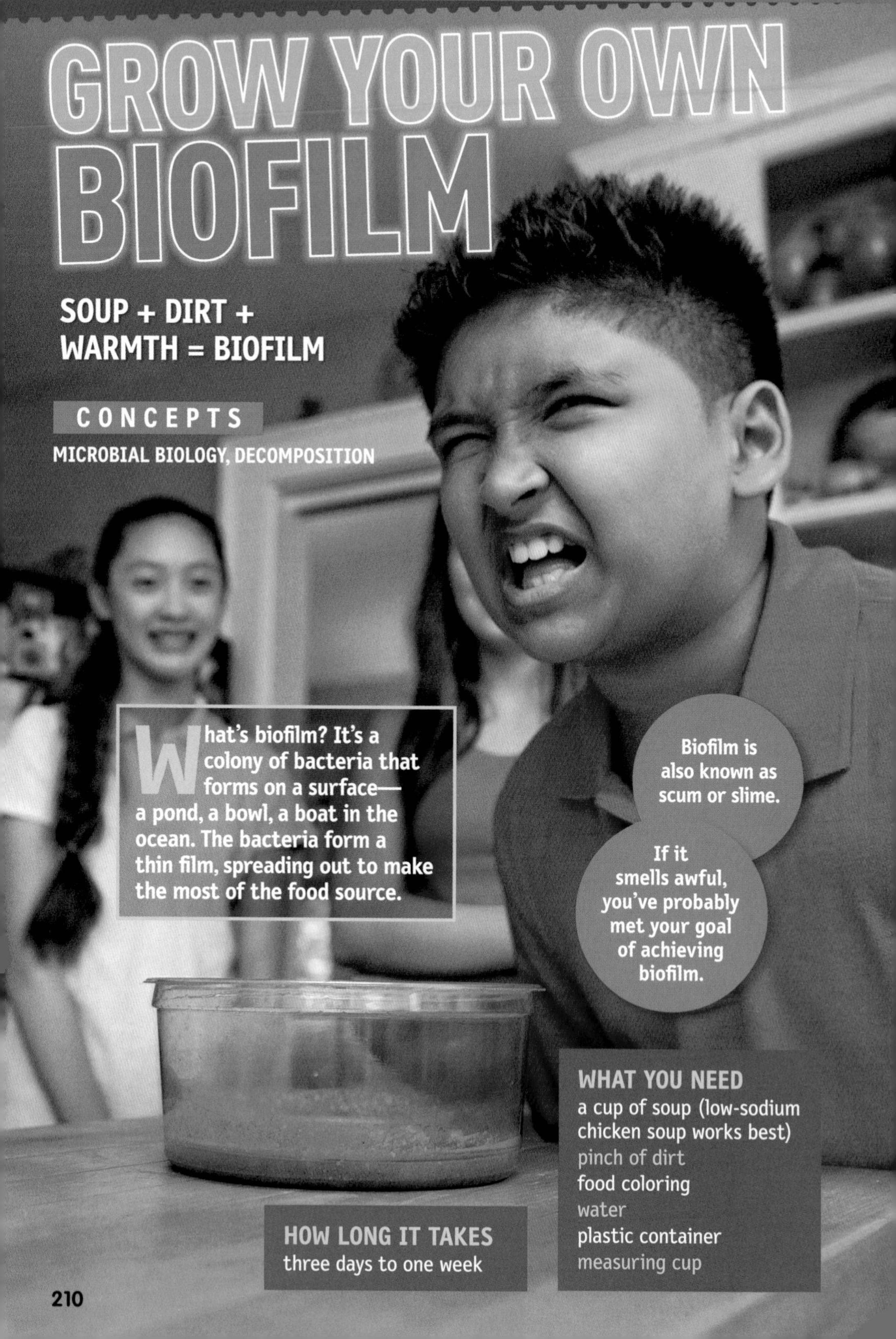

GROW YOUR OWN BIOFILM

SOUP + DIRT + WARMTH = BIOFILM

CONCEPTS

MICROBIAL BIOLOGY, DECOMPOSITION

What's biofilm? It's a colony of bacteria that forms on a surface—a pond, a bowl, a boat in the ocean. The bacteria form a thin film, spreading out to make the most of the food source.

Biofilm is also known as scum or slime.

If it smells awful, you've probably met your goal of achieving biofilm.

WHAT YOU NEED

a cup of soup (low-sodium chicken soup works best)
pinch of dirt
food coloring
water
plastic container
measuring cup

HOW LONG IT TAKES

three days to one week

WHAT TO DO

DAY ONE:

1 **POUR A CUP** (.25 L) **OF SOUP** into the container and add the dirt.

2 **LEAVE THE CONTAINER** in a warm place, uncovered, for four to five days. The ideal temperature is 98.6°F (37°C)—body temperature. You may need to leave it out longer if it's cooler.

DAY TWO AND ON:

3 **WATCH FOR A CHANGE** in the liquid. When it begins to cloud, biofilm is forming.

LAST DAY:

4 **DUMP OUT THE LIQUID** and gently rinse the container with water. No scrubbing. No soap.

5 **DRIP THE FOOD COLORING** down the inside walls of the container. Swirl it round to coat the bottom and sides. Wait 15 minutes, swirling the color again every few minutes.

6 **FILL THE CONTAINER** with water, then dump out the colored water.

7 **THE SMALL SPOTS** of color on the walls of the container are the biofilm.

WHAT TO EXPECT The biofilm will form a ring around the container. It will be difficult to rinse it from the container even with soap, water, and some scrubbing.

WHAT'S GOING ON? Bacteria are tiny organisms that live in two ways: motile (moving freely) and sessile (in a group on a surface). Some motile bacteria become sessile, settling down near a food source that can keep them fed even if they quit moving. A biofilm is a colony of bacteria that live on a surface. If you provide bacteria with a food source, a biofilm may form.

The dirt provided the start-up for the biofilm. One teaspoon (5 mL) of dirt can harbor between 100 million and 1 billion bacteria. In the container, bacteria grow best at the boundary of air and liquid.

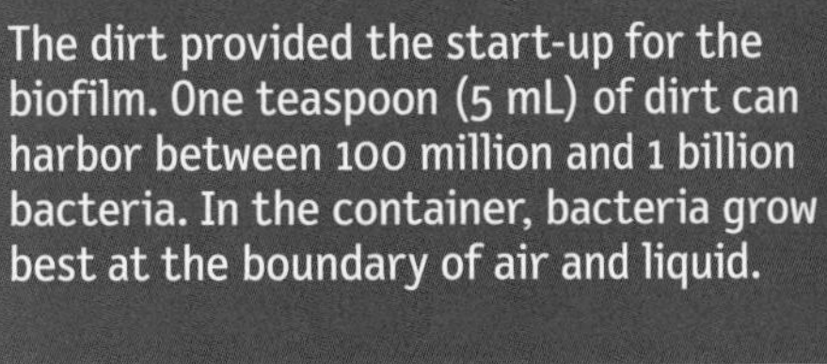

YOU AND YOUR CELLS

Your body is made up of microscopically tiny structures called cells—many trillions of them!

Every living thing—from the tiniest bug to the biggest tree—is made up of cells, too. Cells are the smallest building blocks of life. Some living things, such as an amoeba, are made up of just one cell. Other living things contain many more. Estimates for an adult human, for example, range from 10 trillion to 100 trillion cells!

An animal cell is a bit like the world's tiniest water balloon. It's a jellylike blob surrounded by an oily "skin" called a cell membrane. The membrane works to let some chemicals into the cell and keep others out. The "jelly" on the inside is called cytoplasm. It's speckled with tiny cell parts, called organelles. Some organelles make energy. Others take apart and put together various chemicals, which become ingredients for different body functions such as growth and movement.

CHECK OUT THE BOOK!

SEEING CELLS

The first microscope that clearly showed anything smaller than a flea was invented in the late 1500s. Later, people tinkered with microscopes and lenses to make them even more powerful. One of these people was the English scientist Robert Hooke.

Hooke designed a microscope of his own and drew detailed pictures of what he saw. In 1665, he published his illustrations in a book called *Micrographia*, which means "little pictures." One picture shows boxy spaces in a slice of cork from a tree. Hooke called the spaces "cells" because they looked like little rooms. It would be another 200 years before scientists realized that cells make up all living things.

YOU HAVE A LOT OF NERVE!

Different parts of your brain control different activities, but how does your brain tell all the parts of your body what to do?

And, in return, how do your eyes, ears, and nose tell your brain what they see, hear, and smell? The answer is your nerves!

Nerves—thin, threadlike structures—carry messages between your brain and the rest of your body, in both directions. Nerves run down your spine and branch out all the way to your fingers and toes. This system of nerves controls your body, tells your muscles to move, and lets you experience the wonderful world around you. Nerves are part of your nervous system, which also includes your brain and spinal cord.

Your nerves are made of cells called neurons. Neurons send and receive messages between your brain and the other parts of your body by sending out alternating electrical and chemical signals.

Messages flash from neuron to neuron along your nerves and inside your brain. Signals from your eyes might tell the brain, "There's my school bus." The brain then sends signals that zoom from cell to cell making sense of the message. Then the brain sends signals back down to the nerves connected to your leg muscles to say, "Run to the bus stop!"

TOUR A NEURON

Neurons have four parts:

CELL BODY Contains the nucleus, which controls the activity of the cell and contains its DNA, or deoxyribonucleic acid

AXON Fiber that transmits impulses from the cell body to another nerve cell

DENDRITE Branchlike fiber extending from the cell body that receives signals from other neurons

MYELIN A fatty covering around the axons that insulate the axon, giving the white matter its characteristic color

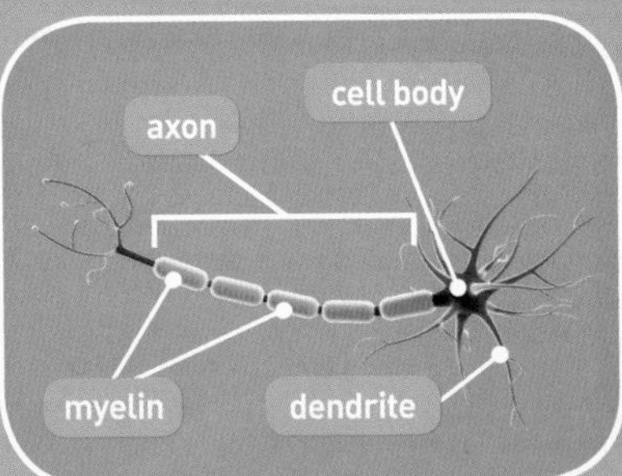

Your Amazing Ears

OUTER EAR
INNER EAR
COCHLEA
MIDDLE EAR
EARDRUM

Listen up! Your ears are so much more than just two funny-looking things stuck to the side of your head. Here's an earful on all that's cool about these awesome organs.

Your entire inner ear can fit inside the tip of your pinkie.

TRIPLE PLAY. The ears are made up of three sections: the outer ear, the middle ear, and the inner ear. Each part plays separate and equally important roles to keep your hearing sharp. Here's how sound travels through your ears.

OUTER EAR: The part you can see and feel, the outer ear consists of the pinna and the ear canal. Sound waves enter here and travel down the ear canal to the ear drum.

MIDDLE EAR: Sound waves create vibrations that strike the eardrum, causing the three tiny bones located here to move. The movement amplifies the sound and delivers it to the inner ear.

INNER EAR: Sound vibrations enter the cochlea, the small, snail-shaped, liquid-filled tube that's lined with tiny hairs. The vibrations make the tiny hairs wave back and forth and tickle the nerve cells. This causes the nerve cells to send messages to your brain that are interpreted as sound.

BETTER BALANCE. Your ears don't just let you hear—they keep you balanced, too. How? Above the cochlea in the inner ear is a set of three fluid-filled canals, called the semicircular canals. When you move your head, tiny hair cells in the canals move too, sending nerve impulses to the brain that tell you where you are. And that dizzy feeling you get when you've spun around in circles one too many times? That happens because the fluid in the semicircular canals continues to swish around even after you stop, confusing your brain into thinking that you're still spinning.

Some people can hear their own eyeballs move.

DRUM ROLL. Despite its name, the eardrum has nothing to do with percussion. Rather, this tiny piece of skin located between the outer and middle ear is called a "drum" because it's such a tightly stretched membrane. Bad ear infections or trauma can cause it to tear, or perforate, but the eardrum usually heals itself within a few months.

WAX ON. It's sticky, it's icky, and it can smell funky. So what's the point of earwax, anyway? The yellowish brown stuff is packed with dead skin cells and chemicals that fight off infections. And it traps dirt and dust, too, keeping your middle and inner ears sparkly clean. So while it may be gunky, it keeps you healthy. And that's not just a ball of wax!

Sense of Smell

Pee-ew! Mammals use their sense of smell to seek out food, avoid predators, and find a mate. But some are better sniffers than others, and the mammals that reign supreme have more olfactory receptors dedicated to smelling. The amount of receptors is determined by the number of scent genes in an animal's DNA—the more you have, the better you sniff! Check out the number of genes devoted to smell in these mammals to see who takes the best whiff.

Your Amazing brain

Inside your body's supercomputer

You carry around a three-pound (1.4-kg) mass of wrinkly material n your head that controls every single thing you will ever do. From enabling you to think, learn, create, and feel emotions to controlling every blink, breath, and heartbeat—this fantastic control center is your brain. It is a structure so amazing that a famous scientist once called it the "most complex thing we have yet discovered in our universe."

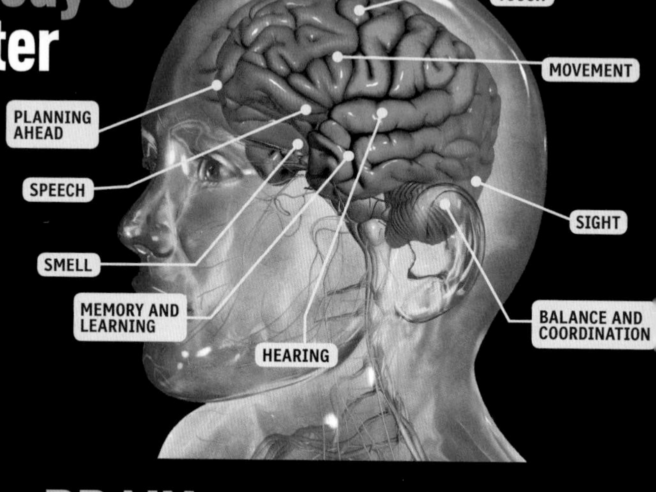

BRAIN MAP

- FRONTAL LOBE
- PARIETAL LOBE
- OCCIPITAL LOBE
- TEMPORAL LOBE

} CEREBRUM

- CEREBELLUM
- BRAIN STEM

THE BIG QUESTION

WHAT TAKES UP TWO-THIRDS OF YOUR BRAIN'S WEIGHT AND ALLOWS YOU TO SWIM, EAT, AND SPEAK?

Answer: The huge hunk of your brain called the cerebrum. It's definitely the biggest part of the brain. The four lobes of the cerebrum house the centers for memory, the senses, movement, and emotion, among other things.

The cerebrum is made up of two hemispheres—the right and the left. Each side controls the muscles of the opposite side of the body.

CHECK YOUR MEMORY

How much can your brain remember? Put it to the test.

CHALLENGE

Take 30 seconds. Memorize as many of these pictures as you can. Cover the pictures. Now get a pencil and a piece of paper. Write down the pictures you remember. How many did you get right?

WHAT EXACTLY IS HAPPENING?

Looking at pictures actually helps your brain to remember better. Short-term memory, also called working memory, relies heavily on the visual cortex. Words that are read are processed very quickly by our brains. They don't stick around for very long. But recording a picture in your brain takes longer. The more time spent looking at the picture, the better the memory. Saying a word out loud does the same thing. It takes longer to speak a word than it does to read it. That's why you remember it better when you say it aloud. The lesson? When you are doing last-minute cramming for a test, look at pictures and speak things out loud. Your memory—and your test score—will thank you.

CHECK OUT THE BOOK!

YOUR SHORT-TERM MEMORY CAN HOLD ONLY ABOUT SEVEN THINGS AT ONE TIME

THE GENE SCENE

Genetics is the study of heredity, or how traits from parents are passed along to their children. And genes are the elements we inherit from each of our parents that combine to make us the individuals we are. By studying genes, scientists have been able to learn not only what makes us similar to and different from one another, but also the causes of certain diseases that are inherited (passed down) from one generation to another.

Amazingly, advances in research have helped scientists discover that there are "disease genes"—genes that indicate that a person who is carrying them may be more likely to get a specific disease. Researchers are also developing ways to test people to see if they have these genes. They are digging deeper into the genetics behind more and more diseases, such as cancer and heart disease, to see which healthy patients could be at risk in the future. Doctors are now even able to know in advance whether a patient will respond well to a particular treatment (medicine) based on their genetic code! Going forward, researchers are working to make genome sequencing (studying a person's unique genetic makeup) more widely available so many people can have access to this amazing medical care. One day we may be able to fix these broken genes.

NATURE'S BLUEPRINT

In 2003, after more than a decade of hard work, scientists completed a very ambitious task called the Human Genome Project. They mapped the entire "sequence" of human DNA—our hereditary "code" containing tens of thousands of genes. DNA is nature's blueprint for human beings, and it makes up the building blocks of life.

Would it surprise you to know that, despite how different individual people seem from one another, more than 99 percent of DNA is the same in all people? It's true! Though there are definite physical and other differences we can identify—such as eye color, hair color, height, and skin color—humans are genetically mostly the same.

ADD IT UP

Ten years ago the number of human genes was thought to be 100,000. Since then, scientists have learned more and revised that number down to between 20,000 and 25,000.

LIMBS FROM LIMBS

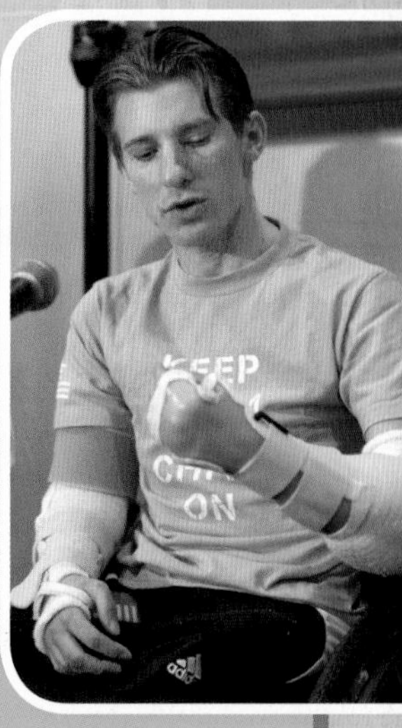

ARMED AND BRAVE

You might have heard of organ transplants, in which a person receives a new organ on the inside of their body, but did you know that some people can receive transplants on the *outside* of their bodies?

In 2012 a U.S. Army soldier who had lost all four limbs after being injured by a roadside bomb in 2009 received a rare double-arm transplant—one of only a small number of people to successfully undergo this risky surgery. In a 13-hour operation, a team of 16 surgeons joined the bone, muscles, blood vessels, nerves, and skin of donor arms with those of former sergeant Brendan Marrocco. With time and physical therapy, these replacement arms have helped Marrocco do many of the things he did before, such as drive a car.

SMART PARTS

A DOLPHIN'S TALE

Maja Kazazic had become used to living with pain—and feeling different. As a teen, Maja lost her leg after she was injured in the Bosnian civil war. Her artificial limb—called a prosthesis—made every movement painful.

Maja's life changed when she met Winter, a dolphin at Clearwater Marine Aquarium in Florida (above). Winter had lost her tail in a crab trap as a baby. When Winter got a high-tech tail to help her swim, Maja wondered if a similar device could help her be pain free. The aquarium put Maja in touch with the company that made Winter's prosthesis. Maja received a new leg out of the same materials that helped Winter. Soon the pair were swimming together—one with a new leg, the other with a new tail.

QUIZ WHIZ

Discover your science smarts by taking this quiz!

Write your answers on a piece of paper. Then check them below.

1. **True or false?** Scientists think life began on Earth 3 million years ago.

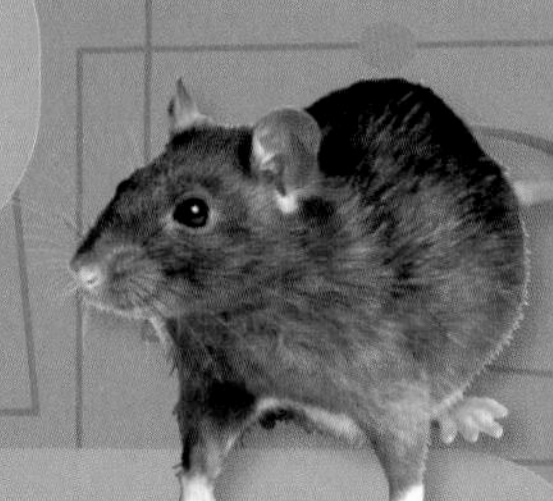

2. **You can't see most fungi because they are ________________.**
   a. invisible
   b. camouflaged
   c. microscopic
   d. super rare

3. **True or False?** An elephant has a better sense of smell than a rat.

4. **The human body is made up of ________ of cells.**
   a. hundreds
   b. thousands
   c. millions
   d. trillions

5. **Your brain's cerebrum controls which of the following?**
   a. memory
   b. senses
   c. movement
   d. all of the above

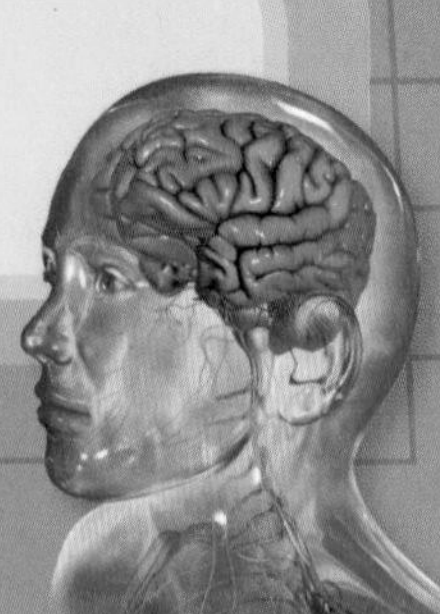

Not **STUMPED** yet? Check out the *NATIONAL GEOGRAPHIC KIDS QUIZ WHIZ* collection for more crazy **SCIENCE** questions!

ANSWERS:
1. False. Scientists estimate that life began about four billion years ago; 2. c; 3. True; 4. d; 5. d

HOMEWORK HELP

Research Like a Pro

There is so much information on the Internet. How do you find what you need and make sure it's accurate?

Be Specific

To come up with the most effective keywords—words that describe what you want to know more about—write down what you're looking for in the form of a question, and then circle the most important words in that sentence. Those are the keywords to use in your search. And for best results, use words that are specific rather than general.

Research

Research on the Internet involves "looking up" information using a search engine (see list below). Type one or two keywords, and the search engine will provide a list of websites that contain information related to your topic.

Use Trustworthy Sources

When conducting Internet research, be sure the website you use is reliable and the information it provides can be trusted. Sites produced by well-known, established organizations, companies, publications, educational institutions, or the government are your best bets.

Don't Copy

Avoid Internet plagiarism. Take careful notes and cite the websites you use to conduct research.

HELPFUL AND SAFE SEARCH ENGINES FOR KIDS

Google Safe Search
squirrelnet.com/search/Google_SafeSearch.asp

GoGooligans
gogooligans.com

AOL Kids
kids.aol.com

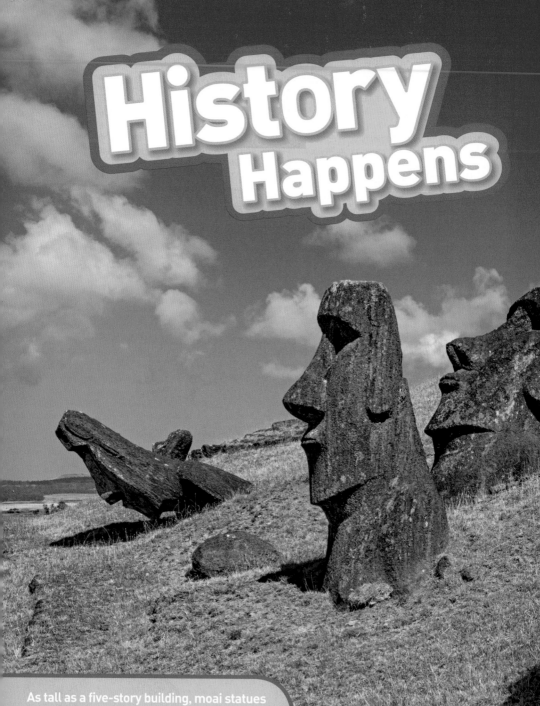

History Happens

As tall as a five-story building, moai statues tower over Easter Island. Scientists believe islanders created them some 800 years ago to honor their ancestors.

awes8me

ROYALLY AMAZING CASTLES

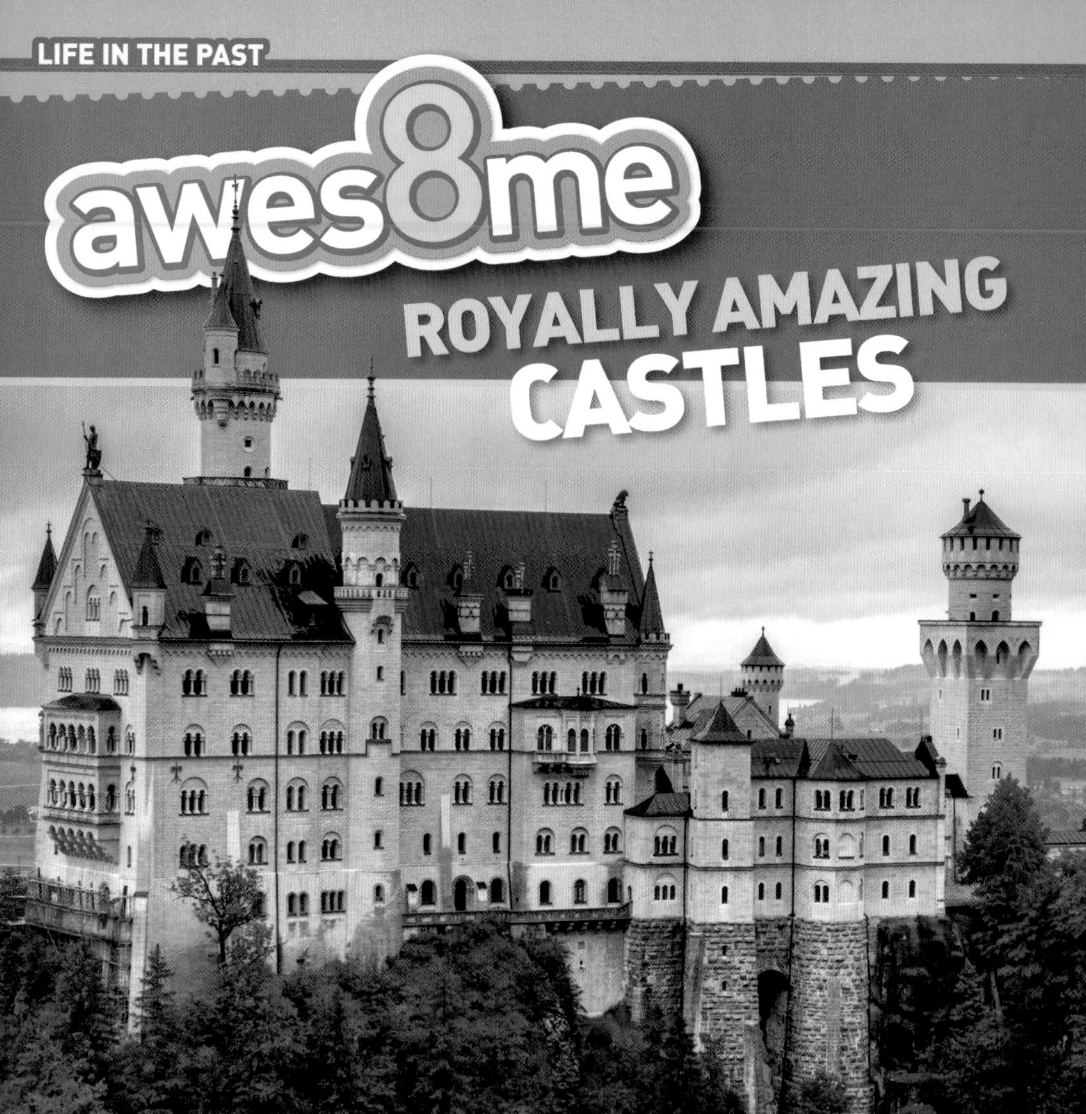

2 KNIGHT LIFE

Walk the paths roamed by medieval knights and princesses at the 14th-century Bodiam Castle in East Sussex, England. The castle's splashiest feature? It's completely surrounded by a moat.

3 FIT FOR A WIZARD

Alnwick Castle, a 900-year-old building in Northumberland, England, was the site of Harry's first flying lesson in the film *Harry Potter and the Sorcerer's Stone.*

4 FIERCE FORTRESS

Perched high in the Austrian Alps, Hohenwerfen Fortress was the site of numerous sieges and attacks for 900 years. The castle was also featured in the 1965 film *The Sound of Music.*

5 DEFYING GRAVITY

The Mont-Saint-Michel abbey is a French monastery that rests on an island surrounded by the English Channel. When the tide rises around the island, the abbey seems to float.

1 TALK ABOUT A FAIRY TALE!

Germany's King Ludwig II built Neuschwanstein Castle on a cliff in Bavaria. Every year more than a million people visit the 19th-century structure, which is said to have been the inspiration for Disneyland's iconic Sleeping Beauty Castle.

7

CASTLE IN FLIGHT

Himeji Castle, the largest castle in Japan, is an 83-building complex! Its look has been likened to a white heron spreading its wings.

8 SPOOKY SPOT

The author who created Count Dracula in 1897 based the vampire's home on Bran Castle in Romania, which is why it's also known as Dracula's Castle. But no bloodthirsty monsters actually live there. This nickname has no teeth!

COLOSSAL CASTLE 6

Founded in the ninth century, Prague Castle in the Czech Republic is the largest ancient castle complex in the world, with an area of more than 750,000 square feet (69,677 sq m).

Jungle of Secrets

Scientists uncover a hidden city near the temple called ANGKOR WAT

In the midst of Cambodia's steamy jungle looms a majestic medieval temple. Called Angkor Wat, the nearly 900-year-old structure was built in the capital of the Khmer Empire, a powerful civilization in Southeast Asia. But until recently, few were aware of something tucked in the forest beyond the temple—a hidden city.

MISSING METROPOLIS

The Khmer Empire thrived between the 9th and 15th centuries. Many people worshipped at the temple of Angkor Wat in the capital city of Angkor, which was about the size (area) of New York City. Scientists believe that in the 14th and 15th centuries, droughts and other extreme natural disasters caused many people to abandon the region and move south. Eventually, thick forests grew over much of the area.

Built in the 12th century to honor a god, Angkor Wat was in continual use even after the capital city was abandoned. When a French explorer came across the temple in the 1800s, he spread word of its beauty, drawing visitors and archaeologists to the area.

Scientists suspected that another, older city from the Khmer Empire called Mahendraparvata was hidden in the jungle around the temple. According to writings found in old texts, the city was built in A.D. 802 and served as the Khmer Empire's capital before it moved to Angkor.

In Cambodia, it's considered an insult to touch someone's head.

AIRBORNE DETECTIVES

In 2012 a team of scientists wanted to investigate the region in search of the remains of Mahendraparvata. A thick tangle of trees

Angkor Wat appears on Cambodia's flag (left).

covering the land made exploring on foot difficult. So instead the team took to the skies.

Crisscrossing over forest canopies in a helicopter, archaeologist Damian Evans used an instrument called LIDAR to scan the ground. LIDAR works by rapidly firing off pulses of laser light. A sensor on the instrument measures how long it takes for each pulse to bounce back from the ground. If a set of laser beams has a shorter return time than the previous pulses sent, it could mean the beams have hit something elevated, such as a building. A longer return time could mean that the beams are bouncing off of a low valley or deep riverbed. Using GPS technology, cartographers then combined all of the measurements to create a map of the terrain.

As the scientists analyzed the map, they noticed an area with a network of roads and canals built into a mountain. It appeared to match the description of Mahendraparvata found in the old texts. Evans and his team knew this had to be the hidden city.

IT'S A JUNGLE OUT THERE

The archaeologists started their expedition north of Angkor Wat under the heat of a sizzling sun. They cut away tree leaves blocking their path with machetes, waded knee-deep in bogs, and dodged dangerous land mines that had been left in the jungle after a war.

Finally they stumbled upon dozens of crumbled temples and evidence of roads and canals, all organized into city blocks. They had reached their destination, and it was indeed Mahendraparvata.

In the coming years, Evans and his team will continue to investigate the area. But the scientists will have their work cut out for them. After all, this jungle is very good at keeping secrets.

Must-See SIGHTS

WHAT: **HERCULANEUM**
WHERE: Ercolano, Italy

WHY IT'S COOL: Buried by ash and lava from the eruption of Mount Vesuvius in A.D. 79, this port town is said to be better preserved than its neighbor Pompeii. Some ruins here stand up to two stories high.

WHAT: **THE GREAT BUDDHA**
WHERE: Kamakura, Japan

WHY IT'S COOL: More than 760 years old, this giant bronze statue has stayed standing through a lot—even surviving a giant tsunami. At 44 feet (13.35 m) tall, it's one of Japan's most famous icons.

WHAT: **U.S.S. *ARIZONA* MEMORIAL**
WHERE: Honolulu, Hawaii, U.S.A.

WHY IT'S COOL: This site, which can be reached by ferry from the visitor's center, marks the memory of Japan's attack on the United States on December 7, 1941.

When you visit these historical landmarks around the world, you'll step into places almost untouched by time.

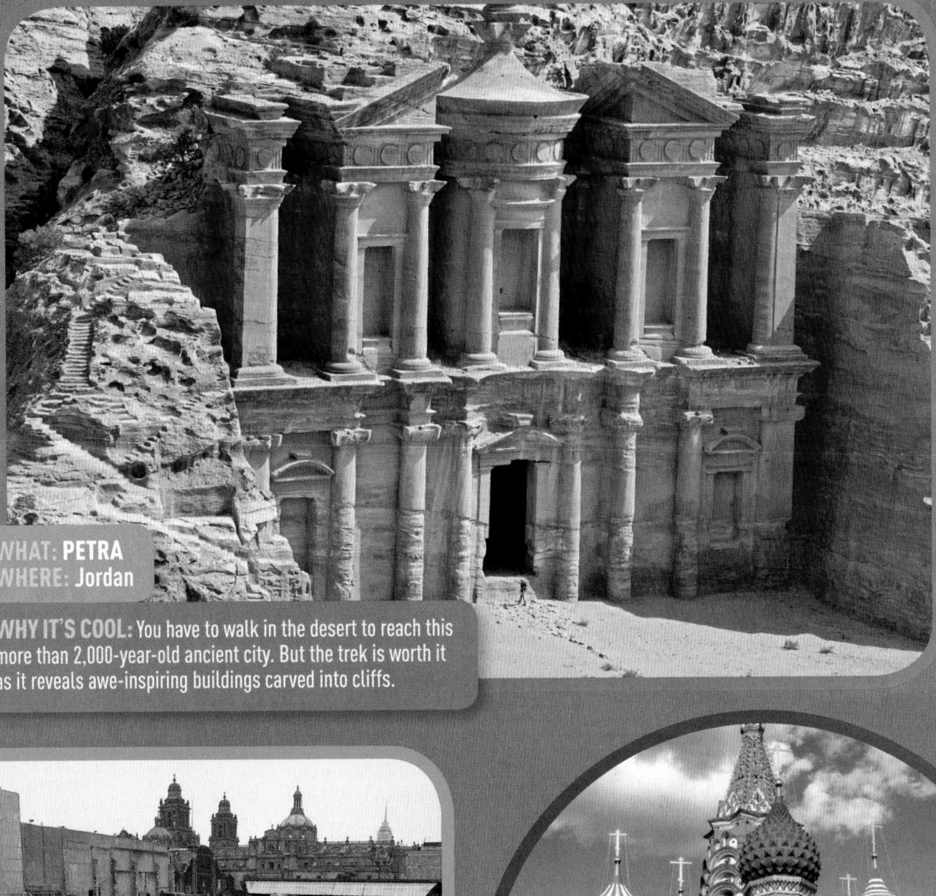

WHAT: PETRA
WHERE: Jordan

WHY IT'S COOL: You have to walk in the desert to reach this more than 2,000-year-old ancient city. But the trek is worth it as it reveals awe-inspiring buildings carved into cliffs.

WHAT: TEMPLO MAYOR
WHERE: Mexico City, Mexico

WHY IT'S COOL: With a pyramid as tall as a 15-story building as its centerpiece, this site was the heart of the Aztec community. The pyramid and temples have since been destroyed, but the artifacts and ruins that remain offer a glimpse of Aztec life over 600 years ago.

WHAT: ST. BASIL'S CATHEDRAL
WHERE: Moscow, Russia

WHY IT'S COOL: This colorful cathedral was commissioned by Ivan the Terrible in 1552 to celebrate a military victory. Today, it remains a stunning symbol of classic Russian architecture.

18 AMAZING FACTS ABOUT

1

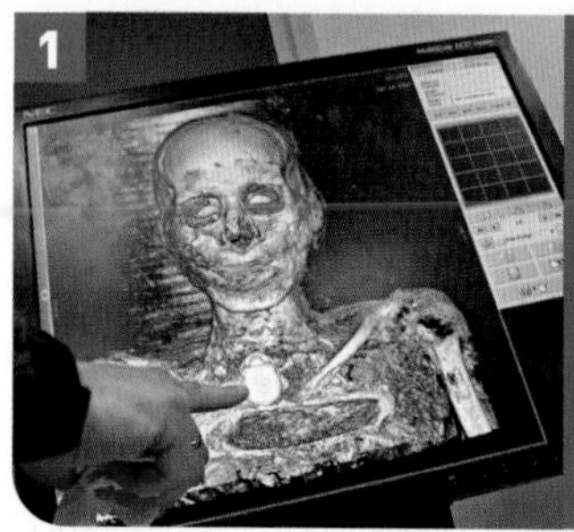

Just as doctors can use machines to look inside your body, they also use them to peer inside mummies.

2

Egyptians **mummified hippopotamuses,** apes, dogs, and cats.

3

WHEN MAKING A MUMMY, ANCIENT EGYPTIANS **THREW OUT THE BRAIN** BUT KEPT THE PERSON'S HEART AND OTHER ORGANS.

4

Mummies aren't just from long ago; the Soviet Union leader Vladimir Lenin was mummified in 1924.

5

Mummies don't weigh much because all of their water content has been dried up.

6

AN EGYPTIAN MUMMY WAS BURIED IN A SARCOPHAGUS, OR STONE COFFIN, THAT SOMETIMES WAS SHAPED LIKE **A HUMAN BODY** AND DECORATED TO LOOK LIKE THE DEAD PERSON.

7

King Tut's tomb was discovered by Howard Carter in 1922, but there is evidence that grave robbers **had gotten there first.**

8

Puruchuco, a site near Lima, Peru, contained more than 2,200 mummies.

9

Preserved by chemicals or by their natural environment, THE BODIES OF MUMMIES **DON'T DECAY.**

10

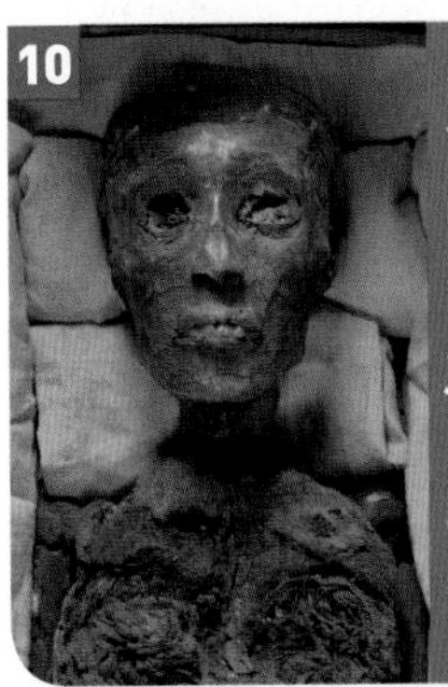

Tutankhamun, or **"King Tut,"** died when he was only **19 years old,** but he had already been **pharaoh for ten years.**

11

The 2,500-year-old Siberian ice maiden mummy was found **frozen in ice;** HER EYEBALLS HAD BEEN REPLACED BY TUFTS OF FUR.

12

EGYPTIAN MUMMIES ARE OFTEN FOUND WITH A RISING SUN AMULET, WHICH SYMBOLIZED ETERNAL LIFE.

13

A MUMMY FROM A.D. 450 THAT WAS DISCOVERED IN A PERU PYRAMID HAD IMAGES OF SPIDERS AND SNAKES TATTOOED ON HER BODY.

14

Scientists can tell that a 5,300-year-old iceman mummy died when someone shot him from behind WITH AN ARROW.

MUMMIES

15

ONE EGYPTIAN MUMMY WAS FOUND WITH HIS TONGUE STICKING OUT.

16

So-called bog mummies are preserved in cold peat bogs in northern Europe. **They look exactly like they did when they died—they even have hair.**

17

In 2007, a reindeer herder found a baby woolly mammoth mummy in the Russian Arctic. She was some 40,000 years old.

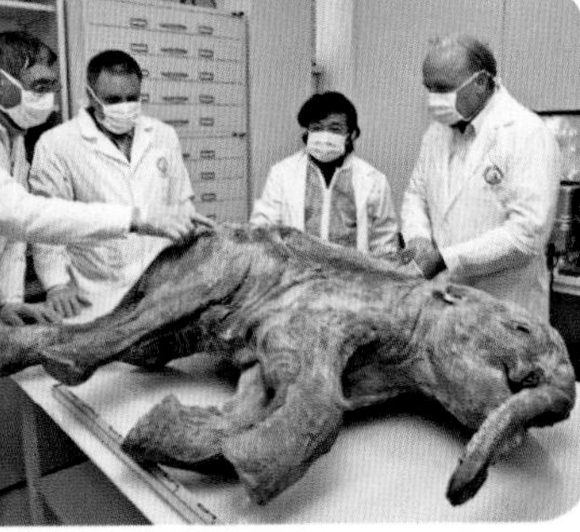

18

THE WORD "MUMMY" COMES FROM THE ARABIC WORD FOR THE BLACK, GOOEY SUBSTANCE THAT PEOPLE BELIEVE WAS USED TO PREPARE EGYPTIAN MUMMIES.

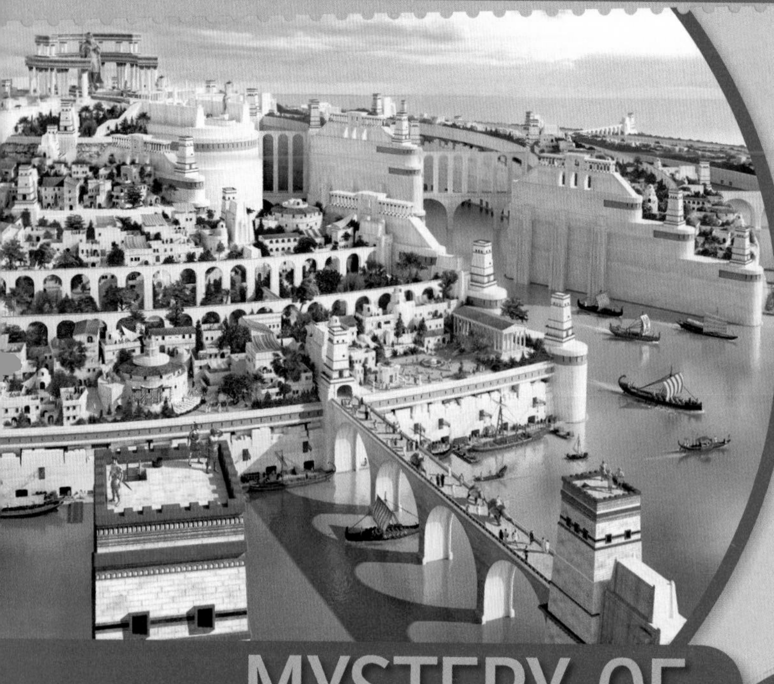

CAN AN ISLAND PARADISE DISAPPEAR IN A DAY? THAT'S WHAT ONE ANCIENT LEGEND SAYS ABOUT THE EMPIRE OF ATLANTIS. TODAY, SCIENTISTS CONTINUE TO TRY TO LOCATE THE LOST ISLAND.

MYSTERY OF ATLANTIS

Plato, an ancient Greek philosopher, described Atlantis as a wealthy city with palaces, a silver-and-gold temple, abundant fruit trees, and elephants roaming the land. But the good times didn't last. Plato wrote that sudden earthquakes jolted Atlantis and whipped up waves that sank the island within a day.

Was Plato's story true? Recently, researchers in Spain used underground radar in search of buried buildings. Results showed something like a crumbled wall in the soil 40 feet (12.1 m) below, but because there was water beneath the site, a dig seemed improbable.

Other explorers think Atlantis is in the Mediterranean Sea, where images supposedly show remains of canals and walls. Others are skeptical about the story entirely. Such an advanced city, they say, couldn't have been built in the Stone Age, when Plato's story was set.

So, was Atlantis real, fake, or something in between? The search continues.

THE SECRETS OF STONEHENGE

Could a new discovery help solve this ancient puzzle?

Dazzling rays from the sun burst through a strange ring of stones set on a grassy field. This huge monument, called Stonehenge, has towered above England's Salisbury Plain for thousands of years—but it's still one of the world's biggest mysteries.

THE UNEXPLAINED

For centuries people have tried to unlock Stonehenge's secrets.

Some theories have suggested that migrants from continental Europe built the site as an astronomical observatory or as a temple to the sun and moon gods. No theories have been proven. But a new discovery may provide more information about the builders of Stonehenge and could help explain why the monument was constructed in this region.

HUNTING FOR CLUES

While digging around a spring about a mile and a half (2.4 km) from Stonehenge, archaeologist David Jacques and his team uncovered hundreds of bones belonging to aurochs—a species of cattle twice the size of a modern-day bull that thrived in ancient times. In fact the site held the largest collection of auroch bones ever found in Europe. That suggests that the spring was a pit stop along an auroch migration route where the animals drank water.

The team also unearthed 31,000 flints, a stone tool used for hunting. "We started to wonder if the area was also a hunting ground and feasting site for ancient people," Jacques says. "Just one auroch could've fed a hundred people, so the place would've been a big draw."

The animal bones and tools date back to 7500 B.C. The age of the artifacts caused Jacques to conclude that people moved to the region around 9,500 years ago to hunt auroch. And he thinks descendants of these settlers assembled the mysterious stone ring.

TREASURE!

Check out these stories of lost treasures found!

SUNKEN GOLD

In the summer of 2013, Rick Schmitt was scuba diving off the coast of eastern Florida when he discovered $300,000 worth of gold chains, coins, and jewelry on the ocean floor. The riches date back to the 1700s, when Spanish ships called galleons often ferried treasure from North and South America to Europe. In July 1715 a hurricane sank 11 galleons near Florida's coast, scattering valuables along the seafloor. Nearly 300 years later, Schmitt found only a portion of this loot. Many more riches still linger at the bottom of the ocean.

MAYA RICHES

During a 2012 expedition to the jungles of northern Guatemala, a team of archaeologists discovered a tomb filled with precious stones and ancient bones dating back to the seventh century. Maya hieroglyphics on a jar in the burial chamber revealed that the bones may have belonged to a warrior queen. The exact worth of the treasure hasn't been calculated—but most people agree that this find is priceless.

PALACE PRIZE

In 2011, workers renovating Hanuman Dhoka, a palace that once housed Nepal's royal family, came upon three safes and a tank filled with gold jewelry, bows with silver arrows, and gold masks. The loot was thought to be at least 500-year-old offerings made to Hindu gods and goddesses, and no one knows for sure why it was placed here. But with the treasure soon on exhibit, the renovated palace museum won't just be spruced up—it'll be blinged out!

CITY IN THE SKY

Scientists search for clues about why the community of Machu Picchu was built.

How do you pronounce Machu Picchu? Like this: MAH-chu PEA-chu.

Peru's Colca Canyon is nearly twice as deep as the Grand Canyon.

Perched nearly 8,000 feet (2,438 m) high is an old city made of stone. Known as Machu Picchu (or "Old Peak" in the local language of Quechua), the site has been here for centuries. But not even the descendants of the builders know for sure why it was built.

THE RISE OF MACHU PICCHU

Machu Picchu was constructed some 500 years ago during the Inca Empire. Archaeologists believe that it took hundreds of builders to construct the mountaintop city, but after the Inca Empire fell in the mid-1500s, Machu Picchu was abandoned.

Few knew about the neglected metropolis until an American explorer stumbled upon its ruins in July 1911. As news of his discovery spread, so did theories about the mysterious sky-high city. Many people thought Machu Picchu was a fortress. Some have even suggested that aliens built it to have a base on Earth. (Yeah, not likely.) Recently scientists digging for clues about the purpose of Machu Picchu have made some interesting finds.

LOVE OF THE LAND

Anthropologist and National Geographic Explorer-in-Residence Johan Reinhard thinks answers to the Machu Picchu puzzle lie in the surrounding landscape. "The Inca believed that gods lived in landforms and bodies of water," Reinhard says. "And they worshipped these sites." During one expedition to Machu Picchu, Reinhard found several large stones carved into the shape of the surrounding peaks. "The area was important to the Inca," Reinhard says. "And Machu Picchu may have been built to honor this cherished landscape where mighty gods were thought to dwell."

STAR POWER

It's likely that the site was also a gathering place during astronomical events such as the summer and winter solstices (the longest and shortest days of the year). Celestial events were important to the Inca, even affecting how buildings were designed. For instance, a temple in the city was built so that the sun shines into its window on the morning of the winter solstice, illuminating a stone shrine.

So are the mysteries of Machu Picchu solved? Not quite. Evidence certainly exists that the site was built to honor sacred land and used as an astronomical observatory. But without written records—or a time machine to travel back and question the Inca—we may never be absolutely sure.

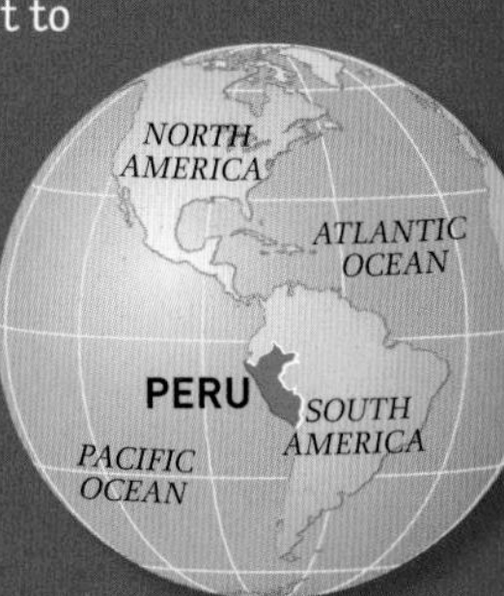

WAR!

Since the beginning of time, different countries, territories, and cultures have feuded with each other over land, power, and politics. Major military conflicts include the following wars:

1095–1291 THE CRUSADES
Starting late in the 11th century, these wars over religion were fought in the Middle East for nearly 200 years.

1337–1453 HUNDRED YEARS' WAR
France and England battled over rights to land for more than a century before the French eventually drove the English out in 1453.

1754–1763 FRENCH AND INDIAN WAR (part of Europe's Seven Years' War)
A nine-year war between the British and French for control of North America.

1775–1783 AMERICAN REVOLUTION
Thirteen British colonies in America united to reject the rule of the British government and to form the United States of America.

1861–1865 AMERICAN CIVIL WAR
Occurred when the northern states (the Union) went to war with the southern states, which had seceded, or withdrawn, to form the Confederate States of America. Slavery was one of the key issues in the Civil War.

1910–1920 MEXICAN REVOLUTION
The people of Mexico revolted against the rule of dictator President Porfirio Díaz, leading to his eventual defeat and to a democratic government.

1914–1918 WORLD WAR I
The assassination of Austria's Archduke Ferdinand by a Serbian nationalist sparked this wide-spreading war. The U.S. entered after Germany sunk the British ship *Lusitania,* killing more than 120 Americans.

1918–1920 RUSSIAN CIVIL WAR
Following the 1917 Russian Revolution, this conflict pitted the Communist Red Army against the foreign-backed White Army. The Red Army won, leading to the establishment of the Union of Soviet Socialist Republics (U.S.S.R.) in 1922.

1936–1939 SPANISH CIVIL WAR
Aid from Italy and Germany helped the Nationalists gain victory over the Communist-supported Republicans. The war resulted in the loss of more than 300,000 lives and increased tension in Europe leading up to World War II.

1939–1945 WORLD WAR II
This massive conflict in Europe, Asia, and North Africa involved many countries that aligned with the two sides: the Allies and the Axis. After the bombing of Pearl Harbor in Hawaii in 1941, the U.S. entered the war on the side of the Allies. More than 50 million people died during the war.

1946–1949 CHINESE CIVIL WAR
Also known as the "War of Liberation," this pitted the Communist and Nationalist parties in China against each other. The Communists won.

1950–1953 KOREAN WAR
Kicked off when the Communist forces of North Korea, with backing from the Soviet Union, invaded their democratic neighbor to the south. A coalition of 16 countries from the United Nations stepped in to support South Korea.

1950s–1975 VIETNAM WAR
Fought between the Communist North, supported by allies including China, and the government of South Vietnam, supported by the United States and other anticommunist nations.

1967 SIX-DAY WAR
A battle for land between Israel and the states of Egypt, Jordan, and Syria. The outcome resulted in Israel's gaining control of coveted territory, including the Gaza Strip and the West Bank.

1991–PRESENT SOMALI CIVIL WAR
Began when Somalia's last president, a dictator named Mohamed Siad Barre, was overthrown. The war has led to years of fighting and anarchy.

2001–2014 WAR IN AFGHANISTAN
After attacks in the U.S. by the terrorist group al Qaeda, a coalition that eventually included more than 40 countries invaded Afghanistan to find Osama bin Laden and other al Qaeda members and to dismantle the Taliban. Bin Laden was killed in a U.S. covert operation in 2011. The North Atlantic Treaty Organization (NATO) took control of the coalition's combat mission in 2003. That combat mission officially ended in 2014.

2003–2011 WAR IN IRAQ
A coalition led by the U.S., and including Britain, Australia, and Spain, invaded Iraq over suspicions that Iraq had weapons of mass destruction.

100th Anniversary

Armistice Day

It was the 11th hour on the 11th day of the 11th month. And on such a profound period in time in 1918, an even more epic moment occurred. The Armistice—an agreement marking the end of four years of fighting in the First World War—began.

100 years have passed since representatives from both sides agreed to end the Great War with a stroke of a pen inside a railway carriage parked in a remote forest north of Paris, France. The Armistice outlined specific rules to ensure that Germany would not restart the war with the Allies—made up of the British Empire, France, Belgium, Russia and the USA. Germany, in particular, had to give up thousands of weapons, airplanes, and submarines and disarm warships. They also had to turn over any prisoners of war they were holding and disclose details on mines and traps they'd set during the war.

While the signing of the Treaty of Versailles half a year later officially ended World War I, this agreement halted the bloodshed and essentially forced Germany to take blame for World War I. Germany was assigned to pay reparations, or war debt, to cover the damage caused over those four years of fighting. It took some 92 years for Germany to pay off the whopping bill, which hovered around $402 billion in today's money.

Today, we honor Armistice Day—also known as Veterans Day or Remembrance Day—on November 11 of every year. It's a time to reflect on World War I and all wars to follow, ensuring that those who made the ultimate sacrifice for their country—and for peace throughout the world—will never be forgotten.

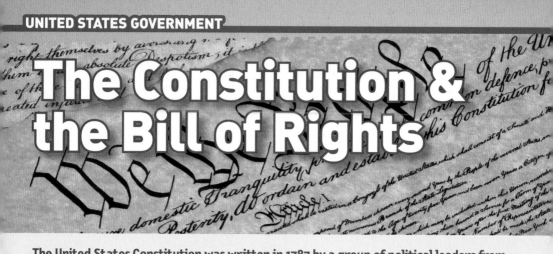

The Constitution & the Bill of Rights

The United States Constitution was written in 1787 by a group of political leaders from the 13 states that made up the U.S. at the time. Thirty-nine men, including Benjamin Franklin and James Madison, signed the document to create a national government. While some feared the creation of a strong federal government, all 13 states eventually ratified, or approved, the Constitution, making it the law of the land. The Constitution has three major parts: the preamble, the articles, and the amendments.

Here's a summary of what topics are covered in each part of the Constitution. Check out the Constitution online or at your local library for the full text.

THE PREAMBLE outlines the basic purposes of the government: ***We the People of the United States,*** *in order to form a more perfect Union, establish justice, insure domestic tranquility, provide for the common defense, promote the general welfare, and secure the blessings of liberty to ourselves and our posterity, do ordain and establish this Constitution for the United States of America.*

SEVEN ARTICLES outline the powers of Congress, the president, and the court system:

Article I outlines the legislative branch—the Senate and the House of Representatives—and its powers and responsibilities.

Article II outlines the executive branch—the Presidency—and its powers and responsibilities.

Article III outlines the judicial branch—the court system—and its powers and responsibilities.

Article IV describes the individual states' rights and powers.

Article V outlines the amendment process.

Article VI establishes the Constitution as the law of the land.

Article VII gives the requirements for the Constitution to be approved.

THE AMENDMENTS, or additions to the Constitution, were put in later as needed. In 1791, the first ten amendments, known as the **Bill of Rights,** were added. Since then another seventeen amendments have been added. This is the Bill of Rights:

1st Amendment: guarantees freedom of religion, speech, and the press, and the right to assemble and petition. The U.S. may not have a national religion.

2nd Amendment: discusses the militia and the right of people to bear arms

3rd Amendment: prohibits the military or troops from using private homes without consent

4th Amendment: protects people and their homes from search, arrest, or seizure without probable cause or a warrant

5th Amendment: grants people the right to have a trial and prevents punishment before prosecution; protects private property from being taken without compensation

6th Amendment: guarantees the right to a speedy and public trial

7th Amendment: guarantees a trial by jury in certain cases

8th Amendment: forbids "cruel and unusual punishments"

9th Amendment: states that the Constitution is not all-encompassing and does not deny people other, unspecified rights

10th Amendment: grants the powers not covered by the Constitution to the states and the people

Read the full text version of the United States Constitution at constitutioncenter.org/constitution/full-text

Branches of Government

The **UNITED STATES GOVERNMENT** is divided into three branches: **executive, legislative**, and **judicial**. The system of checks and balances is a way to control power and to make sure one branch can't take the reins of government. For example, most of the president's actions require the approval of Congress. Likewise, the laws passed in Congress must be signed by the president before they can take effect.

White House

Executive Branch

The Constitution lists the central powers of the president: to serve as commander in chief of the armed forces; make treaties with other nations; grant pardons; inform Congress on the state of the union; and appoint ambassadors, officials, and judges. The executive branch includes the president and the 15 governmental departments.

Legislative Branch

The U.S. Capitol in Washington, D.C.

This branch is made up of Congress—the Senate and the House of Representatives. The Constitution grants Congress the power to make laws. Congress is made up of elected representatives from each state. Each state has two representatives in the Senate, while the number of representatives in the House is determined by the size of the state's population. Washington, D.C., and the territories elect nonvoting representatives to the House of Representatives. The Founding Fathers set up this system as a compromise between big states—which wanted representation based on population—and small states—which wanted all states to have equal representation rights.

Judicial Branch

The judicial branch is composed of the federal court system—the U.S. Supreme Court, the courts of appeals, and the district courts. The Supreme Court is the most powerful court. Its motto is "Equal Justice Under Law." This influential court is responsible for interpreting the Constitution and applying it to the cases that it hears. The decisions of the Supreme Court are absolute—they are the final word on any legal question.

There are nine justices on the Supreme Court. They are appointed by the president of the United States and confirmed by the Senate.

The U.S. Supreme Court Building in Washington, D.C.

The Indian Experience

American Indians are indigenous to North and South America—they are the people who were here before Columbus and other European explorers came to these lands. They lived in nations, tribes, and bands across both continents. For decades following the arrival of Europeans in 1492, American Indians clashed with the newcomers who had ruptured the Indians' way of living.

Tribal Land

During the 19th century, both United States legislation and military action restricted the movement of American Indians, forcing them to live on reservations and attempting to dismantle tribal structures. For centuries Indians were displaced or killed, or became assimilated into the general U.S. population. In 1924 the Indian Citizenship Act granted citizenship to all American Indians. Unfortunately, this was not enough to end the social discrimination and mistreatment that many Indians have faced. Today, American Indians living in the U.S. still face many challenges.

Healing the Past

Many members of the 560-plus recognized tribes in the United States live primarily on reservations. Some tribes have more than one reservation, while others have none. Together these reservations make up less than 3 percent of the nation's land area. The tribal governments on reservations have the right to form their own governments and to enforce laws, similar to individual states. Many feel that this sovereignty is still not enough to right the wrongs of the past: They hope for a change in the U.S. government's relationship with American Indians.

Some American Indians used cranberry juice to dye clothing, rugs, and blankets.

Thousands of years ago, some American Indians may have kept bobcats as pets.

Top: A Navajo youth dances at a powwow.
Middle: A Salish woman in traditional dress in Montana
Bottom: Little Shell men in traditional costume

The president of the United States is the chief of the executive branch, the commander in chief of the U.S. armed forces, and head of the federal government. Elected every four years, the president is the highest policymaker in the nation. The 22nd Amendment (1951) says that no person may be elected to the office of president more than twice. There have been 45 presidencies and 44 presidents.

GEORGE WASHINGTON

1st President of the United States ★ 1789–1797

BORN Feb. 22, 1732, in Pope's Creek, Westmoreland County, VA
POLITICAL PARTY Federalist
NO. OF TERMS two
VICE PRESIDENT John Adams
DIED Dec. 14, 1799, at Mount Vernon, VA

JOHN ADAMS

2nd President of the United States ★ 1797–1801

BORN Oct. 30, 1735, in Braintree (now Quincy), MA
POLITICAL PARTY Federalist
NO. OF TERMS one
VICE PRESIDENT Thomas Jefferson
DIED July 4, 1826, in Quincy, MA

THOMAS JEFFERSON

3rd President of the United States ★ 1801–1809

BORN April 13, 1743, at Shadwell, Goochland (now Albemarle) County, VA
POLITICAL PARTY Democratic-Republican
NO. OF TERMS two
VICE PRESIDENTS 1st term: Aaron Burr
2nd term: George Clinton
DIED July 4, 1826, at Monticello, Charlottesville, VA

***Jeffersonia diphylla* wildflowers** are named after Thomas Jefferson.

JAMES MADISON

4th President of the United States ★ 1809–1817

BORN March 16, 1751, at Belle Grove, Port Conway, VA
POLITICAL PARTY Democratic-Republican
NO. OF TERMS two
VICE PRESIDENTS 1st term: George Clinton
2nd term: Elbridge Gerry
DIED June 28, 1836, at Montpelier, Orange County, VA

JAMES MONROE

5th President of the United States ★ 1817–1825

BORN April 28, 1758, in Westmoreland County, VA
POLITICAL PARTY Democratic-Republican
NO. OF TERMS two
VICE PRESIDENT Daniel D. Tompkins
DIED July 4, 1831, in New York, NY

JOHN QUINCY ADAMS

6th President of the United States ★ 1825–1829

BORN July 11, 1767, in Braintree (now Quincy), MA
POLITICAL PARTY Democratic-Republican
NO. OF TERMS one
VICE PRESIDENT John Caldwell Calhoun
DIED Feb. 23, 1848, at the U.S. Capitol, Washington, DC

ANDREW JACKSON

7th President of the United States ★ 1829–1837

BORN March 15, 1767, in the Waxhaw region, NC and SC
POLITICAL PARTY Democrat
NO. OF TERMS two
VICE PRESIDENTS 1st term: John Caldwell Calhoun
2nd term: Martin Van Buren
DIED June 8, 1845, in Nashville, TN

MARTIN VAN BUREN

8th President of the United States ★ 1837–1841

BORN Dec. 5, 1782, in Kinderhook, NY
POLITICAL PARTY Democrat
NO. OF TERMS one
VICE PRESIDENT Richard M. Johnson
DIED July 24, 1862, in Kinderhook, NY

WILLIAM HENRY HARRISON

9th President of the United States ★ 1841

BORN Feb. 9, 1773, in Charles City County, VA
POLITICAL PARTY Whig
NO. OF TERMS one (cut short by death)
VICE PRESIDENT John Tyler
DIED April 4, 1841, in the White House, Washington, DC

JOHN TYLER

10th President of the United States ★ 1841–1845

BORN March 29, 1790, in Charles City County, VA
POLITICAL PARTY Whig
NO. OF TERMS one (partial)
VICE PRESIDENT none
DIED Jan. 18, 1862, in Richmond, VA

JAMES K. POLK

11th President of the United States ★ 1845–1849

BORN Nov. 2, 1795, near Pineville, Mecklenburg County, NC
POLITICAL PARTY Democrat
NO. OF TERMS one
VICE PRESIDENT George Mifflin Dallas
DIED June 15, 1849, in Nashville, TN

ZACHARY TAYLOR

12th President of the United States ★ 1849–1850

BORN Nov. 24, 1784, in Orange County, VA
POLITICAL PARTY Whig
NO. OF TERMS one (cut short by death)
VICE PRESIDENT Millard Fillmore
DIED July 9, 1850, in the White House, Washington, DC

MILLARD FILLMORE

13th President of the United States ★ 1850–1853

BORN Jan. 7, 1800, in Cayuga County, NY
POLITICAL PARTY Whig
NO. OF TERMS one (partial)
VICE PRESIDENT none
DIED March 8, 1874, in Buffalo, NY

FRANKLIN PIERCE

14th President of the United States ★ 1853–1857

BORN Nov. 23, 1804, in Hillsborough (now Hillsboro), NH
POLITICAL PARTY Democrat
NO. OF TERMS one
VICE PRESIDENT William Rufus De Vane King
DIED Oct. 8, 1869, in Concord, NH

Franklin Pierce was the **FIRST PRESIDENT** to use a **FULL-TIME BODYGUARD.**

JAMES BUCHANAN

15th President of the United States ★ 1857–1861

BORN April 23, 1791, in Cove Gap, PA
POLITICAL PARTY Democrat
NO. OF TERMS one
VICE PRESIDENT John Cabell Breckinridge
DIED June 1, 1868, in Lancaster, PA

ABRAHAM LINCOLN

16th President of the United States ★ 1861–1865

BORN Feb. 12, 1809, near Hodgenville, KY
POLITICAL PARTY Republican (formerly Whig)
NO. OF TERMS two (assassinated)
VICE PRESIDENTS 1st term: Hannibal Hamlin
2nd term: Andrew Johnson
DIED April 15, 1865, in Washington, DC

ANDREW JOHNSON

17th President of the United States ★ 1865–1869

BORN Dec. 29, 1808, in Raleigh, NC
POLITICAL PARTY Democrat
NO. OF TERMS one (partial)
VICE PRESIDENT none
DIED July 31, 1875, in Carter's Station, TN

ULYSSES S. GRANT

18th President of the United States ★ 1869–1877

BORN April 27, 1822, in Point Pleasant, OH
POLITICAL PARTY Republican
NO. OF TERMS two
VICE PRESIDENTS 1st term: Schuyler Colfax
2nd term: Henry Wilson
DIED July 23, 1885, in Mount McGregor, NY

RUTHERFORD B. HAYES

19th President of the United States ★ 1877–1881

BORN Oct. 4, 1822, in Delaware, OH
POLITICAL PARTY Republican
NO. OF TERMS one
VICE PRESIDENT William Almon Wheeler
DIED Jan. 17, 1893, in Fremont, OH

JAMES A. GARFIELD

20th President of the United States ★ 1881

BORN Nov. 19, 1831, near Orange, OH
POLITICAL PARTY Republican
NO. OF TERMS one (assassinated)
VICE PRESIDENT Chester A. Arthur
DIED Sept. 19, 1881, in Elberon, NJ

CHESTER A. ARTHUR

21st President of the United States ★ 1881–1885

BORN Oct. 5, 1829, in Fairfield, VT
POLITICAL PARTY Republican
NO. OF TERMS one (partial)
VICE PRESIDENT none
DIED Nov. 18, 1886, in New York, NY

GROVER CLEVELAND

22nd and 24th President of the United States 1885–1889 ★ 1893–1897

BORN March 18, 1837, in Caldwell, NJ
POLITICAL PARTY Democrat
NO. OF TERMS two (nonconsecutive)
VICE PRESIDENTS 1st administration: Thomas Andrews Hendricks
2nd administration: Adlai Ewing Stevenson
DIED June 24, 1908, in Princeton, NJ

BENJAMIN HARRISON

23rd President of the United States ★ 1889–1893

BORN Aug. 20, 1833, in North Bend, OH
POLITICAL PARTY Republican
NO. OF TERMS one
VICE PRESIDENT Levi Parsons Morton
DIED March 13, 1901, in Indianapolis, IN

WILLIAM MCKINLEY

25th President of the United States ★ 1897–1901

BORN Jan. 29, 1843, in Niles, OH
POLITICAL PARTY Republican
NO. OF TERMS two (assassinated)
VICE PRESIDENTS 1st term: Garret Augustus Hobart
2nd term: Theodore Roosevelt
DIED Sept. 14, 1901, in Buffalo, NY

THEODORE ROOSEVELT

26th President of the United States ★ 1901–1909

BORN Oct. 27, 1858, in New York, NY
POLITICAL PARTY Republican
NO. OF TERMS one, plus balance of McKinley's term
VICE PRESIDENTS 1st term: none
2nd term: Charles Warren Fairbanks
DIED Jan. 6, 1919, in Oyster Bay, NY

WILLIAM HOWARD TAFT

27th President of the United States ★ 1909–1913

BORN Sept. 15, 1857, in Cincinnati, OH
POLITICAL PARTY Republican
NO. OF TERMS one
VICE PRESIDENT James Schoolcraft Sherman
DIED March 8, 1930, in Washington, DC

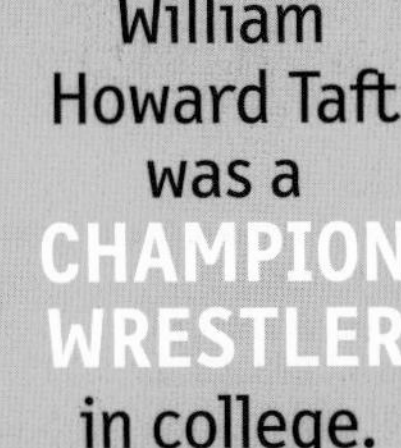

William Howard Taft was a **CHAMPION WRESTLER** in college.

WOODROW WILSON

28th President of the United States ★ 1913–1921

BORN Dec. 29, 1856, in Staunton, VA
POLITICAL PARTY Democrat
NO. OF TERMS two
VICE PRESIDENT Thomas Riley Marshall
DIED Feb. 3, 1924, in Washington, DC

WARREN G. HARDING

29th President of the United States ★ 1921–1923

BORN Nov. 2, 1865, in Caledonia (now Blooming Grove), OH
POLITICAL PARTY Republican
NO. OF TERMS one (died while in office)
VICE PRESIDENT Calvin Coolidge
DIED Aug. 2, 1923, in San Francisco, CA

CALVIN COOLIDGE

30th President of the United States ★ 1923–1929

BORN July 4, 1872, in Plymouth, VT
POLITICAL PARTY Republican
NO. OF TERMS one, plus balance of Harding's term
VICE PRESIDENTS 1st term: none
2nd term: Charles Gates Dawes
DIED Jan. 5, 1933, in Northampton, MA

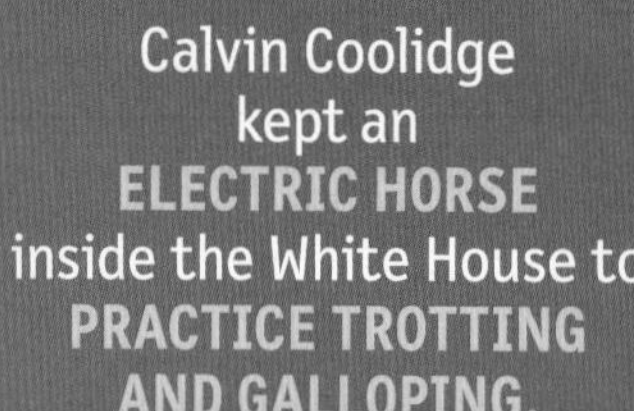

Calvin Coolidge kept an **ELECTRIC HORSE** inside the White House to **PRACTICE TROTTING AND GALLOPING.**

HERBERT HOOVER

31st President of the United States ★ 1929–1933

BORN Aug. 10, 1874, in West Branch, IA
POLITICAL PARTY Republican
NO. OF TERMS one
VICE PRESIDENT Charles Curtis
DIED Oct. 20, 1964, in New York, NY

FRANKLIN D. ROOSEVELT

32nd President of the United States ★ 1933–1945

BORN Jan. 30, 1882, in Hyde Park, NY
POLITICAL PARTY Democrat
NO. OF TERMS four (died while in office)
VICE PRESIDENTS 1st & 2nd terms: John Nance Garner; 3rd term: Henry Agard Wallace; 4th term: Harry S. Truman
DIED April 12, 1945, in Warm Springs, GA

HARRY S. TRUMAN

33rd President of the United States ★ 1945–1953

BORN May 8, 1884, in Lamar, MO
POLITICAL PARTY Democrat
NO. OF TERMS one, plus balance of Franklin D. Roosevelt's term
VICE PRESIDENTS 1st term: none
2nd term: Alben William Barkley
DIED Dec. 26, 1972, in Independence, MO

DWIGHT D. EISENHOWER

34th President of the United States ★ 1953–1961

BORN Oct. 14, 1890, in Denison, TX
POLITICAL PARTY Republican
NO. OF TERMS two
VICE PRESIDENT Richard M. Nixon
DIED March 28, 1969, in Washington, DC

JOHN F. KENNEDY

35th President of the United States ★ 1961–1963

BORN May 29, 1917, in Brookline, MA
POLITICAL PARTY Democrat
NO. OF TERMS one (assassinated)
VICE PRESIDENT Lyndon B. Johnson
DIED Nov. 22, 1963, in Dallas, TX

LYNDON B. JOHNSON

36th President of the United States ★ 1963–1969

BORN Aug. 27, 1908, near Stonewall, TX
POLITICAL PARTY Democrat
NO. OF TERMS one, plus balance of Kennedy's term
VICE PRESIDENTS 1st term: none
2nd term: Hubert Horatio Humphrey
DIED Jan. 22, 1973, near San Antonio, TX

RICHARD NIXON

37th President of the United States ★ 1969–1974

BORN Jan. 9, 1913, in Yorba Linda, CA
POLITICAL PARTY Republican
NO. OF TERMS two (resigned)
VICE PRESIDENTS 1st term & 2nd term (partial): Spiro Theodore Agnew; 2nd term (balance): Gerald R. Ford
DIED April 22, 1994, in New York, NY

GERALD R. FORD

38th President of the United States ★ 1974–1977

BORN July 14, 1913, in Omaha, NE
POLITICAL PARTY Republican
NO. OF TERMS one (partial)
VICE PRESIDENT Nelson Aldrich Rockefeller
DIED Dec. 26, 2006, in Rancho Mirage, CA

JIMMY CARTER

39th President of the United States ★ 1977–1981

BORN Oct. 1, 1924, in Plains, GA
POLITICAL PARTY Democrat
NO. OF TERMS one
VICE PRESIDENT Walter Frederick (Fritz) Mondale

RONALD REAGAN

40th President of the United States ★ 1981–1989

BORN Feb. 6, 1911, in Tampico, IL
POLITICAL PARTY Republican
NO. OF TERMS two
VICE PRESIDENT George H. W. Bush
DIED June 5, 2004, in Los Angeles, CA

GEORGE H.W. BUSH

41st President of the United States ★ 1989–1993

BORN June 12, 1924, in Milton, MA
POLITICAL PARTY Republican
NO. OF TERMS one
VICE PRESIDENT James Danforth (Dan) Quayle III

WILLIAM J. CLINTON

42nd President of the United States ★ 1993–2001

BORN Aug. 19, 1946, in Hope, AR
POLITICAL PARTY Democrat
NO. OF TERMS two
VICE PRESIDENT Albert Gore, Jr.

GEORGE W. BUSH

43rd President of the United States ★ 2001–2009

BORN July 6, 1946, in New Haven, CT
POLITICAL PARTY Republican
NO. OF TERMS two
VICE PRESIDENT Richard Bruce Cheney

BARACK OBAMA

44th President of the United States ★ 2009–2017

BORN Aug. 4, 1961, in Honolulu, HI
POLITICAL PARTY Democrat
NO. OF TERMS two
VICE PRESIDENT Joseph Biden

Donald Trump LIKES CHERRY VANILLA ICE CREAM

DONALD J. TRUMP

45th President of the United States ★ 2017–present

BORN June 14, 1946, in Queens, NY
POLITICAL PARTY Republican
NO. OF TERMS one
VICE PRESIDENT Mike Pence

Cool Things About AIR FORCE ONE

The president of the United States takes a lot of work trips as part of the job. But the commander in chief doesn't fly business class on a regular plane—he or she takes a private jet, *Air Force One*. Here are five reasons why *Air Force One* is the coolest plane in the air.

President Barack Obama flew OVER ONE MILLION MILES (1.6 million km) on more than 940 FLIGHTS aboard *Air Force One*.

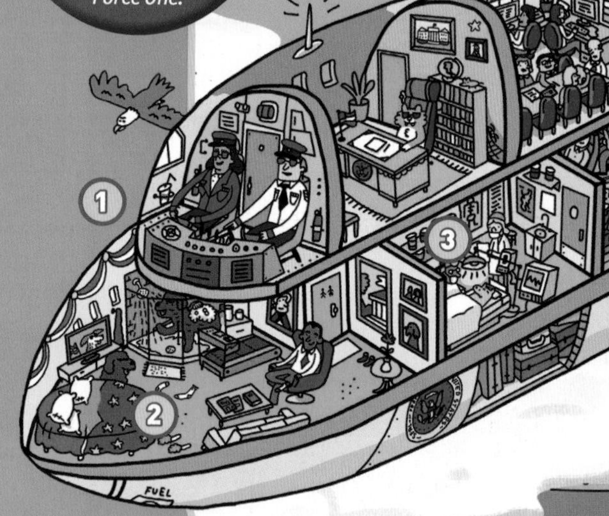

1

JUMBO JET

Most private planes are small. *Air Force One* is definitely *not*. The customized 747 airliner, designed to carry up to 102 passengers, has three levels, stands as tall as a six-story building, and is longer than five school buses. With a full load *Air Force One* can weigh up to a whopping 416 tons (377 t), which is the equivalent of more than 80 big elephants. In the air it's nimble enough to cruise at more than 600 miles an hour (966 km/h).

2

SUPER FIRST-CLASS

The president doesn't just get a big seat on *Air Force One*—there's a whole apartment. Located in the nose of the plane under the cockpit, the presidential suite includes a bedroom, a private bathroom with a shower, and enough space to exercise. The first family even has its own entrance to the plane. The president also has a private office, which explains one of the plane's nicknames, "the Flying White House."

3

DOCTOR ON BOARD

Air Force One doesn't have to make an emergency landing if there's a medical issue, because a doctor is on every flight. The clinic has an office with a small pharmacy, blood supplies, and an emergency operating table.

It costs about $180,000 AN HOUR to fly *Air Force One.*

President Obama visited MORE THAN 45 COUNTRIES during his presidency.

4

AIRPLANE FOOD

Unlike most midair meals, food on *Air Force One* is fine dining. Among the 26 crew members are cooks and several flight attendants who can serve 100 meals at a time from the airplane's two kitchens. The commander in chief can place orders 24/7 for whatever he or she wants—or doesn't want. (President George H.W. Bush banned broccoli from his flights on *Air Force One.*)

5

LIFT TO THE AIRPORT

The president doesn't have to fight traffic on the way to the airport. He or she takes a personal helicopter from the White House. Called *Marine One* because it's operated by the Marine Corps, the chopper lands on the White House lawn and ferries everyone over to the plane.

CIVIL RIGHTS

Although the Constitution protects the civil rights of American citizens, it has not always been able to protect all Americans from persecution or discrimination. During the first half of the 20th century, many Americans, particularly African Americans, were subjected to widespread discrimination and racism. By the mid-1950s, many people were eager to end the bonds of racism and bring freedom to all men and women.

The civil rights movement of the 1950s and 1960s sought to end the racial discrimination against African Americans, especially in the southern states. The movement wanted to restore the fundamentals of economic and social equality to those who had been oppressed.

The Little Rock Nine

The Little Rock Nine study during the weeks when they were blocked from school.

September 4, 1957, marked the first day of school at Little Rock Central High in Little Rock, Arkansas. But this was no ordinary back-to-school scene: Armed soldiers surrounded the entrance, awaiting the arrival of Central's first ever African-American students. The welcome was not warm, however, as the students—now known as the Little Rock Nine—were refused entry into the school by the soldiers and a group of protesters, angry about the potential integration. This did not deter the students, who gained the support of President Dwight D. Eisenhower to eventually earn their right to go to an integrated school. Today, the Little Rock Nine are still considered civil rights icons for challenging a racist system—and winning!

Key Events in the Civil Rights Movement

1954	The Supreme Court case *Brown* v. *Board of Education* declares school segregation illegal.
1955	Rosa Parks refuses to give up her bus seat to a white passenger and spurs a bus boycott.
1957	The Little Rock Nine help to integrate schools.
1960	Four black college students begin sit-ins at a restaurant in Greensboro, North Carolina.
1961	Freedom Rides to southern states begin as a way to protest segregation in transportation.
1963	Martin Luther King, Jr., leads the famous March on Washington.
1964	The Civil Rights Act, signed by President Lyndon B. Johnson, prohibits discrimination based on race, color, religion, sex, and national origin.
1967	Thurgood Marshall becomes the first African American to be named to the Supreme Court.
1968	President Lyndon B. Johnson signs the Civil Rights Act of 1968, which prohibits discrimination in the sale, rental, and financing of housing.

STONE OF HOPE: THE LEGACY OF MARTIN LUTHER KING, JR.

On April 4, 1968, Dr. Martin Luther King, Jr., was shot by James Earl Ray while standing on a hotel balcony in Memphis, Tennessee. The news of his death sent shock waves throughout the world: Dr. King, a Baptist minister and founder of the Southern Christian Leadership Conference (SCLC), was the most prominent civil rights leader of his time. His nonviolent protests and marches against segregation as well as his powerful speeches—including his famous "I Have a Dream" speech—motivated people to fight for justice for all.

Dr. King's dream lives on 50 years after his death through a memorial on the National Mall in Washington, D.C. Built in 2011, the memorial features a 30-foot (9-m) statue of Dr. King carved into a granite boulder named the "Stone of Hope."

Each year, thousands of visitors pay tribute to this inspirational figure, who will forever be remembered as a leader, a peacemaker, and a man who never backed down in his stand against racism.

EQUAL in '63 RIGHTS

"The time is always right to do what is right."

Martin Luther King, Jr. Memorial in Washington, D.C.

Martin Luther King, Jr. is the only non-president to have a national holiday dedicated in his honor.

There are about 900 streets named after Dr. King in the United States.

8 Daring Women in U.S. History!

Who: Dolley Madison
Lived: 1768–1849
Why she's daring: As the nation's First Lady from 1809 to 1817, she single-handedly saved a famous—and valuable—portrait of George Washington when it faced almost certain destruction during the War of 1812. As British troops approached the White House, Madison refused to leave until the painting was taken to safety.

Who: Nellie Tayloe Ross
Lived: 1876–1977
Why she's daring: In 1925, Ross became the nation's first woman governor after boldly campaigning for the Wyoming seat left vacant when her husband suddenly passed away. She went on to run the U.S. Mint from 1933 to 1953.

Who: Bessie Coleman
Lived: 1892–1926
Why she's daring: When U.S. flight schools denied her entry, Coleman traveled to France to earn her pilot's license and became the first African-American female aviator. Later, her high-flying, daredevil stunts in air shows earned her the nickname "Queen Bess."

Who: Sacagawea
Lived: c. 1788–1812
Why she's daring: As the only woman to accompany Lewis and Clark into the American West, Sacagawea's calm presence and smarts saved the expedition many times. She served as a Shoshone interpreter for the explorers, found edible plants to feed the crew, and even saved important documents and supplies from a capsizing boat.

Who: Julia Butterfly Hill
Lived: 1974–
Why she's daring: An environmental activist, Hill spent more than two years (1997–1999) living on a platform in a 1,000-year-old redwood tree named Luna. During her marathon tree-sit to protest aggressive logging practices, Hill endured extreme weather. Hill's efforts eventually lead to a settlement with the lumber company to forever protect Luna, saving the tree and its immediate surroundings.

Who: Annie Smith Peck
Lived: 1850–1935
Why she's daring: After taking up mountain climbing in her late 30s, former professor Smith Peck became the third woman to scale the Swiss Matterhorn. Her shocking choice to climb in pants instead of a skirt brought her international attention. In 1908, she became the first person to climb Peru's Mount Huascarán. Boasting remarkable strength and endurance, Smith Peck continued to climb well into her 80s.

Who: Dolores Huerta
Lived: 1930–
Why she's daring: As a teacher who saw many of her students living in poverty, Huerta rallied to raise awareness for the poor, especially among farmworkers, immigrants, and women. Later, she encouraged Hispanic women to enter politics, helping to increase in the number of women holding offices at the local, state, and federal levels. She received the Presidential Medal of Freedom in 2012.

Who: Lucille Ball
Lived: 1911–1989
Why she's daring: Famous for playing an iconic funny girl in the hit show *I Love Lucy*, Ball worked even more magic behind the screen. A pioneer in the entertainment industry, Ball was the first woman to head a major television studio. At the same time, she made 72 movies, cementing her position as one of the most legendary actresses and comediennes in the world.

Go back in time to seek the answers to this history quiz!

Write your answers on a piece of paper. Then check them below.

1. **Where is St. Basil's Cathedral located?**
   a. Prague, Czech Republic
   b. Moscow, Russia
   c. Ercolano, Italy
   d. Mexico City, Mexico

2. **True or false?** The Hundred Years' War lasted a hundred years.

3. **What do we honor on Armistice Day?**
   a. The first day of school
   b. The right to bear arms
   c. The start of World War I
   d. The end of World War I

4. **True or false?** Ancient Egyptians mummified hippopotamuses.

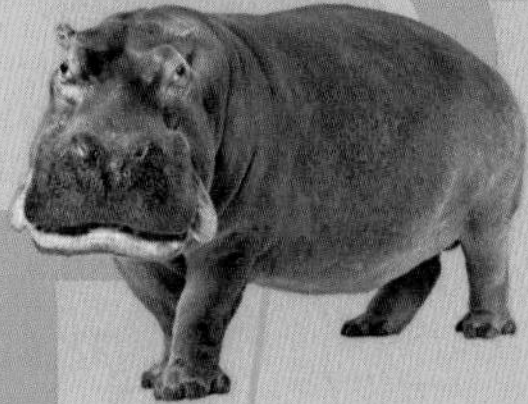

5. **What does Machu Picchu mean in the local Quechua language?**
   a. Where Gods Dwell
   b. Hidden City
   c. Old Peak
   d. Don't Look Down

Not **STUMPED** yet? Check out the *NATIONAL GEOGRAPHIC KIDS QUIZ WHIZ* collection for more crazy **HISTORY** questions!

ANSWERS:
1. b; 2. False. The war lasted longer than 100 years (1337–1453); 3. d; 4. True; 5. c

HOMEWORK HELP

Brilliant Biographies

A biography is the story of a person's life. It can be a brief summary or a long book. Biographers—those who write biographies—use many different sources to learn about their subjects. You can write your own biography of a famous person whom you find inspiring.

How to Get Started

Choose a subject you find interesting. If you think Cleopatra is cool, you have a good chance of getting your reader interested, too. If you're bored by ancient Egypt, your reader will be snoring after your first paragraph.

Your subject can be almost anyone: an author, an inventor, a celebrity, a politician, or a member of your family. To find someone to write about, ask yourself these simple questions:

1. Whom do I want to know more about?
2. What did this person do that was special?
3. How did this person change the world?

Do Your Research

- Find out as much about your subject as possible. Read books, news articles, and encyclopedia entries. Watch video clips and movies, and search the Internet. Conduct interviews, if possible.
- Take notes, writing down important facts and interesting stories about your subject.

Write the Biography

- Come up with a title. Include the person's name.
- Write an introduction. Consider asking a probing question about your subject.
- Include information about the person's childhood. When was this person born? Where did he or she grow up? Whom did he or she admire?
- Highlight the person's talents, accomplishments, and personal attributes.
- Describe the specific events that helped to shape this person's life. Did this person ever have a problem and overcome it?
- Write a conclusion. Include your thoughts about why it is important to learn about this person.
- Once you have finished your first draft, revise and then proofread your work.

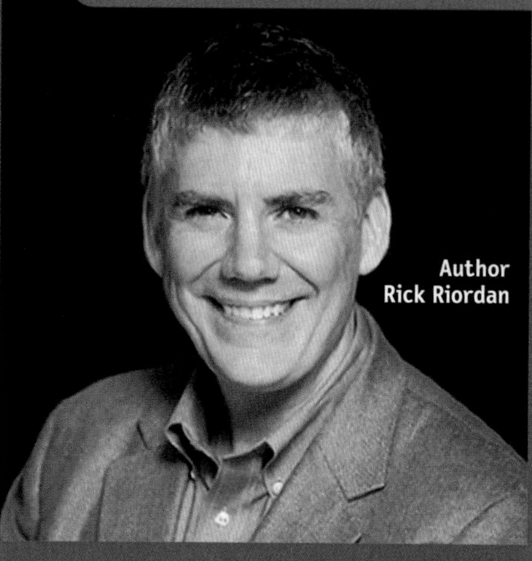
Author Rick Riordan

Here's a SAMPLE BIOGRAPHY of Rick Riordan, best-selling author of series such as Percy Jackson and the Olympians, and Magnus Chase and the Gods of Asgard. Of course, there is so much more for you to discover and write about on your own!

Rick Riordan—Author

Rick Riordan was born on June 5, 1964, in San Antonio, Texas, U.S.A. Born into a creative family—his mom was a musician and artist and his dad was a ceramicist—Riordan began writing in middle school, and he published his first short stories while attending college.

After graduating from University of Texas at Austin, Riordan went on to teach English to middle schoolers, spending his summers as a music director at a summer camp. Writing adult mysteries on the side, Riordan soon discovered his knack for writing for younger readers and published *The Lightning Thief*, the first book in the Percy Jackson series, in 2005. *The Sea of Monsters* soon followed. Before long, Riordan quit his teaching job to become a full-time writer.

Today Riordan has penned dozens of books, firmly establishing himself as one of the most accomplished and well-known authors of our time. When he's not writing, Riordan likes to read, swim, play guitar, and travel with his wife, Becky, and their sons Haley and Patrick.

A diver explores Silfra Canyon—a deep fault between two tectonic plates—at Thingvellir National Park in Iceland.

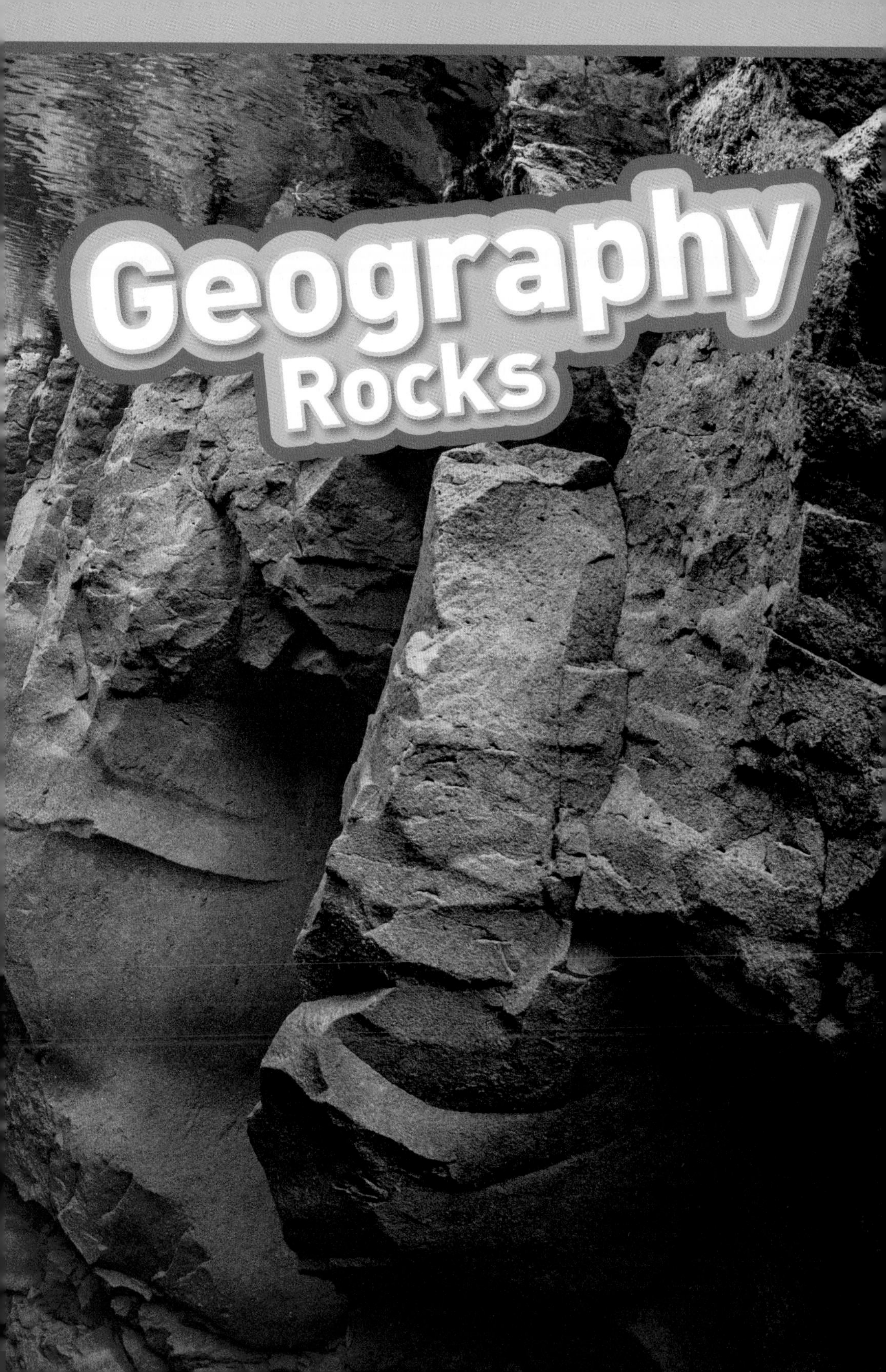
Geography
Rocks

THE POLITICAL WORLD

Earth's land area is made up of seven continents, but people have divided much of the land into smaller political units called countries. Australia is a continent made up of a single country, and Antarctica is used for scientific research. But the other five continents include almost 200 independent countries. The political map shown here depicts boundaries—imaginary lines created by treaties—that separate countries. Some boundaries, such as the one between the United States and Canada, are very stable and have been recognized for many years.

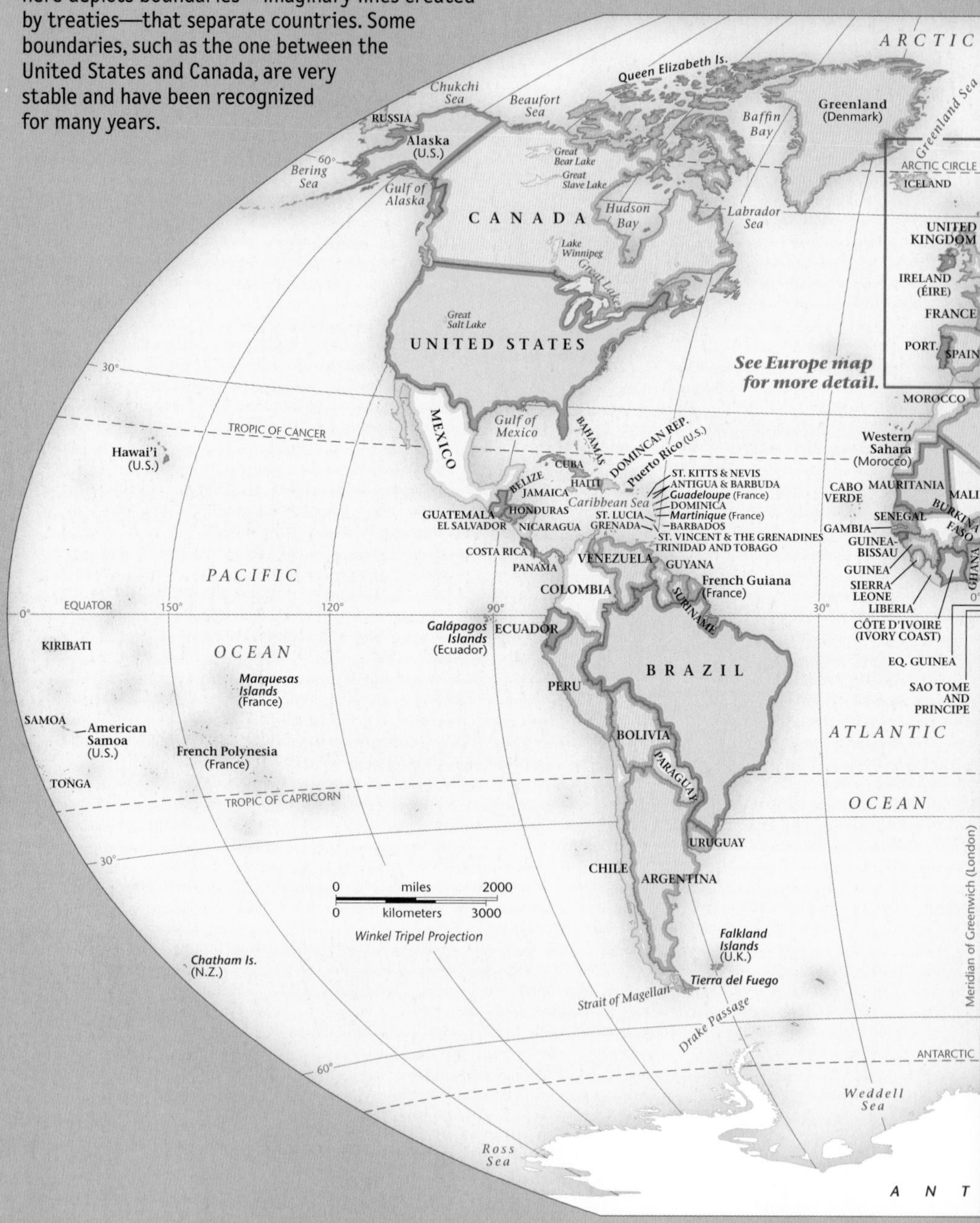

Other boundaries, such as the one between Sudan and South Sudan in northeast Africa, are relatively new and still disputed. Countries come in all shapes and sizes. Russia and Canada are giants; others, such as El Salvador and Qatar, are small. Some countries are long and skinny—look at Chile in South America! Still other countries—such as Indonesia and Japan in Asia—are made up of groups of islands. The political map is a clue to the diversity that makes Earth so fascinating.

TAIWAN
The People's Republic of China claims Taiwan as its 23rd province. Taiwan's government (Republic of China) maintains that there are two political entities.

THE PHYSICAL WORLD

Earth is dominated by large landmasses called continents—seven in all—and by an interconnected global ocean that is divided into four parts by the continents. More than 70 percent of Earth's surface is covered by oceans, and the rest is made up of land areas.

Different landforms give variety to the surface of the continents. The Rocky Mountains divide North America, the Andes mark the western edge of South America, and the Himalaya tower above South Asia. The Plateau of Tibet forms the rugged core of Asia, while

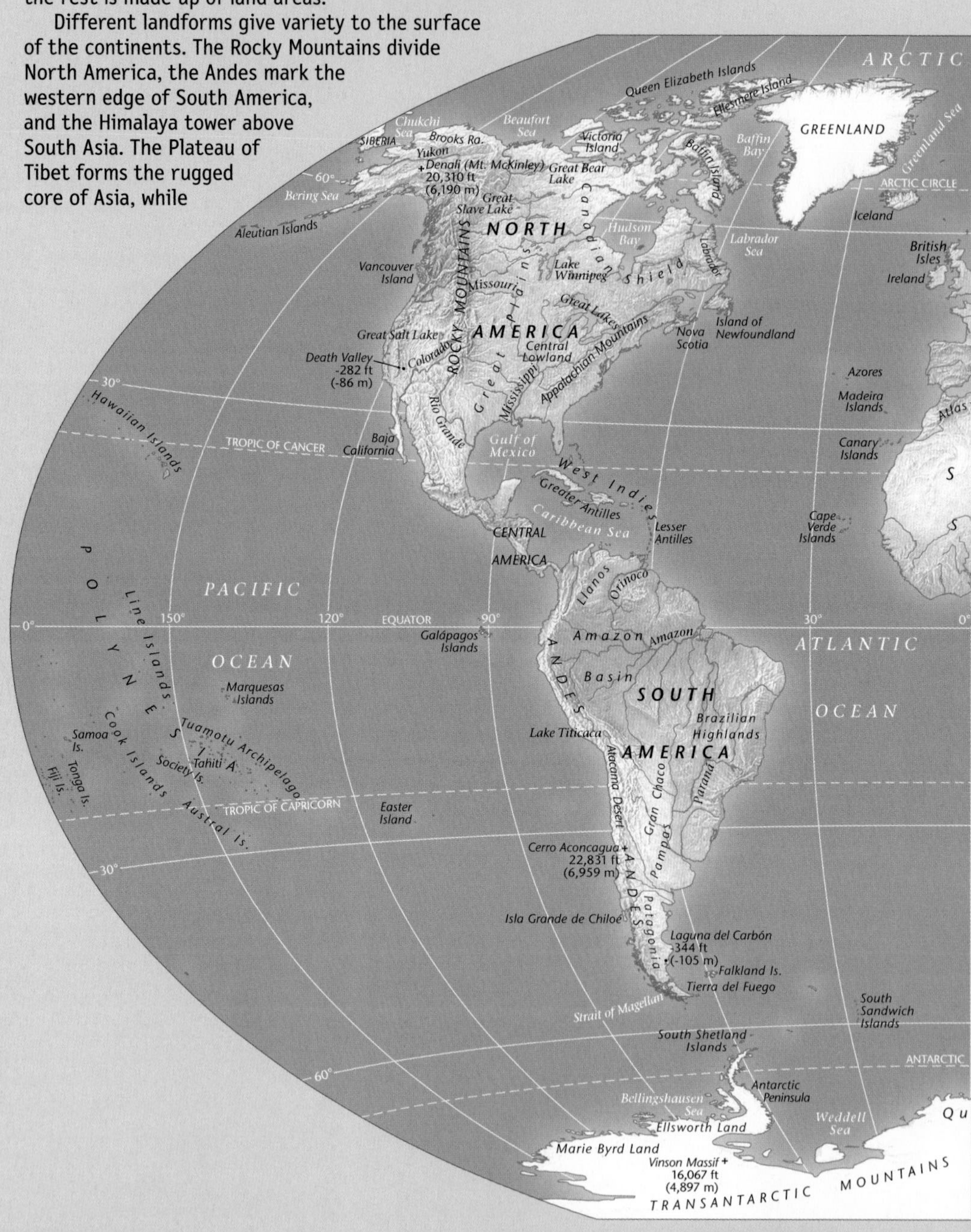

the Northern European Plain extends from the North Sea to the Ural Mountains. Much of Africa is a plateau, and dry plains cover large areas of Australia. Mountains rise more than 16,000 feet (4,877 m) above Antarctica's massive ice sheets. Mountains and trenches make the ocean floors as varied as any continent. A mountain chain called the Mid-Atlantic Ridge runs the length of the Atlantic Ocean. In the western Pacific, trenches drop deep into the ocean floor.

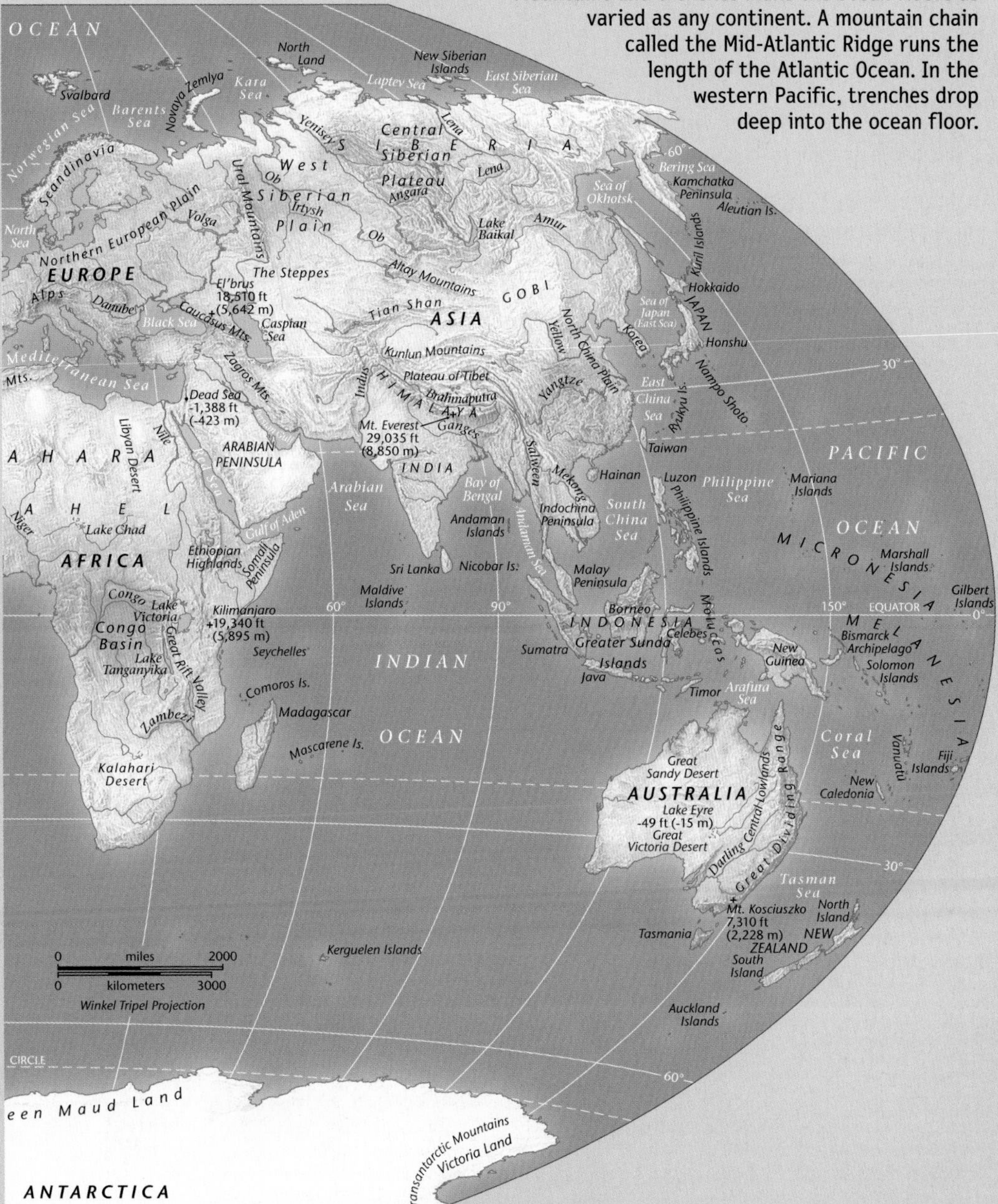

KINDS OF MAPS

Maps are special tools that geographers use to tell a story about Earth. Maps can be used to show just about anything related to places. Some maps show physical features, such as mountains or vegetation. Maps can also show climates or natural hazards and other things we cannot easily see. Other maps illustrate different features on Earth—political boundaries, urban centers, and economic systems.

AN IMPERFECT TOOL

Maps are not perfect. A globe is a scale model of Earth with accurate relative sizes and locations. Because maps are flat, they involve distortions of size, shape, and direction. Also, cartographers—people who create maps—make choices about what information to include. Because of this, it is important to study many different types of maps to learn the complete story of Earth. Three commonly found kinds of maps are shown on this page.

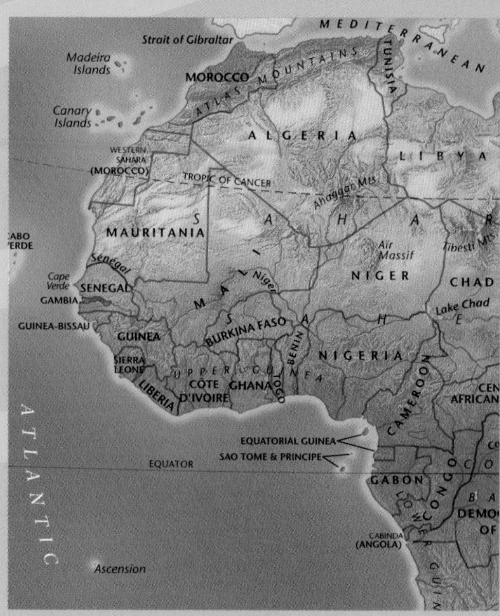

PHYSICAL MAPS. Earth's natural features—landforms, water bodies, and vegetation—are shown on physical maps. The map above uses color and shading to illustrate mountains, lakes, rivers, and deserts of western Africa. Country names and borders are added for reference, but they are not natural features.

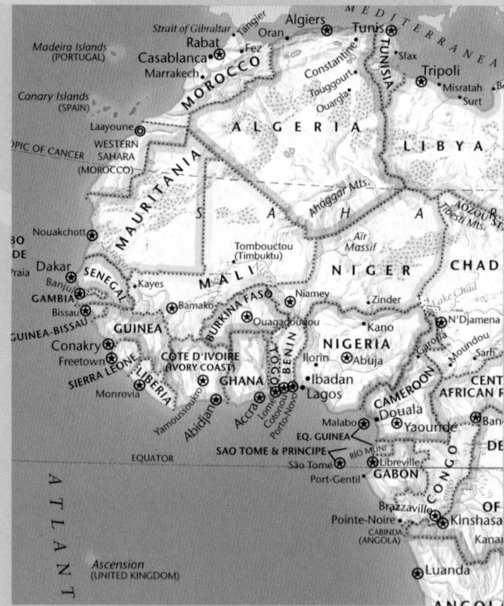

POLITICAL MAPS. These maps represent characteristics of the landscape created by humans, such as boundaries, cities, and place-names. Natural features are added only for reference. On the map above, capital cities are represented with a star inside a circle, while other cities are shown with black dots.

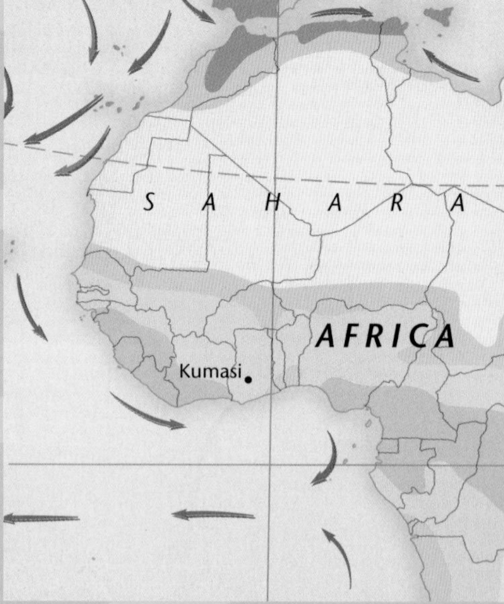

THEMATIC MAPS. Patterns related to a particular topic or theme, such as population distribution, appear on these maps. The map above displays the region's climate zones, which range from tropical wet (bright green) to tropical wet and dry (light green) to semiarid (dark yellow) to arid or desert (light yellow).

MAKING MAPS

Long ago, cartographers worked with pen and ink, carefully handcrafting maps based on explorers' observations and diaries. Today, mapmaking is a high-tech business. Cartographers use Earth data stored in "layers" in a Geographic Information System (GIS) and special computer programs to create maps that can be easily updated as new information becomes available.

The National Geographic staff cartographers Mike McNey and Lauren Tierney, at right, are reviewing a map of Alaska for the *United States Atlas for Young Explorers.*

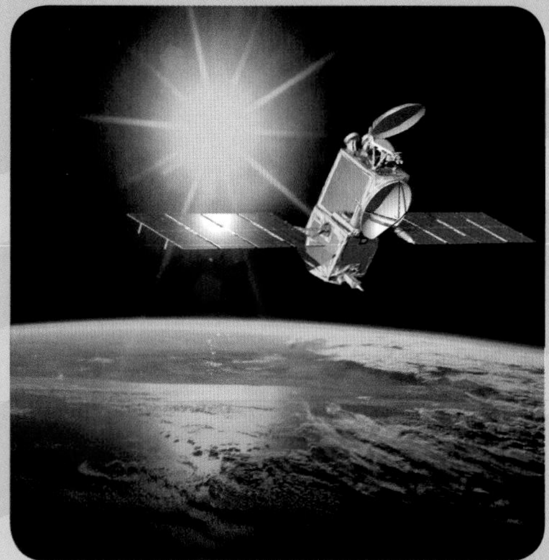

Satellites in orbit around Earth act as eyes in the sky, recording data about the planet's land and ocean areas. The data is converted to numbers that are transmitted back to computers that are specially programmed to interpret the data. They record it in a form that cartographers can use to create maps.

MAP PROJECTIONS

To create a map, cartographers transfer an image of the round Earth to a flat surface, a process called projection. All projections involve distortion. For example, an interrupted projection (bottom map) shows accurate shapes and relative sizes of land areas, but oceans have gaps. Other types of projections are cylindrical, conic, or azimuthal—each with certain advantages, but all with some distortion.

GEOGRAPHIC FEATURES

From roaring rivers to parched deserts, from underwater canyons to jagged mountains, Earth is covered with beautiful and diverse environments. Here are examples of the most common types of geographic features found around the world.

DESERT

Deserts are land features created by climate, specifically by a lack of water. Here, a camel caravan crosses the Sahara in North Africa.

VALLEY

Valleys, cut by running water or moving ice, may be broad and flat or narrow and steep, such as the Indus River Valley in Ladakh, India (above).

RIVER

As a river moves through flatlands, it twists and turns. Above, the Rio Los Amigos winds through a rain forest in Peru.

MOUNTAIN

Mountains are Earth's tallest landforms, and Mount Everest (above) rises highest of all, at 29,035 feet (8,850 m) above sea level.

GLACIER

Glaciers—"rivers" of ice—such as Alaska's Hubbard Glacier (above) move slowly from mountains to the sea. Global warming is shrinking them.

CANYON

Steep-sided valleys called canyons are created mainly by running water. Buckskin Gulch in Utah (above) is the deepest "slot" canyon in the American Southwest.

WATERFALL

Waterfalls form when a river reaches an abrupt change in elevation. Above, Kaieteur Falls, in Guyana, has a sheer drop of 741 feet (226 m).

7 extreme facts about Earth

1 Tropical rain forests began to grow over **100 million** years ago.

2 Millions of years ago, the Earth was covered with **giant** mushrooms that grew taller than a house.

3 **97** percent of water on Earth is undrinkable.

4 There is no land underneath the ice at the North Pole.

5 Earth's longest mountain range is under the sea.

6 The Namib in Africa is the oldest desert in the world, having been dry for 55 million years.

7 Scientists believe that millions of years ago Earth's atmosphere weighed less than half of what it does today.

SPOTLIGHT ON AFRICA

Giraffes sleep for just a few hours a day.

In Nigeria it's considered rude to eat while walking.

Masai giraffes, Masai Mara, Kenya

The massive continent of Africa, where humankind began millions of years ago, is second to only Asia in size. Stretching nearly as far from west to east as it does from north to south, Africa is home to both the longest river in the world (the Nile) and the largest hot desert on Earth (Sahara).

Namibian woman in traditional dress

Wildlife Wonderland

The world's largest population of African elephants can be found in Botswana's Okavango Delta. You'll also spot zebras, hippos, impalas, lions, and leopards splashing around.

Fruit Land

South Africa is one of the world's biggest producers of citrus fruit. The subtropical climate is ideal for growing oranges, grapefruits, tangerines, and lemons.

Star Struck

The force is strong in Tunisia, where the parts of the original *Star Wars* movies were filmed. The sandy scenes were created in various desert locations in the North African nation.

Go Fish

Lake Malawi, the third largest lake in Africa, contains more species of fish than any other lake in the world, including more than 500 species of African cichlids.

Protecting the Environment

Namibia	43.2%*
Seychelles	42.0%
Zambia	37.8%
Botswana	37.2%
Tanzania	32.2%
Congo	30.4%

**Figures represent percent of total land area set aside as protected area*

The Great Sphinx at Giza in Egypt

AFRICA

PHYSICAL

LAND AREA
11,608,000 sq mi (30,065,000 sq km)

LOWEST POINT
Lake Assal, Djibouti -509 ft (-155 m)

LARGEST LAKE
Victoria 26,800 sq mi (69,500 sq km)

HIGHEST POINT
Kilimanjaro, Tanzania 19,340 ft (5,895 m)

LONGEST RIVER
Nile 4,400 mi (7,081 km)

POLITICAL

POPULATION
1,203,435,000

LARGEST METROPOLITAN AREA
Cairo, Egypt Pop. 18,419,000

LARGEST COUNTRY
Algeria 919,595 sq mi (2,381,741 sq km)

MOST DENSELY POPULATED COUNTRY
Mauritius 1,603 people per sq mi (619 per sq km)

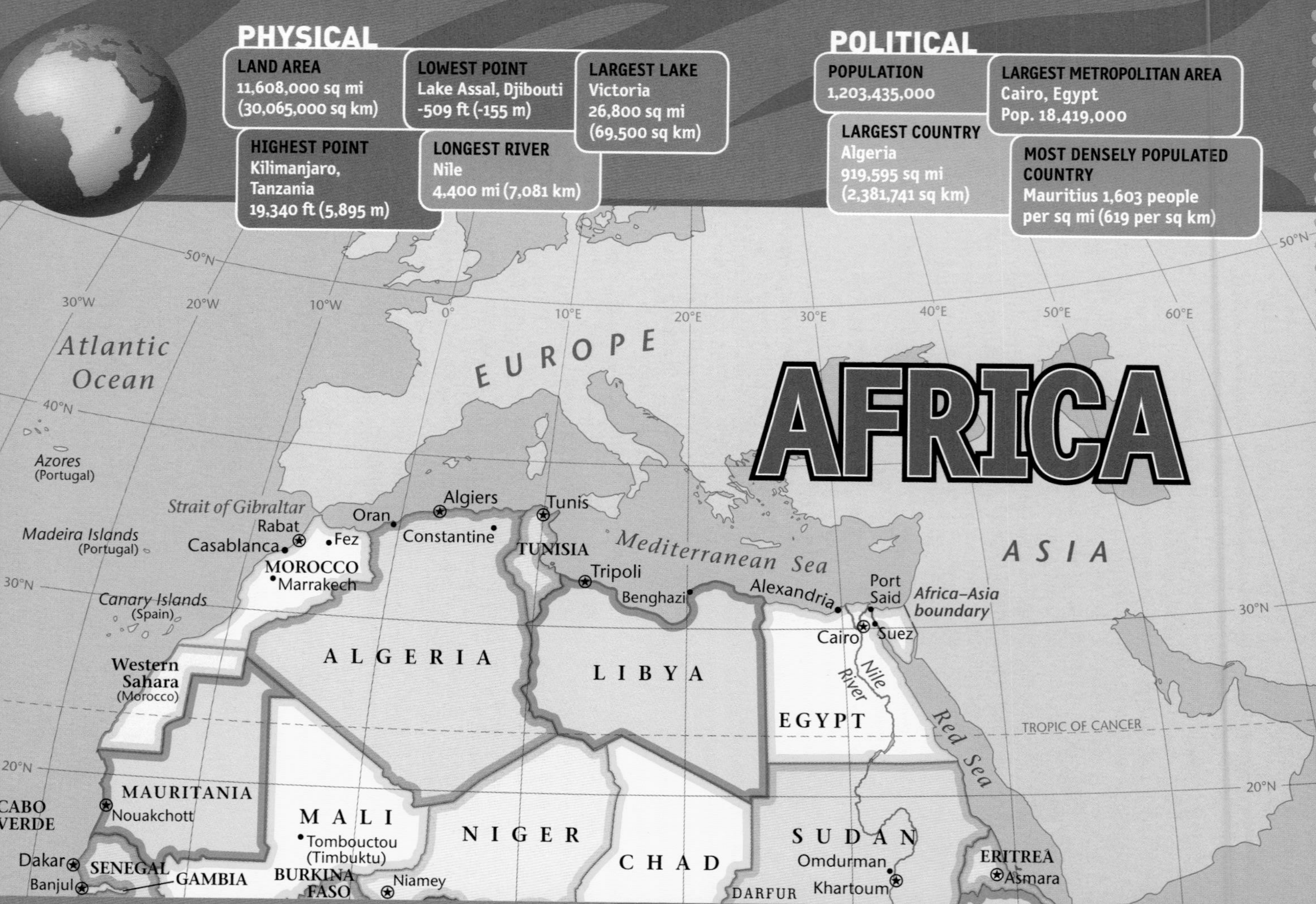

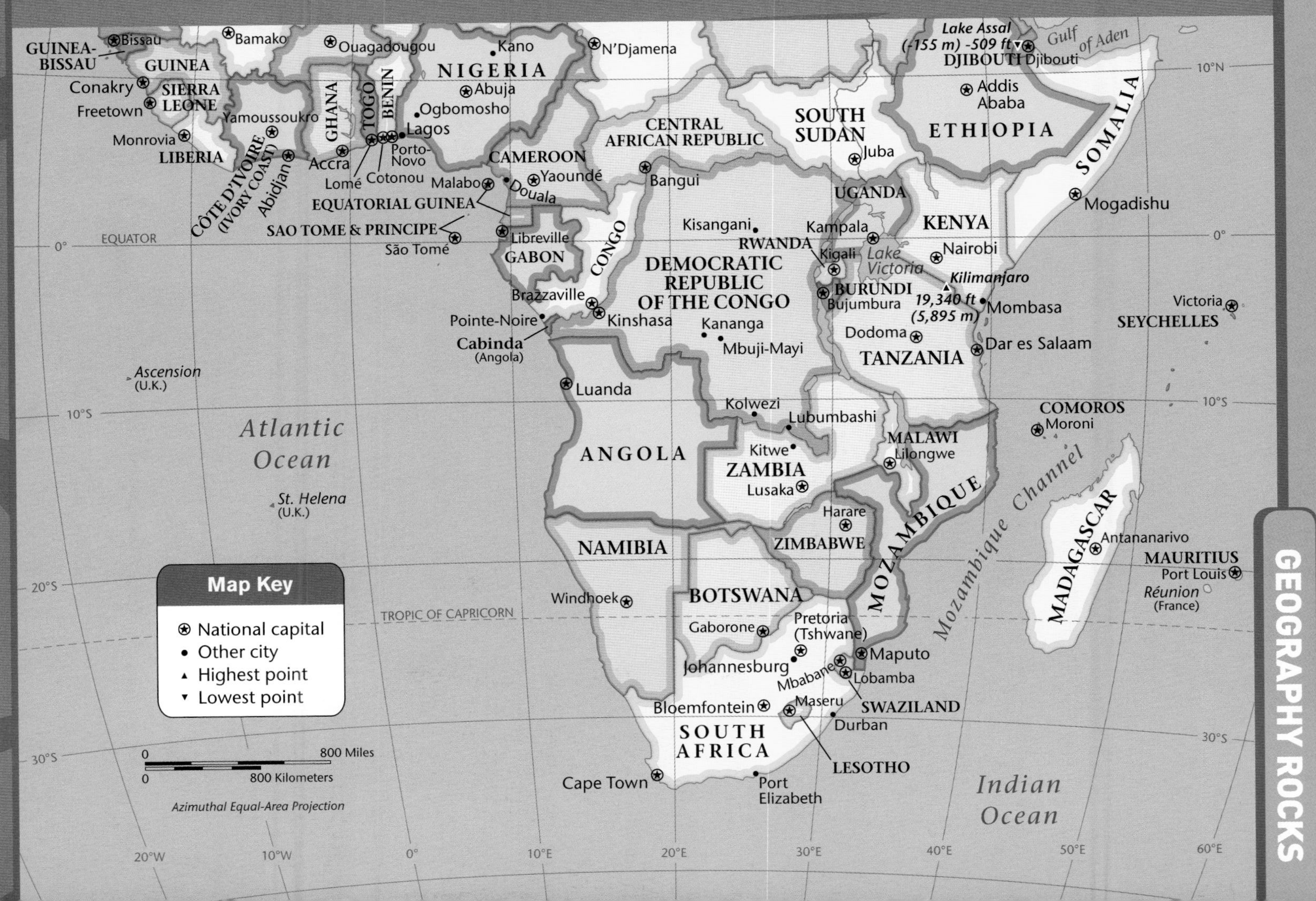
GUINEA-BISSAU
Bissau
Bamako
Ouagadougou
Kano
NIGERIA
N'Djamena
Lake Assal (-155 m) -509 ft
DJIBOUTI
Djibouti
Gulf of Aden
GUINEA
Conakry
SIERRA LEONE
Freetown
Abuja
Addis Ababa
ETHIOPIA
SOMALIA
Yamoussoukro
GHANA
TOGO
BENIN
Ogbomosho
Lagos
CENTRAL AFRICAN REPUBLIC
SOUTH SUDAN
Juba
Monrovia
LIBERIA
CÔTE D'IVOIRE (IVORY COAST)
Abidjan
Accra
Lomé
Cotonou
Porto-Novo
CAMEROON
Yaoundé
Malabo
Douala
Bangui
EQUATORIAL GUINEA
UGANDA
Mogadishu
KENYA
SAO TOME & PRINCIPE
São Tomé
Libreville
GABON
CONGO
Kisangani
RWANDA
Kampala
Kigali
Lake Victoria
Nairobi
EQUATOR
DEMOCRATIC REPUBLIC OF THE CONGO
BURUNDI
Bujumbura
Kilimanjaro 19,340 ft (5,895 m)
Mombasa
Victoria
SEYCHELLES
Brazzaville
Kinshasa
Pointe-Noire
Kananga
Mbuji-Mayi
Dodoma
TANZANIA
Dar es Salaam
Cabinda (Angola)
Ascension (U.K.)
Luanda
Kolwezi
Lubumbashi
COMOROS
Moroni
Atlantic Ocean
ANGOLA
Kitwe
ZAMBIA
Lusaka
MALAWI
Lilongwe
MOZAMBIQUE
Mozambique Channel
St. Helena (U.K.)
Harare
ZIMBABWE
NAMIBIA
MADAGASCAR
Antananarivo
MAURITIUS
Port Louis
Réunion (France)
Windhoek
BOTSWANA
TROPIC OF CAPRICORN
Gaborone
Pretoria (Tshwane)
Maputo
Johannesburg
Mbabane
Lobamba
SWAZILAND
Bloemfontein
Maseru
Durban
SOUTH AFRICA
LESOTHO
Cape Town
Port Elizabeth
Indian Ocean
Map Key
National capital
Other city
Highest point
Lowest point
0 800 Miles
0 800 Kilometers
Azimuthal Equal-Area Projection
10°N
0°
10°S
20°S
30°S
20°W
10°W
0°
10°E
20°E
30°E
40°E
50°E
60°E

SPOTLIGHT ON ANTARCTICA

Emperor penguin with chick

Penguins can spend up to 75 percent of their lives in the water.

No dogs are allowed in Antarctica.

This frozen continent may be a cool place to visit, but unless you're a penguin, you probably wouldn't want to hang out in Antarctica for long. The fact that it's the coldest, windiest, and driest continent helps explain why humans never colonized this ice-covered land surrounding the South Pole.

Russian Orthodox church, South Shetland Islands

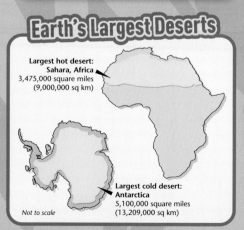

Rock Collection

Researchers have recovered thousands of meteorites in Antarctica over the past few decades. The ice helps preserve the space rocks, some of which date back more than a billion years.

Bug Out

The midge, a wingless insect, is the largest land animal native to Antarctica. This bug is able to dehydrate itself and enter a sleepy state to survive temps close to -4°F (-20°C).

Old Bones

Scientists recently unearthed a trove of ancient fossils in Antarctica. The find includes dinosaur, lizard and prehistoric bird bones that are some 70 million years old.

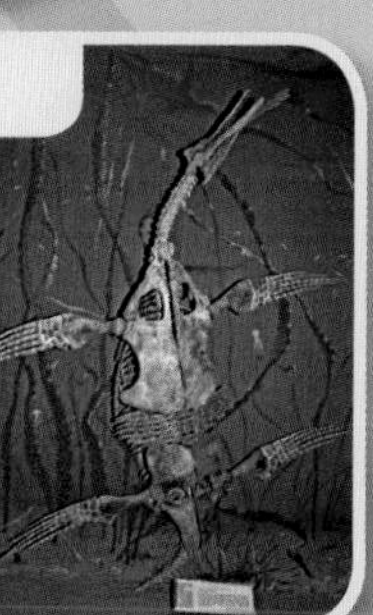

Slippery Landing

Flying into Antarctica is tricky, as many airport runways are made of blue ice. These runways need to be specially prepared to keep the planes from skidding.

Earth's Largest Deserts

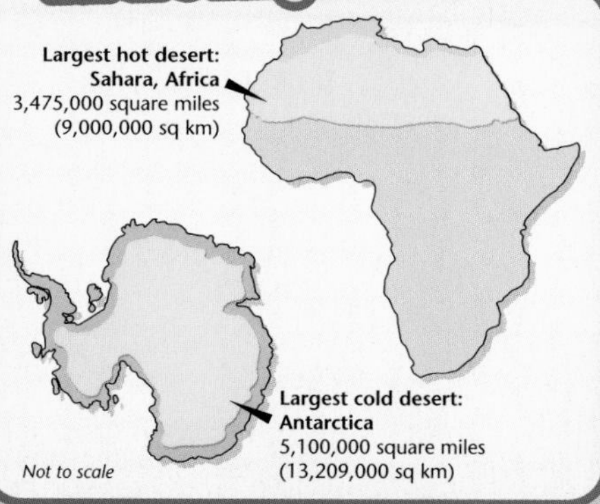

Weddell seal

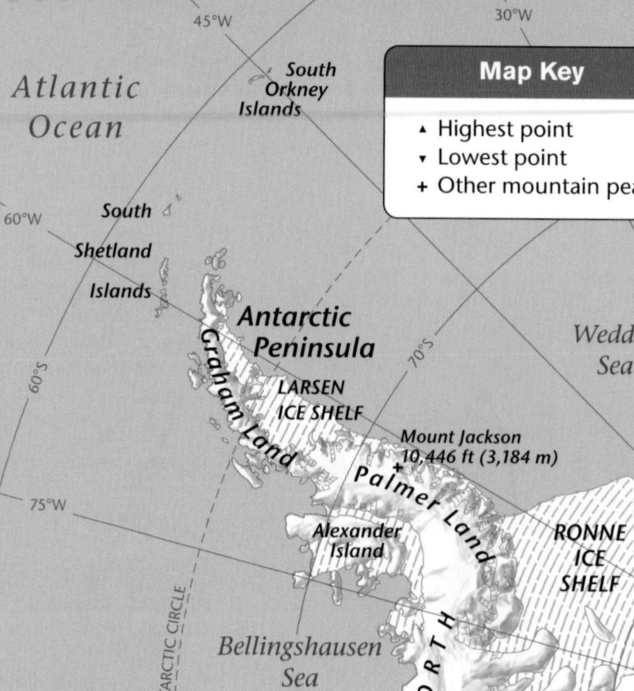

PHYSICAL

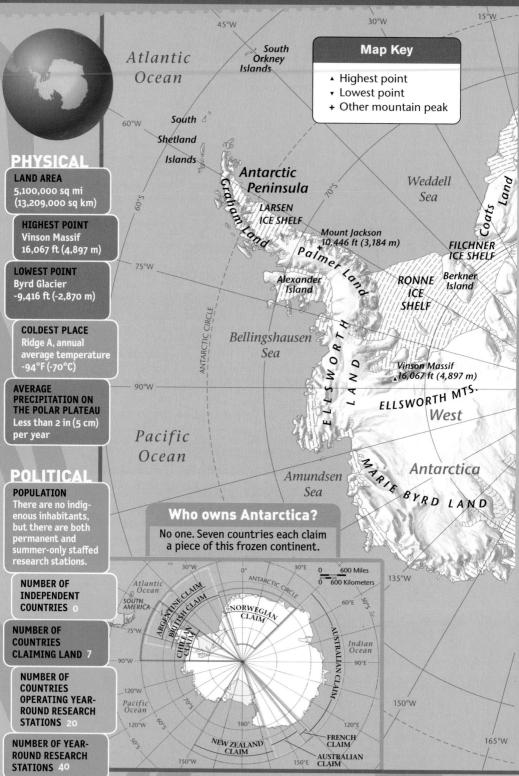

LAND AREA
5,100,000 sq mi (13,209,000 sq km)

HIGHEST POINT
Vinson Massif
16,067 ft (4,897 m)

LOWEST POINT
Byrd Glacier
-9,416 ft (-2,870 m)

COLDEST PLACE
Ridge A, annual average temperature -94°F (-70°C)

AVERAGE PRECIPITATION ON THE POLAR PLATEAU
Less than 2 in (5 cm) per year

POLITICAL

POPULATION
There are no indigenous inhabitants, but there are both permanent and summer-only staffed research stations.

NUMBER OF INDEPENDENT COUNTRIES 0

NUMBER OF COUNTRIES CLAIMING LAND 7

NUMBER OF COUNTRIES OPERATING YEAR-ROUND RESEARCH STATIONS 20

NUMBER OF YEAR-ROUND RESEARCH STATIONS 40

Who owns Antarctica?

No one. Seven countries each claim a piece of this frozen continent.

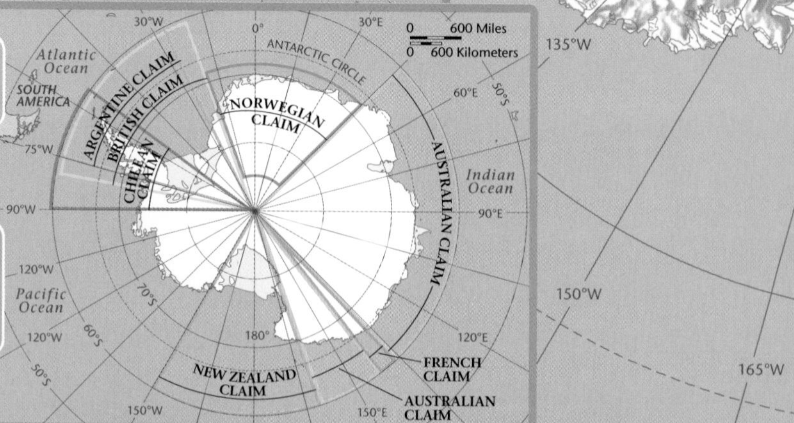

ANTARCTICA

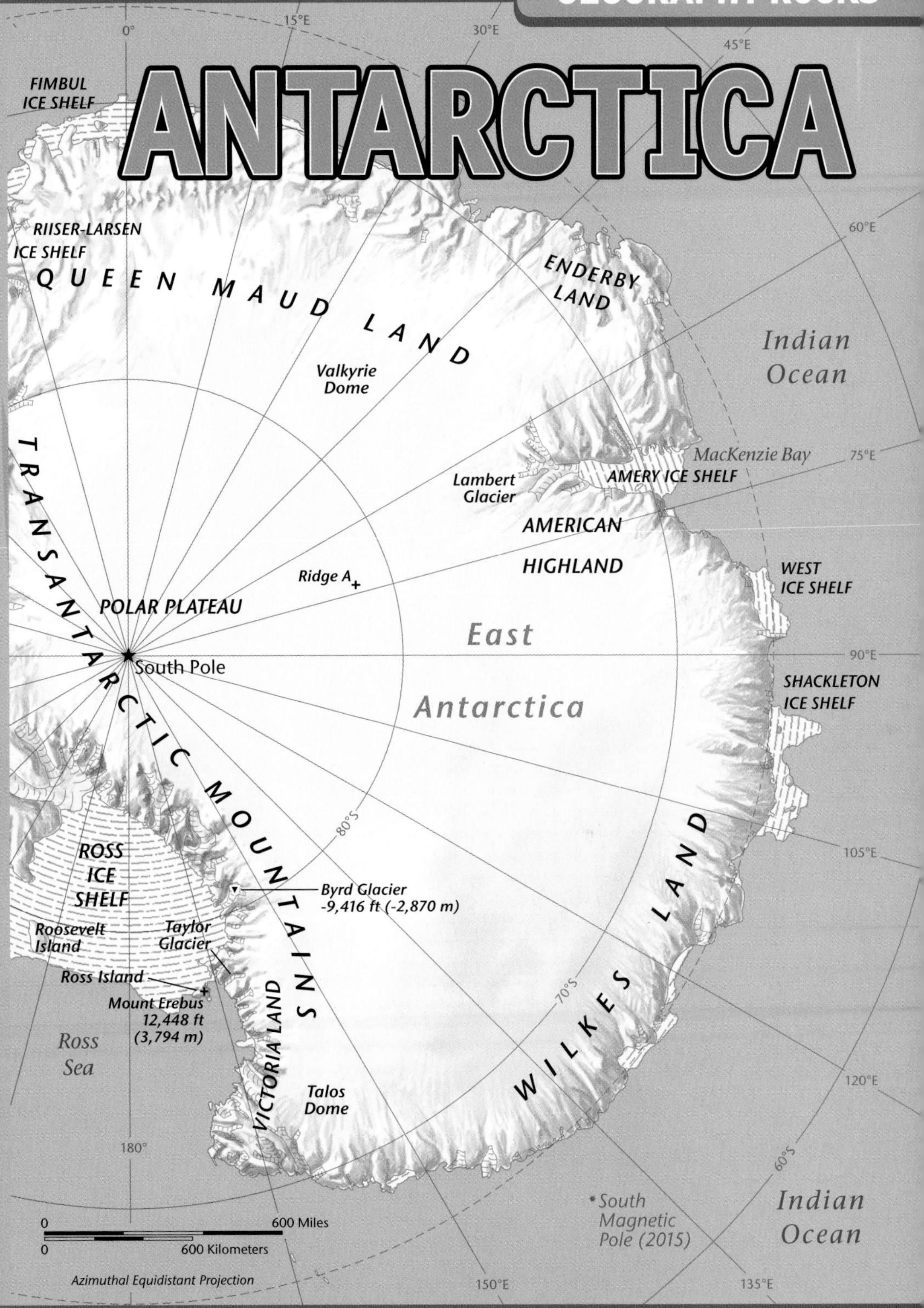

FIMBUL ICE SHELF
RIISER-LARSEN ICE SHELF
QUEEN MAUD LAND
ENDERBY LAND
Indian Ocean
Valkyrie Dome
TRANSANTARCTIC MOUNTAINS
MacKenzie Bay
Lambert Glacier
AMERY ICE SHELF
AMERICAN HIGHLAND
WEST ICE SHELF
Ridge A
POLAR PLATEAU
East Antarctica
South Pole
SHACKLETON ICE SHELF
ROSS ICE SHELF
Byrd Glacier -9,416 ft (-2,870 m)
WILKES LAND
Roosevelt Island
Taylor Glacier
Ross Island
Mount Erebus 12,448 ft (3,794 m)
Ross Sea
VICTORIA LAND
Talos Dome
South Magnetic Pole (2015)
Indian Ocean
0° 15°E 30°E 45°E 60°E 75°E 90°E 105°E 120°E 135°E 150°E 180°
80°S 70°S 60°S
0 600 Miles
0 600 Kilometers
Azimuthal Equidistant Projection

SPOTLIGHT ON ASIA

Laos was once called Lan Xang — which means the "land of a million elephants."

A South Korean baseball team installed cheering robots in its ballpark.

Luang Prabang, Laos, is home to more than 30 temples.

Made up of 46 countries, Asia is the world's largest continent. Just how big is it? From western Turkey to the eastern tip of Russia, Asia spans nearly half the globe! Home to more than four billion citizens—that's three out of five people on the planet—Asia's population is bigger than that of all the other continents combined.

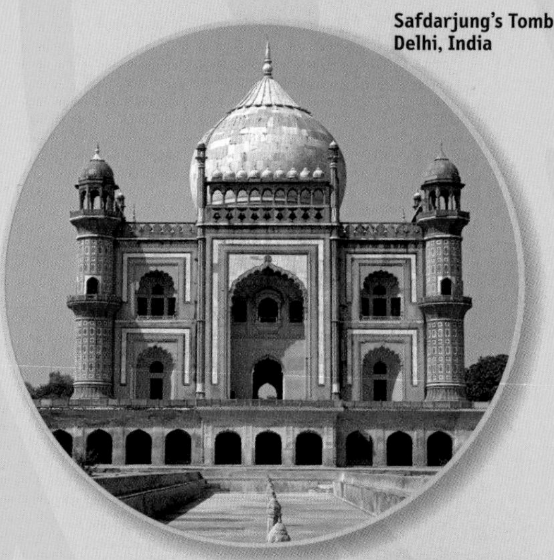

Safdarjung's Tomb, Delhi, India

Transparent Trains

An "invisible" train is set to hit tracks in Tokyo within the next couple of years. Made from a super-reflective material, the high-speed train is designed to blend into the countryside.

Sky High

Hong Kong has about 1,300 skyscrapers in its skyline—more than any other city in the world. The 118-floor International Commerce Center is Hong Kong's tallest tower.

Tiger Aid

More than half of the world's tigers—some 3,900 animals—live in India, mostly in protected nature reserves.

Flower Power

Thailand is one of the world's top orchid exporters. You can find more than 1,000 species of the flower growing wild in Thai forests.

Tallest Peaks by Continent

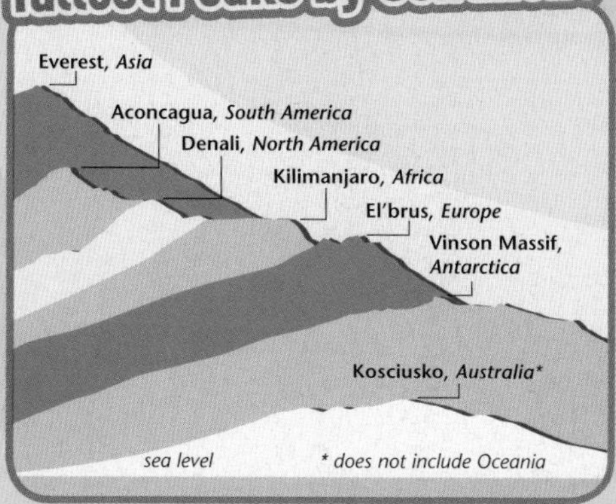

Kuala Lumpur, Malaysia

ASIA

PHYSICAL

LAND AREA
17,208,000 sq mi
(44,570,000 sq km)

HIGHEST POINT
Mount Everest,
China–Nepal
29,035 ft (8,850 m)

LOWEST POINT
Dead Sea,
Israel–Jordan
-1,388 ft (-423 m)

LONGEST RIVER
Yangtze, China
3,880 mi (6,244 km)

LARGEST LAKE ENTIRELY IN ASIA
Lake Baikal, Russia
12,200 sq mi
(31,500 sq km)

POLITICAL

POPULATION
4,436,833,000

LARGEST METROPOLITAN AREA
Tokyo, Japan
Pop. 37,833,000

LARGEST COUNTRY ENTIRELY IN ASIA
China
3,705,405 sq mi
(9,596,960 sq km)

MOST DENSELY POPULATED COUNTRY
Singapore
21,965 people
per sq mi
(8,486 per sq km)

0 800 Miles
0 800 Kilometers
Two-point Equidistant Projection

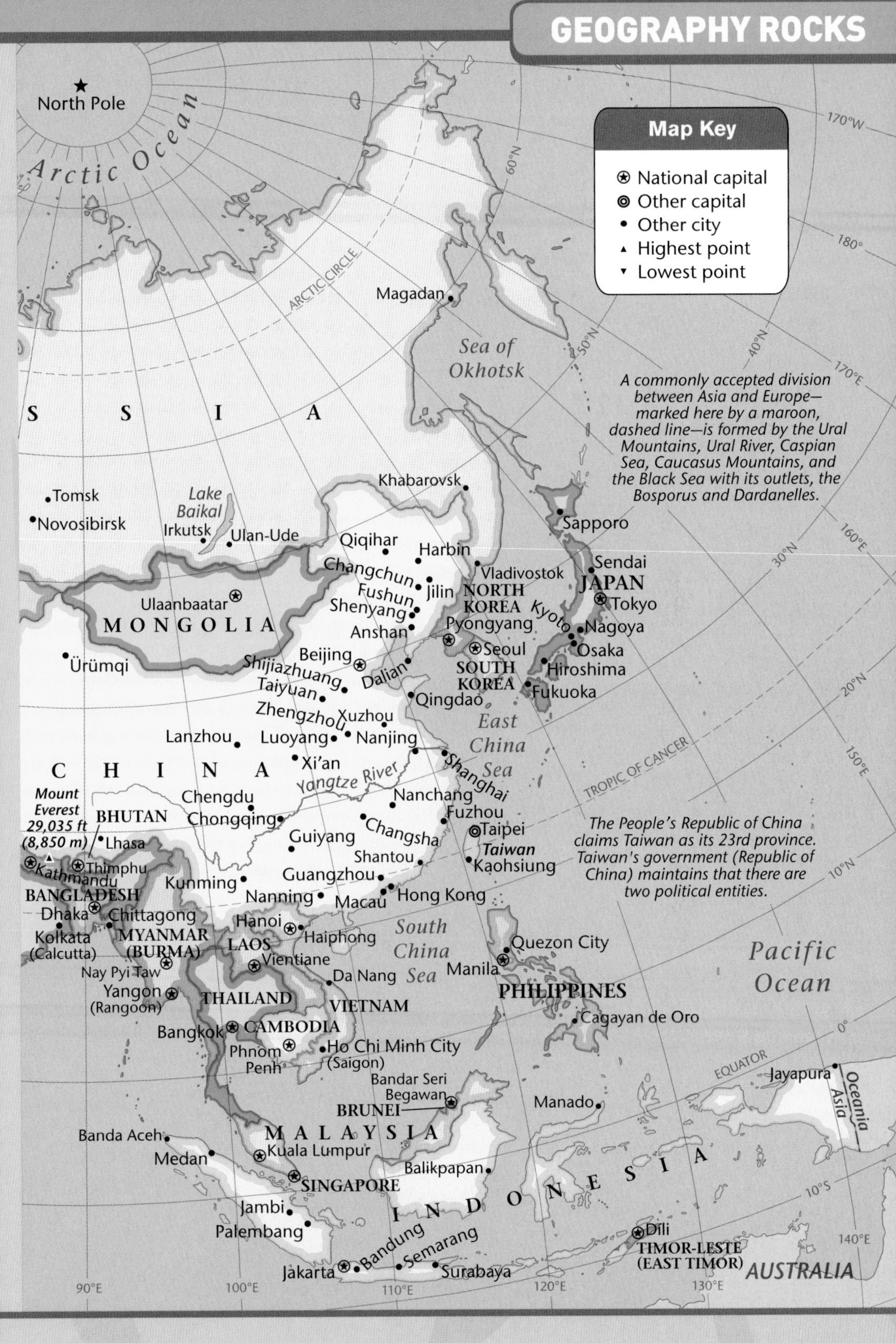
Map Key
National capital
Other capital
Other city
Highest point
Lowest point
North Pole
Arctic Ocean
ARCTIC CIRCLE
Magadan
Sea of Okhotsk
A S I A
A commonly accepted division between Asia and Europe—marked here by a maroon, dashed line—is formed by the Ural Mountains, Ural River, Caspian Sea, Caucasus Mountains, and the Black Sea with its outlets, the Bosporus and Dardanelles.
Tomsk
Novosibirsk
Lake Baikal
Irkutsk
Ulan-Ude
Khabarovsk
Sapporo
Qiqihar
Harbin
Vladivostok
Sendai
Changchun
Jilin
NORTH KOREA
JAPAN
Tokyo
Ulaanbaatar
Fushun
Shenyang
Pyongyang
Kyoto
Nagoya
MONGOLIA
Anshan
Seoul
Osaka
Ürümqi
Beijing
Shijiazhuang
Dalian
SOUTH KOREA
Hiroshima
Fukuoka
Taiyuan
Qingdao
Zhengzhou
Xuzhou
East China Sea
Lanzhou
Luoyang
Nanjing
C H I N A
Xi'an
Shanghai
Yangtze River
TROPIC OF CANCER
Mount Everest 29,035 ft (8,850 m)
Chengdu
Nanchang
BHUTAN
Chongqing
Fuzhou
Lhasa
Changsha
Taipei
Taiwan
The People's Republic of China claims Taiwan as its 23rd province. Taiwan's government (Republic of China) maintains that there are two political entities.
Guiyang
Kathmandu
Thimphu
Shantou
Kaohsiung
Kunming
Guangzhou
BANGLADESH
Nanning
Macau
Hong Kong
Dhaka
Chittagong
Hanoi
Kolkata (Calcutta)
MYANMAR (BURMA)
Haiphong
South China Sea
LAOS
Quezon City
Pacific Ocean
Vientiane
Nay Pyi Taw
Manila
Da Nang
Yangon (Rangoon)
THAILAND
PHILIPPINES
VIETNAM
Bangkok
CAMBODIA
Cagayan de Oro
Phnom Penh
Ho Chi Minh City (Saigon)
EQUATOR
Jayapura
Oceania
Asia
Bandar Seri Begawan
BRUNEI
Manado
Banda Aceh
MALAYSIA
Kuala Lumpur
Medan
Balikpapan
SINGAPORE
INDONESIA
Jambi
Palembang
Dili
TIMOR-LESTE (EAST TIMOR)
Bandung
Semarang
Jakarta
Surabaya
AUSTRALIA
90°E
100°E
110°E
120°E
130°E
140°E
150°E
160°E
170°E
180°
170°W
60°N
50°N
40°N
30°N
20°N
10°N
0°
10°S

SPOTLIGHT ON AUSTRALIA, NEW ZEALAND, AND OCEANIA

A striped sweetlips swims among coral in the Great Barrier Reef.

In New Zealand, trail mix is called scroggin or schmogle.

Australia's Great Barrier Reef isn't one unbroken reef, but a system of more than 3,000 reefs.

G'day, mate! This vast region, covering almost 3.3 million square miles (8.5 million sq km), includes Australia—the world's smallest and flattest continent—and New Zealand, as well as a fleet of mostly tiny islands scattered across the Pacific Ocean. Also known as "down under," most of the countries in this region are in the Southern Hemisphere, and below the Equator.

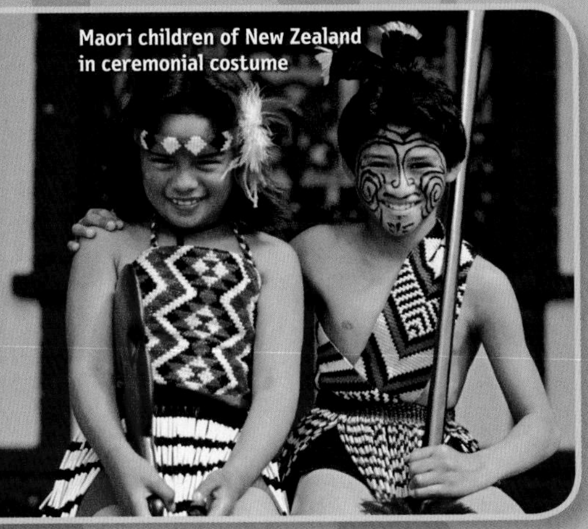
Maori children of New Zealand in ceremonial costume

Sunny Days

If you're seeking sunshine, head to Perth, the capital of Western Australia, which averages eight hours of rays per day. It's said to be the sunniest capital city on the planet.

Pretty Money

New Zealand is known for its colorful cash. The $5 bill—showing famed New Zealand mountaineer Sir Edmund Hillary and a penguin—was named 2015's best banknote of the year.

Vote Here

Registered to vote in Australia? Make sure to show up to the polls! Voting is mandatory for all citizens, and those who don't cast their vote without a valid reason may face a fine.

Protected Waters

The South Pacific island nation of Palau made big waves in 2015 when it became home to one of the world's largest marine sanctuaries, ending most fishing and mining in the area.

Australia
Sizing Up the Great Barrier Reef

Just how big is the Great Barrier Reef Marine Park? It's approximately as large as:

Great Barrier Reef Marine Park

Germany

Vietnam

Australia

or the Republic of Congo

**Based on an area of 133,000 square miles (344,400 sq km)*

Sydney Harbour Bridge in Sydney, Australia

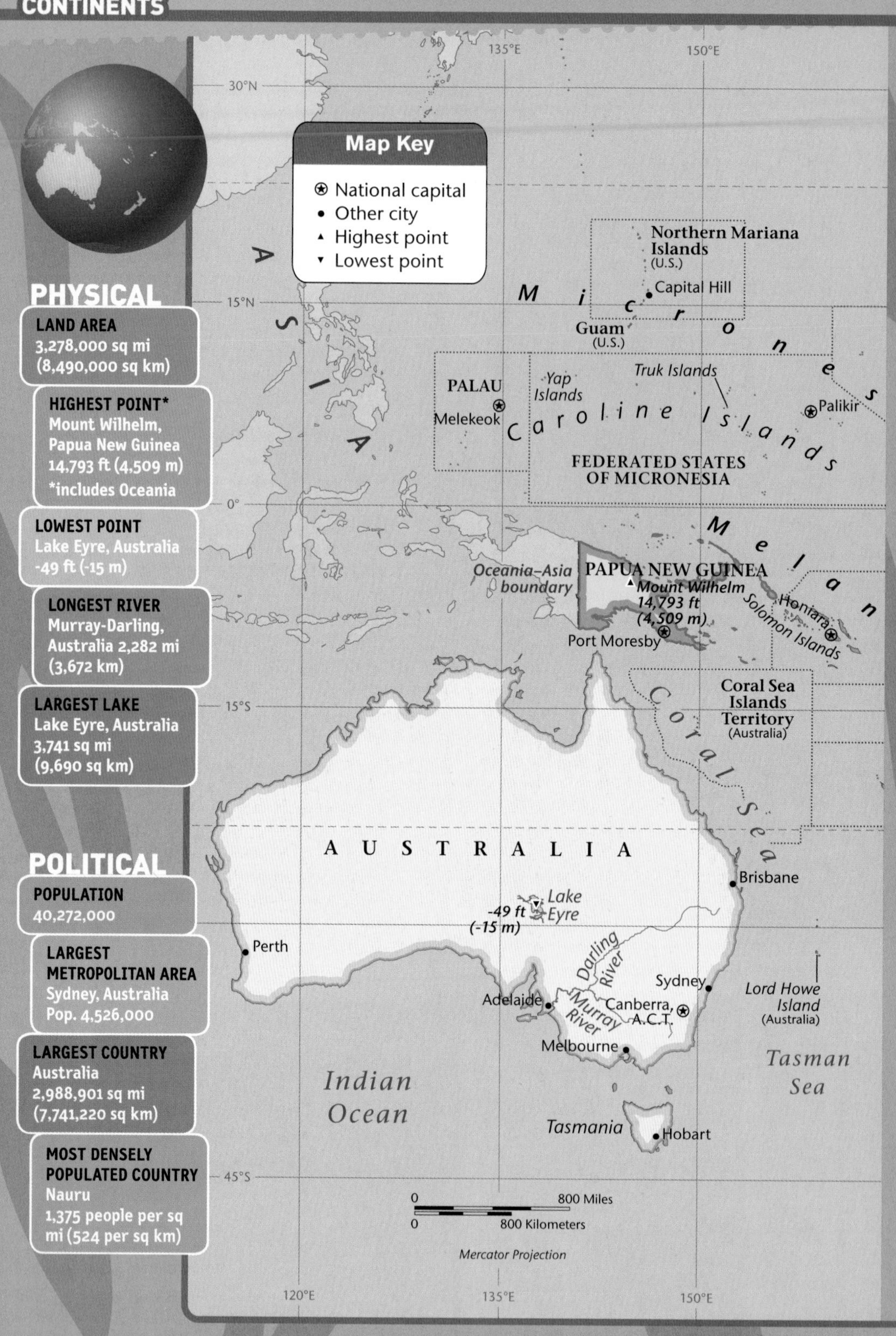

PHYSICAL

LAND AREA
3,278,000 sq mi
(8,490,000 sq km)

HIGHEST POINT*
Mount Wilhelm, Papua New Guinea
14,793 ft (4,509 m)
*includes Oceania

LOWEST POINT
Lake Eyre, Australia
-49 ft (-15 m)

LONGEST RIVER
Murray-Darling, Australia 2,282 mi
(3,672 km)

LARGEST LAKE
Lake Eyre, Australia
3,741 sq mi
(9,690 sq km)

POLITICAL

POPULATION
40,272,000

LARGEST METROPOLITAN AREA
Sydney, Australia
Pop. 4,526,000

LARGEST COUNTRY
Australia
2,988,901 sq mi
(7,741,220 sq km)

MOST DENSELY POPULATED COUNTRY
Nauru
1,375 people per sq mi (524 per sq km)

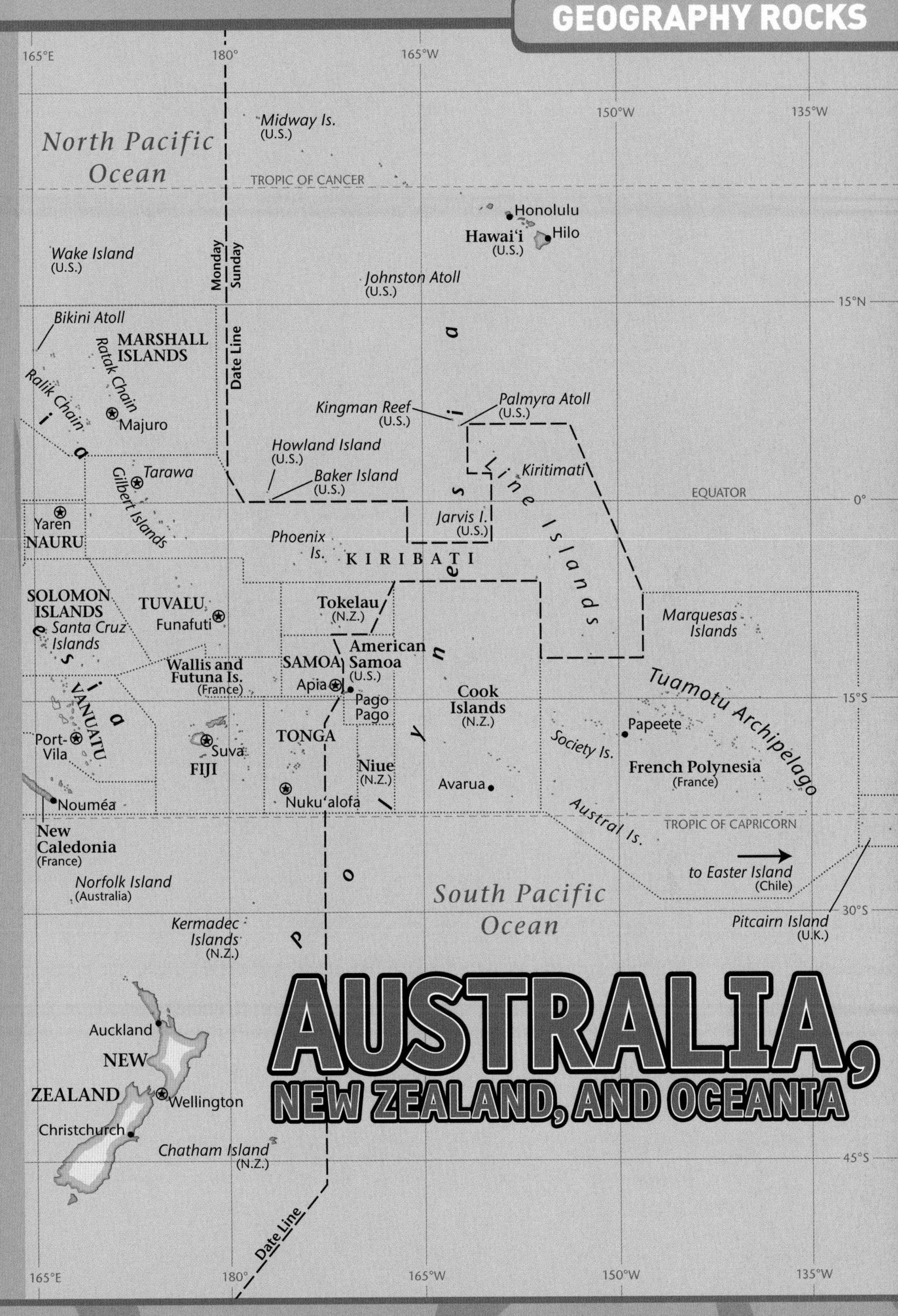
North Pacific Ocean
Midway Is. (U.S.)
TROPIC OF CANCER
Honolulu
Hawai'i (U.S.)
Hilo
Wake Island (U.S.)
Monday
Sunday
Date Line
Johnston Atoll (U.S.)
Bikini Atoll
MARSHALL ISLANDS
Ratak Chain
Ralik Chain
Majuro
Kingman Reef (U.S.)
Palmyra Atoll (U.S.)
Howland Island (U.S.)
Baker Island (U.S.)
Tarawa
Gilbert Islands
Kiritimati
Line Islands
EQUATOR
Yaren
NAURU
Jarvis I. (U.S.)
Phoenix Is.
KIRIBATI
SOLOMON ISLANDS
Santa Cruz Islands
TUVALU
Funafuti
Tokelau (N.Z.)
Marquesas Islands
American Samoa (U.S.)
SAMOA
Apia
Pago Pago
Wallis and Futuna Is. (France)
Cook Islands (N.Z.)
Tuamotu Archipelago
VANUATU
Port-Vila
Suva
FIJI
TONGA
Niue (N.Z.)
Papeete
Society Is.
French Polynesia (France)
Avarua
Nuku'alofa
Nouméa
New Caledonia (France)
Austral Is.
TROPIC OF CAPRICORN
Micronesia
Melanesia
Polynesia
Norfolk Island (Australia)
to Easter Island (Chile)
South Pacific Ocean
Kermadec Islands (N.Z.)
Pitcairn Island (U.K.)
Auckland
NEW ZEALAND
Wellington
Christchurch
Chatham Island (N.Z.)
Date Line
165°E
180°
165°W
150°W
135°W
15°N
0°
15°S
30°S
45°S

AUSTRALIA, NEW ZEALAND, AND OCEANIA

SPOTLIGHT ON EUROPE

The word "robot" comes from the Czech word *robota*, meaning "work."

Roman gladiators consumed an energy drink containing ash.

Dancers in traditional costumes entertain at a festival in Prague, Czech Republic.

A cluster of islands and peninsulas jutting west from Asia, Europe is bordered by the Atlantic and Arctic Oceans and more than a dozen seas. Here you'll find a variety of scenery, from mountains to countryside to coastlines. Europe is also known for its rich culture and fascinating history, which make it one of the most visited continents on Earth.

Hedgehog

Blue Bloods

There are 12 surviving monarchies in western Europe. Denmark's royal family takes the crown for Europe's longest-running monarchy, having lasted more than 1,000 years.

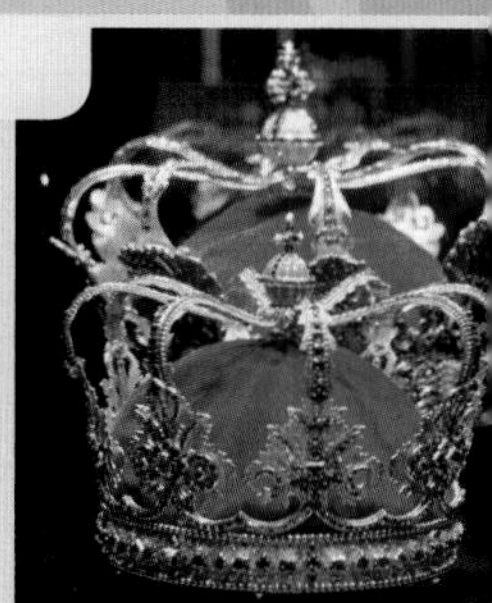

Recycling Star

Sweden takes recycling very seriously. Less than one percent of the country's household garbage ends up in landfills, and an average citizen recycles 146 bottles and cans a year.

Queen's Cards

Brits who turn 100 or celebrate a 60th wedding anniversary can get a truly royal treat: A personalized card from the Queen of England. The tradition dates back to 1917.

Castle Country

Belgium has more castles per square mile than anywhere else in the world. Its 3,000 royal abodes include the 600-year-old Castle of Vêves, still occupied by the original family.

Europe's Longest Rivers

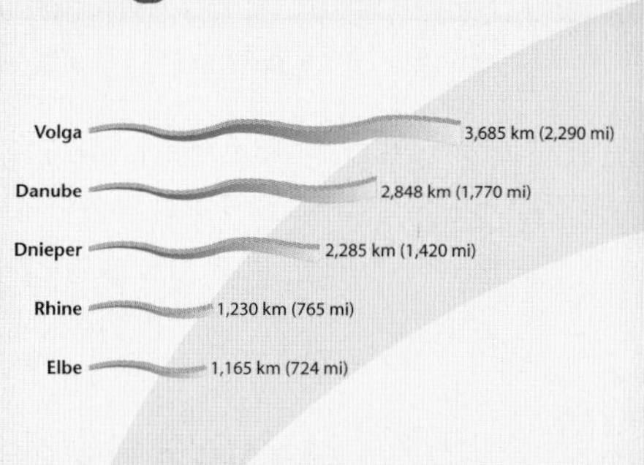

Oia, Greece

PHYSICAL

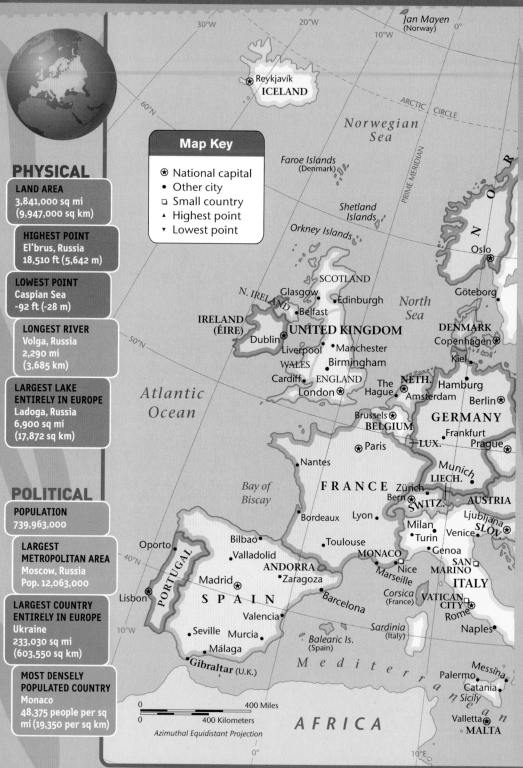

LAND AREA
3,841,000 sq mi
(9,947,000 sq km)

HIGHEST POINT
El'brus, Russia
18,510 ft (5,642 m)

LOWEST POINT
Caspian Sea
-92 ft (-28 m)

LONGEST RIVER
Volga, Russia
2,290 mi
(3,685 km)

LARGEST LAKE ENTIRELY IN EUROPE
Ladoga, Russia
6,900 sq mi
(17,872 sq km)

POLITICAL

POPULATION
739,963,000

LARGEST METROPOLITAN AREA
Moscow, Russia
Pop. 12,063,000

LARGEST COUNTRY ENTIRELY IN EUROPE
Ukraine
233,030 sq mi
(603,550 sq km)

MOST DENSELY POPULATED COUNTRY
Monaco
48,375 people per sq mi (19,350 per sq km)

Map Key

- ⊛ National capital
- • Other city
- ▫ Small country
- ▴ Highest point
- ▾ Lowest point

Jan Mayen (Norway)
Reykjavík
ICELAND
ARCTIC CIRCLE
Norwegian Sea
Faroe Islands (Denmark)
PRIME MERIDIAN
Shetland Islands
Orkney Islands
Oslo
SCOTLAND
N. IRELAND
Glasgow
Edinburgh
North Sea
Göteborg
Belfast
IRELAND (ÉIRE)
Dublin
UNITED KINGDOM
DENMARK
Copenhagen
Liverpool
Manchester
WALES
Birmingham
Kiel
Cardiff
ENGLAND
The Hague
NETH.
Hamburg
London
Amsterdam
Berlin
Atlantic Ocean
Brussels
BELGIUM
GERMANY
Frankfurt
LUX.
Prague
Paris
Nantes
Munich
LIECH.
Bay of Biscay
FRANCE
Zürich
Bern
SWITZ.
AUSTRIA
Bordeaux
Lyon
Ljubljana
SLOV.
Milan
Venice
Turin
Bilbao
Toulouse
Genoa
Oporto
Valladolid
MONACO
SAN MARINO
ANDORRA
Nice
PORTUGAL
Madrid
Zaragoza
Marseille
ITALY
Lisbon
SPAIN
Barcelona
Corsica (France)
VATICAN CITY
Rome
Valencia
Sardinia (Italy)
Naples
Seville
Murcia
Balearic Is. (Spain)
Málaga
Gibraltar (U.K.)
Mediterranean
Messina
Palermo
Catania
Sicily
Valletta
MALTA
AFRICA
30°W
20°W
10°W
0°
10°E
60°N
50°N
40°N

0 — 400 Miles
0 — 400 Kilometers
Azimuthal Equidistant Projection

EUROPE

A commonly accepted division between Asia and Europe—marked here by a maroon, dashed line—is formed by the Ural Mountains, Ural River, Caspian Sea, Caucasus Mountains, and the Black Sea with its outlets, the Bosporus and Dardanelles.

SPOTLIGHT ON NORTH AMERICA

A 95-mile (153 km)-long underground river flows beneath the Yucatán Peninsula in Mexico.

Each year the Cayman Islands holds an 11-day pirate festival.

El Castillo in Chichén Itzá, Mexico

From the Great Plains of the United States and Canada to the rain forests of Panama, North America stretches 5,500 miles (8,850 km) from north to south. The third largest continent, North America can be divided into five regions: the mountainous west (including parts of Mexico and Central America's western coast), the Great Plains, the Canadian Shield, the varied eastern region (including Central America's lowlands and coastal plains), and the Caribbean.

Steel drummers perform in Trinidad and Tobago.

Sloth Sanctuary

Orphaned, injured, and abandoned sloths roam the Sloth Sanctuary in Limon, Costa Rica. Sloths live most of their lives hanging upside down in trees in the dense rain forest canopy.

Hollywood South

Louisiana is one of the top filming locations in the United States. An abandoned Louisiana amusement park served as the setting for the blockbuster hit *Jurassic World*.

Nation's Mammal

Recently named the national mammal of the United States, the bison is North America's largest land animal. Some 500,000 of these animals roam throughout the continent.

Super Smarts

Canada is one of world's most educated countries. More than half of Canadian adults have a college degree. It is the only country other than Russia to achieve this.

World's Longest Coastlines

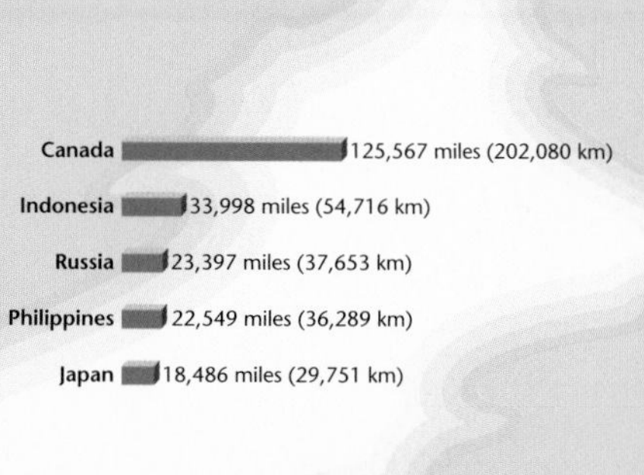

Onlookers celebrate the opening of the Panama Canal expansion in 2016.

PHYSICAL

LAND AREA
9,449,000 sq mi
(24,474,000 sq km)

LOWEST POINT
Death Valley, California
-282 ft (-86 m)

LARGEST LAKE
Lake Superior,
U.S.–Canada
31,700 sq mi
(82,100 sq km)

HIGHEST POINT
Denali, Alaska
20,320 ft (6,194 m)

LONGEST RIVER
Mississippi–Missouri,
United States
3,780 mi (6,083 km)

POLITICAL

POPULATION
578,802,000

LARGEST METROPOLITAN AREA
Mexico City, Mexico
Pop. 20,843,000

LARGEST COUNTRY
Canada
3,855,103 sq mi
(9,984,670 sq km)

MOST DENSELY POPULATED COUNTRY
Barbados / 1,700 people
per sq mi (656 per sq km)

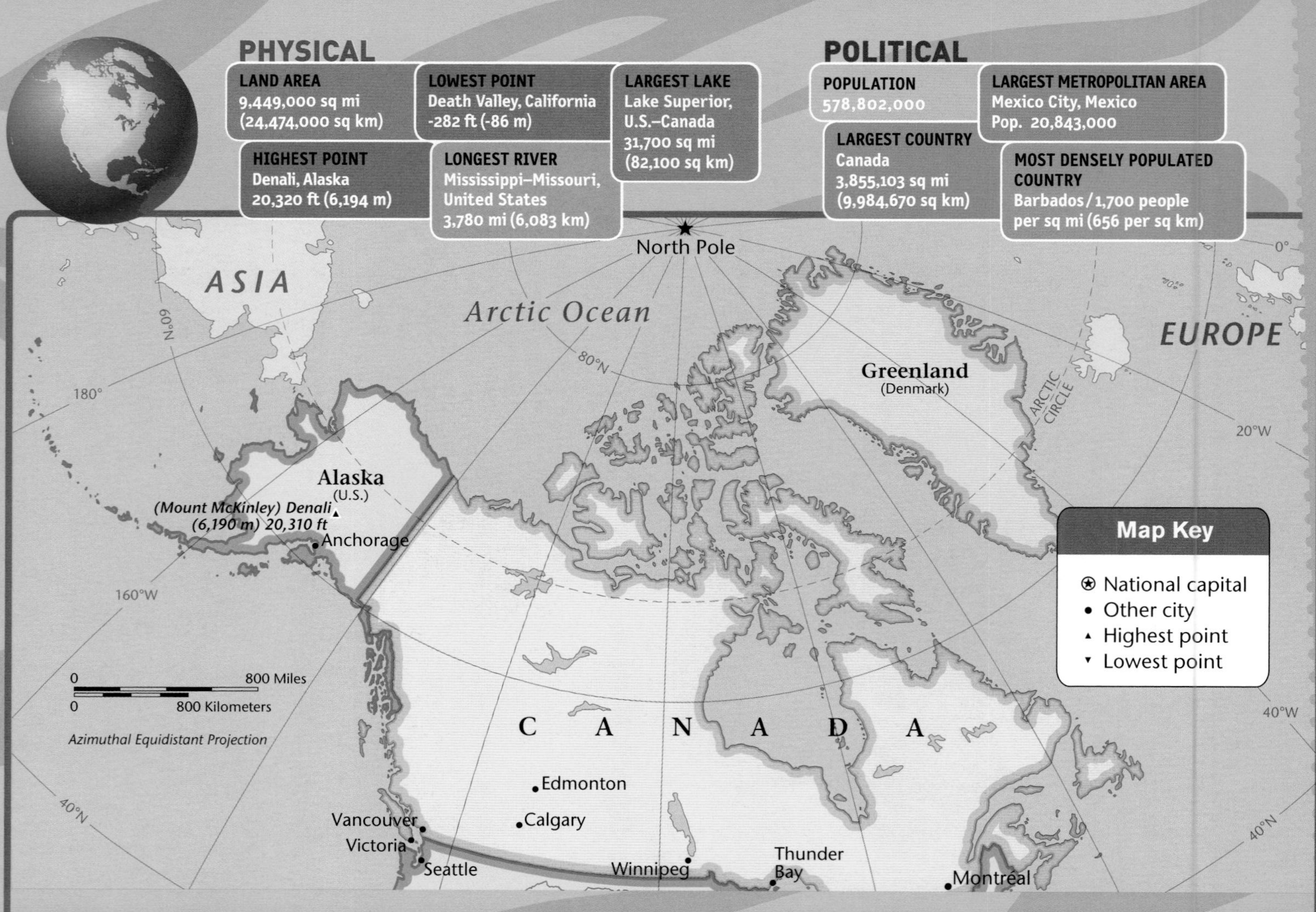

NORTH AMERICA

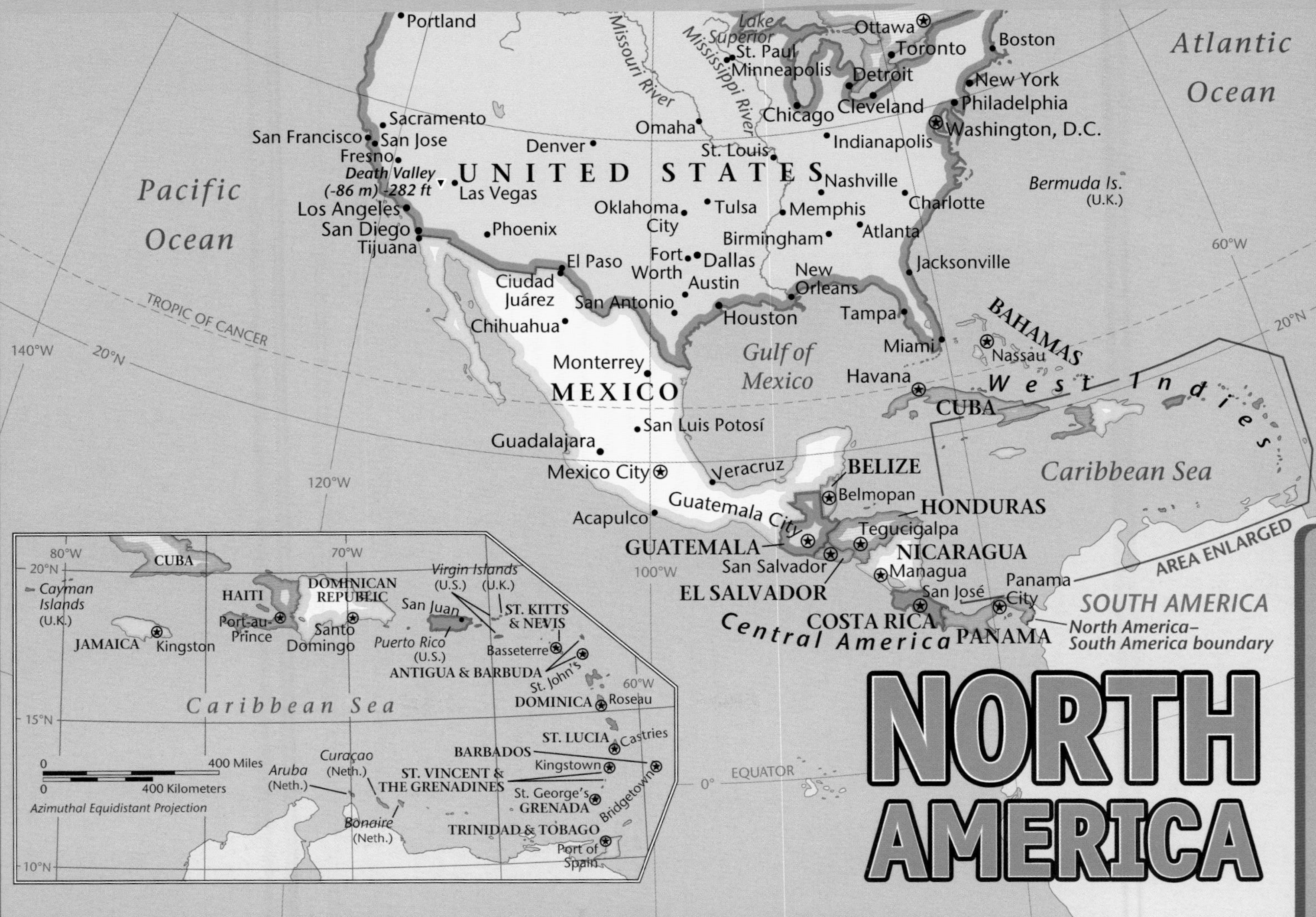

SPOTLIGHT ON SOUTH AMERICA

Nearly 80 percent of Guyana is covered by the rain forest.

You can find yellow, green, and red miniature bananas in Ecuador.

Common tree boa, Iwokrama forest reserve, Guyana

South America is bordered by three major bodies of water—the Caribbean Sea, Atlantic Ocean, and Pacific Ocean. The world's fourth largest continent extends over a range of climates from tropical in the north to subarctic in the south. South America produces a rich diversity of natural resources, including nuts, fruits, sugar, grains, coffee, and chocolate.

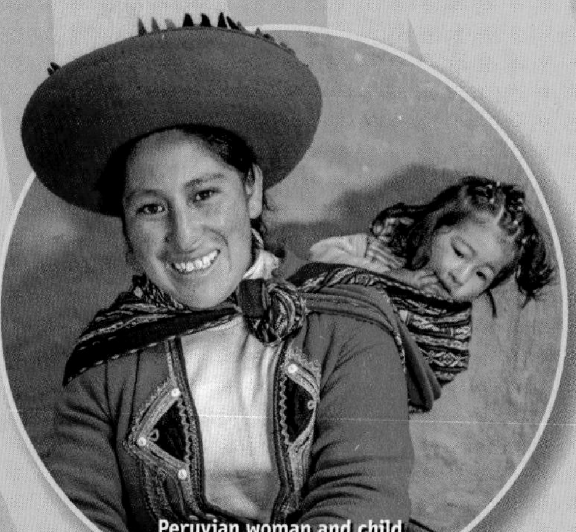
Peruvian woman and child in traditional dress

Hopping With Frogs

Despite its small size Colombia boasts one of the biggest variety of amphibians on the planet. The country is home to 800 species, including the tiny and highly venomous dart frog.

Cool Caves

While Chile's Easter Island is known for its giant moai statues, there's also an extensive cave system beneath the surface. Some are decorated with ancient cave paintings.

Big Horn

Known as the "unicorn bird," the horned screamer gets its name from the spiny, curved horn that juts out from its forehead. The tropical wetland bird is related to ducks and swans.

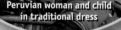

Living in Isolation

Brazil's Amazon rain forest is home to more isolated tribes than anywhere on the planet. There are thought to be at least 77 groups with little to no contact with the outside world.

World's Deepest Canyon

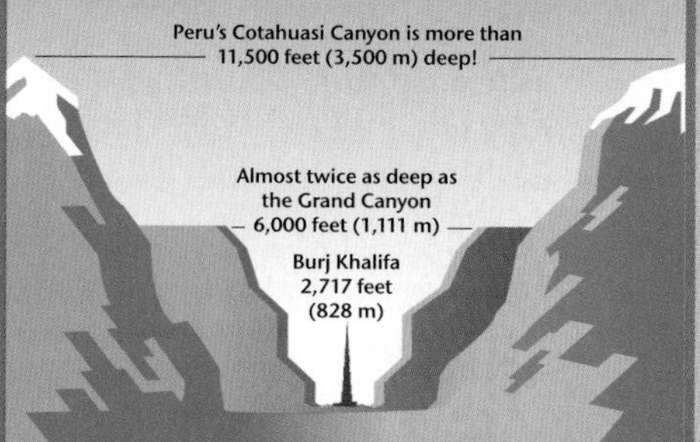
Peru's Cotahuasi Canyon is more than 11,500 feet (3,500 m) deep!
Almost twice as deep as the Grand Canyon 6,000 feet (1,111 m)
Burj Khalifa 2,717 feet (828 m)

Santiago Cathedral in Santiago, Chile

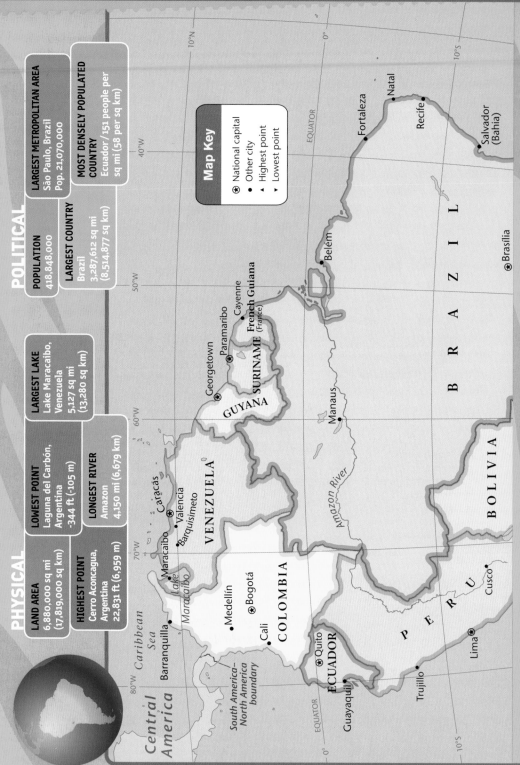

PHYSICAL

LAND AREA
6,880,000 sq mi
(17,819,000 sq km)

HIGHEST POINT
Cerro Aconcagua, Argentina
22,831 ft (6,959 m)

LOWEST POINT
Laguna del Carbón, Argentina
-344 ft (-105 m)

LONGEST RIVER
Amazon
4,150 mi (6,679 km)

LARGEST LAKE
Lake Maracaibo, Venezuela
5,127 sq mi
(13,280 sq km)

POLITICAL

POPULATION
418,848,000

LARGEST COUNTRY
Brazil
3,287,612 sq mi
(8,514,877 sq km)

LARGEST METROPOLITAN AREA
São Paulo, Brazil
Pop. 21,070,000

MOST DENSELY POPULATED COUNTRY
Ecuador / 151 people per sq mi (58 per sq km)

Map Key

- ⍟ National capital
- ● Other city
- ▲ Highest point
- ▼ Lowest point

SOUTH AMERICA
La Paz
Santa Cruz
Sucre
Goiânia
Belo Horizonte
PARAGUAY
Nova Iguaçu
São Paulo
Rio de Janeiro
Santos
TROPIC OF CAPRICORN
Curitiba
Asunción
San Miguel de Tucumán
Atlantic Ocean
Porto Alegre
Santa Fe
Córdoba
Rosario
URUGUAY
Cerro Aconcagua 22,831 ft (6,959 m)
Valparaíso
Santiago
Buenos Aires
La Plata
Montevideo
Pacific Ocean
Mar del Plata
CHILE
ARGENTINA
0
600 Miles
0
600 Kilometers
Azimuthal Equidistant Projection
Laguna del Carbón -344 ft (-105 m)
Stanley
Falkland Islands (U.K.)
Punta Arenas
South Georgia (U.K.)
20°S
30°S
40°S
50°S
100°W
90°W
80°W
60°W
50°W
40°W
30°W
20°W

COUNTRIES OF THE WORLD

The following pages present a general overview of all 195 independent countries recognized by the National Geographic Society, including the newest nation, South Sudan, which gained independence in 2011.

The flags of each independent country symbolize diverse cultures and histories. The statistical data cover highlights of geography and demography and provide a brief overview of each country. They present general characteristics and are not intended to be comprehensive. For example, not every language spoken in a specific country can be listed. Thus, languages shown are the most representative of that area. This is also true of the religions mentioned.

A country is defined as a political body with its own independent government, geographical space, and, in most cases, laws, military, and taxes.

Disputed areas such as Northern Cyprus and Taiwan, and dependencies of independent nations, such as Bermuda and Puerto Rico, are not included in this listing.

Note the color key at the bottom of the pages and the locator map below, which assign a color to each country based on the continent on which it is located. All information is accurate as of press time.

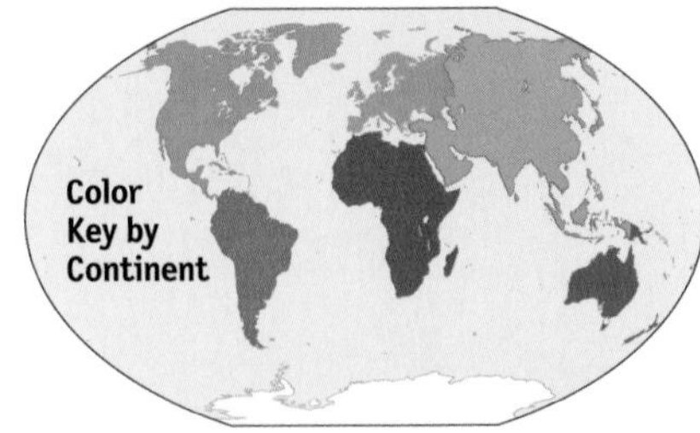

Afghanistan

Area: 251,773 sq mi (652,090 sq km)
Population: 33,403,000
Capital: Kabul, pop. 4,436,000
Currency: afghani
Religions: Sunni Muslim, Shiite Muslim
Languages: Afghan Persian (Dari), Pashto, Turkic languages (primarily Uzbek and Turkmen), Baluchi, 30 minor languages (including Pashai)

Albania

Area: 11,100 sq mi (28,748 sq km)
Population: 2,889,000
Capital: Tirana, pop. 445,000
Currency: lek
Religions: Muslim, Albanian Orthodox, Roman Catholic
Languages: Albanian, Greek, Vlach, Romani, Slavic dialects

Algeria

Area: 919,595 sq mi (2,381,741 sq km)
Population: 40,830,000
Capital: Algiers, pop. 2,559,000
Currency: Algerian dinar
Religion: Sunni Muslim
Languages: Arabic, French, Berber dialects

Andorra

Area: 181 sq mi (469 sq km)
Population: 80,000
Capital: Andorra la Vella, pop. 23,000
Currency: euro
Religion: Roman Catholic
Languages: Catalan, French, Castilian, Portuguese

Angola

Area: 481,354 sq mi (1,246,700 sq km)
Population: 25,830,000
Capital: Luanda, pop. 5,288,000
Currency: kwanza
Religions: indigenous beliefs, Roman Catholic, Protestant
Languages: Portuguese, Bantu, and other African languages

Antigua and Barbuda

Area: 171 sq mi (442 sq km)
Population: 93,000
Capital: St. John's, pop. 22,000
Currency: East Caribbean dollar
Religions: Anglican, Seventh-day Adventist, Pentecostal, Moravian, Roman Catholic, Methodist, Baptist, Church of God, other Christian
Languages: English, local dialects

Argentina

Area: 1,073,518 sq mi (2,780,400 sq km)
Population: 43,625,000
Capital: Buenos Aires, pop. 15,024,000
Currency: Argentine peso
Religion: Roman Catholic
Languages: Spanish, English, Italian, German, French

5 cool things about ARGENTINA

1. Both the coldest (-27°F/-32.8°C) and the hottest (120°F/48.9°C) temperatures in South America were recorded in Argentina.
2. Buenos Aires's subway system is the oldest in the Southern Hemisphere.
3. In 1917, an Argentinian cartoonist created the first-ever full-length animated film.
4. The national sport of Argentina is Pato, a game played on horseback combining elements of polo and basketball.
5. In Argentina, people eat gnocchi—plump pasta dumplings—on the 29th of each month for good luck and happiness.

Armenia

Area: 11,484 sq mi (29,743 sq km)
Population: 2,993,000
Capital: Yerevan, pop. 1,049,000
Currency: dram
Religions: Armenian Apostolic, other Christian
Language: Armenian

Australia

Area: 2,988,901 sq mi (7,741,220 sq km)
Population: 24,103,000
Capital: Canberra, A.C.T., pop. 415,000
Currency: Australian dollar
Religions: Roman Catholic, Anglican
Language: English

Austria

Area: 32,378 sq mi (83,858 sq km)
Population: 8,758,000
Capital: Vienna, pop. 1,743,000
Currency: euro
Religions: Roman Catholic, Protestant, Muslim
Language: German

Azerbaijan

Area: 33,436 sq mi (86,600 sq km)
Population: 9,762,000
Capital: Baku, pop. 2,317,000
Currency: Azerbaijani manat
Religion: Muslim
Language: Azerbaijani (Azeri)

Bahamas

Area: 5,382 sq mi (13,939 sq km)
Population: 382,000
Capital: Nassau, pop. 267,000
Currency: Bahamian dollar
Religions: Baptist, Anglican, Roman Catholic, Pentecostal, Church of God
Languages: English, Creole

Bahrain

Area: 277 sq mi (717 sq km)
Population: 1,446,000
Capital: Manama, pop. 398,000
Currency: Bahraini dinar
Religions: Shiite Muslim, Sunni Muslim, Christian
Languages: Arabic, English, Farsi, Urdu

Bangladesh

Area: 55,598 sq mi (143,998 sq km)
Population: 162,911,000
Capital: Dhaka, pop. 16,982,000
Currency: taka
Religions: Muslim, Hindu
Languages: Bangla (Bengali), English

Barbados

Area: 166 sq mi (430 sq km)
Population: 282,000
Capital: Bridgetown, pop. 90,000
Currency: Barbadian dollar
Religions: Anglican, Pentecostal, Methodist, other Protestant, Roman Catholic
Language: English

Bhutan

Area: 17,954 sq mi (46,500 sq km)
Population: 770,000
Capital: Thimphu, pop. 152,000
Currencies: ngultrum; Indian rupee
Religions: Lamaistic Buddhist, Indian- and Nepalese-influenced Hindu
Languages: Dzongkha, Tibetan dialects, Nepalese dialects

Belarus

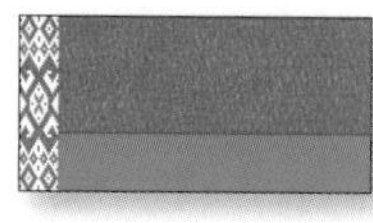

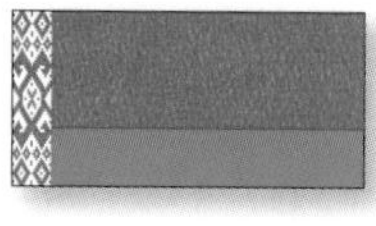

Area: 80,153 sq mi (207,595 sq km)
Population: 9,508,000
Capital: Minsk, pop. 1,905,000
Currency: Belarusian ruble
Religions: Eastern Orthodox, other (includes Roman Catholic, Protestant, Jewish, Muslim)
Languages: Belarusian, Russian

Bhutan is known as "LAND OF THE THUNDER DRAGON."

Belgium

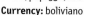

Area: 11,787 sq mi (30,528 sq km)
Population: 11,297,000
Capital: Brussels, pop. 2,029,000
Currency: euro
Religions: Roman Catholic, other (includes Protestant)
Languages: Dutch, French

Bolivia

Area: 424,164 sq mi (1,098,581 sq km)
Population: 10,985,000
Capitals: La Paz, pop. 1,800,000; Sucre, pop. 358,000
Currency: boliviano
Religions: Roman Catholic, Protestant (includes Evangelical Methodist)
Languages: Spanish, Quechua, Aymara

Belize

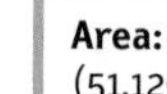

Area: 8,867 sq mi (22,965 sq km)
Population: 378,000
Capital: Belmopan, pop. 17,000
Currency: Belizean dollar
Religions: Roman Catholic, Protestant (includes Pentecostal, Seventh-day Adventist, Mennonite, Methodist)
Languages: Spanish, Creole, Mayan dialects, English, Garifuna (Carib), German

Bosnia and Herzegovina

Area: 19,741 sq mi (51,129 sq km)
Population: 3,519,000
Capital: Sarajevo, pop. 322,000
Currency: konvertibilna marka (convertible mark)
Religions: Muslim, Orthodox, Roman Catholic
Languages: Bosnian, Croatian, Serbian

Benin

Area: 43,484 sq mi (112,622 sq km)
Population: 10,800,000
Capitals: Porto-Novo, pop. 268,000; Cotonou, pop. 680,000
Currency: Communauté Financière Africaine franc
Religions: Christian, Muslim, Vodoun
Languages: French, Fon, Yoruba, tribal languages

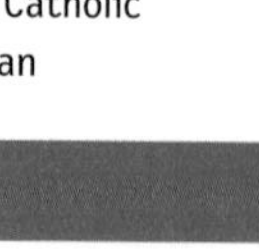

Botswana

Area: 224,607 sq mi (581,730 sq km)
Population: 2,226,000
Capital: Gaborone, pop. 247,000
Currency: pula
Religions: Christian, Badimo
Languages: Setswana, Kalanga

Brazil

Area: 3,287,612 sq mi (8,514,877 sq km)

Population: 206,147,000

Capital: Brasília, pop. 4,074,000

Currency: real

Religions: Roman Catholic, Protestant

Language: Portuguese

Bulgaria

Area: 42,855 sq mi (110,994 sq km)

Population: 7,130,000

Capital: Sofia, pop. 1,222,000

Currency: lev

Religions: Bulgarian Orthodox, Muslim

Languages: Bulgarian, Turkish, Roma

Brunei

Area: 2,226 sq mi (5,765 sq km)

Population: 424,000

Capital: Bandar Seri Begawan, pop. 14,000

Currency: Bruneian dollar

Religions: Muslim, Buddhist, Christian, other (includes indigenous beliefs)

Languages: Malay, English, Chinese

Burkina Faso

Area: 105,869 sq mi (274,200 sq km)

Population: 18,980,000

Capital: Ouagadougou, pop. 2,565,000

Currency: Communauté Financière Africaine franc

Religions: Muslim, indigenous beliefs, Christian

Languages: French, native African languages

You Are There!

North Yungus Road, Bolivia

Feeling brave? Hop on a bike and ride down Bolivia's North Yungus Road—if you dare. Dubbed the world's most dangerous road, this 40-mile (64-km) route attracts thousands of mountain bikers a year who make this risky ride for bragging rights and unrivaled views of the Amazon rain forest. Descending 11,000 feet (3,352 m) from the snowcapped Andes to the rain forest, cyclists navigate the dirt and gravel road, which narrows to just under 10 feet (3 m) at some points. And with no guardrails along the side of the road, there's nothing keeping travelers from tumbling down the cliffs.

Burundi

Area: 10,747 sq mi (27,834 sq km)
Population: 11,099,000
Capital: Bujumbura, pop. 707,000
Currency: Burundi franc
Religions: Roman Catholic, indigenous beliefs, Muslim, Protestant
Languages: Kirundi, French, Swahili

Cambodia

Area: 69,898 sq mi (181,035 sq km)
Population: 15,797,000
Capital: Phnom Penh, pop. 1,684,000
Currency: riel
Religion: Theravada Buddhist
Language: Khmer

Cabo Verde

Area: 1,558 sq mi (4,036 sq km)
Population: 528,000
Capital: Praia, pop. 145,000
Currency: Cape Verdean escudo
Religions: Roman Catholic (infused with indigenous beliefs), Protestant (mostly Church of the Nazarene)
Languages: Portuguese, Crioulo

Cameroon

Area: 183,569 sq mi (475,442 sq km)
Population: 24,361,000
Capital: Yaoundé, pop. 2,930,000
Currency: Communauté Financière Africaine franc
Religions: indigenous beliefs, Christian, Muslim
Languages: 24 major African language groups, English, French

You Are There!

Vancouver Island, British Columbia, Canada

Picture this: You're cruising around Vancouver Island on a ferry boat when you head out to the deck just in time to see a giant, shiny, black-and-white object go flying in the air before plunging back into the water with a huge splash. An orca! Hundreds of these massive mammals—plus other whales, including humpbacks, greys, and minkes—can be found in the waters surrounding Vancouver Island. So it's no wonder this place is one of the world's top whale-watching spots. But there's more than just whales to see as you wonder around Vancouver Island: Sea lions swim alongside octopuses, and you may spot a bald eagle soaring up above or a grizzly bear snagging salmon along the shores. So keep your eyes peeled—and be sure to bring your binoculars!

Canada

Area: 3,855,101 sq mi (9,984,670 sq km)
Population: 36,219,000
Capital: Ottawa, pop. 1,306,000
Currency: Canadian dollar
Religions: Roman Catholic, Protestant (includes United Church, Anglican), other Christian
Languages: English, French

Central African Republic

Area: 240,535 sq mi (622,984 sq km)
Population: 5,004,000
Capital: Bangui, pop. 781,000
Currency: Communauté Financière Africaine franc
Religions: indigenous beliefs, Protestant, Roman Catholic, Muslim
Languages: French, Sangho, tribal languages

Chad

Area: 495,755 sq mi (1,284,000 sq km)
Population: 14,511,000
Capital: N'Djamena, pop. 1,212,000
Currency: Communauté Financière Africaine franc
Religions: Muslim, Catholic, Protestant, animist
Languages: French, Arabic, Sara, more than 120 languages and dialects

Chile

Area: 291,930 sq mi (756,096 sq km)
Population: 18,198,000
Capital: Santiago, pop. 6,472,000
Currency: Chilean peso
Religions: Roman Catholic, Evangelical
Language: Spanish

China

Area: 3,705,406 sq mi (9,596,961 sq km)
Population: 1,378,033,000
Capital: Beijing, pop. 19,520,000
Currency: renminbi (yuan)
Religions: Taoist, Buddhist, Christian
Languages: Standard Chinese or Mandarin, Yue, Wu, Minbei, Minnan, Xiang, Gan, Hakka dialects

Colombia

Area: 440,831 sq mi (1,141,748 sq km)
Population: 48,762,000
Capital: Bogotá, pop. 9,558,000
Currency: Colombian peso
Religion: Roman Catholic
Language: Spanish

Comoros

Area: 863 sq mi (2,235 sq km)
Population: 806,000
Capital: Moroni, pop. 56,000
Currency: Comoran franc
Religion: Sunni Muslim
Languages: Arabic, French, Shikomoro

Congo

Area: 132,047 sq mi (342,000 sq km)
Population: 4,852,000
Capital: Brazzaville, pop. 1,827,000
Currency: Communauté Financière Africaine franc
Religions: Christian, animist
Languages: French, Lingala, Monokutuba, local languages

Costa Rica

Area: 19,730 sq mi (51,100 sq km)
Population: 4,890,000
Capital: San José, pop. 1,160,000
Currency: Costa Rican colón
Religions: Roman Catholic, Evangelical
Languages: Spanish, English

Côte d'Ivoire (Ivory Coast)

Area: 124,503 sq mi (322,462 sq km)
Population: 23,853,000
Capitals: Abidjan, pop. 4,708,000; Yamoussoukro, pop. 259,000
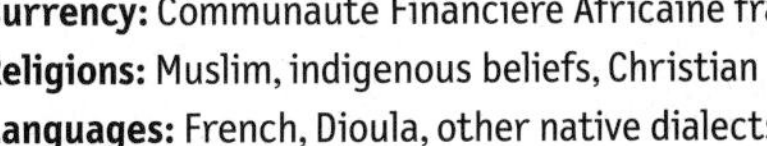
Currency: Communauté Financière Africaine franc
Religions: Muslim, indigenous beliefs, Christian
Languages: French, Dioula, other native dialects

Croatia

Area: 21,831 sq mi (56,542 sq km)
Population: 4,175,000
Capital: Zagreb, pop. 687,000
Currency: kuna
Religions: Roman Catholic, Orthodox
Language: Croatian

Cuba

Area: 42,803 sq mi (110,860 sq km)
Population: 11,208,000
Capital: Havana, pop. 2,146,000
Currency: Cuban peso
Religions: Roman Catholic, Protestant, Jehovah's Witnesses, Jewish, Santería
Language: Spanish

THE CHA-CHA DANCE ORIGINATED IN CUBA.

Cyprus

Area: 3,572 sq mi (9,251 sq km)
Population: 1,177,000
Capital: Nicosia, pop. 251,000
Currencies: euro; new Turkish lira in Northern Cyprus
Religions: Greek Orthodox, Muslim, Maronite, Armenian Apostolic
Languages: Greek, Turkish, English

Czech Republic (Czechia)

Area: 30,450 sq mi (78,866 sq km)
Population: 10,562,000
Capital: Prague, pop. 1,303,000
Currency: koruny
Religion: Roman Catholic
Language: Czech

Democratic Republic of the Congo

Area: 905,365 sq mi (2,344,885 sq km)
Population: 79,799,000
Capital: Kinshasa, pop. 11,116,000
Currency: Congolese franc
Religions: Roman Catholic, Protestant, Kimbanguist, Muslim, syncretic sects, indigenous beliefs
Languages: French, Lingala, Kingwana, Kikongo, Tshiluba

Denmark

Area: 16,640 sq mi (43,098 sq km)
Population: 5,731,000
Capital: Copenhagen, pop. 1,255,000
Currency: Danish krone
Religions: Evangelical Lutheran, other Protestant, Roman Catholic
Languages: Danish, Faroese, Greenlandic, German, English as second language

Djibouti

Area: 8,958 sq mi (23,200 sq km)
Population: 900,000
Capital: Djibouti, pop. 522,000
Currency: Djiboutian franc
Religions: Muslim, Christian
Languages: French, Arabic, Somali, Afar

Dominica

Area: 290 sq mi (751 sq km)
Population: 73,000
Capital: Roseau, pop. 15,000
Currency: East Caribbean dollar
Religions: Roman Catholic, Seventh-day Adventist, Pentecostal, Baptist, Methodist, other Christian
Languages: English, French patois

Dominican Republic

Area: 18,704 sq mi (48,442 sq km)
Population: 10,630,000
Capital: Santo Domingo, pop. 2,873,000
Currency: Dominican peso
Religion: Roman Catholic
Language: Spanish

COLOR KEY ● Africa ● Australia, New Zealand, and Oceania

Ecuador

Area: 109,483 sq mi (283,560 sq km)
Population: 16,529,000
Capital: Quito, pop. 1,699,000
Currency: U.S. dollar
Religion: Roman Catholic
Languages: Spanish, Quechua, other Amerindian languages

Ecuador's Seymour Airport on the Galápagos RUNS ON SOLAR AND WIND ENERGY.

Egypt

Area: 386,874 sq mi (1,002,000 sq km)
Population: 93,492,000
Capital: Cairo, pop. 18,419,000
Currency: Egyptian pound
Religions: Muslim (mostly Sunni), Coptic Christian
Languages: Arabic, English, French

El Salvador

Area: 8,124 sq mi (21,041 sq km)
Population: 6,408,000
Capital: San Salvador, pop. 1,097,000
Currency: U.S. dollar
Religions: Roman Catholic, Protestant
Languages: Spanish, Nahua

Equatorial Guinea

Area: 10,831 sq mi (28,051 sq km)
Population: 870,000
Capital: Malabo, pop. 145,000
Currency: Communauté Financière Africaine franc
Religions: Christian (predominantly Roman Catholic), pagan practices
Languages: Spanish, French, Fang, Bubi

Eritrea

Area: 45,406 sq mi (117,600 sq km)
Population: 5,352,000
Capital: Asmara, pop. 775,000
Currency: nakfa
Religions: Muslim, Coptic Christian, Roman Catholic
Languages: Afar, Arabic, Tigre, Kunama, Tigrinya, other Cushitic languages

Estonia

Area: 17,462 sq mi (45,227 sq km)
Population: 1,317,000
Capital: Tallinn, pop. 392,000
Currency: euro
Religions: Evangelical Lutheran, Orthodox
Languages: Estonian, Russian

Ethiopia

Area: 426,373 sq mi (1,104,300 sq km)
Population: 101,746,000
Capital: Addis Ababa, pop. 3,168,000
Currency: birr
Religions: Christian, Muslim, traditional
Languages: Amharic, Oromigna, Tigrinya, Guaragigna

1. Peaking at 7,610 feet (2,320 m), Addis Ababa is Africa's highest capital city.
2. Ethiopia is the only African country that was never colonized.
3. The oldest remains of modern humans were discovered in Ethiopia. The bones date back about 195,000 years.
4. Ethiopia's Danakil Desert is among the hottest and driest places on Earth. Temperatures regularly top 120°F (49°C).
5. Gelada baboons are only found in Ethiopia. Some 200,000 of the grass-eating monkeys live in the country's high mountain meadows.

Fiji

Area: 7,095 sq mi (18,376 sq km)

Population: 871,000

Capital: Suva, pop. 176,000

Currency: Fijian dollar

Religions: Christian (Methodist, Roman Catholic, Assembly of God), Hindu (Sanatan), Muslim (Sunni)

Languages: English, Fijian, Hindustani

Finland

Area: 130,558 sq mi (338,145 sq km)

Population: 5,494,000

Capital: Helsinki, pop. 1,170,000

Currency: euro

Religion: Lutheran Church of Finland

Languages: Finnish, Swedish

France

Area: 210,026 sq mi (543,965 sq km)

Population: 64,631,000

Capital: Paris, pop. 10,764,000

Currency: euro

Religions: Roman Catholic, Muslim

Language: French

Gabon

Area: 103,347 sq mi (267,667 sq km)

Population: 1,765,000

Capital: Libreville, pop. 695,000

Currency: Communauté Financière Africaine franc

Religions: Christian, animist

Languages: French, Fang, Myene, Nzebi, Bapounou/Eschira, Bandjabi

You Are There!

Mole National Park, Ghana

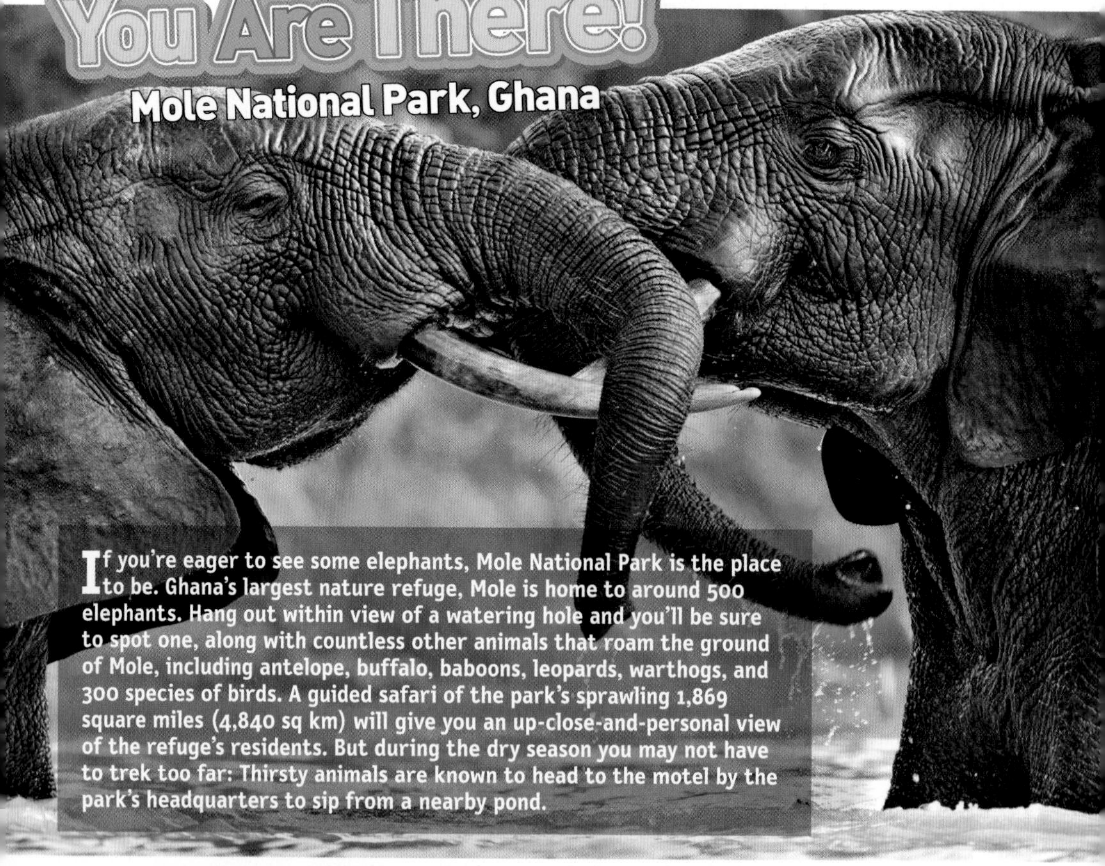

If you're eager to see some elephants, Mole National Park is the place to be. Ghana's largest nature refuge, Mole is home to around 500 elephants. Hang out within view of a watering hole and you'll be sure to spot one, along with countless other animals that roam the ground of Mole, including antelope, buffalo, baboons, leopards, warthogs, and 300 species of birds. A guided safari of the park's sprawling 1,869 square miles (4,840 sq km) will give you an up-close-and-personal view of the refuge's residents. But during the dry season you may not have to trek too far: Thirsty animals are known to head to the motel by the park's headquarters to sip from a nearby pond.

Gambia

Area: 4,361 sq mi (11,295 sq km)
Population: 2,086,000
Capital: Banjul, pop. 489,000
Currency: dalasi
Religions: Muslim, Christian
Languages: English, Mandinka, Wolof, Fula, other indigenous vernaculars

Georgia

Area: 26,911 sq mi (69,700 sq km)
Population: 3,976,000
Capital: Tbilisi, pop. 1,150,000
Currency: lari
Religions: Orthodox Christian, Muslim, Armenian-Gregorian
Languages: Georgian, Russian, Armenian, Azeri, Abkhaz

Germany

Area: 137,847 sq mi (357,022 sq km)
Population: 82,625,000
Capital: Berlin, pop. 3,547,000
Currency: euro
Religions: Protestant, Roman Catholic, Muslim
Language: German

Ghana

Area: 92,100 sq mi (238,537 sq km)
Population: 28,231,000
Capital: Accra, pop. 2,242,000
Currency: Ghana cedi
Religions: Christian (Pentecostal/Charismatic, Protestant, Roman Catholic, other), Muslim, traditional beliefs
Languages: Asante, Ewe, Fante, Boron (Brong), Dagomba, Dangme, Dagarte (Dagaba), Akyem, Ga, English

Greece

Area: 50,949 sq mi (131,957 sq km)
Population: 10,756,000
Capital: Athens, pop. 3,060,000
Currency: euro
Religion: Greek Orthodox
Languages: Greek, English, French

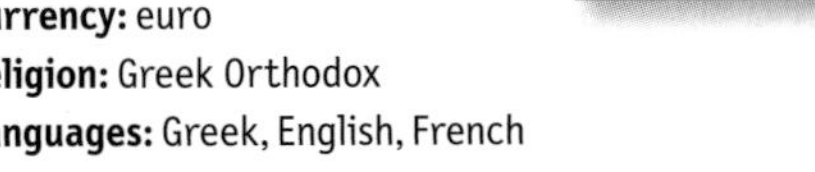

Grenada

Area: 133 sq mi (344 sq km)
Population: 112,000
Capital: St. George's, pop. 38,000
Currency: East Caribbean dollar
Religions: Roman Catholic, Anglican, other Protestant
Languages: English, French patois

Guatemala

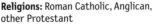

Area: 42,042 sq mi (108,889 sq km)
Population: 16,554,000
Capital: Guatemala City, pop. 2,874,000
Currency: quetzal
Religions: Roman Catholic, Protestant, indigenous Maya beliefs
Languages: Spanish, 23 official Amerindian languages

Guinea

Area: 94,926 sq mi (245,857 sq km)
Population: 11,197,000
Capital: Conakry, pop. 1,886,000
Currency: Guinean franc
Religions: Muslim, Christian, indigenous beliefs
Languages: French, ethnic languages

Guinea-Bissau

Area: 13,948 sq mi (36,125 sq km)
Population: 1,888,000
Capital: Bissau, pop. 473,000
Currency: Communauté Financière Africaine franc
Religions: indigenous beliefs, Muslim, Christian
Languages: Portuguese, Crioulo, African languages

Guyana

Area: 83,000 sq mi (214,969 sq km)
Population: 759,000
Capital: Georgetown, pop. 124,000
Currency: Guyanese dollar
Religions: Christian, Hindu, Muslim
Languages: English, Amerindian dialects, Creole, Hindustani, Urdu

Haiti

Area: 10,714 sq mi (27,750 sq km)
Population: 11,093,000
Capital: Port-au-Prince, pop. 2,376,000
Currency: gourde
Religions: Roman Catholic, Protestant (Baptist, Pentecostal, other)
Languages: French, Creole

Honduras

Area: 43,433 sq mi (112,492 sq km)
Population: 8,200,000
Capital: Tegucigalpa, pop. 1,101,000
Currency: lempira
Religions: Roman Catholic, Protestant
Languages: Spanish, Amerindian dialects

Hungary

Area: 35,919 sq mi (93,030 sq km)
Population: 9,807,000
Capital: Budapest, pop. 1,717,000
Currency: forint
Religions: Roman Catholic, Calvinist, Lutheran
Language: Hungarian

Iceland

Area: 39,769 sq mi (103,000 sq km)
Population: 334,000
Capital: Reykjavík, pop. 184,000
Currency: Icelandic krona
Religion: Lutheran Church of Iceland
Languages: Icelandic, English, Nordic languages, German

India

Area: 1,269,221 sq mi (3,287,270 sq km)
Population: 1,328,853,000
Capital: New Delhi, pop. 24,953,000 (part of Delhi metropolitan area)
Currency: Indian rupee
Religions: Hindu, Muslim
Languages: Hindi, 21 other official languages, Hindustani (popular Hindi/Urdu variant in the north)

Indonesia

Area: 742,308 sq mi (1,922,570 sq km)
Population: 259,448,000
Capital: Jakarta, pop. 10,176,000
Currency: Indonesian rupiah
Religions: Muslim, Protestant, Roman Catholic
Languages: Bahasa Indonesia (modified form of Malay), English, Dutch, Javanese, local dialects

Iran

Area: 636,296 sq mi (1,648,000 sq km)
Population: 79,482,000
Capital: Tehran, pop. 8,353,000
Currency: Iranian rial
Religions: Shiite Muslim, Sunni Muslim
Languages: Persian, Turkic, Kurdish, Luri, Baluchi, Arabic

Iraq

Area: 168,754 sq mi (437,072 sq km)
Population: 38,146,000
Capital: Baghdad, pop. 6,483,000
Currency: Iraqi dinar
Religions: Shiite Muslim, Sunni Muslim
Languages: Arabic, Kurdish, Assyrian, Armenian

Ireland (Éire)

Area: 27,133 sq mi (70,273 sq km)
Population: 4,668,000
Capital: Dublin, pop. 1,155,000
Currency: euro
Religions: Roman Catholic, Church of Ireland
Languages: Irish (Gaelic), English

Israel

Area: 8,550 sq mi (22,145 sq km)
Population: 8,201,000
Capital: Jerusalem, pop. 829,000
Currency: new Israeli sheqel
Religions: Jewish, Muslim
Languages: Hebrew, Arabic, English

Italy

Area: 116,345 sq mi (301,333 sq km)
Population: 60,601,000
Capital: Rome, pop. 3,697,000
Currency: euro
Religions: Roman Catholic, Protestant, Jewish, Muslim
Languages: Italian, German, French, Slovene

Japan

Area: 145,902 sq mi (377,887 sq km)
Population: 125,310,000
Capital: Tokyo, pop. 37,833,000
Currency: yen
Religions: Shinto, Buddhist
Language: Japanese

Jamaica

Area: 4,244 sq mi (10,991 sq km)
Population: 2,732,000
Capital: Kingston, pop. 587,000
Currency: Jamaican dollar
Religions: Protestant (Church of God, Seventh-day Adventist, Pentecostal, Baptist, Anglican, other)
Languages: English, English patois

Jordan

Area: 34,495 sq mi (89,342 sq km)
Population: 8,185,000
Capital: Amman, pop. 1,148,000
Currency: Jordanian dinar
Religions: Sunni Muslim, Christian
Languages: Arabic, English

You Are There!

Blue Lagoon, near Grindavík, Iceland

Tucked away in an ancient, jet-black lava field you'll find the Blue Lagoon, a geothermal spa near Grindavík, Iceland. No matter the temperature outside, this sprawling, steaming spa offers warm waters hovering around 100°F (38°C) to soak in. Slide into the milky blue water and cover yourself with mineral-enriched mud, which softens and nourishes your skin. Or make your way over to the human-made waterfall and let the cascading flow massage your shoulders and back. Did someone say *ahhhh?*

Kazakhstan

Area: 1,049,155 sq mi (2,717,300 sq km)

Population: 17,799,000

Capital: Astana, pop. 741,000

Currency: tenge

Religions: Muslim, Russian Orthodox

Languages: Kazakh (Qazaq), Russian

Kenya

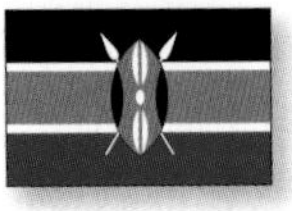

Area: 224,081 sq mi (580,367 sq km)

Population: 45,397,000

Capital: Nairobi, pop. 3,768,000

Currency: Kenyan shilling

Religions: Protestant, Roman Catholic, Muslim, indigenous beliefs

Languages: English, Kiswahili, many indigenous languages

Kiribati

Area: 313 sq mi (811 sq km)

Population: 116,000

Capital: Tarawa, pop. 46,000

Currency: Australian dollar

Religions: Roman Catholic, Protestant (Congregational)

Languages: I-Kiribati, English

Kosovo

Area: 4,203 sq mi (10,887 sq km)

Population: 1,755,000

Capital: Prishtina, pop. 207,500

Currency: euro

Religions: Muslim, Serbian Orthodox, Roman Catholic

Languages: Albanian, Serbian, Bosnian, Turkish, Roma

You Are There!

Bokeo Nature Reserve, Laos

Up for an adventure? Head to the Bokeo Nature Reserve, a lush rain forest in northern Laos. There, you can take a three-day tour exploring the depths of this wilderness while looking out for some of the area's most coveted wildlife, including tigers, black bears, clouded leopards, and black-crested gibbons. Shoot down a series of zip lines cutting through the rain forest's canopy, then cool off in a swimming hole found at the base of a rushing waterfall. And when you need a place to rest your head? Spend the night in a tree house nestled 130 feet (40 m) above the ground. No need to set an alarm clock: The gibbons' screeching call will wake you right up.

Kuwait

Area: 6,880 sq mi (17,818 sq km)
Population: 4,049,000
Capital: Kuwait City, pop. 2,680,000
Currency: Kuwaiti dinar
Religions: Sunni Muslim, Shiite Muslim
Languages: Arabic, English

Kyrgyzstan

Area: 77,182 sq mi (199,900 sq km)
Population: 6,083,000
Capital: Bishkek, pop. 858,000
Currency: som
Religions: Muslim, Russian Orthodox
Languages: Kyrgyz, Uzbek, Russian

Laos

Area: 91,429 sq mi (236,800 sq km)
Population: 7,077,000
Capital: Vientiane, pop. 946,000
Currency: kip
Religions: Buddhist, animist
Languages: Lao, French, English, various ethnic languages

Latvia

Area: 24,938 sq mi (64,589 sq km)
Population: 1,964,000
Capital: Riga, pop. 629,000
Currency: Latvian lat
Religions: Lutheran, Roman Catholic, Russian Orthodox
Languages: Latvian, Russian, Lithuanian

Lebanon

Area: 4,036 sq mi (10,452 sq km)
Population: 6,238,000
Capital: Beirut, pop. 2,179,000
Currency: Lebanese pound
Religions: Muslim, Christian
Languages: Arabic, French, English, Armenian

Lesotho

Area: 11,720 sq mi (30,355 sq km)
Population: 2,163,000
Capital: Maseru, pop. 267,000
Currencies: loti; South African rand
Religions: Christian, indigenous beliefs
Languages: Sesotho, English, Zulu, Xhosa

Liberia

Area: 43,000 sq mi (111,370 sq km)
Population: 4,615,000
Capital: Monrovia, pop. 1,224,000
Currency: Liberian dollar
Religions: Christian, indigenous beliefs, Muslim
Languages: English, some 20 ethnic languages

Libya

Area: 679,362 sq mi (1,759,540 sq km)
Population: 6,330,000
Capital: Tripoli, pop. 1,126,000
Currency: Libyan dinar
Religion: Sunni Muslim
Languages: Arabic, Italian, English

Liechtenstein

Area: 62 sq mi (160 sq km)
Population: 38,000
Capital: Vaduz, pop. 5,000
Currency: Swiss franc
Religions: Roman Catholic, Protestant
Languages: German, Alemannic dialect

Lithuania

Area: 25,212 sq mi (65,300 sq km)
Population: 2,872,000
Capital: Vilnius, pop. 519,000
Currency: litas
Religions: Roman Catholic, Russian Orthodox
Languages: Lithuanian, Russian, Polish

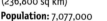

Luxembourg

Area: 998 sq mi (2,586 sq km)
Population: 583,000
Capital: Luxembourg, pop. 107,000
Currency: euro
Religions: Roman Catholic, Protestant, Jewish, Muslim
Languages: Luxembourgish, German, French

Macedonia

Area: 9,928 sq mi (25,713 sq km)
Population: 2,073,000
Capital: Skopje, pop. 501,000
Currency: Macedonian denar
Religions: Macedonian Orthodox, Muslim
Languages: Macedonian, Albanian, Turkish

Madagascar

Area: 226,658 sq mi (587,041 sq km)
Population: 23,667,000
Capital: Antananarivo, pop. 2,487,000
Currency: Madagascar ariary
Religions: indigenous beliefs, Christian, Muslim
Languages: English, French, Malagasy

Malawi

Area: 45,747 sq mi (118,484 sq km)
Population: 17,225,000
Capital: Lilongwe, pop. 867,000
Currency: Malawian kwacha
Religions: Christian, Muslim
Languages: Chichewa, Chinyanja, Chiyao, Chitumbuka

Malaysia

Area: 127,355 sq mi (329,847 sq km)
Population: 30,791,000
Capital: Kuala Lumpur, pop. 6,629,000
Currency: ringgit
Religions: Muslim, Buddhist, Christian, Hindu
Languages: Bahasa Malaysia, English, Chinese, Tamil, Telugu, Malayalam, Panjabi, Thai, indigenous languages

Maldives

Area: 115 sq mi (298 sq km)
Population: 414,000
Capital: Male, pop. 156,000
Currency: rufiyaa
Religion: Sunni Muslim
Languages: Maldivian Dhivehi, English

Mali

Area: 478,841 sq mi (1,240,192 sq km)
Population: 17,260,000
Capital: Bamako, pop. 2,386,000
Currency: Communauté Financière Africaine franc
Religions: Muslim, indigenous beliefs
Languages: Bambara, French, numerous African languages

Malta

Area: 122 sq mi (316 sq km)
Population: 433,000
Capital: Valletta, pop. 197,000
Currency: euro
Religion: Roman Catholic
Languages: Maltese, English

Marshall Islands

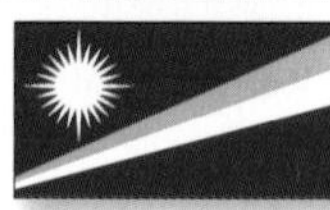

Area: 70 sq mi (181 sq km)
Population: 55,000
Capital: Majuro, pop. 31,000
Currency: U.S. dollar
Religions: Protestant, Assembly of God, Roman Catholic
Language: Marshallese

THE HIGHEST POINT on the Marshall Islands is a 32-foot (10-m) hill.

Mauritania

Area: 397,955 sq mi (1,030,700 sq km)
Population: 4,166,000
Capital: Nouakchott, pop. 945,000
Currency: ouguiya
Religion: Muslim
Languages: Arabic, Pulaar, Soninke, French, Hassaniya, Wolof

Mauritius

Area: 788 sq mi (2,040 sq km)
Population: 1,263,000
Capital: Port Louis, pop. 135,000
Currency: Mauritian rupee
Religions: Hindu, Roman Catholic, Muslim, other Christian
Languages: Creole, Bhojpuri, French

Mexico

Area: 758,449 sq mi (1,964,375 sq km)
Population: 128,632,000
Capital: Mexico City, pop. 20,843,000
Currency: Mexican peso
Religions: Roman Catholic, Protestant
Languages: Spanish, Mayan, other indigenous languages

Micronesia

Area: 271 sq mi (702 sq km)
Population: 103,000
Capital: Palikir, pop. 7,000
Currency: U.S. dollar
Religions: Roman Catholic, Protestant
Languages: English, Trukese, Pohnpeian, Yapese, other indigenous languages

Moldova

Area: 13,050 sq mi (33,800 sq km)
Population: 3,552,000
Capital: Chisinau, pop. 721,000
Currency: Moldovan leu
Religion: Eastern Orthodox
Languages: Moldovan, Russian, Gagauz

Monaco

Area: 0.8 sq mi (2.0 sq km)
Population: 39,000
Capital: Monaco, pop. 38,000
Currency: euro
Religion: Roman Catholic
Languages: French, English, Italian, Monegasque

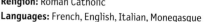

5 cool things about MONACO

1. The second smallest country in the world, Monaco would fit inside New York City's Central Park.
2. Both the Prince and Princess of Monaco are Olympians. Prince Albert competed in the bobsleigh, while Princess Charlene was a champion swimmer for South Africa.
3. Each May, race cars zoom through the country's narrow streets for the Monaco Grand Prix, a world-famous car race.
4. The changing-of-the-guard outside of the Prince's Palace has occurred every day at 11:55 a.m. for more than 100 years.
5. A native of Monaco is called a Monegasque.

Mongolia

Area: 603,909 sq mi (1,564,116 sq km)
Population: 3,094,000
Capital: Ulaanbaatar, pop. 1,334,000
Currency: togrog/tugrik
Religions: Buddhist Lamaist, Shamanist, Christian
Languages: Khalkha Mongol, Turkic, Russian

Montenegro

Area: 5,333 sq mi (13,812 sq km)
Population: 619,000
Capital: Podgorica, pop. 165,000
Currency: euro
Religions: Orthodox, Muslim, Roman Catholic
Languages: Serbian (Ijekavian dialect), Bosnian, Albanian, Croatian

Asia • Europe • North America • South America

Morocco

Area: 172,414 sq mi (446,550 sq km)
Population: 34,705,000
Capital: Rabat, pop. 1,932,000
Currency: Moroccan dirham
Religion: Muslim
Languages: Arabic, Berber dialects, French

Myanmar (Burma)

Area: 261,218 sq mi (676,552 sq km)
Population: 52,414,000
Capitals: Nay Pyi Taw, pop. 1,016,000; Yangon (Rangoon), pop. 4,802,000
Currency: kyat
Religions: Buddhist, Christian, Muslim
Languages: Burmese, minority ethnic languages

Mozambique

Area: 308,642 sq mi (799,380 sq km)
Population: 27,181,000
Capital: Maputo, pop. 1,174,000
Currency: metical
Religions: Roman Catholic, Muslim, Zionist Christian
Languages: Emakhuwa, Xichangana, Portuguese, Elomwe, Cisena, Echuwabo, other local languages

Namibia

Area: 318,261 sq mi (824,292 sq km)
Population: 2,537,000
Capital: Windhoek, pop. 356,000
Currencies: Namibian dollar; South African rand
Religions: Lutheran, other Christian, indigenous beliefs
Languages: Afrikaans, German, English

Milford Sound, New Zealand

Cascading waterfalls, mountaintop glaciers, and towering cliffs: These are just some of the reasons why New Zealand's Milford Sound is often referred to as the "eighth wonder of the world." An inlet of the Tasman Sea, this 7.5-mile (12-km) body of water is not actually a sound but a fjord carved by a glacier. The deep blue water is framed by majestic mountains, including Mitre Peak, soaring some 5,550 feet (1,690 m) into the sky. Take a hike around the trails and discover unrivaled natural beauty, or head down to an enclosed, underwater observatory where you can spot 11-legged sea stars and rainbow-hued tropical fish swimming around the black coral. Really want to take it all in? Hop on a helicopter and enjoy a bird's-eye view of the entire area, from ancient forest valleys to jagged peaks, while keeping an eye out for wildlife like dolphins, seals, and penguins.

Nauru

Area: 8 sq mi (21 sq km)
Population: 11,000
Capital: Yaren, pop. 10,000
Currency: Australian dollar
Religions: Protestant, Roman Catholic
Languages: Nauruan, English

Nepal

Area: 56,827 sq mi (147,181 sq km)
Population: 28,431,000
Capital: Kathmandu, pop. 1,142,000
Currency: Nepalese rupee
Religions: Hindu, Buddhist, Muslim, Kirant
Languages: Nepali, Maithali, Bhojpuri, Tharu, Tamang, Newar, Magar

Netherlands

Area: 16,034 sq mi (41,528 sq km)
Population: 17,020,000
Capital: Amsterdam, pop. 1,084,000
Currency: euro
Religions: Roman Catholic, Dutch Reformed, Calvinist, Muslim
Languages: Dutch, Frisian

New Zealand

Area: 104,454 sq mi (270,534 sq km)
Population: 4,698,000
Capital: Wellington, pop. 380,000
Currency: New Zealand dollar
Religions: Anglican, Roman Catholic, Presbyterian, other Christian
Languages: English, Maori

Nicaragua

Area: 50,193 sq mi (130,000 sq km)
Population: 6,328,000
Capital: Managua, pop. 951,000
Currency: gold cordoba
Religions: Roman Catholic, Evangelical
Language: Spanish

Niger

Area: 489,191 sq mi (1,267,000 sq km)
Population: 19,749,000
Capital: Niamey, pop. 1,058,000
Currency: Communauté Financière Africaine franc
Religions: Muslim, other (includes indigenous beliefs and Christian)
Languages: French, Hausa, Djerma

Nigeria

Area: 356,669 sq mi (923,768 sq km)
Population: 186,510,000
Capital: Abuja, pop. 2,301,000
Currency: naira
Religions: Muslim, Christian, indigenous beliefs
Languages: English, Hausa, Yoruba, Igbo (Ibo), Fulani

North Korea

Area: 46,540 sq mi (120,538 sq km)
Population: 25,115,000
Capital: Pyongyang, pop. 2,856,000
Currency: North Korean won
Religions: Buddhist, Confucianist, some Christian and syncretic Chondogyo
Language: Korean

Norway

Area: 125,004 sq mi (323,758 sq km)
Population: 5,238,000
Capital: Oslo, pop. 970,000
Currency: Norwegian krone
Religion: Church of Norway (Lutheran)
Languages: Bokmal Norwegian, Nynorsk Norwegian, Sami

Oman

Area: 119,500 sq mi (309,500 sq km)
Population: 4,351,000
Capital: Muscat, pop. 812,000
Currency: Omani rial
Religions: Ibadhi Muslim, Sunni Muslim, Shiite Muslim, Hindu
Languages: Arabic, English, Baluchi, Urdu, Indian dialects

Pakistan

Area: 307,374 sq mi (796,095 sq km)
Population: 203,447,000
Capital: Islamabad, pop. 1,297,000
Currency: Pakistani rupee
Religions: Sunni Muslim, Shiite Muslim
Languages: Punjabi, Sindhi, Siraiki, Pashto, Urdu, Baluchi, Hindko, English

Palau

Area: 189 sq mi (489 sq km)
Population: 19,000
Capital: Melekeok, pop. 1,000
Currency: U.S. dollar
Religions: Roman Catholic, Protestant, Modekngei, Seventh-day Adventist
Languages: Palauan, Filipino, English, Chinese

Panama

Area: 29,157 sq mi (75,517 sq km)
Population: 4,041,000
Capital: Panama City, pop. 1,638,000
Currencies: balboa; U.S. dollar
Religions: Roman Catholic, Protestant
Languages: Spanish, English

Papua New Guinea

Area: 178,703 sq mi (462,840 sq km)
Population: 8,151,000
Capital: Port Moresby, pop. 338,000
Currency: kina
Religions: indigenous beliefs, Roman Catholic, Lutheran, other Protestant
Languages: Melanesian Pidgin, 820 indigenous languages

Paraguay

Area: 157,048 sq mi (406,752 sq km)
Population: 7,033,000
Capital: Asunción, pop. 2,307,000
Currency: guarani
Religions: Roman Catholic, Protestant
Languages: Spanish, Guarani

Peru

Area: 496,224 sq mi (1,285,216 sq km)
Population: 31,489,000
Capital: Lima, pop. 9,722,000
Currency: nuevo sol
Religion: Roman Catholic
Languages: Spanish, Quechua, Aymara, minor Amazonian languages

Philippines

Area: 115,831 sq mi (300,000 sq km)
Population: 102,572,000
Capital: Manila, pop. 12,764,000
Currency: Philippine peso
Religions: Roman Catholic, Muslim, other Christian
Languages: Filipino (based on Tagalog), English

Poland

Area: 120,728 sq mi (312,685 sq km)
Population: 38,417,000
Capital: Warsaw, pop. 1,718,000
Currency: zloty
Religion: Roman Catholic
Language: Polish

Portugal

Area: 35,655 sq mi (92,345 sq km)
Population: 10,303,000
Capital: Lisbon, pop. 2,869,000
Currency: euro
Religion: Roman Catholic
Languages: Portuguese, Mirandese

Qatar

Area: 4,448 sq mi (11,521 sq km)
Population: 2,477,000
Capital: Doha, pop. 699,000
Currency: Qatari rial
Religions: Muslim, Christian
Languages: Arabic; English commonly a second language

Romania

Area: 92,043 sq mi (238,391 sq km)

Population: 19,756,000

Capital: Bucharest, pop. 1,872,000

Currency: new leu

Religions: Eastern Orthodox, Protestant, Roman Catholic

Languages: Romanian, Hungarian

Russia

Area: 6,592,850 sq mi (17,075,400 sq km)

Population: 144,326,000

Capital: Moscow, pop. 12,063,000

Currency: ruble

Religions: Russian Orthodox, Muslim

Languages: Russian, many minority languages

**Note: Russia is in both Europe and Asia, but its capital is in Europe, so it is classified here as a European country.*

Rwanda

Area: 10,169 sq mi (26,338 sq km)

Population: 11,896,000

Capital: Kigali, pop. 1,223,000

Currency: Rwandan franc

Religions: Roman Catholic, Protestant, Adventist, Muslim

Languages: Kinyarwanda, French, English, Kiswahili

Samoa

Area: 1,093 sq mi (2,831 sq km)

Population: 195,000

Capital: Apia, pop. 37,000

Currency: tala

Religions: Congregationalist, Roman Catholic, Methodist, Church of Jesus Christ of Latter-day Saints, Assembly of God, Seventh-day Adventist

Languages: Samoan (Polynesian), English

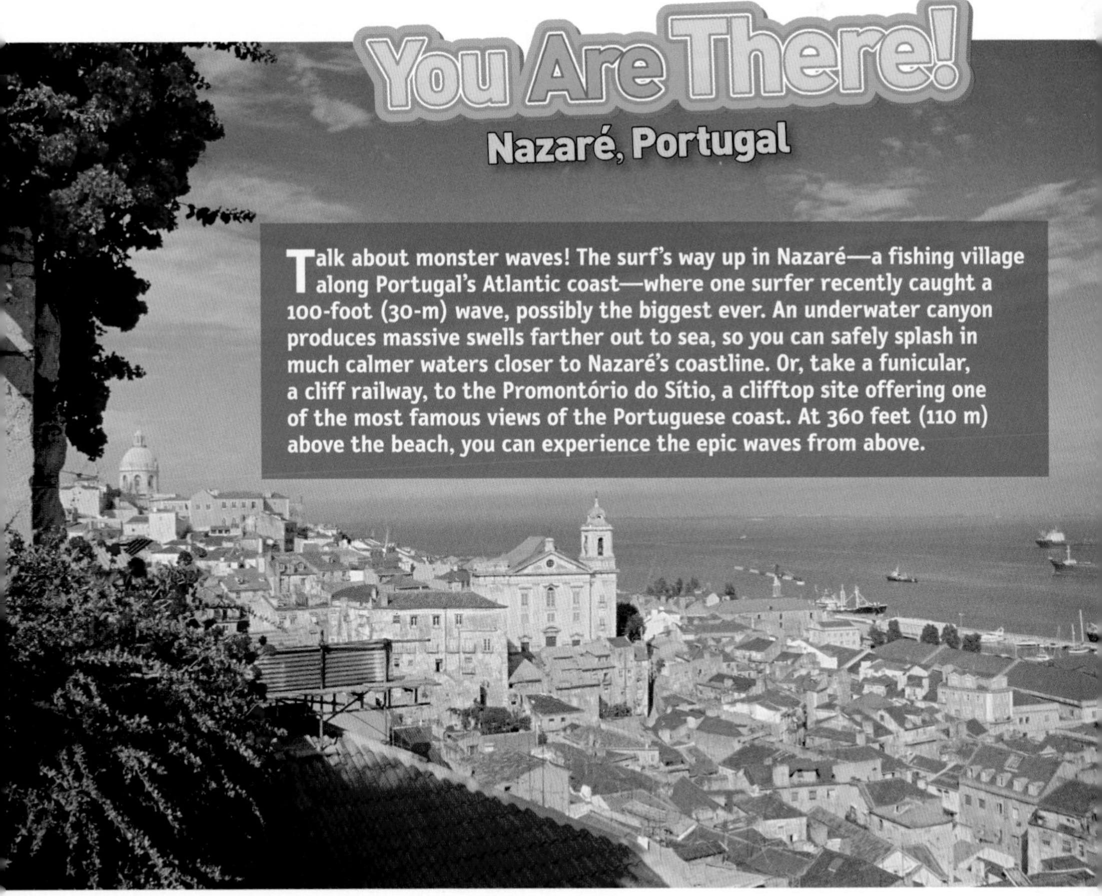

You Are There!

Nazaré, Portugal

Talk about monster waves! The surf's way up in Nazaré—a fishing village along Portugal's Atlantic coast—where one surfer recently caught a 100-foot (30-m) wave, possibly the biggest ever. An underwater canyon produces massive swells farther out to sea, so you can safely splash in much calmer waters closer to Nazaré's coastline. Or, take a funicular, a cliff railway, to the Promontório do Sítio, a clifftop site offering one of the most famous views of the Portuguese coast. At 360 feet (110 m) above the beach, you can experience the epic waves from above.

San Marino

Area: 24 sq mi (61 sq km)
Population: 33,000
Capital: San Marino, pop. 4,000
Currency: euro
Religion: Roman Catholic
Language: Italian

Sao Tome and Principe

Area: 386 sq mi (1,001 sq km)
Population: 198,000
Capital: São Tomé, pop. 71,000
Currency: dobra
Religions: Roman Catholic, Evangelical
Language: Portuguese

Saudi Arabia

Area: 756,985 sq mi (1,960,582 sq km)
Population: 31,677,000
Capital: Riyadh, pop. 6,195,000
Currency: Saudi riyal
Religion: Muslim
Language: Arabic

Senegal

Area: 75,955 sq mi (196,722 sq km)
Population: 14,800,000
Capital: Dakar, pop. 3,393,000
Currency: Communauté Financière Africaine franc
Religions: Muslim, Christian (mostly Roman Catholic)
Languages: French, Wolof, Pulaar, Jola, Mandinka

Serbia

Area: 29,913 sq mi (77,474 sq km)
Population: 7,063,000
Capital: Belgrade, pop. 1,181,000
Currency: Serbian dinar
Religions: Serbian Orthodox, Roman Catholic, Muslim
Languages: Serbian, Hungarian

Seychelles

Area: 176 sq mi (455 sq km)
Population: 94,000
Capital: Victoria, pop. 26,000
Currency: Seychelles rupee
Religions: Roman Catholic, Anglican, other Christian
Languages: Creole, English

Sierra Leone

Area: 27,699 sq mi (71,740 sq km)
Population: 6,567,000
Capital: Freetown, pop. 986,000
Currency: leone
Religions: Muslim, indigenous beliefs, Christian
Languages: English, Mende, Temne, Krio

Singapore

Area: 255 sq mi (660 sq km)
Population: 5,601,000
Capital: Singapore, pop. 5,517,000
Currency: Singapore dollar
Religions: Buddhist, Muslim, Taoist, Roman Catholic, Hindu, other Christian
Languages: Mandarin, English, Malay, Hokkien, Cantonese, Teochew, Tamil

Slovakia

Area: 18,932 sq mi (49,035 sq km)
Population: 5,429,000
Capital: Bratislava, pop. 403,000
Currency: euro
Religions: Roman Catholic, Protestant, Greek Catholic
Languages: Slovak, Hungarian

Slovenia

Area: 7,827 sq mi (20,273 sq km)
Population: 2,065,000
Capital: Ljubljana, pop. 279,000
Currency: euro
Religions: Roman Catholic, Muslim, Orthodox
Languages: Slovene, Croatian, Serbian

COLOR KEY ● Africa ● Australia, New Zealand, and Oceania

Solomon Islands

Area: 10,954 sq mi (28,370 sq km)
Population: 658,000
Capital: Honiara, pop. 73,000
Currency: Solomon Islands dollar
Religions: Church of Melanesia, Roman Catholic, South Seas Evangelical, other Christian
Languages: Melanesian pidgin, 120 indigenous languages

Somalia

Area: 246,201 sq mi (637,657 sq km)
Population: 11,079,000
Capital: Mogadishu, pop. 2,014,000
Currency: Somali shilling
Religion: Sunni Muslim
Languages: Somali, Arabic, Italian, English

South Africa

Area: 470,693 sq mi (1,219,090 sq km)
Population: 55,654,000
Capitals: Pretoria (Tshwane), pop. 1,991,000; Bloemfontein, pop. 496,000; Cape Town, pop. 3,624,000
Currency: rand
Religions: Zion Christian, Pentecostal, Catholic, Methodist, Dutch Reformed, Anglican, other Christian
Languages: IsiZulu, IsiXhosa, Afrikaans, Sepedi, English

South Korea

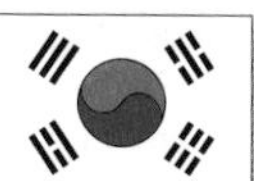

Area: 38,321 sq mi (99,250 sq km)
Population: 50,801,000
Capital: Seoul, pop. 9,775,000
Currency: South Korean won
Religions: Christian, Buddhist
Languages: Korean, English

South Sudan

Area: 248,777 sq mi (644,329 sq km)
Population: 12,733,000
Capital: Juba, pop. 307,000
Currency: South Sudan pound
Religions: animist, Christian
Languages: English, Arabic, regional languages (Dinke, Nuer, Bari, Zande, Shilluk)

Spain

Area: 195,363 sq mi (505,988 sq km)
Population: 43,285,000
Capital: Madrid, pop. 6,133,000
Currency: euro
Religion: Roman Catholic
Languages: Castilian Spanish, Catalan, Galician, Basque

Sri Lanka

Area: 25,299 sq mi (65,525 sq km)
Population: 21,163,000
Capitals: Colombo, pop. 704,000; Sri Jayewardenepura Kotte, pop. 128,000
Currency: Sri Lankan rupee
Religions: Buddhist, Muslim, Hindu, Christian
Languages: Sinhala, Tamil

5 cool things about SRI LANKA

1. A 2,300-year-old sacred fig tree in Anuradhapura, Sri Lanka, is believed to be the world's oldest tree planted by a human.
2. Some 3,000 elephants roam throughout Sri Lanka's protected national parks.
3. Volleyball is the national sport of Sri Lanka.
4. The world's biggest blue star sapphire—weighing more than 1,400 carats and valued at $100 million—was recently found in Sri Lanka.
5. There are hundreds of waterfalls flowing throughout Sri Lanka, including Bambarakanda Falls, which feature a sheer drop of 863 feet (263 m).

St. Kitts and Nevis

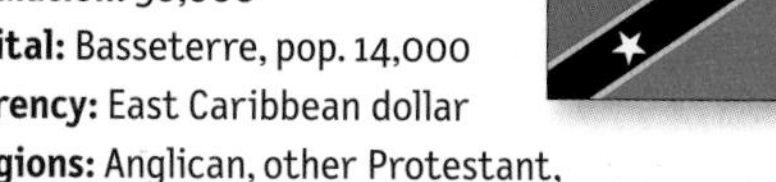

Area: 104 sq mi (269 sq km)
Population: 50,000
Capital: Basseterre, pop. 14,000
Currency: East Caribbean dollar
Religions: Anglican, other Protestant, Roman Catholic
Language: English

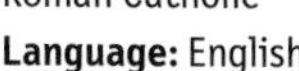

St. Lucia

Area: 238 sq mi (616 sq km)
Population: 177,000
Capital: Castries, pop. 22,000
Currency: East Caribbean dollar
Religions: Roman Catholic, Seventh-day Adventist, Pentecostal
Languages: English, French patois

St. Vincent and the Grenadines

Area: 150 sq mi (389 sq km)
Population: 110,000
Capital: Kingstown, pop. 27,000
Currency: East Caribbean dollar
Religions: Anglican, Methodist, Roman Catholic
Languages: English, French patois

Sudan

Area: 718,722 sq mi (1,861,484 sq km)
Population: 42,127,000
Capital: Khartoum, pop. 5,000,000
Currency: Sudanese pound
Religions: Sunni Muslim, indigenous beliefs, Christian
Languages: Arabic, Nubian, Ta Bedawie, many diverse dialects of Nilotic, Nilo-Hamitic, Sudanic languages

Suriname

Area: 63,037 sq mi (163,265 sq km)
Population: 548,000
Capital: Paramaribo, pop. 234,000
Currency: Suriname dollar
Religions: Hindu, Protestant (predominantly Moravian), Roman Catholic, Muslim, indigenous beliefs
Languages: Dutch, English, Sranang Tongo, Hindustani, Javanese

Swaziland

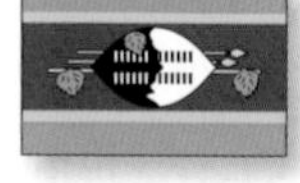

Area: 6,704 sq mi (17,363 sq km)
Population: 1,304,000
Capitals: Mbabane, pop. 66,000; Lobamba, pop. 4,600
Currency: lilangeni
Religions: Zionist, Roman Catholic, Muslim
Languages: English, siSwati

Sweden

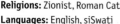

Area: 173,732 sq mi (449,964 sq km)
Population: 9,903,000
Capital: Stockholm, pop. 1,464,000
Currency: Swedish krona
Religion: Lutheran
Languages: Swedish, Sami, Finnish

Switzerland

Area: 15,940 sq mi (41,284 sq km)
Population: 8,387,000
Capital: Bern, pop. 358,000
Currency: Swiss franc
Religions: Roman Catholic, Protestant, Muslim
Languages: German, French, Italian, Romansh

Syria

Area: 71,498 sq mi (185,180 sq km)
Population: 17,185,000
Capital: Damascus, pop. 2,574,000
Currency: Syrian pound
Religions: Sunni, other Muslim (includes Alawite, Druze), Christian
Languages: Arabic, Kurdish, Armenian, Aramaic, Circassian

Tajikistan

Area: 55,251 sq mi (143,100 sq km)
Population: 8,645,000
Capital: Dushanbe, pop. 801,000
Currency: somoni
Religions: Sunni Muslim, Shiite Muslim
Languages: Tajik, Russian

Tanzania

Area: 364,900 sq mi (945,087 sq km)
Population: 54,207,000
Capitals: Dar es Salaam, pop. 5,116,000; Dodoma, pop. 228,000
Currency: Tanzanian shilling
Religions: Muslim, indigenous beliefs, Christian
Languages: Kiswahili, Kiunguja, English, Arabic, local languages

Thailand

Area: 198,115 sq mi (513,115 sq km)
Population: 65,323,000
Capital: Bangkok, pop. 9,098,000
Currency: baht
Religions: Buddhist, Muslim
Languages: Thai, English, ethnic dialects

Tunisia

Area: 63,170 sq mi (163,610 sq km)
Population: 11,303,000
Capital: Tunis, pop. 1,978,000
Currency: Tunisian dinar
Religion: Muslim
Languages: Arabic, French

Timor-Leste (East Timor)

Area: 5,640 sq mi (14,609 sq km)
Population: 1,266,000
Capital: Dili, pop. 228,000
Currency: U.S. dollar
Religion: Roman Catholic
Languages: Tetum, Portuguese, Indonesian, English, indigenous languages

STUDENTS IN TUNISIA once created the world's LARGEST PAIR OF JEANS— measuring longer than a 16-story building is tall.

Togo

Area: 21,925 sq mi (56,785 sq km)
Population: 7,505,000
Capital: Lomé, pop. 930,000
Currency: Communauté Financière Africaine franc
Religions: indigenous beliefs, Christian, Muslim
Languages: French, Ewe, Mina, Kabye, Dagomb

Turkey

Area: 300,948 sq mi (779,452 sq km)
Population: 79,472,000
Capital: Ankara, pop. 4,644,000
Currency: new Turkish lira
Religion: Muslim (mostly Sunni)
Languages: Turkish, Kurdish, Dimli (Zaza), Azeri, Kabardian, Gagauz

Tonga

Area: 289 sq mi (748 sq km)
Population: 103,000
Capital: Nuku'alofa, pop. 25,000
Currency: pa'anga
Religion: Christian
Languages: Tongan, English

Turkmenistan

Area: 188,456 sq mi (488,100 sq km)
Population: 5,439,000
Capital: Ashgabat, pop. 735,000
Currency: Turkmen manat
Religions: Muslim, Eastern Orthodox
Languages: Turkmen, Russian, Uzbek

Trinidad and Tobago

Area: 1,980 sq mi (5,128 sq km)
Population: 1,355,000
Capital: Port of Spain, pop. 34,000
Currency: Trinidad and Tobago dollar
Religions: Roman Catholic, Hindu, Anglican, Baptist
Languages: English, Caribbean Hindustani, French, Spanish, Chinese

Tuvalu

Area: 10 sq mi (26 sq km)
Population: 11,000
Capital: Funafuti, pop. 6,000
Currencies: Australian dollar; Tuvaluan dollar
Religion: Church of Tuvalu (Congregationalist)
Languages: Tuvaluan, English, Samoan, Kiribati

Uganda

Area: 93,104 sq mi (241,139 sq km)

Population: 36,593,000

Capital: Kampala, pop. 1,863,000

Currency: Ugandan shilling

Religions: Protestant, Roman Catholic, Muslim

Languages: English, Ganda, other local languages, Kiswahili, Arabic

United Arab Emirates

Area: 30,000 sq mi (77,700 sq km)

Population: 9,267,000

Capital: Abu Dhabi, pop. 1,114,000

Currency: Emirati dirham

Religion: Muslim

Languages: Arabic, Persian, English, Hindi, Urdu

Ukraine

Area: 233,090 sq mi (603,700 sq km)

Population: 42,677,000

Capital: Kiev, pop. 2,917,000

Currency: hryvnia

Religions: Ukrainian Orthodox, Orthodox, Ukrainian Greek Catholic

Languages: Ukrainian, Russian

United Kingdom

Area: 93,788 sq mi (242,910 sq km)

Population: 65,627,000

Capital: London, pop. 10,189,000

Currency: British pound

Religions: Anglican, Roman Catholic, Presbyterian, Methodist

Languages: English, Welsh, Scottish form of Gaelic

You Are There!

Dubai, United Arab Emirates

Can you say dream destination? There's tons to do in Dubai, a city sitting on the coast of the Persian Gulf in the United Arab Emirates. Need a quick itinerary? First, take a lightning-quick elevator ride up to the top of Burj Khalifa, the tallest building in the world. From 148 stories up, watch the cars and people, as tiny as ants, mill below you. Once you're back on the ground, head on over to Ski Dubai, the Middle East's first indoor ski resort. No matter the weather, you can schuss down the slopes on human-made snow at this giant arena, complete with a black diamond run and a chairlift. While you're there, check out the resident king and gentoo penguins—you can even feed and hug one if you'd like. End your day with a fountain and light show on Burj Khalifa Lake in downtown Dubai. With the spray synched up to music and lights, it's literally a can't-miss sight: The water sprays as high as a 50-story building, making it the world's largest dancing fountain.

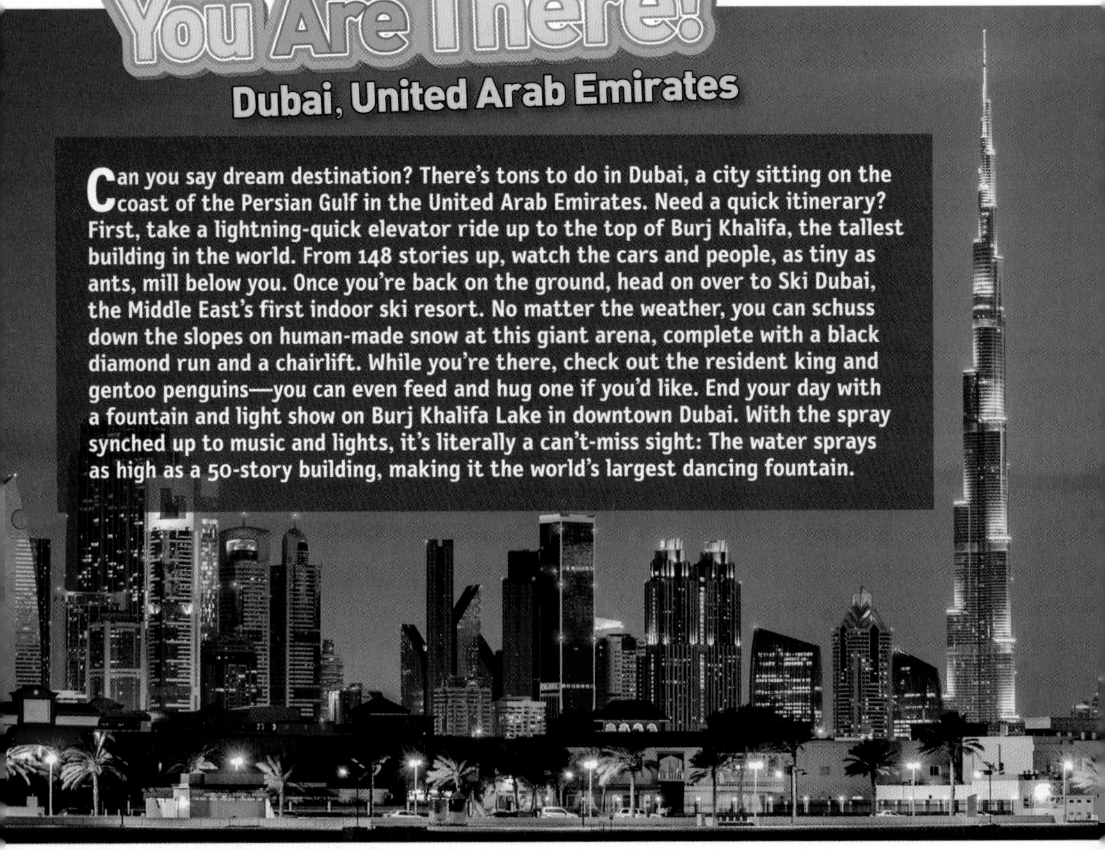

United States

Area: 3,794,083 sq mi (9,826,630 sq km)

Population: 323,890,000

Capital: Washington, D.C., pop. 646,449

Currency: U.S. dollar

Religions: Protestant, Roman Catholic

Languages: English, Spanish

Uruguay

Area: 68,037 sq mi (176,215 sq km)

Population: 3,480,000

Capital: Montevideo, pop. 1,698,000

Currency: Uruguayan peso

Religion: Roman Catholic

Language: Spanish

Uzbekistan

Area: 172,742 sq mi (447,400 sq km)

Population: 31,855,000

Capital: Tashkent, pop. 2,241,000

Currency: Uzbekistani sum

Religions: Muslim (mostly Sunni), Eastern Orthodox

Languages: Uzbek, Russian, Tajik

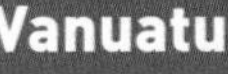

Vanuatu

Area: 4,707 sq mi (12,190 sq km)

Population: 284,000

Capital: Port Vila, pop. 53,000

Currency: vatu

Religions: Presbyterian, Anglican, Roman Catholic, other Christian, indigenous beliefs

Languages: more than 100 local languages, pidgin (known as Bislama or Bichelama)

Vatican City

Area: 0.2 sq mi (0.4 sq km)

Population: 800

Capital: Vatican City, pop. 800

Currency: euro

Religion: Roman Catholic

Languages: Italian, Latin, French

Venezuela

Area: 352,144 sq mi (912,050 sq km)

Population: 31,029,000

Capital: Caracas, pop. 2,912,000

Currency: bolivar

Religion: Roman Catholic

Languages: Spanish, numerous indigenous dialects

Vietnam

Area: 127,844 sq mi (331,114 sq km)

Population: 92,699,000

Capital: Hanoi, pop. 3,470,000

Currency: dong

Religions: Buddhist, Roman Catholic

Languages: Vietnamese, English, French, Chinese, Khmer

Yemen

Area: 207,286 sq mi (536,869 sq km)

Population: 27,460,000

Capital: Sanaa, pop. 2,833,000

Currency: Yemeni rial

Religions: Muslim, including Shaf'i (Sunni) and Zaydi (Shiite)

Language: Arabic

Zambia

Area: 290,586 sq mi (752,614 sq km)

Population: 15,934,000

Capital: Lusaka, pop. 2,078,000

Currency: Zambian kwacha

Religions: Christian, Muslim, Hindu

Languages: English, Bemba, Kaonda, Lozi, Lunda, Luvale, Nyanja, Tonga, about 70 other indigenous languages

Zimbabwe

Area: 150,872 sq mi (390,757 sq km)

Population: 15,987,000

Capital: Harare, pop. 1,495,000

Currency: Zimbabwean dollar

Religions: Syncretic (part Christian, part indigenous beliefs), Christian, indigenous beliefs

Languages: English, Shona, Sindebele, tribal dialects

THE POLITICAL UNITED STATES

9:00AM
PACIFIC TIME
10:00AM
MOUNTAIN TIME
Cape Flattery
Seattle
Olympia
Tacoma
Columbia
WASHINGTON
Spokane
Yakima
Portland
Lewiston
Columbia
Salem
Cascade Range
Eugene
OREGON
Medford
Klamath Falls
Eureka
Redding
Coast Ranges
Sacramento
Sierra Nevada
Reno
Carson City
Lake Tahoe
San Francisco
Oakland
San Jose
Salinas
Fresno
CALIFORNIA
NEVADA
Great Basin
Mojave Desert
Bakersfield
Point Conception
Los Angeles
Long Beach
Riverside
Salton Sea
San Diego
IDAHO
Boise
Snake
Idaho Falls
Pocatello
Great Falls
Missouri
MONTANA
Helena
Butte
Billings
ROCKY MOUNTAINS
Cody
Yellowstone L.
WYOMING
Casper
N. Platte
Cheyenne
Laramie
Great Salt Lake
Ogden
Salt Lake City
Provo
UTAH
Grand Junction
Fort Collins
Boulder
Denver
COLORADO
Colorado
Lake Powell
St. George
Las Vegas
Lake Mead
Grand Canyon
Colorado Springs
Pueblo
Flagstaff
ARIZONA
Colorado
Phoenix
Mesa
Yuma
Tucson
Santa Fe
Albuquerque
NEW MEXICO
Rio Grande
Roswell
Las Cruces
El Paso
Minot
NORTH DAKOTA
Bismarck
Aberdeen
SOUTH DAKOTA
Pierre
Rapid City
Missouri
NEBRASKA
S. Platte
Grand Island
Platte
GREAT PLAINS
KANSAS
Dodge City
Arkansas
Wichita
OKLAH
Oklahoma City
Amarillo
Lawton
Red
Wichita Falls
Lubbock
Fort Worth
Abilene
Midland
Odessa
Waco
TEXAS
Austin
San Antonio
Rio Grande
Corpus Christi
Laredo
Brownsville
7:00AM
HAWAI'I-ALEUTIAN TIME
North Slope
Brooks Range
Yukon
Alaska Range
Juneau
Anchorage
ALASKA
Alaska Peninsula
ALEUTIAN ISLANDS
0 400 miles
0 400 kilometers
8:00AM
ALASKA TIME
Kaua'i
Ni'ihau
O'ahu
Honolulu
Moloka'i
Lana'i
Maui
Kaho'olawe
Hilo
Hawai'i
HAWAI'I
0 150 mi
0 150 km
7:00AM
HAWAI'I-ALEUTIAN TIME

The United States is made up of 50 states joined like a giant quilt. Each is unique, but together they make a national fabric held together by a constitution and a federal government. State boundaries, outlined in dotted lines on the map, set apart internal political units within the country. The national capital—Washington, D.C.—is marked by a star in a double circle. The capital of each state is marked by a star in a single circle.

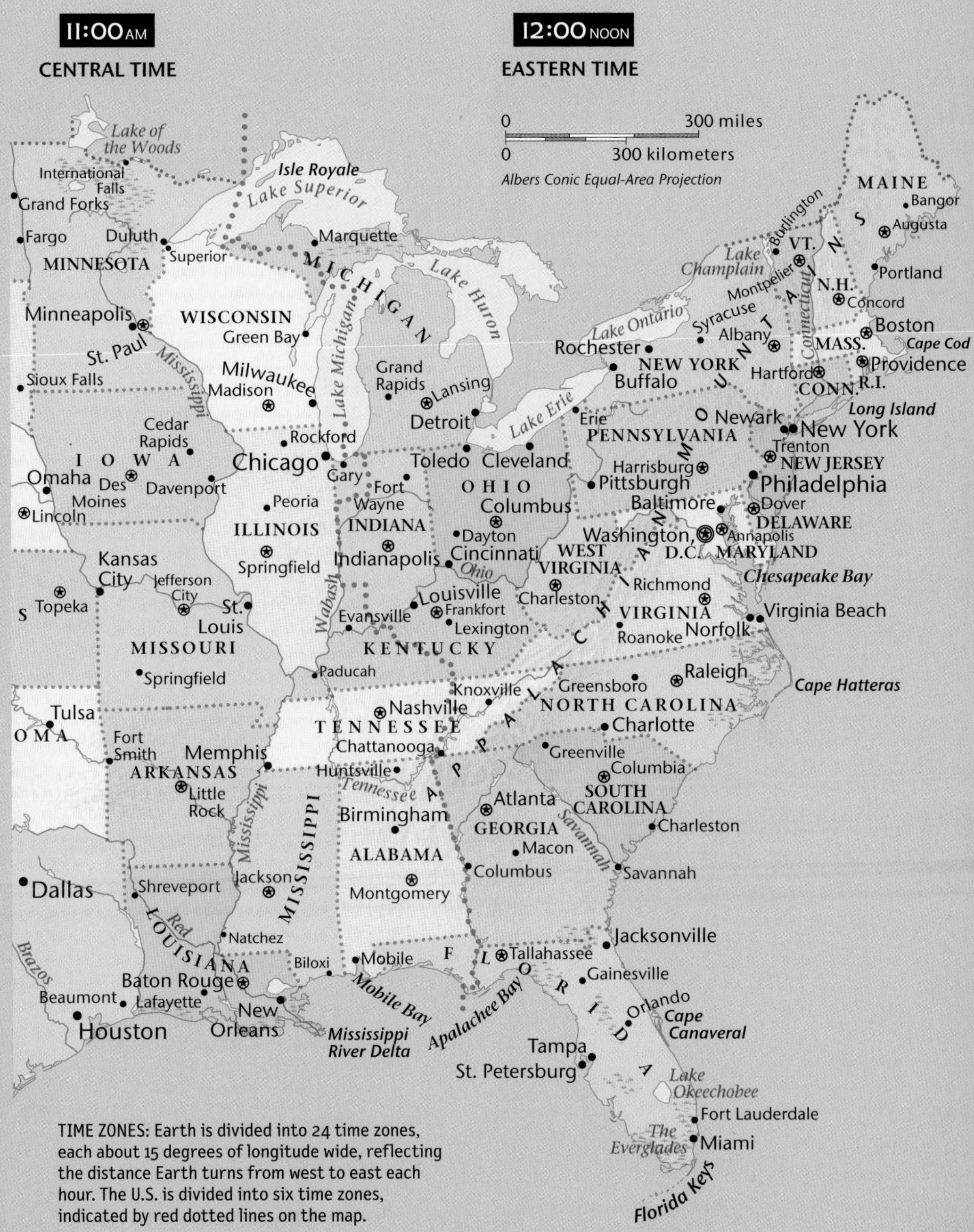

TIME ZONES: Earth is divided into 24 time zones, each about 15 degrees of longitude wide, reflecting the distance Earth turns from west to east each hour. The U.S. is divided into six time zones, indicated by red dotted lines on the map.

THE PHYSICAL UNITED STATES

ALASKA AND HAWAII:
In addition to the states located on the main landmass, the U.S. has two states—Alaska and Hawaii—that are not directly connected to the other 48 states. If Alaska and Hawaii were shown in their correct relative sizes and locations, the map would not fit on these pages.

Stretching from the Atlantic Ocean in the east to the Pacific Ocean in the west, the United States is the third largest country (by area) in the world. Its physical diversity ranges from mountains to fertile plains and dry deserts. Shading on the map indicates changes in elevation, while colors show different vegetation patterns.

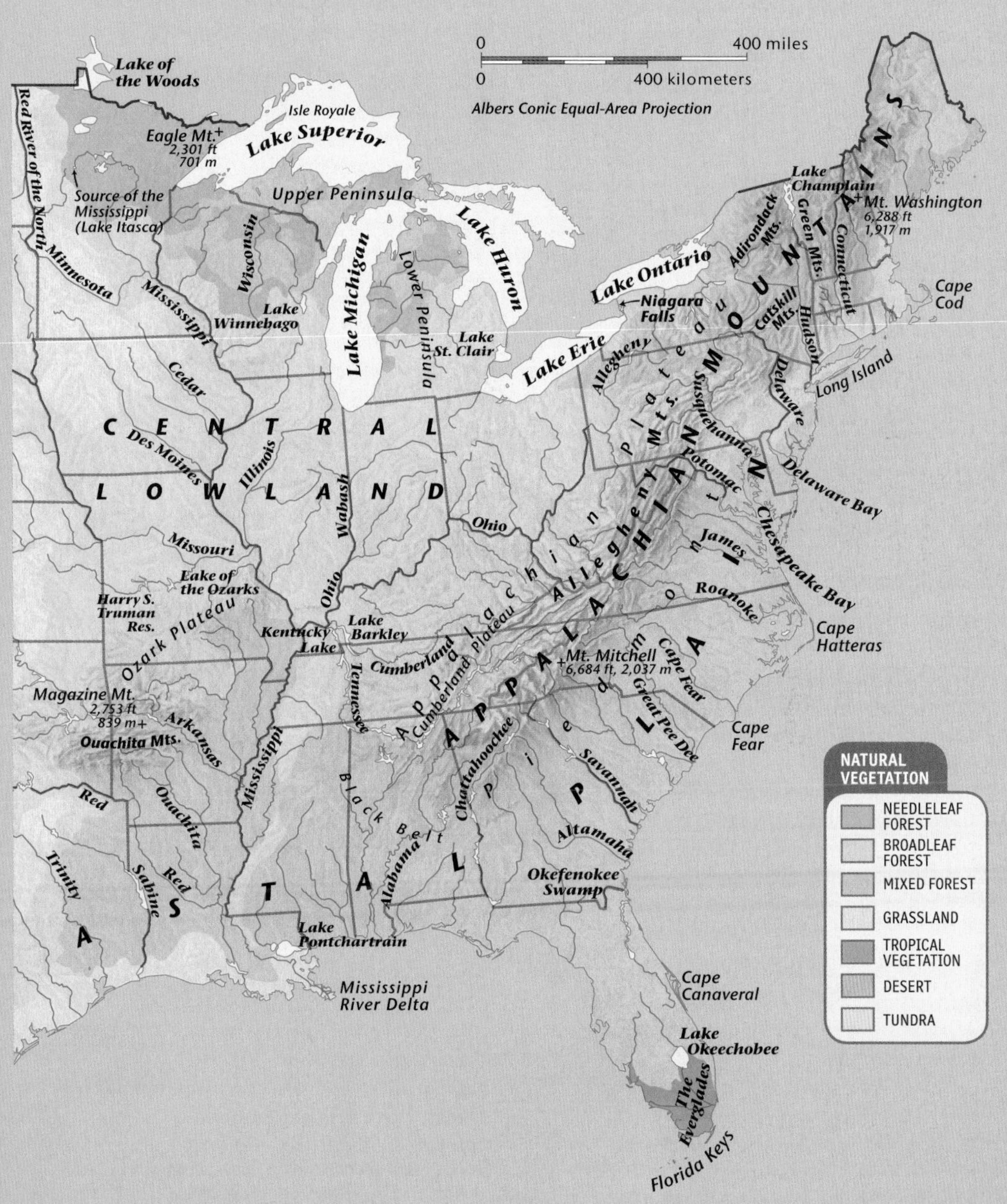

THE STATES

From sea to shining sea, the United States of America is a nation of diversity. In the 241 years since its creation, the nation has grown to become home to a wide range of peoples, industries, and cultures. The following pages present a general overview of all 50 states in the U.S.

The country is generally divided into five large regions: the Northeast, the Southeast, the Midwest, the Southwest, and the West. Though loosely defined, these zones tend to share important similarities, including climate, history, and geography. The color key below provides a guide to which states are in each region.

Flags of each state and highlights of demography and industry are also included. These details offer a brief overview of each state.

In addition, each state's official flower and bird are identified.

Color Key by Region

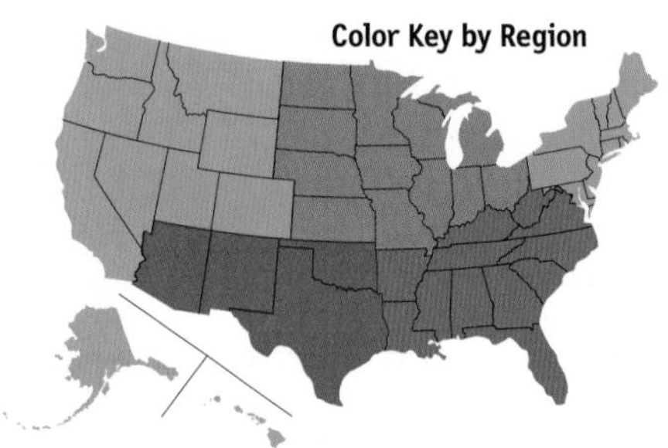

Arizona

Area: 113,998 sq mi (295,256 sq km)
Population: 6,828,065
Capital: Phoenix, pop. 1,563,025
Largest city: Phoenix, pop. 1,563,025
Industry: Real estate, manufactured goods, retail, state and local government, transportation and public utilities, wholesale trade, health services
State flower/bird: Saguaro/cactus wren

Arkansas

Area: 53,179 sq mi (137,732 sq km)
Population: 2,978,204
Capital: Little Rock, pop. 197,992
Largest city: Little Rock, pop. 197,992
Industry: Services, food processing, paper products, transportation, metal products, machinery, electronics
State flower/bird: Apple blossom/mockingbird

The World Championship Duck Calling Contest is held each year in Stuttgart, Arkansas.

Alabama

Area: 52,419 sq mi (135,765 sq km)
Population: 4,858,979
Capital: Montgomery, pop. 200,602
Largest city: Birmingham, pop. 212,461
Industry: Retail and wholesale trade, services, government, finance, insurance, real estate, transportation, construction, communication
State flower/bird: Camellia/northern flicker

Alaska

Area: 663,267 sq mi (1,717,862 sq km)
Population: 738,432
Capital: Juneau, pop. 32,756
Largest city: Anchorage, pop. 298,695
Industry: Petroleum products, government, services, trade
State flower/bird: Forget-me-not/willow ptarmigan

California

Area: 163,696 sq mi (423,972 sq km)
Population: 39,144,818
Capital: Sacramento, pop. 490,712
Largest city: Los Angeles, pop. 3,971,883
Industry: Electronic components and equipment, computers and computer software, tourism, food processing, entertainment, clothing
State flower/bird: Golden poppy/California quail

Colorado

Area: 104,094 sq mi (269,602 sq km)
Population: 5,456,574
Capital: Denver, pop. 682,545
Largest city: Denver, pop. 682,545
Industry: Real estate, government, durable goods, communications, health and other services, nondurable goods, transportation
State flower/bird: Columbine/lark bunting

COLOR KEY ● Northeast ● Southeast

Connecticut

Area: 5,543 sq mi (14,357 sq km)
Population: 3,590,886
Capital: Hartford, pop. 124,006
Largest city: Bridgeport, pop. 147,629
Industry: Transportation equipment, metal products, machinery, electrical equipment, printing and publishing, scientific instruments, insurance
State flower/bird: Mountain laurel/robin

Delaware

Area: 2,489 sq mi (6,447 sq km)
Population: 945,934
Capital: Dover, pop. 37,522
Largest city: Wilmington, pop. 115,933
Industry: Food processing, chemicals, rubber and plastic products, scientific instruments, printing and publishing, financial services
State flower/bird: Peach blossom/blue hen chicken

Florida

Area: 65,755 sq mi (170,304 sq km)
Population: 20,271,272
Capital: Tallahassee, pop. 189,907
Largest city: Jacksonville, pop. 868,031
Industry: Tourism, health services, business services, communications, banking, electronic equipment, insurance
State flower/bird: Orange blossom/mockingbird

Georgia

Area: 59,425 sq mi (153,910 sq km)
Population: 10,214,860
Capital: Atlanta, pop. 463,878
Largest city: Atlanta, pop. 463,878
Industry: Textiles and clothing, transportation equipment, food processing, paper products, chemicals, electrical equipment, tourism
State flower/bird: Cherokee rose/brown thrasher

Hawaii

Area: 10,931 sq mi (28,311 sq km)
Population: 1,431,603
Capital: Honolulu, pop. 352,769
Largest city: Honolulu, pop. 352,769
Industry: Tourism, trade, finance, food processing, petroleum refining, stone, clay, glass products
State flower/bird: Hibiscus/Hawaiian goose (nene)

Idaho

Area: 83,570 sq mi (216,447 sq km)
Population: 1,654,930
Capital: Boise, pop. 218,281
Largest city: Boise, pop. 218,281
Industry: Electronics and computer equipment, tourism, food processing, forest products, mining
State flower/bird: Syringa (Lewis's mock orange)/ mountain bluebird

Illinois

Area: 57,914 sq mi (149,998 sq km)
Population: 12,859,995
Capital: Springfield, pop. 116,565
Largest city: Chicago, pop. 2,720,546
Industry: Industrial machinery, electronic equipment, food processing, chemicals, metals, printing and publishing, rubber and plastics, motor vehicles
State flower/bird: Violet/cardinal

Indiana

Area: 36,418 sq mi (94,322 sq km)
Population: 6,619,680
Capital: Indianapolis, pop. 853,173
Largest city: Indianapolis, pop. 853,173
Industry: Transportation equipment, steel, pharmaceutical and chemical products, machinery, petroleum, coal
State flower/bird: Peony/cardinal

There is
a town called
SANTA CLAUS,
INDIANA.

Iowa

Area: 56,272 sq mi (145,743 sq km)
Population: 3,123,899
Capital: Des Moines, pop. 210,330
Largest city: Des Moines, pop. 210,330
Industry: Real estate, health services, industrial machinery, food processing, construction
State flower/bird: Wild rose/American goldfinch

Kansas

Area: 82,277 sq mi (213,097 sq km)
Population: 2,911,641
Capital: Topeka, pop. 127,265
Largest city: Wichita, pop. 389,965
Industry: Aircraft manufacturing, transportation equipment, construction, food processing, printing and publishing, health care
State flower/bird: Sunflower/western meadowlark

Kentucky

Area: 40,409 sq mi (104,659 sq km)
Population: 4,425,092
Capital: Frankfort, pop. 27,830
Largest city: Louisville, pop. 615,366
Industry: Manufacturing, services, government, finance, insurance, real estate, retail trade, transportation, wholesale trade, construction, mining
State flower/bird: Goldenrod/cardinal

Louisiana

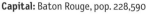

Area: 51,840 sq mi (134,265 sq km)
Population: 4,670,724
Capital: Baton Rouge, pop. 228,590
Largest city: New Orleans, pop. 389,617
Industry: Chemicals, petroleum products, food processing, health services, tourism, oil and natural gas extraction, paper products
State flower/bird: Magnolia/brown pelican

Maine

Area: 35,385 sq mi (91,646 sq km)
Population: 1,329,328
Capital: Augusta, pop. 18,471
Largest city: Portland, pop. 66,881
Industry: Health services, tourism, forest products, leather products, electrical equipment
State flower/bird: White pine cone and tassel/chickadee

Maryland

Area: 12,407 sq mi (32,133 sq km)
Population: 6,006,401
Capital: Annapolis, pop. 39,474
Largest city: Baltimore, pop. 621,849
Industry: Real estate, federal government, health services, business services, engineering services
State flower/bird: Black-eyed Susan/northern (Baltimore) oriole

Massachusetts

Area: 10,555 sq mi (27,336 sq km)
Population: 6,794,422
Capital: Boston, pop. 667,137
Largest city: Boston, pop. 667,137
Industry: Electrical equipment, machinery, metal products, scientific instruments, printing and publishing, tourism
State flower/bird: Mayflower/chickadee

The Boston Terrier IS THE OFFICIAL STATE DOG of Massachusetts.

Michigan

Area: 96,716 sq mi (250,495 sq km)
Population: 9,922,576
Capital: Lansing, pop. 115,056
Largest city: Detroit, pop. 677,116
Industry: Motor vehicles and parts, machinery, metal products, office furniture, tourism, chemicals
State flower/bird: Apple blossom/robin

Minnesota

Area: 86,939 sq mi (225,172 sq km)
Population: 5,489,594
Capital: St. Paul, pop. 300,851
Largest city: Minneapolis, pop. 410,939
Industry: Real estate, banking and insurance, industrial machinery, printing and publishing, food processing, scientific equipment
State flower/bird: Showy lady's slipper/common loon

Mississippi

Area: 48,430 sq mi (125,434 sq km)
Population: 2,992,333
Capital: Jackson, pop. 170,674
Largest city: Jackson, pop. 170,674
Industry: Petroleum products, health services, electronic equipment, transportation, banking, forest products, communications
State flower/bird: Magnolia/mockingbird

COLOR KEY 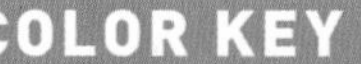 Northeast  Southeast

Missouri

Area: 69,704 sq mi (180,534 sq km)
Population: 6,083,672
Capital: Jefferson City, pop. 43,169
Largest city: Kansas City, pop. 475,378
Industry: Transportation equipment, food processing, chemicals, electrical equipment, metal products
State flower/bird: Hawthorn/eastern bluebird

Montana

Area: 147,042 sq mi (380,840 sq km)
Population: 1,032,949
Capital: Helena, pop. 30,581
Largest city: Billings, pop. 110,263
Industry: Forest products, food processing, mining, construction, tourism
State flower/bird: Bitterroot/western meadowlark

Nebraska

Area: 77,354 sq mi (200,346 sq km)
Population: 1,896,190
Capital: Lincoln, pop. 277,348
Largest city: Omaha, pop. 443,885
Industry: Food processing, machinery, electrical equipment, printing and publishing
State flower/bird: Goldenrod/western meadowlark

Nevada

Area: 110,561 sq mi (286,352 sq km)
Population: 2,890,845
Capital: Carson City, pop. 93,281
Largest city: Las Vegas, pop. 623,747
Industry: Tourism and gaming, mining, printing and publishing, food processing, electrical equipment
State flower/bird: Sagebrush/mountain bluebird

A hotel in LAS VEGAS, NEVADA, HAS A TWO-STORY-TALL chocolate fountain.

New Hampshire

Area: 9,350 sq mi (24,216 sq km)
Population: 1,330,608
Capital: Concord, pop. 42,620
Largest city: Manchester, pop. 110,229
Industry: Machinery, electronics, metal products
State flower/bird: Purple lilac/purple finch

New Jersey

Area: 8,721 sq mi (22,588 sq km)
Population: 8,958,013
Capital: Trenton, pop. 84,225
Largest city: Newark, pop. 281,944
Industry: Machinery, electronics, metal products, chemicals
State flower/bird: Violet/American goldfinch

New Mexico

Area: 121,590 sq mi (314,917 sq km)
Population: 2,085,109
Capital: Santa Fe, pop. 84,099
Largest city: Albuquerque, pop. 559,121
Industry: Electronic equipment, state and local government, real estate, business services, federal government, oil and gas extraction, health services
State flower/bird: Yucca/roadrunner

New York

Area: 54,556 sq mi (141,300 sq km)
Population: 19,795,791
Capital: Albany, pop. 98,469
Largest city: New York City, pop. 8,550,405
Industry: Printing and publishing, machinery, computer products, finance, tourism
State flower/bird: Rose/eastern bluebird

North Carolina

Area: 53,819 sq mi (139,390 sq km)
Population: 10,042,802
Capital: Raleigh, pop. 451,066
Largest city: Charlotte, pop. 827,097
Industry: Real estate, health services, chemicals, tobacco products, finance, textiles
State flower/bird: Flowering dogwood/cardinal

● Midwest ● Southwest ● West

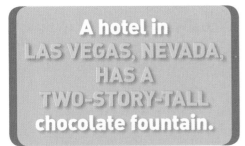

North Dakota

Area: 70,700 sq mi (183,113 sq km)
Population: 756,927
Capital: Bismarck, pop. 71,167
Largest city: Fargo, pop. 118,523
Industry: Services, government, finance, construction, transportation, oil and gas
State flower/bird: Wild prairie rose/ western meadowlark

Rhode Island

Area: 1,545 sq mi (4,002 sq km)
Population: 1,056,298
Capital: Providence, pop. 179,207
Largest city: Providence, pop. 179,207
Industry: Health services, business services, silver and jewelry products, metal products
State flower/bird: Violet/Rhode Island red

Ohio

Area: 44,825 sq mi (116,097 sq km)
Population: 11,613,423
Capital: Columbus, pop. 850,106
Largest city: Columbus, pop. 850,106
Industry: Transportation equipment, metal products, machinery, food processing, electrical equipment
State flower/bird: Scarlet carnation/cardinal

South Carolina

Area: 32,020 sq mi (82,932 sq km)
Population: 4,896,146
Capital: Columbia, pop. 133,803
Largest city: Columbia, pop. 133,803
Industry: Service industries, tourism, chemicals, textiles, machinery, forest products
State flower/bird: Yellow jessamine/Carolina wren

Oklahoma

Area: 69,898 sq mi (181,036 sq km)
Population: 3,911,338
Capital: Oklahoma City, pop. 631,346
Largest city: Oklahoma City, pop. 631,346
Industry: Manufacturing, services, government, finance, insurance, real estate
State flower/bird: Mistletoe/scissor-tailed flycatcher

South Dakota

Area: 77,117 sq mi (199,732 sq km)
Population: 858,469
Capital: Pierre, pop. 14,002
Largest city: Sioux Falls, pop. 171,544
Indus try: Finance, services, manufacturing, government, retail trade, transportation and utilities, wholesale trade, construction, mining
State flower/bird: Pasqueflower/ring-necked pheasant

Oregon

Area: 98,381 sq mi (254,806 sq km)
Population: 4,028,977
Capital: Salem, pop. 164,549
Largest city: Portland, pop. 632,309
Industry: Real estate, retail and wholesale trade, electronic equipment, health services, construction, forest products, business services
State flower/bird: Oregon grape/western meadowlark

Pennsylvania

Area: 46,055 sq mi (119,283 sq km)
Population: 12,802,503
Capital: Harrisburg, pop. 49,081
Largest city: Philadelphia, pop. 1,567,442
Industry: Machinery, printing and publishing, forest products, metal products
State flower/bird: Mountain laurel/ruffed grouse

5 cool things about OREGON

1. With a depth of 1,943 feet (592 m), Oregon's Crater Lake is the deepest lake in the United States.
2. Oregon is the only state with a flag featuring different images on each side.
3. Oregon's D River is just 120 feet (37 m) long.
4. Some 98 square miles (255 sq km) of Oregon is dedicated to Christmas tree farms, with the state producing more than six million trees annually.
5. The University of Oregon's mascot, the Oregon Duck, is based on Donald Duck.

COLOR KEY ● Northeast ● Southeast

Tennessee

Area: 42,143 sq mi (109,151 sq km)
Population: 6,600,299
Capital: Nashville, pop. 654,610
Largest city: Memphis, pop. 655,770
Industry: Service industries, chemicals, transportation equipment, processed foods, machinery
State flower/bird: Iris/mockingbird

Texas

Area: 268,581 sq mi (695,624 sq km)
Population: 27,469,114
Capital: Austin, pop. 931,830
Largest city: Houston, pop. 2,296,224
Industry: Chemicals, machinery, electronics and computers, food products, petroleum and natural gas, transportation equipment
State flower/bird: Bluebonnet/mockingbird

One of the WORLD'S FIRST DRIVE-THROUGH BANKS opened in Dallas, Texas, in 1938.

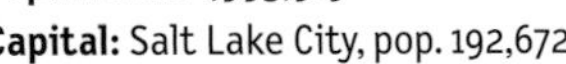

Utah

Area: 84,899 sq mi (219,888 sq km)
Population: 2,995,919
Capital: Salt Lake City, pop. 192,672
Largest city: Salt Lake City, pop. 192,672
Industry: Government, manufacturing, real estate, construction, health services, business services, banking
State flower/bird: Sego lily/California gull

Vermont

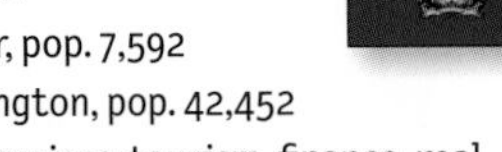

Area: 9,614 sq mi (24,901 sq km)
Population: 626,042
Capital: Montpelier, pop. 7,592
Largest city: Burlington, pop. 42,452
Industry: Health services, tourism, finance, real estate, computer components, electrical parts, printing and publishing, machine tools
State flower/bird: Red clover/hermit thrush

Virginia

Area: 42,774 sq mi (110,785 sq km)
Population: 8,382,993
Capital: Richmond, pop. 220,289
Largest city: Virginia Beach, pop. 452,745
Industry: Food processing, communication and electronic equipment, transportation equipment, printing, shipbuilding, textiles
State flower/bird: Flowering dogwood/cardinal

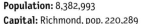

Washington

Area: 71,300 sq mi (184,666 sq km)
Population: 7,170,351
Capital: Olympia, pop. 50,302
Largest city: Seattle, pop. 684,451
Industry: Aerospace, tourism, food processing, forest products, paper products, industrial machinery, printing and publishing, metals, computer software
State flower/bird: Coast rhododendron/Amer. goldfinch

West Virginia

Area: 24,230 sq mi (62,755 sq km)
Population: 1,844,128
Capital: Charleston, pop. 49,736
Largest city: Charleston, pop. 49,736
Industry: Tourism, coal mining, chemicals, metal manufacturing, forest products, stone, clay, oil, glass products
State flower/bird: Rhododendron/cardinal

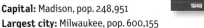

Wisconsin

Area: 65,498 sq mi (169,639 sq km)
Population: 5,771,337
Capital: Madison, pop. 248,951
Largest city: Milwaukee, pop. 600,155
Industry: Industrial machinery, paper products, food processing, metal products, electronic equipment, transportation
State flower/bird: Wood violet/robin

Wyoming

Area: 97,814 sq mi (253,337 sq km)
Population: 586,107
Capital: Cheyenne, pop. 63,335
Largest city: Cheyenne, pop. 63,335
Industry: Oil and natural gas, mining, generation of electricity, chemicals, tourism
State flower/bird: Indian paintbrush/western meadowlark

● Midwest ● Southwest ● West

THE TERRITORIES

The United States has 14 territories— political divisions that are not states. Three of these are in the Caribbean Sea, and the other 11 are in the Pacific Ocean.

St. John, U.S. Virgin Islands

Convention Center, San Juan, Puerto Rico

Talofofo Falls, Guam

U.S. CARIBBEAN TERRITORIES

Puerto Rico

Area: 3,508 sq mi (9,086 sq km)
Population: 3,474,182
Capital: San Juan, pop. 366,726
Languages: Spanish, English

U.S. Virgin Islands

Area: 149 sq mi (386 sq km)
Population: 103,000
Capital: Charlotte Amalie, pop. 52,000
Languages: English, Spanish or Spanish Creole, French or French Creole

U.S. PACIFIC TERRITORIES

American Samoa

Area: 77 sq mi (199 sq km)
Population: 54,000
Capital: Pago Pago, pop. 48,000
Language: Samoan

Guam

Area: 217 sq mi (561 sq km)
Population: 163,000
Capital: Hagåtña (Agana), pop. 143,000
Languages: English, Chamorro, Philippine languages

Northern Mariana Islands

Area: 184 sq mi (477 sq km)
Population: 53,000
Capital: Saipan, pop. 49,000
Languages: Philippine languages, Chinese, Chamorro, English

Other U.S. Territories

Baker Island, Howland Island, Jarvis Island, Johnston Atoll, Kingman Reef, Midway Islands, Palmyra Atoll, Wake Island, Navassa Island (in the Caribbean)

Figures for capital cities vary widely between sources because of differences in the way the area is defined and other projection methods.

THE U.S. CAPITAL

District of Columbia

Area: 68 sq mi (177 sq km)
Population: 672,228

Abraham Lincoln, who was President during the Civil War and a strong opponent of slavery, is remembered in the Lincoln Memorial, located at the opposite end of the National Mall from the U.S. Capitol Building.

COLOR KEY ● Territories ● Northeast

DESTINATION GUIDE

New Orleans, Louisiana

City Park

Mississippi riverboat

Mardi Gras World Museum

New Orleans street car

Happy Birthday, New Orleans! In 2018, the Crescent City turns 300 years old. And it's showing no sign of its age: From historical sights to sweet eats, there's so much to see and do in NOLA. Here's where to begin.

WHAT TO DO:

ROLL DOWN THE RIVER: Take a cruise on an iconic riverboat down the Mississippi and listen to live jazz, munch on classic New Orleans foods, and take in the sights on the shore while you chug along.

EAT SWEETS: A trip to New Orleans is not complete without indulging in a beignet (pronounced ben-yay)—or three. The staple sweet of the city, beignets are puffs of fried dough dusted with confectioner's sugar. Cafe Du Monde in the centrally located French Quarter is world-famous for its beignets, but you can find equally-as-delicious treats throughout the city.

TAKE A STREET CAR: Take a trip back in time by riding on a street car, the classic trolleys that run from downtown throughout the city. Rumble down scenic St. Charles Avenue or along the riverfront while imagining what life was like in the city centuries ago.

PARK IT: Stretch your legs in New Orleans' City Park, where you can clamber around Storyland, a playground decorated with larger-than-life fairy tale characters. Want to relax? Float along Big Lake in a pedal boat while exploring the park's bayous and lagoons.

PARTY ON: Experience the magic of Mardi Gras year-round at Blaine Kern's Mardi Gras World, a museum dedicated to the festive celebration. Check out parade floats, try on a traditional costume, and learn about the history of the holiday, held each February or March.

New Orleans is nicknamed the Crescent City because it was built along a sharp bend in the Mississippi River.

Because of the high water table, tombs lie aboveground in cemeteries in New Orleans.

The city of New Orleans is about 6 feet (2 m) below sea level on average.

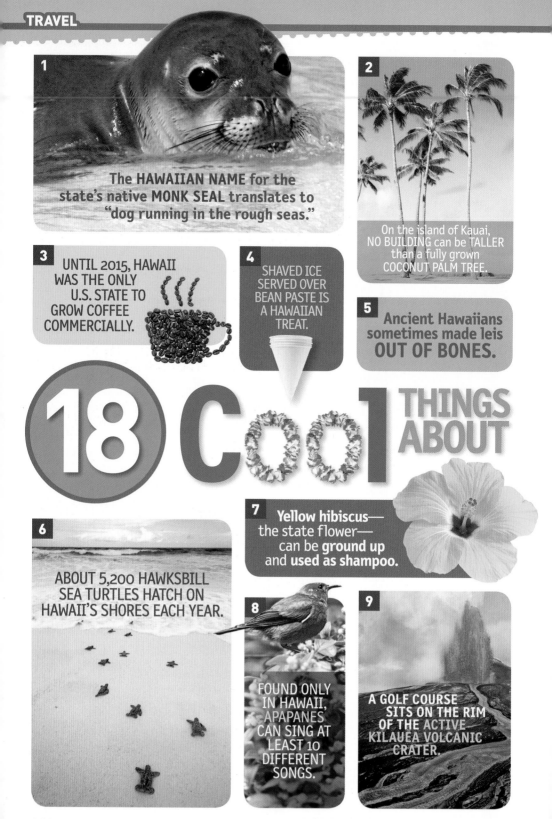

1 The HAWAIIAN NAME for the state's native MONK SEAL translates to "dog running in the rough seas."

2 On the island of Kauai, NO BUILDING can be TALLER than a fully grown COCONUT PALM TREE.

3 UNTIL 2015, HAWAII WAS THE ONLY U.S. STATE TO GROW COFFEE COMMERCIALLY.

4 SHAVED ICE SERVED OVER BEAN PASTE IS A HAWAIIAN TREAT.

5 Ancient Hawaiians sometimes made leis **OUT OF BONES.**

18 Cool THINGS ABOUT

7 **Yellow hibiscus**—the state flower—can be **ground up** and **used as shampoo.**

6 ABOUT 5,200 HAWKSBILL SEA TURTLES HATCH ON HAWAII'S SHORES EACH YEAR.

8 FOUND ONLY IN HAWAII, APAPANES CAN SING AT LEAST 10 DIFFERENT SONGS.

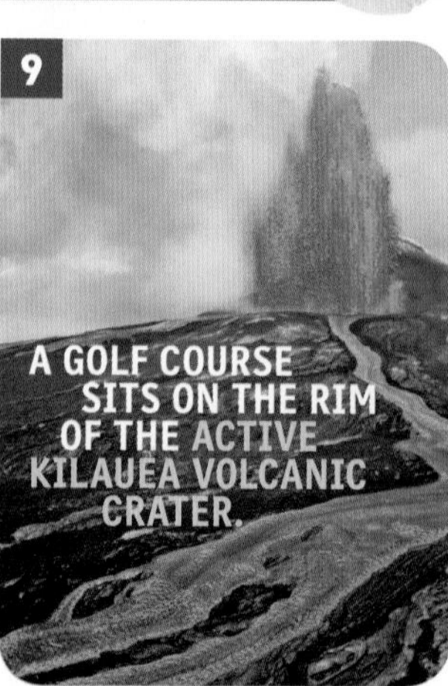

9 A GOLF COURSE SITS ON THE RIM OF THE ACTIVE KILAUEA VOLCANIC CRATER.

10

SOME OF THE STATE'S BEACHES HAVE BLACK, RED, OR GREEN SAND.

11

ONCE HOME TO HAWAIIAN ROYALS, IOLANI PALACE HAD ELECTRICITY FOUR YEARS BEFORE THE WHITE HOUSE.

12

Around **40** shark species **inhabit** the **waters** off **Hawaii.**

13

Hawaii once produced about **900,000 tons (816,466 t) of pineapples** a year.

HAWAII

14

The abdomen of one Hawaiian spider species resembles a **smiling face.**

15

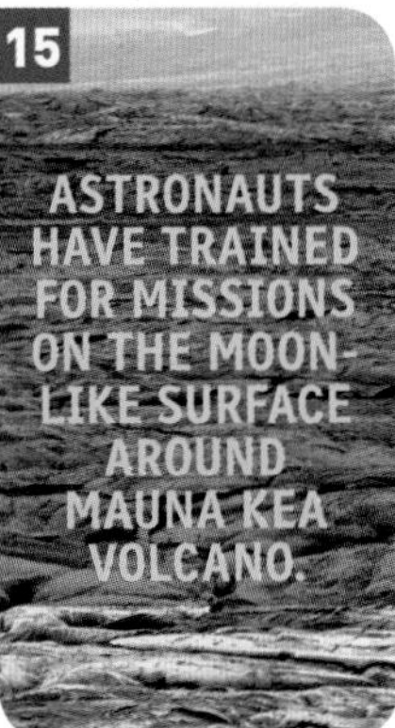

ASTRONAUTS HAVE TRAINED FOR MISSIONS ON THE MOON-LIKE SURFACE AROUND MAUNA KEA VOLCANO.

16

Early Hawaiian surfboards could weigh up to 200 pounds (91 kg).

17

HAWAII CONSISTS OF EIGHT MAIN ISLANDS AND MORE THAN A HUNDRED SMALLER ISLANDS.

18

Hawaiian SILVERSWORD plants can live for 40 YEARS—and ONLY FLOWER ONCE in their life span.

Wild Vacation

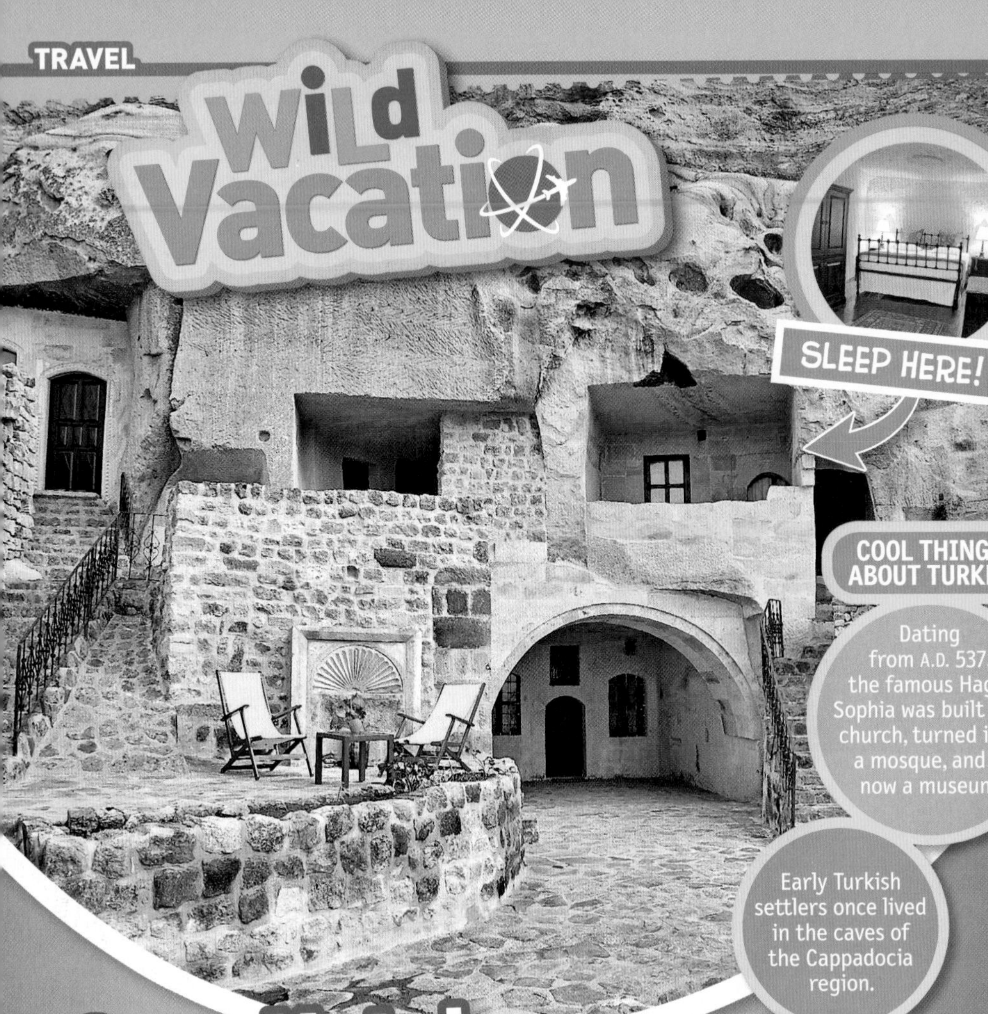

COOL THINGS ABOUT TURKEY

Dating from A.D. 537, the famous Hagia Sophia was built as a church, turned into a mosque, and is now a museum.

Early Turkish settlers once lived in the caves of the Cappadocia region.

Yogurt was invented in Turkey and is a main ingredient in local food—from soups to desserts.

King Midas may not have really turned all he touched into gold. But he did rule over the kingdom of Phrygia, in what is now Turkey, in the eighth century B.C.

Cave Hotel

YUNAK EVLERI HOTEL

WHERE Cappadocia region, Turkey

WHY IT'S COOL Here's a hotel that really rocks. The Yunak Evleri is built into caves left by volcanic activity 10 million years ago. Follow narrow passageways and stone stairs to rooms that are a cool 57°F (14°C). Spend the day hiking rocky terrain, exploring caverns, or hot-air ballooning over "fairy chimneys"—tall rock formations that dot the skyline. At night you won't have to worry about being awakened by eruptions since the Cappadocia volcanoes are now dormant. So they're "sleeping," too!

THINGS TO DO IN TURKEY

- Ride a camel to tour the bizarre rock formations around Cappadocia.
- Take a boat ride up the Bosporus strait to get from Asia to Europe in 15 minutes.
- Haggle with shopkeepers in the bustling market of Istanbul's Grand Bazaar.

EXTREME WEIRDNESS

AT EASE, GORILLAS!

GORILLA FOOLS HUMANS

WHAT Ape robot

WHERE Bristol, England

DETAILS Call it *Planet of the Fake Apes.* The Bristol Zoo Gardens' "Wow! Gorillas" exhibit featured an animatronic ape and several five-foot (1.5-m)-tall fiberglass gorilla sculptures. The sculptures were later painted and decorated by local artists. What's next—papier-mâché penguins?

STRAW MAN

MEET STRAW MAN, TIN MAN'S LONG-LOST COUSIN.

WHAT Straw bears

WHERE Heldra, Germany

DETAILS Somebody went overboard with their winter coat. In colder months, some Germans have a tradition of wearing outfits made of straw while attending seasonal festivals. These "straw bears" date back to an old belief that the outfits would scare winter away. All this guy needs is a straw scarf.

BIIIGGG BINOCULARS

NOT SURE HOW TO WATCH BIRDS WITH THESE.

WHAT Binocular-shaped entrance

WHERE Venice, California, U.S.A.

DETAILS Did somebody ask for a better view? Sculptors Claes Oldenburg and Coosje van Bruggen designed this 45-foot (14-m)-tall set of binoculars that now serves as an office entrance for Google. So *that's* what they mean by "Internet search."

TOWER POWER

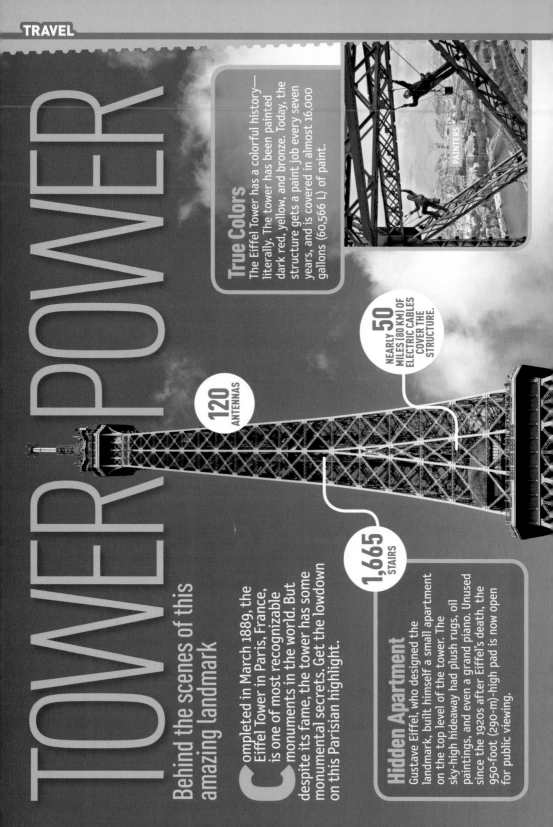

Behind the scenes of this amazing landmark

Completed in March 1889, the Eiffel Tower in Paris, France, is one of most recognizable monuments in the world. But despite its fame, the tower has some monumental secrets. Get the lowdown on this Parisian highlight.

120 ANTENNAS

1,665 STAIRS

NEARLY **50** MILES (80 KM) OF ELECTRIC CABLES COVER THE STRUCTURE.

True Colors

The Eiffel Tower has a colorful history—literally. The tower has been painted dark red, yellow, and bronze. Today, the structure gets a paint job every seven years, and is covered in almost 16,000 gallons (60,566 L) of paint.

PAINTERS

Hidden Apartment

Gustave Eiffel, who designed the landmark, built himself a small apartment on the top level of the tower. The sky-high hideaway had plush rugs, oil paintings, and even a grand piano. Unused since the 1920s after Eiffel's death, the 950-foot (290-m)-high pad is now open for public viewing.

Sky Lab

Atop the Eiffel tower you'll find two small laboratories where Eiffel conducted experiments. To learn about how objects move against air, he dropped items attached to cords from the second level of the tower (about 380 feet/116 m aboveground.)

THE TOWER IS MADE OF **18,000** IRON PIECES BOLTED TOGETHER BY OVER 2.5 MILLION RIVETS.

Green Scene

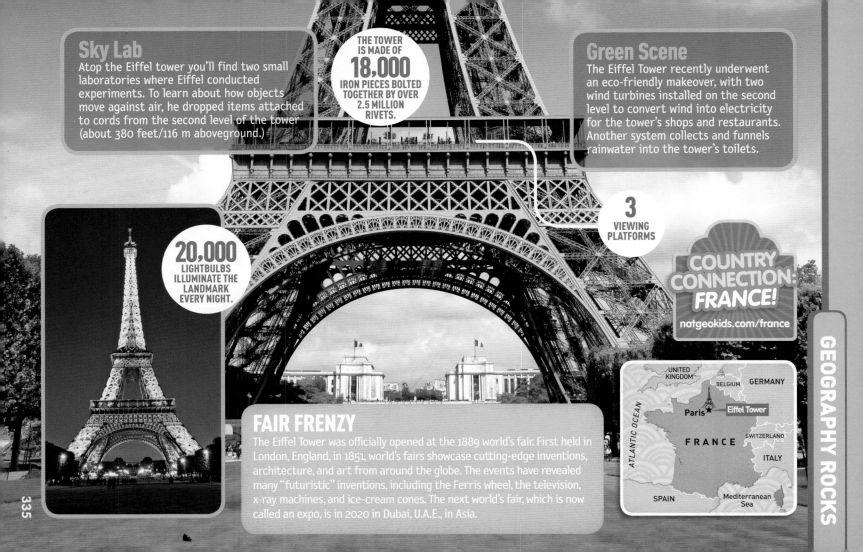

The Eiffel Tower recently underwent an eco-friendly makeover, with two wind turbines installed on the second level to convert wind into electricity for the tower's shops and restaurants. Another system collects and funnels rainwater into the tower's toilets.

3 VIEWING PLATFORMS

20,000 LIGHTBULBS ILLUMINATE THE LANDMARK EVERY NIGHT.

COUNTRY CONNECTION: *FRANCE!*
natgeokids.com/france

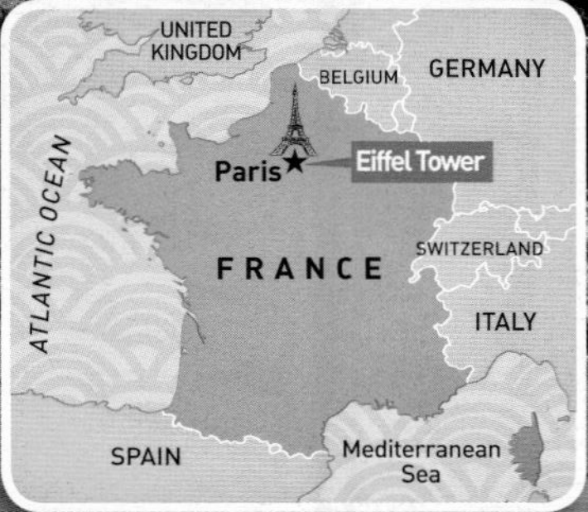

UNITED KINGDOM
BELGIUM
GERMANY
Paris
Eiffel Tower
ATLANTIC OCEAN
FRANCE
SWITZERLAND
ITALY
SPAIN
Mediterranean Sea

FAIR FRENZY

The Eiffel Tower was officially opened at the 1889 world's fair. First held in London, England, in 1851, world's fairs showcase cutting-edge inventions, architecture, and art from around the globe. The events have revealed many "futuristic" inventions, including the Ferris wheel, the television, x-ray machines, and ice-cream cones. The next world's fair, which is now called an expo, is in 2020 in Dubai, U.A.E., in Asia.

Is your geography knowledge off the map? Quiz yourself to find out!

Write your answers on a piece of paper. Then check them below.

1. **97 percent of water on Earth is:**
   a. undrinkable
   b. frozen
   c. fresh
   d. underground

2. **Hong Kong has more ________ than any other city in the world.**
   a. museums
   b. birds
   c. people
   d. skyscrapers

3. **Both the coldest and the hottest temperatures in South America were recorded in __________.**

4. **Scientists recently unearthed a trove of ancient fossils in Antarctica containing the bones of which species?**
   a. birds
   b. lizards
   c. dinosaurs
   d. all of the them

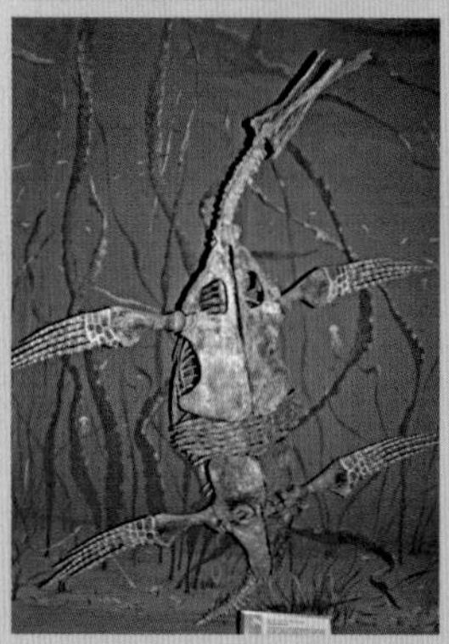

5. **True or false?** Yogurt was invented in Turkey.

Not **STUMPED** yet? Check out the *NATIONAL GEOGRAPHIC KIDS QUIZ WHIZ* collection for more crazy **GEOGRAPHY** questions!

ANSWERS:
1. a; 2. d; 3. Argentina; 4. d; 5. True

HOMEWORK HELP

Finding Your Way Around

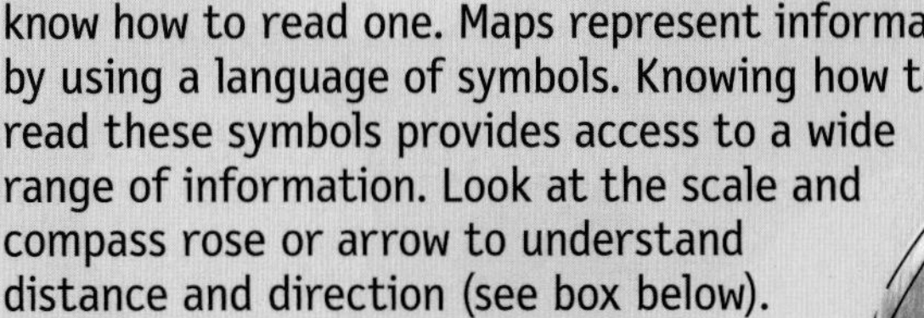

Every map has a story to tell, but first you have to know how to read one. Maps represent information by using a language of symbols. Knowing how to read these symbols provides access to a wide range of information. Look at the scale and compass rose or arrow to understand distance and direction (see box below).

To find out what each symbol on a map means, you must use the key. It's your secret decoder—identifying information by each symbol on the map.

LATITUDE AND LONGITUDE

Latitude and longitude lines (above) help us determine locations on Earth. Every place on Earth has a special address called absolute location. Imaginary lines called lines of latitude run west to east, parallel to the Equator. These lines measure distance in degrees north or south from the Equator (0° latitude) to the North Pole (90°N) or to the South Pole (90°S). One degree of latitude is approximately 70 miles (113 km).

Lines of longitude run north to south, meeting at the Poles. These lines measure distance in degrees east or west from 0° longitude (prime meridian) to 180° longitude. The prime meridian runs through Greenwich, England.

SCALE AND DIRECTION

The scale on a map can be shown as a fraction, as words, or as a line or bar. It relates distance on the map to distance in the real world. Sometimes the scale identifies the type of map projection. Maps may include an arrow or compass rose to indicate north on the map.

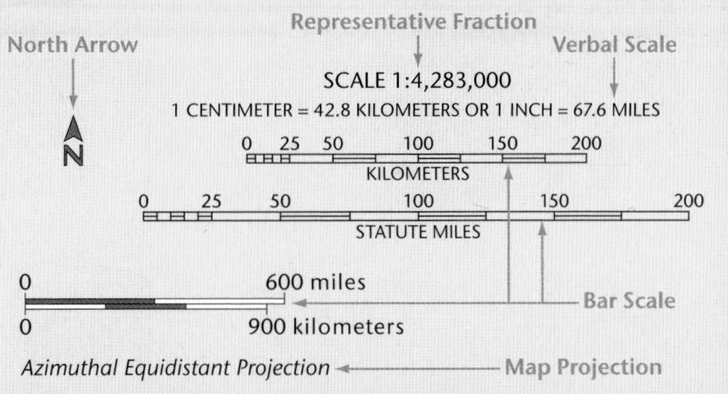

GAME ANSWERS

Find the Hidden Animals, page 142
1. **B**, 2. **C**, 3. **A**, 4. **E**, 5. **D**.

What in the World? page 143
Top row: **pig, walking worm, lobster.**
Middle row: **moth, river dolphin, katydid.**
Bottom row: **flamingo, frog, coral.**
Bonus: **tweethearts**

Grand Teton Adventure, page 144

Spring Fever, page 146

Penguin Party, page 147
1. **B**, 2. **D**, 3. **F**, 4. **H**, 5. **C**, 6. **A**, 7. **G**, 8. **J**, 9. **I**, 10. **E**.

What in the World? page 148
Top row: **snowball, globe, basketball.**
Middle row: **marble, Saturn, bowling ball.**
Bottom row: **rubber ball, orange, disco ball.**
Bonus: **a ball hog.**

Fishy Business, page 150

Redwood Roundup, page 153

Go Fish! page 155

Want to Learn More?

Find more information about topics in this book in these National Geographic Kids resources.

5,000 Awesome Facts (About Everything!) series

Awesome 8 series

By the Numbers series

Funny Fill-In series

Weird But True series

Animal Ark
Joel Sartore, Kwame Alexander
February 2017

The Book of Heroines
Stephanie Warren Drimmer
November 2016

Everything World War I
Karen L. Kenny
September 2014

Mission Shark Rescue:
Ruth A. Musgrave
March 2016

Oceanpedia
Christina Wilsdon
November 2016

Our Country's Presidents
Ann Bausum
January 2017

Science Encyclopedia
October 2016

Tales From the Arabian Nights
Donna Jo Napoli and Christina Balit
October 2016

Ultimate Explorer Guide
Nancy Honovich
March 2017

Welcome to Mars
Buzz Aldrin and Marianne Dyson
September 2015

Your World 2018 (8–17)

All articles in section by Sarah Wassner Flynn.

Awesome Exploration (18–35)

pp. 22–25 "Dare to Explore" by C.M. Tomlin; p. 30 "Meerkat Close Encounter" by Kitson Jazynka; 31–32 "Frozen in Time" and "Photo Ark" by Sarah Wassner Flynn.

Amazing Animals (36–91)

pp. 38–39 "Extraordinary Animals" by Kay Boatner (dog); Kristin Baird Rattini (parrot); Heather E. Schwartz (chimp); and Kitson Jazynka (koala); pp. 40–41 "Incredible Animal Friends" by Kitson Jazynka (fox/terrier) and Angela Modany (dolphin/sea lion); pp. 42–43 "Frog Versus Fungus" by Ruth A. Musgrave; p. 44 "Spying on Sloths" by Karen De Seve; p. 45 "Snow Leopard Selfies" by Scott Elder; pp. 46–47 "What Is Taxonomy?" & "Vertebrates"/"Invertebrates" by Susan K. Donnelly; p. 48 "Tips for Being a Coati" by Ruth A. Musgrave; p. 49 "Tough Cats" by Karen De Seve; pp. 50–51 "Goofballs" by Avery Elizabeth Hurt; p. 52 "Mistaken Identity" by Scott Elder; p. 53 "Wolverine!" by Stephanie Warren; pp. 54–55 "Wild Hamsters" by Kate Jaimet; pp. 56–57 "18 Cool Things About Reptiles" by Christina Wilsdon; pp. 58–59 "Brain Waves" by Crispin Boyer; pp. 60–61 "Name That Tide Pool Animal" by Nancy Honovich; pp. 62–63 "Mission Animal Rescue: Sea Turtle" by Scott Elder; pp. 64–65 "Awesome Insect Awards" by Sarah Wassner Flynn; pp. 66–67 "Big Cats" by Elizabeth Carney; pp. 68–69 "Top Spot" by Scott Elder; pp. 70–71 "Lifestyles of the Rich & Furry" by Patricia J. Murphy; p. 73 "7 Facts about Pet Rodents ..." by Andrea Silen; pp. 74–75 "Famous Pets of History" by April Capochino Myers; p. 76 "What Killed the Dinosaurs?" by Sarah Wassner Flynn; pp. 76–79 "Prehistoric Timeline" & "Who Ate What?" by Susan K. Donnelly; p. 78 "What If Dinos Hadn't Gone Extinct?" by Rose Davidson; p. 79 "A Great Discovery!" by Sarah Wassner Flynn; p. 80 "Dino Classification" by Susan K. Donnelly; pp. 84–89 "18 Cutest Animals of 2018" by Sarah Wassner Flynn.

Going Green (92–105)

p. 94 "The Arctic's Disappearing Ice," by Sarah Wassner Flynn; pp. 96–98 "5 Animals Battling Climate Change," & "6 Tips to Save the Earth" by Sarah Wassner Flynn; p. 99 "Pollution" by David George Gordon; pp. 99–100 "What a Prince!" and "Ugly Food" by Sarah Wassner Flynn.

Engineering and Technology (106–117)

pp. 108–109 "Cool Inventions" by Crispin Boyer (plane, lamp, speaker), Andrea Silen (watch), and Cathy Lu (car); p. 110 "The Buzz on Drones" by Sarah Wassner Flynn; p. 111 "Robotics" by Jamie Kiffel-Alcheh; p. 114 "George Washington Carver" by Kay Boatner; p. 115 "Accidents Happen" by Renee Skelton.

Wonders of Nature (118–139)

p. 120 "Weather and Climate" by Mark Bockenhauer; p. 122 "Types of Clouds" by Kathy Furgang; p. 123 "Make a Barometer" by Nancy Honovich; pp. 126–127 "Typhoon!" & "Earthquake" & "Flood!" by Sarah Wassner Flynn; pp. 128–129 "Wildfire!" by Stephanie Warren Drimmer; p. 130 "How Does Your Garden Grow?" by Susan K. Donnelly; pp. 132–133 "Biomes" by Susan K. Donnelly; pp. 136–137 "Pristine Seas" by Sarah Wassner Flynn.

Space and Earth (160–179)

pp. 162–163 "Big Bang" by David A. Aguilar; p. 162 "Powerful Particle" by Sarah Wassner Flynn; p. 166 "Dwarf Planets" by Sarah Wassner Flynn; p. 167 "Destination Space: Black Hole" by Stephanie Warren Drimmer; p. 172 "Rock Stars" by Steve Tomecek; p. 173 "What if You Could Dig ...?" by Crispin Boyer; pp. 173–175 "A Look Inside" and "What Is a Volcano?" by Kathy Furgang; pp. 176–177 "Hot Spot" by Scott Elder.

Culture Connection (180–203)

pp. 182–183 "Food That Fools You" by Lisa Sonne; p. 184 "Mango Lassi" by Kay Boatner; p. 185 "7 Bite-Size Facts ..." by Erin Whitmer; p. 188 "What's Your Chinese Horoscope?" by Geoff Williams; p. 191 "Treat Your Pet" by Kay Boatner; pp. 192–193 "Money Around the World!" by Kristin Baird Rattini; pp. 198–199 "Monster Myths" by Kitson Jazynka; pp. 200–201 "World Religions" by Mark Bockenhauer; p. 201 "Technology Meets Tradition" by Sarah Wassner Flynn.

Life Science (204–221)

p. 207 "The Three Domains of Life" by Susan K. Donnelly; pp. 210–211 "Grow Your Own Biofilm" by Karen Romano Young; pp. 212–213 "You and Your Cells" & "You Have a Lot of Nerve!" by Christina Wilsdon, Patricia Daniels, and Jen Agresta; p. 214 "Your Amazing Ears" by Sarah Wassner Flynn; p. 216 "Your Amazing Brain" by Douglas E. Richards; p. 217 "Check Your Memory" by Jennifer Swanson; pp. 218–219 "The Gene Scene," "Limbs from Limbs" & "Smart Parts!" by Christina Wilsdon, Patricia Daniels, and Jen Agresta.

History Happens (222–253)

pp. 224–225 "Royally Amazing Castles" by Jen Agresta; pp. 226–227 "Jungle of Secrets" by John Micklos, Jr.; pp. 228–229 "Must-See Sights" by Sarah Wassner Flynn; p. 232 "Mystery of Atlantis" by John Micklos, Jr.; p. 233 "The Secrets of Stonehenge" by Kristin Baird Rattini; p. 234 "Treasure!" by Jamie Kiffel-Alech; p. 235 "City in the Sky" by Kristin Baird Rattini; pp. 236–237 "War!" by Susan K. Donnelly and Sarah Wassner Flynn; p. 237 "Armistice Day" by Sarah Wassner Flynn; pp. 238–239 "The Constitution & the Bill of Rights" & "Branches of Government" by Susan K. Donnelly; p. 240 "The Indian Experience" by Martha B. Sharma; pp. 246–247 "Cool Things About *Air Force One*" by Scott Elder; pp. 248–249 "Civil Rights" & "Stone of Hope" by Susan K. Donnelly and Sarah Wassner Flynn; pp. 250–251 "8 Daring Women in U.S. History!" by Sarah Wassner Flynn.

Geography Rocks (254–337)

pp. 256–262 by Mark Bockenhauer; pp. 264–291 by Sarah Wassner Flynn, Mark Bockenhauer, and Susan K. Donnelly; pp. 292–317 "You Are There!" by Sarah Wassner Flynn; p. 329 "Destination Guide: New Orleans, Louisiana" by Sarah Wassner Flynn; pp. 330–331 "18 Cool Things About Hawaii" by Alicia Klepeis; p. 332 "Wild Vacation" by C.M. Tomlin; p. 333 "Extreme Weirdness From Around the World" by Kay Boatner; pp. 334–335 "Tower Power" by Sean McCollum.

All "Homework Help" by Vicki Ariyasu, except p.117 "This is How It's Done!" by Sarah Wassner Flynn.

ABBREVIATIONS:
CO: Corbis
DS: Dreamstime
GI: Getty Images
IS: iStockphoto
MP: Minden Pictures
NGC: National Geographic Creative
SS: Shutterstock
WHHA: White House Historical Association

All Maps
By National Geographic unless otherwise noted

All Illustrations & Charts
By Stuart Armstrong unless otherwise noted

Front Cover/Spine
(shark), Tim Davis/CO/VCG/GI; (lion cub), amrishw/SS; (penguin), Parry Grip/NG; (phone), Mark Thiessen, NG Staff; (bottom insert), © 2017 WildWorks Inc. All rights reserved.; (tiger), iStockphoto; (drone), Richard Newstead/GI; (chameleon), Kuttelvaserova Stuchelova/SS; (volcano), AvDe/SS

Back Cover
(Earth), Alex Staroseltsev/SS; (boy hiking), Julia Kuznetsova/SS; (chameleon), Kuttelvaserova Stuchelova/SS; (*T. rex* skeleton), Marques/SS; (drone), Richard Newstead/GI; (tiger), iStockphoto; (volcano), AvDe/SS; (hat), Steve Collender/SS

Inside Front Cover
(dolphin), ArchMan/SS; (sea turtle), David Carbo/SS

Front Matter (2–7)
2–3, Jordi Chias/NPL/MP; 5 (RT), SS; 5 (UP), Eric Isselée/SS; 5 (UP CTR), Peter Macdiarmid/GI; 5 (CTR), Design Pics Inc./NGC; 5 (LO CTR), Jasper Doest/MP; 5 (LO), Shulzie/GI; 6 (UP LE), Pau Barrena/Bloomberg/GI; 6 (UP RT), Patrick Tehan/MCT/Newscom; 6 (UP CTR LE), Birgitte Wilms/MP; 6 (CTR LE), IS; 6 (CTR RT), Rinie Van Meurs/Foto Natura/MP; 6 (LO CTR LE), Peter Bollinger; 6 (LO LE), gregobagel/GI; 6 (LO RT), Digital Storm/SS; 7 (RT), Steve Gschmeissner/Photo Researchers, Inc.; 7 (UP LE), Eye of Science/Science Source; 7 (CTR LE), Michael Melfordê/NGC; 7 (LO LE), Alex Mustard/Nature Picture Library

Your World 2018 (8–17)
8–9, Peter Macdiarmid/GI; 10 (UP), courtesy National Aquarium of New Zealand; 10 (LO), Norbert Wu/MP; 11 (UP), AsiaPac/GI; 11 (LO LE), PCN Photography/Alamy Stock Photo; 11 (LO RT), Robbie Shone/Alamy Stock Photo; 12 (UP LE), Brian Edwards; 12 (UP RT), Brian Edwards; 12 (CTR LE), WPA Pool/GI; 12 (CTR RT), Anadolu Agency/GI; 12 (LO LE), Ocean Exploration Trust/NOAA; 13 (UP), John Lund/GI; 13 (CTR), courtesy Plume Labs/Digitas LBI; 13 (LO), AP Photo/Eric Vandeville/Sipa USA; 14, NASA; 15 (UP), Graham Monro/gm photographics/GI; 15 (CTR), Universal Images Group/GI; 15 (LO LE), Natthawat/GI; 15 (LO RT), satriaangga7/GI; 16 (A), Daniel Dempster Photography/Alamy Stock Photo; 16 (B), sampics/GI; 16 (C) Lesya Gapchuk/GI; 16 (D), Craig Lovell/Eagle Visions Photography/Alamy Stock Photo; 16 (E), Robynrg/SS; 16 (F), bunya541/GI; 16 (G), Krzysztof Dydynski/GI; 16 (H), Hannah Peters/GI; 16 (I), Ascent Xmedia/GI; 17 (UP), NASA; 17 (CTR), courtesy Waverly Labs; 17 (CTR RT), courtesy Waverly Labs; 17 (LO), Paul Hameister

Awesome Exploration (18–35)
18–19, Design Pics Inc./NGC; 20 (UP LE), Jennie Miller; 20 (UP CTR), Sean Macdiarmid/DS; 20 (UP RT), Peter Chadwick/GI; 20 (UP CTR LE), f9photos/SS; 20 (UP CTR RT), blackred/GI; 20 (LO LE), Iershova Khrystyna/SS; 20 (LO CTR LE), SanderStock/GI; 20 (LO CTR), shama65/SS; 20 (LO RT), restyler/SS; 21 (UP LE), Skoda/SS; 21 (UP RT), Ruslan Kudrin/SS; 21 (UP CTR LE), Bernard Prost/GI; 21 (UP CTR RT), Vaclav Mach/SS; 21 (LO LE), drohn/SS; 21 (LO CTR), Claudio Divizia/SS; 21 (LO RT), Justin Bailie/GI; 22 (UP), Jenny Daltry and Andrea Otto; 22 (LO LE), Joe McDonald/Visuals Unlimited, Inc./Nature Picture Library; 22 (LO CTR), Jenny Daltry; 22 (LO RT), Jenny Daltry; 23 (UP RT), Charles Trout; 23 (LE), African People & Wildlife Fund; 23 (LO RT), Mitsuaki Iwago/MP; 24, Cory Richards/NGC; 25 (UP), Godfrey Merlen/NGC; 25 (CTR), Sue Moore/NGC; 25 (LO), Pete Oxford/MP; 26 (UP), NadyaEugene/SS; 26 (CTR), Vasin Lee/SS; 26 (LO RT), Stephen Bonk/SS; 26 (LO LE), Duplass/SS; 27 (UP LE), Kuttelvaserova Stuchelova/SS; 27 (UP RT), Marques/SS; 27 (LO), Julia Kuznetsova/SS; 28 (LE), Dave McAloney/National Geographic Pristine Seas; 28 (RT) Shane Gross/SS; 29 (UP RT), My Shot User INIMINIMO; 29 (LO LE), My Shot User Ferretopia; 29 (LO RT), My Shot User allid126; 30, Will Burrard-Lucas; 31 (UP), Alasdair Turner/Aurora Photos/CO/GI; 31 (LO LE), Popperfoto/GI; 31 (LO RT), Ashley Cooper pics/Alamy; 32 (UP), Joel Sartore/NGC; 32 (CTR), courtesy Columbus Zoo and Aquarium; 32 (LO), Joel Sartore/NGC; 33 (UP LE), FishyMan; 33 (UP RT), creatifxpressions; 33 (CTR LE), Lomax; 33 (CTR RT), Funnysweetlicious; 33 (LO LE), s07gra0983; 33 (LO RT), Bunny; 34 (UP), courtesy Columbus Zoo and Aquarium; 34 (CTR), Jennie Miller; 34 (LO), Mitsuaki Iwago/MP; 35 (UP RT), Grady Reese/IS

Amazing Animals (36–91)
36–37, Jasper Doest/MP; 38 (UP), ImagoStock/Newscom; 38 (LO), Juniors Bildarchiv GmbH/Alamy; 39 (UP RT), Tetsuro Matsuzawa/PRI/Kyoto University; 39 (CTR RT), Tetsuro Matsuzawa/PRI/Kyoto University; 39 (LO LE), Ben Beaden/Australia Zoo; 39 (LO RT), Ben Beaden/Australia Zoo; 40, Rex USA/Richard Bowler/Rex; 41, Nathan Edwards/Newspix/Rex/Rex USA; 42, Gil Wizen; 43 (UP), age fotostock/Alamy; 43 (CTR), Paul D. Lemke; 43 (LO), Mark Kostich/Vetta/GI; 44 (UP), Thomas Marent/MP; 44 (CTR), Suzi Eszterhas/MP; 44 (LO LE), Ingo Arndt/MP; 44 (LO RT), Thomas Marent/MP; 45 (UP), Paul Sangeorzan; 45 (CTR), Sean Shui/Snow Leopard Trust/Panthera; 45 (LO), Peter Bolliger; 46 (UP RT), Diane McAllister/Nature Picture Library; 46 (CTR LE), Eric Isselée/SS; 46 (LO RT), Joel Sartore/NGC; 47 (UP LE), FloridaStock/SS; 47 (UP RT), cbpix/SS; 47 (CTR LE), mashe/SS; 47 (LO RT), Karen Massier/IS; 47 (LO), Eric Isselée/SS; 48 (LE), Claus Meyer/MP; 48 (UP RT), Luciano Candisani/MP; 48 (CTR RT), Pete Oxford/MP; 48 (LO CTR), imageBROKER/Alamy; 48 (CTR LE), Mark Taylor/Nature Picture Library; 48 (LO RT), Christian Ziegler/MP; 49 (UP), Arco Images GmbH/Alamy; 49 (LO), Lisa & Mike Husar/Team Husar; 50 (UP), Heidi & Hans-Juergen Koch/MP; 50 (LO), M. Watson/Ardea; 51 (UP LE), Bianca Lavies/NGC; 51 (UP RT), Mark Payne-Gill/Nature Picture Library; 51 (LO LE), Bianca Lavies/NGC; 51 (CTR RT), Claus Meyer/MP; 51 (LO RT), Jason Tharp; 52 (UP), Joe McDonald/CO/GI; 52 (LO LE), Jean Paul Ferrero/Ardea; 52 (LO RT), Roland Seitre/MP; 53 (Background), Sergey Gorshkov/MP; 53 (LO), Daniel J. Cox/Oxford Scientific/GI; 53 (RT), A. & J. Visage/Peter Arnold/GI; 53 (LO LE), Igor Shpilenok/Nature Picture Library; 54–55, Eric Baccega/Nature Picture Library; 56 (1), Andrew Burgess/SS; 56 (2), bluedogroom/SS; 56 (3), iStock.com/amwu; 56 (4), Kistina Mahlau/DS; 56 (5), Isselée/DS; 56 (6), Mgkuijpers/DS; 56 (7), Stephen Dalton/MP; 56 (8), Photo2008a/DS; 56 (9), Michael & Patricia Fogden/MP; 57 (10), Marcel Auret/DS; 57 (11 LE), Kim Taylor/MP; 57 (11 RT), Kim Taylor/MP; 57 (12), Satoshi Kuribayashi/MP; 57 (13), Isselée/DS; 57 (14), Eric Isselée/SS; 57 (15), Farinoza/DS; 57 (16), Pascal Kobeh/Nature Picture Library; 57 (17), reptiles4all/SS; 57 (18), Bence Mate/MP; 58–59, Brian Skerry/NGC; 60, apsimo1/IS; 61 (B), Lars Johansson/IS; 61 (C), Nancy Nehring/IS; 61 (D), Brendan Hunter/IS; 61 (E), AtWaG/IS; 61 (F), Lee Rogers/IS; 62–63, Brian J. Skerry/NGC; 62 (LO), New England Aquarium Rescue; 63 (UP RT), Terry Dickson/Florida Times-Union; 63 (LO LE), Connie Merigo/New England Aquarium; 63 (LO RT), Jekyll Island Authority; 64 (UP LE), Stephen Dalton/MP; 64 (UP RT), Gregory Hoover; 64 (LO), Elio Della Ferrera/MP; 65 (UP LE), Stephen Dalton/Nature Picture Library; 65 (UP RT), Mitsuhiko Imamori/MP; 65 (LO LE), Studio Times Ltd/MP; 65 (LO RT), Bruce Davidson/MP; 66, Staffan Widstrand/Nature Picture Library; 67 (UP LE), worldswildlifewonders/SS; 67 (UP CTR LE), Kesu/SS; 67 (UP CTR RT), WitR/SS; 67 (UP RT), Eric Isselée/SS; 67 (CTR LE), Dlillc/CO/GI; 67 (CTR RT), Eric Isselée/SS; 67 (LO LE), Eric Isselée/SS; 67 (LO RT), Eric Isselée/SS; 68 (LE), Mark Newman/FLPA/MP; 68 (RT), Frans Lanting; 69 (UP), Suzi Eszterhas/MP; 69 (LO), Nick Gordon/Ardea; 70 (LE), Yoshitsugu Kimura/Fifi & Romeo; 70 (RT), Meredith Parmelee/Stone/GI; 71 (UP), courtesy of La Petite Maison; 71 (CTR LE), Britt Erlanson/The Image Bank/GI; 71 (CTR), James Kegley; 71 (CTR RT), James Kegley; 71 (LO LE), Augustus Butera/Taxi/GI; 71 (LO RT), courtesy of Three Dog Bakery LLC; 72 (UP LE), Jean Michel Labat/Ardea; 72 (UP RT), Johan de Meester/Ardea; 72 (LO LE), John Daniels/Ardea; 72 (LO RT), Jaromir Chalabala/SS; 73, Arco Images GmbH/Alamy; 74 (UP), Krissi Lundgren/SS; 74 (CTR), Jagodka/SS; 74 (LO), World History Archive/Newscom; 75 (UP), Juniors Bildarchiv GmbH/Alamy; 75 (UP CTR LE), iStock/fotojagodka; 75 (UP CTR RT), David Douglas Duncan/Photography Collection/Harry Ransom Center; 75 (LO CTR), Sir Edwin Landseer/Royal Collection Trust/© Her Majesty Queen Elizabeth II 2015; 75 (LO), The White House/Pete Souza/GI; 76 (UP), Chris Butler/Science Photo Library/Photo Researchers, Inc.; 76 (CTR), Publiphoto/Photo Researchers, Inc.; 76 (LO), Pixeldust Studios/NGC; 77 (A), Publiphoto/Photo Researchers, Inc.; 77 (B), Laurie O'Keefe/Photo Researchers, Inc.; 77 (C), Chris Butler/Photo Researchers, Inc.; 77 (D), Publiphoto/Photo Researchers, Inc.; 77 (E), image courtesy of Project Exploration; 78, Joe Rocco; 78–79 (CTR), Pixeldust Studios/NGC; 79, Mark Witton; 80 (UP), Paul B. Moore/SS; 80 (LO), Andrea Meyer/SS; 81 (UP LE), art by Mark Klinger, courtesy Carnegie Museum of Natural History, Section of Vertebrate Paleontology; 81 (UP RT), Franco Tempesta/NG; 81 (LO),

Jorge Gonzalez and Pablo Lara; 82–83, Franco Tempesta; 84 (UP), Denver Bryan/KimballStock; 84 (LO), Ann and Steve Toon/NPL/MP; 85 (UP LE), Klein and Hubert/MP; 85 (UP RT), David Tipling Photo Library/Alamy Stock Photo; 85 (LO), Barcroft Media/GI; 86 (UP LE), Theo Bosboom/NPL/MP; 86 (UP RT), Thomas Marent/MP; 86 (LO), Thiebaud Gontard/Biosphoto/MP; 87 (UP), Cyril Ruoso/MP; 87 (LO LE), Weidong Li; 87 (LO RT), Sylvain Cordier/Biosphoto/MP; 88 (UP LE), Ross Hoddinott/NPL/MP; 88 (UP RT), Suzi Eszterhas/MP; 88 (LO LE), Image Source/Alamy Stock Photo; 88 (LO RT), Carmelka/GI; 89 (UP LE), Jelger Herder/Buiten-beeld/MP; 89 (UP RT), Hisham Atallah/NiS/MP; 89 (LO), Ferrero-Labat/Ardea; 90 (UP), Suzi Eszterhas/MP; 90 (CTR), Pixeldust Studios/NGC; 90 (LO), ÊSnowleopard1/GI; 91 (UP RT), CampCrazy Photography/SS

Going Green (92–105)

92–93, schulzie/GI; 95, Albo003/SS; 95 (school bus), Rob Wilson/SS; 95 (Statue of Liberty), Steve Smith/SS; 95 (orca), Christian Musat/SS; 96 (UP), outdoorsman/SS; 96 (LO), Richard McManus/GI; 97 (UP), Perry de Graaf/NiS/MP; 97 (CTR), Joel Sartore/NGC; 97 (LO), Tim Flach/GI; 98 (LO), Jono Halling; 99 (Background), Mujka Design Inc./IS; 99 (CTR), Giorgio Cosulich/GI; 99 (LO), Featureflash/SS; 100–101, James Yamasaki; 100–101 (wooden floor background, all), Lilkar/DS; 100 (bananas), Martina_L/GI; 100 (carrots), tBoyan/GI; 100 (peach), Jimejume/GI; 100 (lettuce), manulito/SS; 100 (BACK), mangiurea/SS; 101 (BACK), Walter Zerla/GI; 101 (UP LE), Jiang Hongyan/SS; 101 (UP RT), lucielang/IS; 101 (UP CTR LE), PeJo29/IS; 101 (UP CTR), Imagesbybarbara/IS; 101 (UP CTR RT), toddtaulman/IS; 101 (LO CTR RT), nilsz/IS; 101 (LO CTR LE), talevr/IS; 101 (LO LE), PhotosbyAbby/IS; 101 (LO RT), kedsanee/IS; 102 (2), courtesy of Miller Hull; 102 (3), Jonathan Karwacki/SS; 102 (4), Sam Yeh/AFP/GI; 102 (5), Maks Narodenko/SS; 102 (6), Ian 2010/SS; 102 (7), K Link Photography/SS; 102 (8), Kim Petersen/Alamy Stock Photo; 102 (9), Martin Bond/Alamy Stock Photo; 103 (10), S. Borisov/SS; 103 (11), Sean Hsu/SS; 103 (13), Manfred Ruckszio/SS; 103 (14), David Patterson; 103 (15), Denis Kichatof/SS; 103 (16), Wiskerke/Alamy Stock Photo; 103 (17), robert_s/SS; 104 (UP), IS; 104 (CTR), robert_s/SS; 104 (LO), Mujka Design Inc./IS

Engineering and Technology (106–117)

106–107, Pau Barrena/Bloomberg/GI; 108 (UP LE), DeepFlight; 108 (UP RT), Photo courtesy of Laucala Island Resort; 108 (LO LE), DeepFlight; 108 (CTR RT), Paladone Products Ltd.; 108 (LO RT), Paladone Products Ltd.; 109 (UP LE), Heimplanet; 109 (UP RT), courtesy VTech Electronics; 109 (LO BOTH), courtesy of Parajet International Limited; 110 (UP), Richard Newstead/GI; 110 (LO LE), Paul Souders/GI; 110 (LO RT), GI; 111 (UP LE), Benebot Remote Sales Robot Ecovacs Robotics, Inc.; 111 (UP RT), AP Photo/Keith Srakocic; 111 (CTR), Patrick Tehan/MCT/Newscom; 111 (LO LE), Patrick Tehan/MCT/Newscom; 111 (LO RT), Michael Bahlo/EPA/Newscom; 112 (1), Bloomberg/Contributor/GI; 112 (2), Minneapolis Star Tribune/MC/Newscom; 112 (3), heromen30/SS; 112 (4), Tobias Schwarz/AFP/GI; 112 (5), Luke J. Roberts/Maryland Robotics Center, University of Maryland; 112 (7), Issei Kato/Reuters/GI; 112 (8), Shebeko/SS; 113 (10), Aki Inomata; 113 (11), courtesy Air Wolf 3-D; 113 (12), Mandel Ngan/AFP/GI; 113 (13), Makushin Alexey/SS; 113 (14), Bloomberg/Contributor/GI; 113 (15), epa european pressphoto agency b.v/Alamy Stock Photo; 113 (16), BSIP/UIG/GI; 113 (18), Chakrapong Zyn/SS; 114–115, art by Joe Rocco; 116 (UP), Art by Joe Rocco; 116 (CTR), Joe Rocco; 116 (LO), Patrick Tehan/MCT/Newscom; 117, Klaus Vedfelt/GI

Wonders of Nature (118–139)

118–119, Birgitte Wilms/MP; 120 (CTR), Humming Bird Art/SS; 121 (UP), Stuart Armstrong; 122 (LO), Richard Peterson/SS; 122 (1), Leonid Tit/SS; 122 (2), Frans Lanting/NGC; 122 (3), Daniel Loretto/SS; 122 (4), Lars Christensen/SS; 123 (UP LE), Lori Epstein/NG Staff; 123 (UP CTR), GrigoryL/SS; 123 (UP RT), Richard Griffin/SS; 123 (LO LE), Lori Epstein/NG Staff; 123 (LO RT), Lori Epstein/NG Staff; 124 (1), Aneese/SS; 124 (2), SuperStock/GI; 124 (3), urfin/SS; 124 (4), Alberto Incrocci/GI; 124 (5), ScreenProd/Photononstop/Alamy Stock Photo; 124 (6), Keystone-France/Gamma-Keystone/GI; 124 (7), imageBROKER/Alamy Stock Photo; 125 (11), Zastolskiy Victor/SS; 125 (12), Serj Malomuzh/SS; 125 (13), GI; 125 (14), NASA; 125 (15), Topical Press Agency/Hulton Archive/GI; 125 (16), Lysogor Roman/SS; 125 (17), Mario Tama/GI; 125 (18), Ron Dahlquist/GI; 126 (UP), Dan Kitwood/GI; 127 (UP LE), KalypsoWorldPhotography/GI; 127 (LO LE), KalypsoWorldPhotography/GI; 127 (UP RT), Michael B. Thomas/GI; 127 (LO RT), Michael B. Thomas/GI; 128–129, Frans Lanting/NGC; 128 (LE), AP Photo/U.S. California Air National Guard, Master Sgt. Julie Avey; 128 (RT), Justin Sullivan/GI; 129 (UP LE), Robert Winslow; 129 (UP RT), National Interagency Fire Center; 129 (LO LE), Brian Cahn/Zuma Press/Newscom; 130 (UP), FotograFFF/SS; 130 (LO), Craig Tuttle/CO/GI; 131 (UP LE), NASA/Goddard Space Flight Center; 131 (LO LE), Image Source/SuperStock; 131 (LO RT), Andrey_Kuzmin/SS; 132 (LE), AVTG/IS; 132 (RT), Brad Wynnyk/SS; 133 (A), Rich Carey/SS; 133 (B), Richard Walters/IS; 133 (C), Karen Graham/IS; 133 (D), Michio Hoshino/MP/NGC; 134–135 (UP), Jason Edwards/NGC; 134 (LO LE), Brandon Cole; 134 (LO RT), Reinhard Dirscherl/Visuals Unlimited, Inc.; 135 (LO LE), Dray van Beeck/SS; 135 (LO RT), Brandon Cole; 136–137, Enric Sala/NGC; 136 (LO LE), Rebecca Hale/NGC; 137 (UP), Danita Delimont/Alamy; 137 (CTR RT), Dan Burton/Nature Picture Library; 137 (LO), Brian J. Skerry/NGC; 138 (UP), Kalypso World Photography/GI; 138 (CTR), Richard Walters/IS; 138 (LO), Dan Kitwood/GI

Fun and Games (140–159)

140–141, IS; 140 (LE), Talia Goldsmith; 142 (UP), Thomas Marent/MP; 142 (CTR LE), Steve Knell/Nature Picture Library; 142 (CTR RT), Rolf Nussbaumer/Nature Picture Library; 142 (LO LE), Thomas Marent/MP; 142 (LO RT), Malisa Nicolau/Alamy; 143 (UP LE), Johny87/iStock; 143 (UP CTR), Brian Rogers/Natural Visions; 143 (UP RT), Gary Bell/CO/GI; 143 (CTR LE), Fred Siskind; 143 (CTR), Kevin Schafer/MP; 143 (CTR RT), Basco/GT Photo; 143 (LO LE), kyoko kiyama/EyeEm/GI; 143 (LO CTR), Basco/GT Photo; 143 (LO RT), Jeffrey L. Rotman/CO/GI; 144, Alice Feagan; 145, Jason Tharpe; 146, CTON; 147 (A), Fred Bavendam/MP; 147 (B), Rinie Van Meurs/Foto Natura/MP; 147 (C), Tui de Roy/MP; 147 (D), Tony Heald/Nature Picture Library; 147 (E), Peter Steyn/Ardea London Ltd.; 147 (F), Dlillc/CO/GI; 147 (G), Yongyut Kumsri/SS; 147 (H), David Tipling/GI; 147 (I), Tim Davis/CO/GI; 147 (J), Kevin Schafer; 148 (UP LE), Photodisc Green/GI; 148 (UP CTR), Mark Thiessen/NG Staff; 148 (UP RT), Skypixel/DS; 148 (CTR LE), Silberkorn/DS; 148 (CTR), MarcelClemens/SS; 148 (CTR RT), Comstock/PictureQuest; 148 (LO LE), Brand X Pictures/PictureQuest; 148 (LO CTR), StockDisc/PictureQuest; 148 (LO RT), Ingram/PictureQuest; 149 (UP LE), Brand X Pictures/GI; 149 (UP RT), Steven Hunt/GI; 149 (LO LE), Andy Rouse/GI; 149 (LO RT), Design Pics/Keith Levit/GI; 150, CTON; 151 (UP LE), Chris Ware; 151 (UP RT), Chris Ware; 151 (CTR RT), Karen Sneider; 151 (LO), Jean GalvŒo; 152, Marty Baumann; 153, Dan Sipple; 154 (UP), Keren Su/CO/GI; 154 (CTR RT), Jim Craigmyle/CO/GI; 154 (LO LE), Image Source/GI; 154 (LO CTR), 68/Don Mason/Ocean/CO/GI; 154 (LO RT), FineArt/Alamy; 155, James Yamasaki; 156–157, Strika Entertainment; 158, Dan Sipple; 159 (UP), Haroldo Palo Jr./NHPA/Photoshot; 159 (CTR LE), Science Photo Library/Alamy; 159 (CTR), Skip Brown/NGC; 159 (CTR RT), Photodisc Green/GI; 159 (LO), All Canada Photos/Alamy

Space and Earth (160–179)

160–161, Peter Bollinger; 162–179 (Background), Take 27 Ltd/Photo Researchers, Inc.; 162–163, Rakita/SIPA/Newscom; 163 (A–E), David Aguilar; 164–165 (UP), David Aguilar; 166 (UP), David Aguilar; 166 (LO RT), NASA/JHUAPL/SwRI; 167, Mondolithic Studios Inc.; 168 (Background UP), Alexxandar/GI; 168 (UP RT), Walter Myers/Stocktrek Images/CO/GI; 168 (CTR RT), Tony & Daphne Hallas/Photo Researchers, Inc.; 168 (LO RT), NASA; 169, Moment RM/GI; 170 (1), ESB Professional/SS; 170 (2), Digital Storm/SS; 170 (4), Maks Narodenko/SS; 170 (6), AvDe/SS; 170 (7), EyeEm/Alamy Stock Photo; 170 (8), Bronwyn Photo/SS; 171 (10), robert_s/SS; 171 (11), apdesign/SS; 171 (12), Fotos593/SS; 171 (13), Makitalo/SS; 171 (14), Robert Crum/SS; 171 (15), Poul Riishede/SS; 171 (16 BACK), MarcelClemens/SS; 171 (16 FRONT), Mega Pixel/SS; 171 (17), ChrisVanLennepPhoto/SS; 172 (UP), Ralph Lee Hopkins/NGC; 172 (UP CTR LE), Visuals Unlimited/GI; 172 (UP CTR RT), Visuals Unlimited/GI; 172 (LO CTR LE), Doug Martin/Photo Researchers, Inc.; 172 (LO CTR RT), DEA/C. Dani/GI; 172 (LO LE), Michael Baranski/SS; 172 (LO RT), Terry Davis/SS; 172–191 (A), Jeff Goulden/IS; 173 (LO), Joe Rocco; 174 (LE), Cynthia Turner; 174 (BACK), Bychkov Kirill Alexandrovich/SS; 174 (UP RT), Robert Crow/SS; 174 (LO LE), Carsten Peter/NGC; 175 (UP LE), Mark Thiessen NG Staff; 175 (UP [1]), M. Unal Ozmen/SS; 175 (UP [2]), design56/SS; 175 (UP [3]), 4Kodiak/IS; 175 (UP [4]), Scott Bolster/SS; 175 (UP [5]), Picsfive/SS; 175 (LO), NASA; 176–177, Prisma/Superstock; 178 (UP), Doug Martin/Science Source; 178 (CTR), EyeEm/Alamy Stock Photo; 178 (LO), Moment RM/GI

Culture Connection (180–203)

180–181, gregobagel/GI; 182, David Aguilar; 182–183, Renee Comet, Food Styling by Lisa Cherkasky; 182 (LO LE), Renee Comet, Food Styling by Lisa Cherkasky; 182 (LO CTR), Renee Comet, Food Styling by Lisa Cherkasky; 182 (LO RT), Renee Comet, Food Styling by Lisa Cherkasky; 182 (lemon), Mark Thiessen/NG Staff; 182 (jam), Mark Thiessen/NG Staff; 182 (whipped cream), Mark Thiessen/NG Staff; 183, Mark Thiessen/NG Staff; 184 (RT), Tim Hill/Alamy; 184 (UP LE), Margo555/DS; 184 (UP CTR),

Danny Smythe/DS; 184 (LO CTR), Natika/DS; 184 (LO), Angelo Gilardelli/DS; 185, FoodCollection/Punchstock; 186 (1), fotohunter/SS; 186 (3), Ar2r/SS; 186 (4), Tubol Evgeniya/SS; 186 (6), Maarten Wouters/GI; 186 (8), Mike Clarke/GI; 186 (9), Supachita Ae/SS; 187 (12), Dinodia/age fotostock; 187 (14), Zee/Alamy; 187 (15), wacpan/SS; 189 (UP), Rebecca Hale/NG Staff; 189 (RT), Rebecca Hale/NG Staff; 189 (LO LE), Rebecca Hale/NG Staff; 189 (LO RT), Cathy Crawford/Nonstock/Jupiterimages; 190 (CTR), Robyn Beck/AFP/GI; 190 (LO LE), Timothy Clary/AFP/GI; 190 (LO RT), Barbara Ries; 191, Barbara Ries; 192 (UP LE), Ivan Vdovin/Alamy; 192 (UP RT CTR), B.A.E. Inc./Alamy; 192 (UP RT), B.A.E. Inc./Alamy; 192 (UP RT BACK), apomare/iStock; 192 (CTR LE), Mlenny/iStock; 192 (CTR RT), Zoonar GmbH/Alamy; 192 (LO LE), courtesy womenon20s.org; 192 (LO RT), Ninette Maumus/Alamy; 193 (UP LE), Kiev.Victor/SS; 193 (UP RT), Comstock/GI; 193 (UP CTR LE), Aleaimage/iStock; 193 (LO CTR LE), Splash News/Newscom; 193 (LO LE), Nataliya Evmenenko/DS; 193 (LO CTR), D. Hurst/Alamy; 193 (LO RT), Kelley Miller/NG Staff; 194, Sergey Novikov/SS; 195 (BACK), Subbotina Anna/SS; 195 (RT), Mark Thiessen/NG Staff; 196 (1), Newscom; 196 (2), Africa Studio/SS; 196 (3), Cliff Hide/Newscom; 196 (4), Dionisvera/SS; 196 (5), Sebastian Willnow/Newscom; 196 (6), ER_09/SS; 196 (7), Ralph Orlowski/GI; 196 (8), Mikael Damkier/SS; 197 (10), titov dmitriy/SS; 197 (11), Haryadi Be/Newscom; 197 (12), Mitsuhiko Imamori/MP; 197 (14), Gladcov/SS; 197 (15), Pierre Teyssot/Splash News/Newscom; 197 (16), Marco La Melia/SS; 197 (17), Alex Milan Tracy/Newscom; 197 (18), chuhail/SS; 198–199, Dean Macadam; 200 (UP), Randy Olson; 200 (LO LE), Martin Gray/NGC; 200 (LO RT), Sam Panthaky/AFP/GI; 201 (UP), Filippo Monteforte/GI; 201 (LO LE), Reza/NGC; 201 (LO RT), Richard Nowitz/NGC; 202 (UP), Marco La Melia/SS; 202 (LO), IS; 203 (UP LE), catwalker/SS; 203 (UP RT), dimitris_k/SS; 203 (UP CTR), oconnelll/SS; 203 (LO), Steve Allen/SS

Life Science (204–221)

204–205, Eye of Science/Science Source; 206 (LO), David Aguilar; 207 (A), Sebastian Kaulitzki/SS; 207 (B), Steve Gschmeissner/Photo Researchers, Inc.; 207 (C), Volker Steger/Christian Bardele/Photo Researchers, Inc.; 207 (D), Fedor A. Sidorov/SS; 207 (E), Marie C. Fields/SS; 207 (F), sgame/SS; 207 (G), Benjamin Jessop/IS; 208 (1), LeventeGyori/SS; 208 (3), Katstudio/SS; 208 (4), Dariusz Majgier/SS; 208 (6), NGC; 208 (7), Arterra/UIG via GI; 208 (9), dariagarnik/SS; 209 (10), hxdbzxy/SS; 209 (11), James P. Blair/NGC; 209 (12), Ben Nottidge/Alamy; 209 (13), mehmetakgul/IS; 209 (14), Anand Varma/GI; 209 (15), Guntars Grebezs/IS; 209 (18), kislev/IS; 210–211, Matthew Rakola; 212 (UP), Brand X/GI; 212 (LO), SSPL/Science Museum/GI; 212 (3), Matthew Rakola; 213 (UP), Mike Agliolo/Science Source; 213 (LO), martan/SS; 214 (UP), Cynthia Turner; 214 (LO), Jason Lugo/GI; 215 (UP LE), Vaclav Volrab/SS; 215 (UP CTR), Arkhipov/iStock; 215 (UP RT), Vitalii Hulai/SS; 215 (UP CTR LE), AnetaPics/SS; 215 (CTR RT), HughStoneIan/SS; 215 (LO CTR LE), Eric Isselée/SS; 215 (LO LE), delihayat/iStock; 215 (LO RT), Alexia Khruscheva/SS; 216, Cynthia Turner; 217 (UP), DS; 218, 4X-image/IS; 219 (UP), Jose Luis Magana/Reuters; 219 (LO), Digital Beach Media/Rex/Rex USA; 220 (UP), Vitalii Hulai/SS; 220 (CTR), Sciepro/GI; 220 (LO), Cynthia Turner; 221 (UP), Avava/SS; 221 (LO), Chris Gorgio/IS

History Happens (222–253)

222–223, Michael Melfordê/NGC; 224–225, Alessandro Colle/SS; 225 (UP), S.R.Lee Photo Traveller/SS; 225 (LO), warmcolors/iStock; 226–227, Jose Fuste Raga/CO/GI; 227, 145/Marcaux/Ocean/CO/GI; 228 (UP LE), Dea/G. Carfagna/GI; 228 (UP RT), Somyote Tiraphon/SS; 228 (LO), Robert Cravens/GI; 229 (UP), DaleBHalbur/GI; 229 (LO LE), Dea/G.Dagli Orti/GI; 229 (LO RT), alex83/SS; 230 (1), Bruno Ferrandez/AFP/GI; 230 (2), Eric Isselée/SS; 230 (3), Marc Bruxelle/SS; 230 (4), AFP/GI; 230 (5), rangizzz/SS; 230 (6), SuperStock/GI; 230 (7), Pictorial Parade/GI; 230 (8), Ira Block/NGC; 231 (10), Kenneth Garrett/NGC; 231 (12), Necklace of the Rising Sun, from the tomb of Tutankhamun (c.1370-52 BC) New Kingdom (gold inlaid with semi-precious stones) (detail of 153788)/Bridgeman Images; 231 (13), paulrommer/SS; 231 (14), Andrey Burmakin/SS; 231 (15), Bobboz/Alamy Stock Photo; 231 (16), Werner Forman/Universal Images Grou/GI; 231 (17), ITAR-TASS Photo Agency/Alamy; 232, Art by Mondolithic; 233, Jason Hawkes/CO/GI; 234 (VARIOUS), Cidepix/DS; 234 (RT), Cloki/DS; 234 (VARIOUS), Byjeng/DS; 234 (LO), Andrey57641/DS; 234 (VARIOUS), Luba V Nel/DS; 234 (LO RT), Kupka/Mauritius/Superstock; 235, Kelly Cheng Travel Photography/GI; 236–237 (LE), AP Images/Adam Butler; 237 (RT), A. R. Coster/Topical Press Agency/GI; 238 (UP), Scott Rothstein/SS; 239 (UP), Aleksandar Nakic/IS; 239 (LO), Gary Blakely/SS; 240 (UP), Marc Dozier/GI; 240 (CTR), Wolfgang Kaehler/GI; 240 (LO), Education Images/UIG/GI; 241 (B), WHHA; 241 (C), WHHA; 241 (D), WHHA; 241 (E), WHHA; 241 (G), WHHA; 241 (H), WHHA; 241 (I), WHHA; 241 (A), WHHA; 241 (LO LE), Larry West/FLPA/MP; 242 (A), WHHA; 242 (B), WHHA; 242 (C), WHHA; 242 (D), WHHA; 242 (E), WHHA; 242 (F), WHHA; 242 (G), WHHA; 242 (H), WHHA; 242 (J), WHHA; 243 (A), WHHA; 243 (B), WHHA; 243 (C), WHHA; 243 (D), WHHA; 243 (E), WHHA; 243 (F), WHHA; 243 (G), WHHA; 243 (H), WHHA; 243 (I), WHHA; 243 (J), WHHA; 243 (LO RT), Daniel Hurst Photography/GI; 244 (A), WHHA; 244 (B), WHHA; 244 (C), WHHA; 244 (D), WHHA; 244 (E), WHHA; 244 (F), WHHA; 244 (G), WHHA; 244 (H), WHHA; 245 (A), WHHA; 245 (C), WHHA; 245 (D), WHHA; 245 (F), WHHA; 245 (G), WHHA; 245 (J), WHHA; 245 (K), WHHA; 245 (I), WHHA; 245 (LO RT), AP Photo/John Locher; 246–247, CTON; 248 (UP), Bettmann/CO/GI; 248 (LO), Bettmann/CO/GI; 249 (Background), Reuters/Mannie Garcia/Alamy; 249 (CTR), Division of Political History, National Museum of American History, Smithsonian Institution; 249 (LO CTR), Charles Kogod/NGC; 250 (UP LE), Archive Photos/GI; 250 (UP RT), Bettmann/CO/GI; 250 (LO LE), Michael Ochs Archives/GI; 250 (INSET), Underwood & Underwood/CO/GI; 250 (LO RT), Patrick Faricy; 250 (UP CTR LE), Stuart, Gilbert (1755-1828)/Art Resource, NY; 251 (UP LE), Jesse Grant/WireImage/GI; 251 (UP RT), Jason Reed/Reuters/CO/GI; 251 (LO LE), Library of Congress Prints and Photographs Division; 251 (LO RT), 2011 Silver Screen Collection/GI; 252 (UP), SS; 252 (CTR), Eric Isselée/SS; 252 (LO), GI; 253 (UP RT), Michael Frost/Disney Publishing Worldwide

Geography Rocks (254–337)

254–255, Alex Mustard/Nature Picture Library; 261 (UP), Lori Epstein/NG Staff; 261 (LE), NASA; 262 (UP), Carsten Peter/NGC; 262 (CTR LE), Thomas J. Abercrombie/NGC; 262 (CTR CTR), Maria Stenzel/NGC; 262 (CTR RT), Gordon Wiltsie/NGC; 262 (LO LE), James P. Blair/NGC; 262 (LO CTR), Bill Hatcher/NGC; 262 (LO RT), Bill Curtsinger/NGC; 263, Dirk Ercken/SS; 264, Anup Shah/MP; 265 (UP LE), Dennis Walton/GI; 265 (UP RT), Hillary Leo; 265 (UP CTR RT), Martin Harvey/Alamy Stock Photo; 265 (LO LE), Letiziag84/DS; 265 (LO CTR), Kumar Sriskandan/Alamy Stock Photo; 265 (LO RT), Glowimages/GI; 268, Keith Szafranski/GI; 269 (UP LE), Izzet Keribar/GI; 269 (UP RT), Antarctic Search for Meteorites Project; 269 (LO LE), Stephen J. Krasemann/Science Source; 269 (UP CTR RT), Rick Lee; 269 (LO CTR RT), Dean Lewins/epa/CO; 269 (LO RT), Achim Baque/SS; 269 (LO RT), Achim Baque/SS; 272, Marc Dozier/GI; 273 (UP LE), narvikk/GI; 273 (UP RT), Kazuyo Sejima and Associates; 273 (UP CTR LE), SeanPavonePhoto/GI; 273 (LO CTR RT), Universal Images Group/GI; 273 (CTR LE), Gudkov Andrey/SS; 273 (LO CTR), ullstein bild/GI; 276, Louise Murray/Robert Harding/GI; 277 (UP LE), Jon Arnold/Alamy; 277 (UP RT), Jason Knott/Alamy Stock Photo; 277 (UP CTR RT), Zig Urbanski/Alamy Stock Photo; 277 (LO CTR RT), Allan Seiden/Robert Harding World Imagery; 277 (CTR LE), Philip Game/Alamy Stock Photo; 277 (LO RT), robertcicchetti/GI; 280, ale_flamy/GI; 281 (UP LE), Alexander Klemm/GI; 281 (UP RT), Bob Krist/CO/GI; 281 (UP CTR RT), Johner Images/Alamy Stock Photo; 281 (CTR LE), G. Bowater/GI; 281 (LO CTR RT), Sergey Novikov/Alamy Stock Photo; 281 (LO RT), Grafissimo/GI; 284, JoseIgnacioSoto/GI; 285 (UP LE), Pablo Corral V/CO/GI/VCG/GI; 285 (UP RT), Suzi Eszterhas/MP; 285 (UP CTR RT), ©Universal/Courtesy Everett Collection; 285 (CTR LE), Darren Baker/SS; 285 (LO CTR RT), Hero Images/GI; 285 (LO RT), Rodrigo Arangua/GI; 288, Pete Oxford/MP; 289 (UP LE), hadynyah/GI; 289 (UP RT), ZSSD/MP; 289 (UP CTR RT), Lee Foster/Alamy Stock Photo; 289 (CTR LE), Mark Bowler/NPL/MP; 289 (LO CTR RT), Cristina Mittermeier/NGC; 289 (LO RT), Soberka Richard/hemis.fr/GI; 295, Steffen Foerster/SS; 296, Chris Cheadle/GI; 300, Mint Images-Frans Lanting/GI; 303, Annie Griffiths/NGC; 304, Tim Gerard Barker/GI; 308, Katarina S/SS; 311, Hans-Peter Merten/Robert Harding World Imagery; 316, krivinis/SS; 328 (UP RT), Panoramic Images/GI; 328 (UP CTR LE), SS; 328 (UP CTR RT), SS; 328 (LO RT), PhotoDisc; 329 (UP), Rebeccaannphotography/DS; 329 (UP CTR), Cafebeanzphoto/DS; 329 (LO CTR), Brian Cahn/Newscom; 329 (LO), Trox Photo/SS; 330 (1), Stephen Frink Collection/Alamy; 330 (2), Ellensmile/DS; 330 (3), Tamás Horváth/DS; 330 (4), Design56/DS; 330 (6), Martin Harvey/GI; 330 (7), Rosamund Parkinson/DS; 330 (8), Cornforth Images/Alamy; 330 (9), Douglas Peebles Photography/Alamy; 330 (CTR), Stephen Coburn/DS.; 331 (10), Yu-he Zhang/DS; 331 (11), James Crawford/DS; 331 (12), Michael Patrick O'Neill/Alamy; 331 (14), Darlyne A. Murawski/NGC; 331 (15), Tobias Peciva/Alamy; 331 (16), Epicstock/DS; 331 (17), Serban Bogdan/DS; 331 (18), Frans Lanting/CO/GI; 331 (CTR), Twlvsx/DS; 332 (UP LE), courtesy of Yunak Evleri Cave Hotel; 333 (UP LE), Matt Cardy/GI; 333 (UP RT), Uwe Zucch/Alamy; 333 (LO), Reuters/Lucy Nicholson; 334–335, Chris Hill/NGC; 334 (UP), Bertrand Rieger/Hemis/CO/GI; 335 (LO), John Harper/Photolibrary/GI; 336 (UP), Dirk Ercken/SS; 336 (CTR), SeanPavonePhoto/GI; 336 (LO), Stephen J. Krasemann/Science Source

E

F

G

L

M

N

U

V

W

Y

Z

Since 1888, the National Geographic Society has funded more than 12,000 research, exploration, and preservation projects around the world. The Society receives funds from National Geographic Partners, LLC, funded in part by your purchase. A portion of the proceeds from this book supports this vital work. To learn more, visit www.natgeo.com/info.

For more information, visit www.nationalgeographic.com, call 1-800-647-5463, or write to the following address:
National Geographic Partners
1145 17th Street N.W.
Washington, D.C. 20036-4688 U.S.A.

Visit us online at nationalgeographic.com/books

For librarians and teachers: ngchildrensbooks.org

More for kids from National Geographic:
kids.nationalgeographic.com

For information about special discounts for bulk purchases, please contact National Geographic Books Special Sales:
specialsales@natgeo.com

For rights or permissions inquiries, please contact National Geographic Books Subsidiary Rights:
bookrights@natgeo.com

Art directed by Kathryn Robbins
Designed by Ruthie Thompson

The publisher would like to thank everyone who worked to make this book come together: Angela Modany, associate editor; Mary Jones, project editor; Sarah Wassner Flynn, writer; Michelle Harris, researcher; Lori Epstein, photo director; Hillary Leo, photo editor; Mike McNey, map production; Stuart Armstrong, illustrator; Sean Philpotts, production director; Anne LeongSon and Gus Tello, design production assistants; Sally Abbey, managing editor; Joan Gossett, editorial production manager; and Molly Reid, production editor.

Paperback ISBN: 978-1-4263-2772-8
Hardcover ISBN: 978-1-4263-2773-5

Printed in the United States of America
17/QGT-QGL/1